Imagination Shaped

D1291914

Imagination Shaped

OLD TESTAMENT PREACHING
— IN THE —
ANGLICAN TRADITION

Ellen F. Davis

TRINITY PRESS INTERNATIONAL
Valley Forge, Pennsylvania

Trinity Press International, P.O. Box 851, Valley Forge, PA 19482-0851

Library of Congress Cataloging-in-Publication Data

Davis, Ellen F.
    Imagination shaped : Old Testament preaching in the Anglican
tradition / Ellen F. Davis.
        p.   cm.
    Includes bibliographical references and index.
    ISBN 1-56338-121-4
    1. Preaching—England—History.   2. Bible. O.T.—Homiletical use.
3. Church of England—Sermons.   4. Church of England—Sermons—
History and criticism.   5. Sermons, English.   6. Sermons, English—
History and criticism.   7. Anglican Communion—Sermons.
8. Anglican Communion—Sermons—History and criticism.   I. Title.
BV4208.G7D35   1995
251'.008'823–dc20   95-11558
                                                                      CIP

Printed in the United States of America

95   96   97   98   99   10   9   8   7   6   5   4   3   2   1

For Brevard S. Childs

and

for Jane Anderson Morse, priest
(March 20, 1943–February 18, 1995)

"THE LIPS OF THE RIGHTEOUS FEED MANY."
—Proverbs 10:21

Poetry is not imagination, but imagination shaped; not feeling, but feeling expressed symbolically — the formless suggested indirectly through form.

— FREDERICK ROBERTSON

THE HOLY SCRIPTURES II

Oh that I knew how all thy lights combine,
*   And the configurations of their glory!*
*   Seeing not only how each verse doth shine,*
But all the constellations of the story.

This verse marks that, and both do make a motion
*   Unto a third, that ten leaves off doth lie;*
*   Then as dispersed herbs do watch a potion,*
These three make up some Christian's destiny.

Such are thy secrets, which my life makes good,
*   And comments on thee: for in every thing*
*   Thy words do find me out, and parallels bring,*
And in another make me understood.

*   Stars are poor books, and oftentimes do miss;*
*   This book of stars lights to eternal bliss.*

— GEORGE HERBERT (1593–1633)

Contents

PREFACE AND ACKNOWLEDGMENTS

The present book comes out of two moments of recognition in the course of my education. First, as a seminarian doing research for a project on the Psalms, I (almost accidentally) read some of John Donne's sermons and realized that for the first time I had found clear guidance for my own development as a preacher. Several years later, as a fledgling biblical scholar reading and teaching in the area of literary interpretations of Scripture, I discovered that few modern "literary treatments" show much interest in questions of theological meaning — that is, in what was traditionally understood as *the* meaning of Scripture — and therefore, that they were of surprisingly little interest to my students, even at a university-related divinity school of no pietistic bent. Consequently, I began increasingly to use the traditional *belles lettres* of Christian biblical interpretation, namely sermons, in my teaching.

This *apologia* is offered by way of explanation that my own credentials for writing this book are not those of a homiletician but rather a biblical scholar and occasional preacher. Yet the book is written primarily for preachers, most of them with far more pulpit experience and responsibility than I have had. Insofar as this book is intended to address the "crisis in contemporary preaching" (and I suppose no one writes a book where she does not see a problem as well as an opportunity), it is based on the belief that the central element of that crisis is an impoverished understanding of the meaning and uses of Scripture, and that biblical scholars must work to relieve that crisis, as we have indeed contributed to it.

This book treats the work of five men who are, in my judgment, the most important biblical preachers within the Anglican tradition. They represent a style of preaching that stretches like a fine (in both senses) strand across three centuries and is characterized by close, imaginative attention to the *words* of Scripture as the chief means by which God's nature and will are known. The selection of preachers necessarily involves personal preference; doubtless some readers will find that their favorite preacher was omitted. My chief criterion for selection was a simple one: I looked for preachers whose essential frame of reference is the language and concepts of the Bible. Traditionally, at least, most Christian preaching has begun with the Bible, but often the motivating force lies elsewhere; that is, the text serves merely to pose a question or an idea that is then explored along lines suggested by philosophy, ethics, psychology, the social sciences, and so on. I chose people who exercised active pastoral ministries (in various settings), of which preaching was the central element. Finally, I have chosen preachers who worked frequently with Old Testament texts, in part because it is my own field of specialization, and, more important, because so many present-day preachers seem to lack the confidence to handle it — despite or due to the benefit of substantial formal study in seminary.

To them, these sermons are offered as encouragement rather than as direct models. All five preachers had approximately an hour of pulpit time at their disposal, as well as extraordinary talent and many hours for preparation. But we who lack any or all of these things can yet learn much from them, as my students have shown me, far beyond my own expectations. Specifically, we can be instructed by the care with which they shaped their own language to lead their listeners more deeply into the language of Scripture. That care in opening up the Scriptures reflects their conviction that the gulf of time separating us from the biblical writers in no way diminishes the cogency or urgency of their message. With respect to biblical interpretation, the premodern Christianity represented by these preachers departs most significantly from the contemporary view — common among biblical scholars, clergy, and ordinary churchgoers — in its recognition that it is sin, not historical distance, which keeps us from hearing the message of Scripture as "relevant," that is, life-giving. It follows from this that the quality of the preacher's own life bears directly on the effectiveness with which the biblical message is conveyed; preaching involves an essential unity of person and doctrine, as George Herbert's poem at the front of this volume suggests. The format of this book reflects that unity: each section is an essay treating the preacher's life and use of Scripture in preaching, and is followed by unabridged sermon texts, lightly annotated. The final essay looks at the contemporary task of biblical preaching and explores the role played by the imagination in the work of interpretation.

Several difficulties should be anticipated by readers coming to this material for the first time. First, the sermons are very demanding of their audience, in terms of complexity of both thought and language, as well as length. This is especially true of the sermons in the first two sections. They were, of course, meant to be heard; and Andrewes and Donne in particular have a highly rhythmical style. Many readers will find them more readily comprehensible — and far more beautiful — when read aloud. Second, each preacher is to some extent confined by the social vision of his own time, and modern Christians will find them at points insensitive on issues (e.g., of gender, race, religious difference) where we have come to recognize insensitivity as dangerous. It is not my place to excuse them, but only to ask that readers consider these points of offense within the preacher's whole social, moral, and theological vision presented, which in each case transcends much of the narrow popular wisdom of their own age — and, sometimes in different respects, of our own. We do well if we can achieve as much in our own preaching.

The format closely reflects the design of courses taught at Yale Divinity School and the College of Preachers in Washington, D.C. I hope that others (and not only Anglicans) will find it useful for teaching in the fields of homiletics and church history, as well as biblical interpretation. The sermons printed here are, of course, only a starting place. Each of the five preachers produced substantial bodies of work that are available in most theological libraries; the endnotes point to a wide range of secondary literature.

Over the years of conceiving and executing this project, I needed more than the average amount of encouragement to wander so far afield from biblical studies "proper." Special thanks go to the members of my dedicated class at Yale Divinity School with whom I first explored this approach, and who convinced me that it worked; to John Archer, for his excellent collaboration in the early stages; to Erica Wood and the College of Preachers for giving me a testing ground, at some cost to themselves; to Peter Hawkins and Rowan Greer, for their careful reading and detailed comments; to Sr. Catherine Grace, CHS, for her patient and cheerful editorial work; and to Dwayne and Gillian Huebner, for showing consistent interest and making our home a peaceful place for work and other forms of life. I dedicate this book to two colleagues who have inspired me by their own commitment to scholarship that serves the needs of the church: Brevard Childs, who first encouraged my interest in Donne, and Jane Morse, who shared my joy in this project and died just as it was coming to completion. They have my deep affection and gratitude.

INTRODUCTION

FIVE BIBLICAL PREACHERS

The preachers whose work follows (Lancelot Andrewes, John Donne, Joseph Hall, Frederick Robertson, Henry Parry Liddon) are surely among those who have labored most successfully to render not only the message but also the tone of Scripture in the English language. Do they, considered as a group, tell us anything about the dispositions or conditions that produce great biblical preaching?

Certainly one factor that links these preachers to one another, and further links them to preachers of our own day, is cultural change of bewildering proportion and speed. They cluster in the two great ages of preaching in the English-speaking church, roughly coinciding with the reigns of James I (1603–25) and Victoria (1837–1901). The times were similar to those in which much of the Bible itself was written, when not only social structures but also symbolic worlds that had stood fast for centuries were being drastically eroded. The first age of preaching felt the shockwaves following the final collapse of the medieval hierarchy of feudal lords and monastics, the devastations of plague, and on the other hand, the exhilaration of Renaissance humanism. The second age watched, with both hope and fear, socialist revolutions on the Continent and industrial revolution in England; it grappled with radical new ideas about the origins of the Bible and of the human species. These five preachers were deeply involved in the ideas and events of their time; and they worked both to bring the biblical message to bear on contemporary discussions of theology, politics, science, and literature and, conversely, to identify new avenues into eternal truths. All had a strong pastoral sense; and they made it the chief task of their ministries to equip their hearers with the words, images, and communal memories — primarily but not exclusively those of Scripture — that had through centuries sustained Christians in periods of massive upheaval. With keen insight into human nature and extraordinary fluency in biblical language and history, they erected against confusion, skepticism,

1

and despair strong verbal bulwarks so effective that people flocked to hear them by hundreds and even by thousands.

The aim of their preaching is invariably practical; the emotional power of the rhetoric, but more, the intellectual force with which Scripture is interpreted, is bent upon fortifying the will and enlisting it in God's service. The distinctive quality of these five preachers is just this practical address to the "heart," to use the biblical word that encompasses the several faculties later theologians would distinguish as affect, intellect, and will. For the effectiveness of their *comprehensive* appeal to the moral center of the human spirit — which, as I shall argue in the final essay, is in modern parlance best designated as "imagination" — they stand out in the history of English-language preaching. Most strikingly, their imaginative preaching differs widely from the "plain style" of preaching that dominated the nearly two centuries intervening between Joseph Hall and Frederick Robertson.

Probably it is no coincidence that the three seventeenth-century preachers treated here were poets, albeit in very different modes — all of them highly sensitive to the motive force of language (including but not exclusively figurative language) crafted with care. Early in the seventeenth century, George Herbert struck the keynote for the poetic preachers of classical Anglicanism with his Country Parson's advice for moving "thick and heavy" folk: first "by choosing...moving and ravishing texts, whereof the scriptures are full" and then "by dipping and seasoning all our words and sentences in our hearts, before they come into our mouths, truly affecting and cordially expressing all we say, so that the auditors may plainly perceive that every word is heart-deep."[1] But beginning in the middle of the seventeenth century, a marked shift occurred in English preaching, among Puritans as well as Anglicans. The sermon came to be viewed no longer as communication between ravished hearts, but rather as reasonable discourse addressed to enlightened minds — or at least minds susceptible to enlightenment. Archbishop John Tillotson's (1630–94) sermon "The Wisdom of Being Religious," preached in 1663 before the lord mayor and aldermen of London, sounds the main themes of Restoration preaching: the reasonableness of Christianity and the absurdity of irreligion, the nature of operative faith and the necessity of virtue.

"The triumph of Tillotson" was to establish the plain style as the norm of English preaching. Early seventeenth-century audiences, learned or not, reveled in skillful wordplay in the pulpit as in the theater. But now "an unnecessary mixture of various languages, affected wit, and puerile rhetoric" was rejected in favor of simple diction and the relaxed prose of ordinary speech.[2] For Andrewes, Hall, and Donne the sermon was a liturgical poem, a meditation on Scripture, a journey through Scripture into another world. For Tillotson, it was a moral essay, and the Bible a sourcebook of propositions about the moral life. The ascendancy of the plain style marked the English church's definite move out of the deeply shaded atmosphere of the medieval world into the full light of eighteenth-century thought.

Tillotson's victory represents more than a changing aesthetic within the church; it is part of a fundamental epistemological shift in Western culture, a change in the way truth itself is understood, or at least how we may grasp the truth. Stanley Fish describes the nature of the shift that made the poetic style obsolete:

> ...the assumption that the apprehension of ultimate truth is beyond the capacity of the rational understanding is no longer respectable. No one is now willing to say, with Donne, that he intends to "trouble the understanding, to displace, and to discompose, and disorder the judgment"; and indeed everyone is loudly professing exactly the opposite intention, not to trouble the judgment, but to conform in every way possible to its procedures, to dispose arguments in a methodical and orderly progression and so affirm... "a faith in the instructed intellect."[3]

This epistemological shift ramified throughout the learned culture of seventeenth-century England. The Royal Society of London for the Improving of Natural Knowledge was chartered in that same year, 1663, and the declared aim of the Restoration scientists (a number of whom were clergy) parallels that of Tillotson:

> to separate the knowledge of nature from the colors of rhetoric, the devices of fancy, or the delightful deceit of fables...to return back to the primitive purity, and shortness, when men delivered so many things, almost in an equal number of words...bringing all things as near the mathematical plainness as they can.[4]

The yearning for verbal simplicity was expressed in experiments with a univocal language, free of ambiguity. Tillotson himself was elected a Fellow of the Royal Society in 1671, probably in recognition of his collaboration with his father-in-law John Wilkins on his Essay towards a Real Character and Philosophical Language (1668). Identifying the "real character" meant developing a system of signs to represent words, which, in the interest of economy, required grouping near-synonyms. This project was congenial with and may well have contributed to the young clergyman's lack of concern for verbal nuances.[5] So in "The

Wisdom of Being Religious," he requires four pages to resolve the words of his text — "And unto man he said, Behold! the fear of the Lord that is wisdom, and to depart from evil is understanding" (Job 28:28) — into a proposition: "Religion is the best knowledge," and fifty more to expound that proposition in nonbiblical terms. Tillotson's attempt to translate the biblical text into discursive language stands in sharp contrast to the "wit" practiced by the early seventeenth-century "metaphysical preachers,"[6] who used puns, metaphors, and wordplays in English, Latin, Greek, and even Hebrew to tease out spiritual truths hidden in familiar things and to show surprising relations among seemingly disparate phenomena. In the sermon on Isaiah 7:14 that follows here, Andrewes takes his cue from the Angel Gabriel and draws out his message from the verse "word by word...not so much as the *ecce* [behold] left out." In a sermon half the length of Tillotson's, the one word *ecce* gets as much attention as the archbishop gives to the biblical text altogether.

The triumph of the plain style was swift and thorough; its implicit confidence in the ability of the human mind to command the truth and set it forth fully lasted through the eighteenth century. Perhaps the metaphysical style had required too much ingenuity from preachers, and it never regained ground. But the Romantic poets of the early nineteenth century once again awakened an awareness that deep truths can be intimated but not exhausted, and that poetry yields insight precisely because it is respectful of mystery. It is then not surprising that the Romantic poets fostered the development of a preacher, Frederick Robertson, who combined simplicity of style with the early seventeenth-century preachers' fascination with the words of Scripture in their capacity to conceal as well as to reveal.

This brief look at the shift in seventeenth-century preaching may be helpful in thinking about the current crisis in preaching, for we are still affected by Tillotson's triumph in establishing the sermon as rationalistic moral discourse. Within Anglicanism and most strains of "liberal" Protestant Christianity, the chief aim of the sermon is to call reasonable people to right thinking about the virtuous life, to help them be good people, just neighbors, and functional family members. The preachers whose work is represented here challenge the adequacy of that aim and, further, the view of Scripture that underlies it. Consistently they affirm that biblical faith is concerned with much more than the virtuous life; its central matters are God's goodness and the salvation of souls. Moreover, they probe the words of the text because they understand that the

Bible is something other and vastly more than a moral treatise, where the essential thing is the content, the form being incidental and, ideally, as unnoticeable as possible.

But the form of biblical literature is hardly unnoticeable. It is notoriously difficult, if often beautiful. Judging from much of the preaching of the last three centuries, the form of Scripture is a problem to be dealt with firmly and without sentiment; the tough husk is to be broken and discarded, so that something useful can be made of the kernel. Yet from the perspective of the poet, interest lies chiefly in difficulties or peculiarities of form; and it is this perspective that makes the poetic preachers such excellent exegetes. The Bible does indeed offer guidance to the moral life, but it does so artfully — indirectly rather than discursively. Which is to say, the Bible is a *text* in the strong sense; the words are "woven" (Latin *textum*) into a unique shape and texture. A textbook, upon which modern educational systems depend so heavily, is designed to be skimmed for content; a text has a significant surface over which the wise reader moves slowly. One who reads a literary text and remembers only the "gist" has missed most of what was set there for our learning.

One more "environmental factor" (arguably the most important) shared by these preachers is the catholic Anglican tradition, which four of the five (Andrewes excepting) chose as adults. Since that tradition housed and presumably shaped their preaching over decades, it is reasonable to ask what in the general atmosphere of Anglicanism may have been conducive to their full development as preachers — or, putting the question the other way around, to ask whether one can identify in their work certain consistent elements of what might be called Anglican biblical preaching.

The most obvious element is, of course, the liturgy itself. These sermons often stood at the end of the service, and their very length made them the main event of the day. Nonetheless they are very much liturgical events, in which the language of the Book of Common Prayer is frequently evident; and often the sermon itself turns into prayer, being punctuated by apostrophes addressed to God and concluding with a prayer that is more than formulaic. But even beyond these overt allusions, the influence of the liturgy is felt in the way Scripture is treated. The influence is subtle but pervasive, and I suggest that it is no less real for the fact that it may have operated most of the time below the level of consciousness. The preacher whose mind has been sensitized by countless repetitions of the great poem of the liturgy comes to

Scripture already attuned to echoes and cadences, dramatic movement, visual and verbal symbolism.[7] In other words, the poetics of the liturgy makes one attentive to the poetics of Scripture.

Further, the catholic liturgy is itself the product of the medieval church's sustained communal reflection upon Scripture. To read Scripture against that background is to read through a centuries-long tradition that contains within it multiple options for interpretation, while also serving as a guard against idiosyncrasy. For the place of Scripture in the liturgy is a reminder that its meaning cannot be fully discerned apart from the common life of prayer and sacraments. Indeed, the catholic side of Anglicanism affirms that, *abstracted from the context of public worship*, the Bible is not a comprehensible and reliable guide to the Christian life. In complementary fashion, the Reformation tradition within Anglicanism emphasizes that it is through regular reflection on Scripture by *all* its members that the community remains both healthy and identifiably Christian.

A second element that is often named as belonging to the special genius of Anglican preaching is application of the text to the lives of the hearers. In the formative period of Anglicanism, the emphasis on application distinguished Anglican sermons from Puritan expositions. Much of the power of these five preachers lies in the skill with which they draw the connection between text and life; yet they do not (as one might expect) achieve this by "updating" the text, modernizing its concepts in conformity with our normal thought categories and advanced state of knowledge. The movement is rather in the reverse direction. They invite their hearers to enter into the past through the text, which is all the more valuable for the present life of faith because of the antiquity of its witness to God's revelation. "The art of salvation is but the art of memory";[8] the Scriptures expand our active memory by giving us access to experiences that belong to us solely by virtue of participation in the community of faith. The basic concept is, of course, biblical: "It was not with our ancestors that the LORD made this covenant but with us — *us*, the ones here today, all of us alive" (Deut. 5:3). Behind the frequent injunction to Israel, "Remember!" (Deut. 5:15, 7:18, 8:24, *et al.*), is the premise that grateful orientation to God's action in the past is the best guard against egotistical involvement in the present.

This same premise is, of course, fundamental to the structure of Christian liturgy; the shape of the eucharistic liturgy evidences the fact that proper worship is entirely dependent upon cultivating the art of memory:

The service of the Word, like the Passover *haggada*, relates the second part of the service to the redemptive events of the past, without which the Godward act would be meaningless. Unless the Eucharist proper is preceded by the ministry of the Word, the liturgy becomes a Pelagian affair, a work of man, a purely human offering. It is then an arrogant attempt of man to storm the heights of heaven and to establish communion with God for himself. This would reduce the liturgy to the status of a mystery cult. . . . If the mighty acts of God in Christ are to become the stuff of Christian worship, stuff for recital before God in thanksgiving — and it is this, and this alone, which distinguishes Christian worship from pagan — . . . then the congregation must first be confronted anew with these same mighty acts, before it can make them the material of its worship.[9]

Sound biblical preaching provides direction for the application of text to life within the environment of worship.

Finally, as the title of this book suggests, these preachers share a quality of mind that I believe is best described as imagination shaped by tradition. I do not use the word "imagination" in the sense of mere fancifulness or self-deception, which was in fact its meaning in seventeenth-century English: "He hath scattered the proud in the imagination of their hearts" (Luke 1:51b). Rather, by it I designate the intellectual, affective, intuitive, and even sensuous faculties that, as I have noted, together constitute what the Bible calls "heart." Imagination is the faculty by which we strive to form a holistic picture of the subject under consideration. Richard Kroner, speaking of the function of the imagination in the life of faith, observes:

Its peculiar excellency consists exactly in its capacity of making visible what is invisible and of detecting the invisible element in the visible situation. Imagination binds together what the thinking separates; or, more precisely, it maintains the original unity of the elements separated by abstract thought.[10]

I certainly would not wish to defend the claim that Anglicans are, generally speaking, more imaginative than other preachers (were I to attempt that, the present volume would have to include many more than five preachers out of several centuries). I suggest only that the tradition *at its best* encourages a certain kind of holistic, concrete, and practical thinking, marked by (1) a deep reverence for God and also for the material world as God's creation; (2) a feeling for the "ordered loveliness" of language[11] — both these characteristics being fostered by study of Scripture and absorption of the liturgy; and (3) a broad understanding of human nature (itself derived in no small part from the Bible). When this kind of thinking is applied to the task of proclaiming the revealed Word of God, it becomes a keen instrument of theological insight and pastoral guidance, enabling the hearers to map their own experience and aspirations on the map of Scripture. The preachers whose work follows exemplify that particular style of excellence.

CHAPTER ONE

LANCELOT ANDREWES
(1555–1626)
"The Day of Small Things"

And hear you, you are to begin with *datum*, "not to despise the day of small things" [Zech. 4:10]. It is the Prophet's counsel, to learn to see God in them. "Caesar's image" [Matt. 22:21], not only in his coin of gold, but even upon the poor "penny." See God in small, or you shall never see him in great; in "good," or never in "perfect."[1]

The sermons of Lancelot Andrewes are unparalleled in the history of Anglican preaching for their comprehensive instruction in the basic understandings and practices of Christian living. His sermons are among the foundational documents of Anglican moral theology, at the heart of which lies the experience of the sacraments and the major festivals of the church year. Andrewes was preeminently a festal preacher, and the great majority of his 123 surviving sermons were preached at court in observance of the great feasts and fasts: the Nativity, Ash Wednesday and Lent, the Passion, Easter, Pentecost, and the two "political festivals" celebrating James I's safe deliverance from Catholic and Protestant enemies respectively in the Gunpowder Plot (1605) and the alleged Gowrie Conspiracy (1600).[2] With an earnestness that does not weary, this "diligent and painful preacher"[3] produced a catechesis for the English Church, setting forth over and over the few essential points of Christian doctrine in language that fulfills his friend George Herbert's prescription for holy preaching: "so that the auditors may plainly perceive that every word is heart-deep."[4] Perhaps the most significant aspect of his achievement is its modesty. By insisting repeatedly on the distinction between essential and accessory matters, and confining himself to explicating the former, he staked out a large area of freedom within the Church: room for disagreement, agnosticism, and exercise of private judgment on all but the central articles of faith.

9

The recurrent events of the church year fired Andrewes's imagination, and probably no one since the Middle Ages has framed the significance of those events in more striking, if generally homely terms: of the relation between the Ascension of Christ and the Sending of the Holy Spirit, he asks, "Are they like two buckets? one cannot go down, unless the other go up?"[5] But like the monastic theologians of the early and medieval Church upon whom he continually drew, he understood that doctrine serves not only or even primarily to instruct the intellect. Rather, properly taught, it touches the conscience, shapes character, and makes us capable of response to God. The preaching of doctrine is then for Andrewes a thoroughly practical matter:

> The only true praise of a sermon is, some evil left, or some good done upon the hearing of it....And sure it is, on whom a sermon works aright, it leaves him not leisure to say much, to use many words, but rather makes him full of thoughts. And when all comes to all, *fructus factus* [when the fruit is formed], "the deed done" is it. And it is no good sign in a tree when all the sap goes up into the leaves, is spent that way; nor in an auditor, when all is verbal that comes and nothing else — no reality at all.[6]

If Andrewes, with his steady imaginative appeal to conscience, laid the foundations for moral theology in the English Church, he may also be credited with the origins of its mystical theology.[7] Indeed, for him the two are not separate; the theological question that is most profitable to ordinary Christians is the question of practical mysticism, "namely, how we may get into the partnership of this mystery [of godliness]."[8] And the ultimate outcome of the moral life, life lived in full and proper response to God, is resemblance to God. Andrewes continually draws out the implications of the patristic principle of *theosis*: "God became as we are that we might become as God is."[9] The Nativity sermons in particular display an estimation of humanity that differs markedly from the tone of much Puritan preaching of his time: "And the very Angels who this day adored Him in our flesh and it in Him, thereby showed plainly not the purging only but the exalting of it also by this day's work."[10] The Passion offers the occasion for him to take up the negative as well as the positive aspects of the correspondence, "in calling to mind and taking to regard what this day the Son of God did and suffered for us; and all for this end, that what He was then we might not be, and what He is now we might be for ever."[11]

Andrewes's preaching throughout expresses an optimism that links him with both patristic thought and Renaissance humanism, which differs fundamentally from modern secular humanism, being grounded in the conviction that human dignity is conferred by God's love. Despite the regular emphasis on repentance, the dominant tones of his preaching are wonder and joy derived from reflection upon that love, as expressed above all in the Incarnation. The charter for Andrewes's whole program of preaching can be understood in light of the observation made by his favorite Father, Augustine, on how the Incarnation of God in Christ brought happiness to humanity:

> First we had to be persuaded how much God loved us, in case out of sheer despair we lacked the courage to reach up to him. Also we had to be shown what sort of people we are that he loves, in case we should take pride in our own worth, and so bounce even further away from him and sink even more under our own strength.[12]

Andrewes's pastoral task is to awaken in his hearers, first, an acute consciousness of what God has done for us, and second, a penitential but not morbid awareness of the need in which we stand. Guiding them repeatedly through the seasons of the liturgical year, he provides steady encouragement and remarkable insight into the dynamics of Christian living. Although firmly anchored in early Christian thought, he speaks directly to present conditions, pointing to the new evidences of God's grace witnessed in the establishment of a faithful Church. Andrewes offers his contemporaries encouragement that through that Body they may enter into full partnership in the mystery of godliness.

Andrewes's Life

For more than two decades Andrewes was, despite his retiring nature, a close advisor to a king who put religion at the head of matters of state and was himself a theologian of some ability. Andrewes served James I as confessor, Bible translator, and most favored preacher; he was appointed as bishop successively of three important sees (Chichester, Ely, and Winchester), which placed him on the king's Privy Council. But in order to understand the earnest and even urgent tone that characterizes his pulpit catechesis, it is well to remember that he was not born in a nation with an established church but rather in Mary's England, in the year (1555) when John Rogers, one of the translators of the Bible, was burned at the stake in Smithfield. Within a few months Hugh Latimer and Nicholas Ridley were burned in Oxford, and the English Church

had its first company of martyrs. The thirty years prior to the Settlement made at the beginning of Elizabeth's reign (1559) were the most
turbulent in European religious history, when England went through
six different forms of Christian faith and practice and emerged as a Reformed nation based upon the comprehension of Protestant opinion and
the uniformity of public worship.

Although Andrewes is usually remembered as a Jacobean preacher,
it was Elizabeth who first chose him as chaplain. In his sermon on Lot's
wife (printed below), he praises the perseverance of the queen who
steadfastly opposed the casual intermingling of civil and ecclesiastical
affairs and thus encouraged the Church to adapt itself to the needs of
the people and resist the narrowing orthodoxy of much Western Christianity. Although Elizabeth's reign also had its (Catholic) martyrs, the
steadfastness of "England's Deborah" spared her realm the widespread
destruction which the Thirty Years' War wreaked on the Continent.

Andrewes's temperament is well described in terms used of Gregory
the Great, the patristic theologian he most closely resembles: he was "a
contemplative condemned to action."[13] Study and prayer were his natural occupations. He was born in London, the first of thirteen children
of parents whom he remembered as "honest and good." His father was
a well-to-do merchant sailor, but Lancelot's first teacher insisted that
his abilities demanded a classical education rather than apprenticeship
to a trade. His parents agreed, and so the six-year-old was sent to the
Merchant-Taylors' School, famed for its rigorous and excellent master,
Richard Mulcaster. Andrewes's friend and biographer Henry Isaacson
records that he was from childhood "totally addicted to the study of
good letters";[14] he would awaken the school ushers for admittance well
before dawn. Throughout his life, long daily walks were the only form
of recreation he chose, and many lovely passages in his sermons show
keen attention to nature and its rhythms. A Greek scholarship sent him
to Cambridge at 16, where he was to live for nearly twenty years as student, Fellow, and finally Master of Pembroke College. During the Easter
holiday he would walk from Cambridge to London (although his friends'
teasing about penury eventually drove him to take a coach). There he
would spend a month with his family, reportedly each year studying a
new language with a tutor engaged through his father's connections. In
addition to Latin, Greek, and Hebrew, which he had studied at school,
he became proficient in Aramaic, Syriac, classical Arabic, and fifteen
modern languages.

At a time when theology was vital to statecraft, breadth of knowledge no less than his preaching ability brought Andrewes to eminence. He was well known as a biblical and patristic scholar, and his knowledge of the ancient liturgies was unparalleled in Europe (not a small achievement in an age of liturgical reform). He is generally identified with the position of the Arminians, those within the English Church who, over against the Puritans, appealed to the authority of the ancient Church as well as of Scripture and emphasized a holy life lived in cooperation with God's grace.[15] But the years in Cambridge had brought him into regular contact with English Puritans[16] and also Continental scholars; and James relied on him as an arbiter and controversialist with both Roman Catholics and Puritans. Despite Andrewes's personal dislike for contention, the role was nonetheless compatible with his ideal of a unified Church. This ideal is set forth especially in his Pentecost sermons, the last of which gives clear expression to the theological basis for ecumenicity, namely, that the Church's unity is not a distant goal but rather its original and essential character, given by God: "All our multitude is from unity. All our diversity is from identity. All our divisions from integrity; from 'one and the same' entire 'Spirit.'"[17]

The habit of daily study continued throughout Andrewes's lifetime. As best he could, he confined administrative work to a few hours in the afternoon and considered that "they were no true scholars, that came to speak with him before noon."[18] But equally formative for his singular style of preaching was Andrewes's practice of prayer, in which he is reported to have spent nearly five hours each day.[19] Certainly Andrewes's best-known work is one he never intended others to read: Preces Privatae, the private prayer book that, found and published only after his death, has made a permanent contribution to the Anglican devotional tradition.

These verse prayers, written in Latin and Greek, show the continuity between his intense inner life and his preaching. Especially they demonstrate that it was through examination of his own soul that Andrewes developed acute insight into the sources and nature of sin, and further, that the pastoral preacher was also a conscientious intercessor. The prayers, like the sermons, display the originality peculiar to a mind steeped in tradition. Andrewes draws from an astonishingly broad range of sources (including the Bible; Jewish, Greek, and Latin liturgies; Sophocles and Virgil; the Fathers; the medieval theologians, both monastics and schoolmen; John Knox's Book of Common Order; and the Book of Common Prayer). Through long usage, he has blended them into a new composition that is unmistakably heartfelt and yet free from idiosyncrasy.[20]

A penitential mood dominates the *Preces;* the manuscript copy is said to have been badly stained by Andrewes's own tears. Yet there is nothing grim about these prayers, whose organizing theme is the wondrous work of creation. The aim of the whole is a positive one: namely, through detailed praise, confession, intercession, and prayers for grace, to restore his own wandering heart and indeed the whole world to God. And it is precisely the tone of penitence, properly understood, that is the key to Andrewes's whole character: "Penitence is often the unsuspected secret of joyousness, simplicity, evenness of mind, a childlike spirit, and thoughtful tenderness for others."[21]

These qualities account for the (initially surprising) fact that Andrewes, for all his scholarly brilliance, excelled as a teacher of children. As dean of Westminster (1601–5), Andrewes supervised and often taught in the Westminster School. He took the young children with him on his daily walks, "and in that wayfaring leisure had a singular dexterity to fill those narrow vessels with a funnel." In the evenings, from 8 to 11, he invited the senior students to his rooms for lessons in Greek and Hebrew. A former student reports: "All this he did to boys without any compulsion of correction; nay I never heard him utter so much as a word of austerity among us."[22] No doubt it was in part the trust of the children and the young men who studied with him that enabled Andrewes to become a remarkably astute and gentle guide for those taking their first steps in the spiritual life.

The years at Westminster brought him the assignment by which he left his best-known (albeit anonymous) legacy to the English Church — indeed, to all English-speaking Christianity. When James acceded to the Puritans' request to authorize a new English version of the Bible, he appointed Andrewes to head the committee responsible for the translation of Genesis through Kings. Andrewes's qualifications were threefold: eminence as a Hebrew scholar, experience in working with people of diverse theological positions, and perhaps most important, a spare, refined English prose style. It is in no small part due to his abilities that the translation published in 1611 is the only work produced by committee to be established as a classic of English literature.

Moreover, his activity as a linguist and translator was not incidental to his preaching and accounts for a feature of his style that is foreign to most modern readers. Andrewes often derives meaning from the elements of Hebrew, Greek, and Latin grammar and even engages in multilingual wordplay, the most famous example being the "Immanu-el/ Immanu-hell" pun in the Nativity sermon of 1614. It is important to

remember that many members of his learned court audience were flu-
ent in Latin, had studied Greek, and, in this age of translation, liked
hearing Hebrew. Yet his aim was not primarily to please them. Rather,
it was to pass on to them the full richness and subtlety of God's word
in human language: "For my part, I wish no word every narrowed by a
translation, but as much as might be left in the latitude of the original
tongue."[23]

Andrewes finally resigned his mastership at Pembroke and fully entered into public life in 1605, when he was consecrated bishop of
Chichester. Twice in Elizabeth's reign he had refused episcopal appointment, in opposition to the queen's policy of appropriating part of the
revenues of the see. As a member of James's Privy Council, he did not
welcome the opportunity to become widely active in the affairs of state.
It is reported that when the council convened, he would inquire: "Is
there anything to be done today for the church?" If the answer was
"no," he would leave.[24] The story is characteristic even if it should
be apocryphal; for in a time when bishops of important sees were the
busiest government officials, Andrewes trained his attention closely on
ecclesiastical affairs. He earned the nickname "Gamaliel," the learned
teacher of the Apostle Paul, for both his studiousness and his cautious
attitude toward public controversies (Acts 5:33–39, 22:3).

The question arises whether Andrewes's inclination toward silence
in government affairs is a culpable desertion of the public sphere[25] or
whether, on the other hand, it represents a realistic assessment of where
he could work to good effect. With respect to James, he has been accused of "servility and sycophancy and the sale of justice."[26] Certainly
Andrewes upheld the divine right of kings in language that is vituper-
ative toward James's enemies;[27] yet he also called into question the
official account of the so-called Gowrie Conspiracy, saying he could
not preach about it in ignorance of the truth, and he dissuaded the
king from appropriating diocesan lands to ameliorate his financial problems.[28] James was salacious, self-indulgent, and vain, if also somewhat
learned; and Andrewes's praise at times strikes the reader as obsequious.
But he does not exempt his sovereign from the call to repentance that
is a frequent element of his preaching, distinguishing between the king
as God's representative, to whom homage is due, and the king as sinner, of whom penitence is required.[29] Andrewes must have experienced
disappointments and probably also crises of conscience[30] in thirty years'
attendance at court; and it is likely that the sermons themselves are the
chief fruit of that experience, that the long-held tension between world-

liness and personal asceticism which gave fervency to his private prayers also impelled Andrewes to forge a complex public statement about the life of faith.

Andrewes understood himself as a Christian subject of a Christian king, an identity that is not readily comprehensible in our own day. But there is no reason to doubt the good faith of his intention to uphold James in his role of supreme governor of the Church, nor the sincerity of his hopes that this reign would serve God's cause. The sermon of Easter Sunday, 1611, the eighth anniversary of James's ascension to the throne of England, concludes with a pronouncement of grace, not only *in christo Domino* ("in Lord Christ") but also *in christo Domini* ("on the Lord's anointed"), as Andrewes charges him to make God "your stone of chief trust and your mark of highest regard in all your counsels and purposes ... and seek to reduce the *disjecta latera*, 'the sides and walls flying off,' of this great building for which the world itself was built, his Church, and reduce them to one great angle, the greatest service that can be done him on earth."[31]

The standard view of James as an ineffectual fop has recently undergone reevaluation; and it seems that he did indeed contribute to the strength and unity of the Church, even if not always in ways the bishop himself approved. He was personally involved in the selection of bishops, eased their financial burdens, and greatly improved the standards for their education: all but one of the forty bishops consecrated during James's reign held a doctorate in divinity. He made concessions to allow moderate Puritans to remain in the established Church, the most important being granting their request for a retranslation of the Bible, as well as improving catechesis and making minor emendations in the Prayer Book. James placed less emphasis on matters of ceremony (including kneeling and bowing) and, ironically, more on preaching than Andrewes thought wise. He revived the old practice of choosing his closest advisors from among the clergy; and he balanced them off carefully one against the other, so that for more than a decade Andrewes served as a counterweight to the staunchly Calvinist Archbishop George Abbott (1611–33). Thus James maintained, deliberately and with no little skill, a tense unity that, if it "ultimately satisfied no one, in the short term it gave encouragement to all," and staved off, at least for one generation, the tragedy of religious warfare that was already engulfing the Continent.[32]

Andrewes was one of the most conscientious patrons and disciplinarians of the Jacobean episcopate; he was instrumental in raising the standards for ministry over those of the sixteenth century, when many clergy lacked a basic knowledge of Scripture and were not licensed to preach. Andrewes deplored the ignorance even of university graduates who "hazard men's souls." Of the very few candidates he accepted for ordination, most were M.A.s, and he gave generously for the education of poor scholars. The bishop was fair-minded, advancing Calvinists as well as Arminians, yet unusually firm in ousting nonresident clergy; he was frequently sued by men to whom he refused benefices. The wealth that came from his several preferments Andrewes used liberally in repairing the episcopal estates and churches and furnishing them properly for eucharistic worship. He also established endowments for schools and hospitals, gave relief to debtors, and was noted for his exceptional hospitality at home.

Andrewes's episcopal service was more administrative than pastoral. Although he spent the summer months in his see, he departed from the norm established by Calvinist bishops, the majority of whom functioned as itinerant preachers, in making few visitations to preach and confirm. This departure signified not laziness but the different view of ministry held by the Arminians, who saw the bishop as custodian of church order rather than a preaching prelate. Although himself the most celebrated preacher of the day, Andrewes was skeptical of the unprecedented enthusiasm for sermons that characterized the early seventeenth century, so that clergy indulged in impassioned, unpremeditated utterances, and the laity in "evil-proportioned hearing" that left the heart untouched: "For a wonderful thing it is, how many sermons, and sermons upon sermons, as it were so many measures of seed, are thrown in daily, and what becomes of them no man can tell. Turn they all to wind? or run they all through? for fruit there comes none."[33]

Andrewes in fact disapproved of the common practice of frequent preaching and said of himself that "when he preached twice a day at St. Giles' [his parish charge in London] he prated once."[34] His care in preparation was exceptional, so that the sermons were printed (after his death) exactly as they had been preached. The fact that Andrewes did not publish them in his lifetime is telling with respect to his own understanding of ministry. Andrewes intended his sermons primarily for an audience of intimates, albeit highly influential ones. Moreover, preaching is always subordinated, in his view, to the primary work of prayer.[35] Priests are "the Lord's remembrancers," bringing the people before God in prayer, both private and public, and God before them in preaching.[36] The constant aim of his preaching is to move his hearers to offer themselves to God in prayer and encourage them that their offering will be accepted.[37] By making frequent use of the language and basic concepts of the liturgy, Andrewes seeks to make the sacrament available to his hearers as a means of personal reconciliation.

Andrewes went little to court in his last few years, as the physical strain of preaching became too great. "A sore fit of the stone and gout"[38] prevented him from attending James on his deathbed in April 1625, and he never preached before Charles I. He was present in Parliament on several occasions during the next year, for the last time in June 1626. The deaths of two beloved brothers within a short time made Andrewes certain that his own would soon follow, "and from that time till the hour of his dissolution he spent all his time in prayer; and his prayer-book, when he was private, was seldom seen out of his hands."[39] He died on September 25, 1626, peaceably, as he had prayed:

> And, with thy other blessings, send
> (best gift of all) a holy end;
> a good and holy end of life,
> a glorious and joyful resurrection.[40]

Andrewes's Preaching

Andrewes's liturgical preaching constituted a revolution in English preaching, presenting a fully developed alternative to both the thematic oration of the Roman Church (modeled on medieval scholastic discourse) and the Puritan lecture, with its verse-by-verse exposition of the biblical text.[41] Andrewes created a sermon form woven out of the three compositional elements of early Anglicanism: (1) Scripture; (2) the tradition of text-centered exegesis developed by ancient and medieval commentators; (3) sacramental worship and the great poem of the liturgy as the context for preaching. He is relentlessly exegetical, never more than momentarily turning aside from the language of the text, digging into it with a playful rigor that confounds our modern sensibilities. While the sermon is tightly reasoned and ordered in direct response to text, its stylistic freedom and poise make it a genuine work of literary art.

Andrewes was in his own day lauded (and by the end of the seventeenth century vilified) for introducing the "metaphysical style" of poetic preaching, which was paralleled by a new vogue in verse. The metaphysical preachers drew their material from traditional sources: the medieval stock of patristic and classical writings; examples from nature, history, and daily life; above all the words and images of Scripture. The distinctiveness of the new style came from the adoption of a certain perspective commonly known as "wit." Toward the end of the century, Joseph Glanvill defined wit as "a perfection of our faculties, chiefly in the *understanding and imagination*" and further, "a sagacity to find out the nature, relations, and consequences of things."[42]

Drawing unexpected connections among familiar phenomena was a common feature of learned speech of the day: witness James's address to Parliament advocating the union of England and Scotland, in which he argues that as a king he is wedded to his nation, and as a Christian he cannot be a polygamist.[43] The witty preacher drew startling parallels, sometimes casting new light on the biblical text, traditional faith concepts, the design of creation. The playful use of reason, which is the essence of wit, afforded the flexibility for deep exploration of the central Christian paradox: the Incarnation of divine grace in human nature, "The God whom 'the heavens and the heaven of heavens cannot contain' [1 Kgs. 8:27; 2 Chron. 2:6, 6:18] in a little child not a span long."[44] With their exquisite analyses of heart and mind (in a time when these two were not yet held to be distinct) and frequent emphasis on the individual soul, the best of the metaphysicals — Andrewes, Donne, and perhaps Andrewes's younger colleague at Cambridge, Mark Frank — produced a strain of what might be called psychological preaching. By offering their analyses wholly within the framework of the liturgy and basic catechesis, they preserved their art from overrefinement and made an enduring contribution to the literature of Christian character formation.

The immediate practical effect of this surprising sermon style was to seize and hold the attention — an act of mercy to a congregation for whom church attendance was compulsory. But the deeper practical aim was a moral one: to focus that attention on God's intricate and comprehensive design for the world, and to move the hearers, through careful appeals to memory and conscience, to take their place within it. Andrewes's style is superbly designed for memorability; he is, in T. S. Eliot's phrase, "master of the short sentence."[45]

> But it fareth with sentences as with coins: in coins, they that in smallest compass contain greatest value are best esteemed; and in sentences, those that in fewest words comprise most matter, are most praised.... The shorter the better; the better, the better carried away, and the better kept; and the better called for when we need it.[46]

His prose comes in breath-units; it advances through repetition and variation on themes of sound and sense, much in the manner of verse. Indeed, a portion of a Nativity sermon was taken up, with slight change, as the opening lines of Eliot's poem *Journey of the Magi:*

> It was no summer progress. A cold coming they had of it at this time of the year, just the worst time of the year to take a journey, and specially a long journey in. The ways deep, the weather sharp, the days short, the sun farthest off, *in solstitio brumali*, "the very dead of winter."[47]

The attention to concrete detail is typical; the setting evoked by the text gives the sermon a locale more vividly real than the royal chapel in which Andrewes preached. But observations about geography, weather, the natural and social world, do more than impress the scene on our minds. They point always to the moral dimensions of the story. Here he dwells on the inclement season of Christ's birth in order to emphasize the Magi's perseverance in coming to worship him. With pointed irony, which penetrates rather than berates and implicates preacher as well as hearer, he contrasts their cheerfulness and haste with our own mistaken leisure:

> We love to make no very great haste. To other things perhaps; not to *adorare*, the place of the worship of God. Why should we? Christ is no wildcat. What talk ye of twelve days? And if it be forty days hence, ye shall be sure to find His Mother and Him; she cannot be churched till then.... Best get us a new Christmas in September; we are not like to come to Christ at this feast.[48]

If the season of Christ's birth is significant, even more so is the place, since the prophet Micah takes special note of it (5:2). Bethlehem is in Andrewes's thought a chief symbol of the moral significance of the In-carnation. To someone with Andrewes's superb linguistic training and philological imagination, the name is, of course, suggestive: "It is inter-preted *domus panis*, 'the house of bread.' What place more proper for him who is 'the living bread that came down from heaven' [John 6:51], to give life to the world?"[49] But more profoundly he is struck by the fact that Micah designates this village especially as "little," and so he dwells upon its "very *miniminess:*"

> It was the least and the lowest of all "the thousands of Judah." What little and low is in things natural, that lowliness and humility is in spiri-tual. This natural birthplace of his showeth his spiritual. Humility is his place — humility, as I may call it, the Bethlehem of virtues; where you find it, "Lo, there is he born." So born in us, as born for us.[50]

The overwhelming tone of virtually all the sermons is awe at God's stupendous humility in bridging "'so great a gulf' [Luke 16:26], so huge a space, so infinite a distance between those two, between God and dust, God and hay, God and corruption, as no coming of one at the other."[51] Repeatedly he uses sharp antitheses and wordplays to underscore the magnitude of the mystery whereby God joins radical incompatibles in order to enter into our world: "It speaketh humility, I am sure, and great love that so would humble itself, if we have ears to hear it; when He, That was 'the brightness of His Father's glory,' should be so eclipsed, He that sits on the throne be thrown in a manger."[52] From this central strangeness of God manifested in flesh unfolds the whole "mystery of godliness" (1 Tim. 3:16), from Incarnation, through Passion, to glory: "We may well begin with Christ in the Cratch [manger]; we must end with Christ on the Cross";[53] "He that cometh here in clouts [swaddling clothes], He will come in the clouds one day."[54]

In his magisterial study of the metaphysical preachers and poets, Horton Davies identifies as one of the sources of their style the renaissance emphasis on instruction, both grammatical and poetic, in classical languages. Noting that an extraordinary number of them had been pupils at the Westminster School, where Andrewes was dean, he concludes: "There can be no question that the rigorous instruction in the school's curriculum, in Latin and Greek versification and retranslation into English verse, was the training ground of imagination and wit that made the metaphysical mode in verse and prose possible."[55] Doubtless this is the case, but with respect to Andrewes's distinctly *theological* application of wit, there is in fact a much nearer model than the classical pagan poets, and one with which no other English churchman was so familiar. His rhythms and antitheses often show striking similarity to the poems of the Greek liturgy. A Vespers hymn for Christmas Day uses them, exactly as Andrewes does, to underscore the wonder of the Incarnate God:

> O Lord, Thou art come to Bethlehem and hast made Thy dwelling in a cave. Thou who hast heaven as Thy throne art laid in a manger. Thou whom the hosts of angels attend on every side hast come down among shepherds, that in Thy compassion Thou mightest save our kind. Glory to Thee![56]

Andrewes's terse images contrast with the remarkably extended metaphors so characteristic of John Donne; but even that flamboyant poet does not exceed the boldness of Andrewes's imagination. Christ is considered variously as wildcat, grammatical particle, embryo, and herb;

the compassionate God as though possessed of multiple wombs filled with the pity of many mothers; the congregation as elephants who decline to bend their knees in worship. Nor does he engage in the sort of fanciful abstraction that often occupies Donne. The way they treat the theme of death shows something of the different qualities of imagination belonging to these two Jacobean preachers. There is a fascinated indignation to Donne's reflection on the process of "vermiculation" by which worms reduce the body to earth; with grim gusto he imagines our parents' dust blowing in our faces as we walk past a graveyard on a windy day; he wonders how in the resurrection God will gather limbs lost on foreign battlefields. Above all, Donne is dazzled by the prospect of heaven, which he often strains to envision or symbolize in the abstract figures of geometry.

Andrewes's interest, by comparison, is immediate and practical. His aim is to represent to his hearers the present conditions and dangers of our life in this world as they are most accurately depicted in the Scriptures. Death provides the perspective point for his artistry: "Our charge is to preach to men, *non quae volunt audire, sed quae volunt audisse,* 'not what for the present they would hear, but what another day they would wish they had heard.' "[57] The unwavering yet constantly varied appeal to the conscience which motivates his exegesis expresses with particular clarity the view that informs all premodern biblical interpretation and marks the great divide between that and modern historical critical study: namely, that there is no fixed distance between the world of the text and our own. That is, the Scriptures delineate a moral world, and not primarily a historical one, open to all who repent.

Andrewes's adherence to the full Gospel as the context for treating any text or occasion leads to surprising effects: the justly famed Nativity sermons refer to Christ's death as often as to his birth. But it is a practice of real ethical significance and is perhaps the aspect of Andrewes's preaching that is most worth emulation by modern preachers. Bonhoeffer aptly warns against the distortion of the Christian life that arises from absolutization of any one part of the Gospel: "A Christian ethic constructed solely on the basis of the incarnation would lead directly to the compromise solution. An ethic which was based solely on the cross or the resurrection of Jesus would fall victim to radicalism and enthusiasm. Only in the unity is the conflict resolved."[58]

As I have suggested, Andrewes's own moral imagination is fundamentally philological, informed by superb linguistic training, nourished and guided by a poet's love of language. The words of Scripture are to be "scrutinized in their every detail" (Ps. 111:2), for they are the most reliable means of access to spiritual truth. His exegetical sensibility allies him with such monastic theologians as Gregory the Great and Bernard of Clairvaux. Like them, he most often enters the passage by means of a single word or phrase, dissecting it grammatically and semantically, tracing it through Scripture and the ancient translations, punning on it, using it as the theme or refrain for his own exposition. To later tastes, fascination with the particular words of Scripture is sometimes carried to the point of absurdity. But the strength of this tireless exploration is that the words are never removed from their context or explained away. The text remains throughout clearly in view, "a plain mystery," its meaning enriched and rendered more susceptible of absorption by what the monastic exegetes described as "chewing" on the word to extract its full savor and nourishment. Very likely it is more than coincidence that, in a time when England's churches had been stripped of images, Andrewes treats the words of Scripture as palpable symbols by which we may see, handle, and even taste, not the whole mystery of faith, but all that is necessary for us to comprehend.

It was Andrewes's remarkable mastery of language that made his play with it of permanent significance for the English Church. He dedicated himself to the development in English of a rich and flexible theological idiom, both scriptural and liturgical, that shuns obscurantism, yet refuses to subsume the essential mysteries to rationalistic categories. In evaluating his achievement, it is well to remember that Andrewes was both a radical traditionalist and a politician who admitted to being addicted to peace "both by nature and choice."[59] If, on the one hand, he put the emerging culture of Anglicanism in full conversation with the ancient and medieval Church, on the other hand, his very reliance on the language of Scripture is a timely response to the mounting religious crisis between Reform and Counter-Reform movements that, fifteen years after Andrewes's death, would cost a king his head.[60] Following the Reformers' view that the perspicuity of Scripture is the basis for Christian unity, he charted "a way of peace . . . even in the midst of a world of controversies" with the principle that became formative for Anglicanism: "Those [points of religion] that are necessary [God] hath made plain; those that [are] not plain not necessary."[61]

The very firmness with which he adheres to the biblical text, as well as the architectonic structure of his sermons, does not make Andrewes the most quotable of preachers. It is essential to follow him as hard as he follows the biblical text, which he often examines at three levels. Briefly he refers to the (ostensible) historical context, for example, within the life of Moses, David, Jeremiah; then, at much greater length, he treats it prophetically, as pointing to Christ. It is a mark of a new kind of critical consciousness within the Reformation Church that Andrewes explicitly defends his hermeneutical moves to the audience, showing his warrants in the church fathers, in rabbinic tradition, or (as he prefers) in the New Testament, for reading an Old Testament text christologically; sometimes he explains the choice of a particular text for the present occasion.[62] Andrewes is a pastoral exegete *par excellence;* invariably and usually at greatest length, he works with the text "morally," as it denotes some benefit to ourselves — notably, ourselves as members of the gathered Body of Christ. If Donne often entertains a vision of the individual, rapt soul entering into eternal life, Andrewes consistently calls attention to the small preparatory steps that the Church as a whole takes through its common prayer and sacramental worship.

The magnificent Good Friday sermon of 1604 is one of the best examples of his judicious care in applying the text to the present life of the Church. His text is Lamentations 1:12: "Have ye no regard, O all ye that pass by the way? Consider and behold, if ever there were sorrow like my sorrow." The entire meditation revolves around a single concept, indeed, a single word: "Regard is the main point.... If you considered as you should, you would regard as you ought."[63] To bring us to this proper regard, Andrewes sets forth in the first two sections of his sermons the nature of Christ's suffering, to which there is *non sicut* (no like) and the cause of it, "which bringeth home this text to us, even unto our own bosoms":

> No reason can be given but because he regarded us — mark that reason. And what were we? Verily, utterly unworthy even His least regard, not worth the taking up, not worth the looking after. *Cum inimici essemus,* saith the Apostle; "we were his enemies" [Rom. 5:8], when he did it, without all desert before, and without all regard after he had done and suffered all this for us; and yet he would regard us that so little regard him. For when he saw us a sort of forlorn sinners, *non prius natos quam damnatos,* "damned as fast as born," as being "by nature children of wrath" [Eph. 2:3], and yet still "heaping up wrath against the day of wrath" [Rom. 2:5], by the errors of our life, till the time of our passing hence; and then the "fierce wrath of God" ready to overwhelm us, and to make us endure the terror and torments of a never dying death, another *non sicut* yet — when, I say, he was in this case, he was moved with compassion over us and undertook all this for us. Even then in

his love he regarded us, and so regarded us that he regarded not himself, to regard us...; and shall this regard find no regard at our hands? (2:152–53)

In the final part of the sermon he establishes the absurdity of our utter lack of regard:

Yes sure, his complaint is just, "Have ye no regard?" None? and yet never the like? None? and it pertains unto you? "No regard?" As if it were some common ordinary matter, and the like never was? "No regard?" As if it concerned you not a whit, and it toucheth you so near?... What will move you? Will pity? Here is distress never the like. Will duty? Here is a Person never the like. Will fear? Here is wrath never the like. Will remorse? Here are sins never the like. Will kindness? Here is love never the like. Will bounty? Here are benefits never the like. Will all these? Here they be all, all above any *sicut*, all in the highest degree. (2:155–56)

Despite the drastic disparity between God's action and our response, the sermon ends characteristically with encouragement and a surprising modesty in its demand. Christ's suffering and his love "should have... our highest regard. But if that cannot be had, our nature is so heavy, and flesh and blood so dull of apprehension in spiritual things, yet at least some regard. Some I say; the more the better; but in any wise some, and not as here no regard, none at all" (2:157). The wise pastor concludes by putting the initial demand of faith within the reach of every member of the audience: simply to regard now, this day, in this place, for a short time, what God has done — and so show a kindness to God!

It is kindly to consider *opus diei in die suo*, "the work of the day in the day it was wrought," and this day it was wrought. This day therefore, whatsoever business be, to lay them aside a little; whatsoever our haste, yet to stay a little, and to spend a few thoughts in calling to mind and taking to regard what this day the Son of God did and suffered for us; and all for this end, that what he was then we might not be, and what he is now we might be for ever. Which Almighty God grant we may do, more or less, even every one of us, according to the several measures of his grace in us! (2:158)

Ironically, the inimitability of Andrewes's exegetical and linguistic mastery may have contributed to the disrepute of metaphysical preaching. Few of Andrewes's followers could match what T. S. Eliot aptly calls his "relevant intensity." Within a few years of his death, George Herbert derided the practice, evidently by this time popular among provincial preachers of very ordinary ability, of "crumbling a text into small parts…since the words apart are not scripture, but a dictionary, and may be considered alike in all the Scripture."[64] By the middle of the century, both Anglican and Puritan preachers had moved decisively in the direction of moral and philosophical discourse, demonstrating that the truths of religion are consonant with both nature and reason. In view of the scientific search for a streamlined language of explanation rather than of wonder, it is telling that the first attack on Andrewes himself for "the great corruption of the oratory of the pulpit" came (in 1752) from the Reverend Thomas Birch, who was secretary to the Royal Society and the biographer of Archbishop Tillotson, the famed exemplar of the plain style.[65] There was no further interest in Andrewes's sermons until the Tractarians rediscovered (and reprinted) them in the nineteenth century, when Romanticism had again produced a widespread awareness of the incomparable richness of poetic language that is essential to the work of catechesis.

Introduction to "Remember Lot's Wife"

One of Andrewes's earliest court sermons, "Remember Lot's Wife" uses some of his characteristic effects, and at this early stage of his learned preaching there is a simplicity of organization that shows them to best advantage. The whole is essentially a meditation on the single word "remember," which appears in English or Latin some sixty times. The theme of perseverance is captured in the image of salt, treated both positively (as a preservative) and negatively (as the residue of the "melting virtue" of security). His concern for the moral implications of narrative is particularly clear as he teaches his audience, "So to read stories past, as we make not ourselves matter for story to come."

Andrewes's view of human nature is typically sympathetic but unsentimental. Lot's wife is not a cardboard moral type but a real person, admirable yet ultimately and tragically frail: with terrible suddenness, thirty years of constancy are undone. She is contrasted with Mary Magdalene, perhaps Andrewes's favorite biblical character,[66] who exemplifies a necessary lack of constancy in sin. The theme of perseverance in faithfulness complements Andrewes's regular Lenten preaching on repentance and reminds an audience grown sanguine through the long stability of Elizabeth's reign and the recent victory over the Armada that many fall away "in these dangerous days of ours." The concluding section is framed as a commendation of the queen's perseverance, but the final note of warning suggests that he addresses her as a Christian in need of continual strengthening as well as an example of virtue. At this season, it was Andrewes's custom to set aside regular hours for private spiritual conversation with any who might seek it; and his sermons for Ash Wednesday and Lent contain his most specific teachings on the habits of faith. Here, following the practice of other prominent Elizabethan preachers, he makes the holiest season of the year an occasion to recall governors, and especially the Sovereign, to their vocation of setting a godly example for the people.[67]

REMEMBER LOT'S WIFE

Preached before Queen Elizabeth at Hampton Court
on March 6, 1594

A part of the chapter read this morning, by order of the Church, for the second lesson.

Remember Lot's wife.
Memores estote uxoris Lot.
—LUKE 17:32

The words are few, and the sentence short; no one in Scripture so short. But it fareth with sentences as with coins: in coins, they that in smallest compass contain greatest value are best esteemed; and in sentences, those that in fewest words comprise most matter are most praised. Which, as of all sentences it is true; so specially of those that are marked with *memento*. In them, the shorter the better; the better, and the better carried away, and the better kept; and the better called for when we need it. And such is this here; of rich contents, and withal exceeding compendious. So that we must needs be without all excuse, it being but three words and but five syllables, if we do not remember it.

The sentence is our Savior's, uttered by him upon this occasion. Before, in verse 18, he had said that "the days of the Son of Man should be as the days of Lot," in two respects: (1) in respect of the suddenness of the destruction that should come; and (2) in respect of the security of the people on whom it should come. For the

Sodomites laughed at it; and Lot's wife, it should seem, but slightly regarded it. Being then in Lot's story, very fitly and by good consequence out of that story, he leaveth us a *memento* before he leaveth it.

There are in Lot's story two very notable monuments of God's judgment: the lake of Sodom, and Lot's wife's pillar. The one the punishment of resolute sin; the other of faint virtue. For the Sodomites are an example of impenitent willful sinners, and Lot's wife of imperseverant [failing to be constant in the face of discouragement] and relapsing righteous persons.

Both these are in it; but Christ, of both these, taketh the latter only. For two sorts of men there are, for which these two items are to be fitted: (1) to those in state of sin that are wrong, the lake of Sodom; (2) to those in state of grace that are well, if so they can keep them, Lot's wife's pillar. To the first in state of sin, Moses propoundeth "the vine of Sodom and grapes of Gomorrah" [Deut. 32:32], *quæ contacta cinerescunt*, 'that if ye but touch them turn to ashes.' To the other in state of grace, Christ here, Lot's wife's pillar. To the one Jeremy crieth, *Qui cecidit, adjiciat ut resurgat* [Let the one who has fallen strive to rise (Jer. 8:4)]. To the other St. Paul; *Qui stat, videat ne cadat* [Let the one who stands take care not to fall (1 Cor. 10:12)]. [H]Agar, that is departed from Abraham's house with her face toward Egypt, the angel calleth to return and not to persevere [Gen. 16:9]: Lot's wife, that is gone out of Sodom and in the right way to Zoar, the angel willeth to persevere and not to return [Gen. 19:17]. So that to them this *memento* is by Christ directed, that being departed from the errors of Ur are gone out from the sins of Sodom, are entered into the profession of the truth or into the course of a virtuous life. So that if we lay it to ourselves, we shall lay it aright; that Lot's wife be our example, and that we sprinkle ourselves with the salt of her pillar, *ne putrescamus* [lest we rot], that we turn not again to folly, or fall away from our own steadfastness. And, if it be meant to us, needful it is that we receive it. A point no doubt of important consideration and necessity, as well for religion to call on, as for our nature to hear of. First, for religion: her glory it is no less to be able to show *antiquos discipulos*, "old professors," as Mnason was [Acts 21:16], than daily to convert and make new proselytes. And therefore, with Christ we must not ever be dealing with *venite ad me* [come to me (Matt. 11:28)]; but sometimes too, with *manete in me* [remain in me (John 15:4)]. That hath his place — not ever with *stimuli,* 'goads' to incite men to, but otherwise with *clavi,* 'nails' to fasten them in. For as nature hath thought requisite as well the breasts to bring up, as the womb to bring forth; and philosophy holdeth *tueri* [to protect/maintain] of no less regard than *quærere* [to seek]; and with the lawyers, *habendum* [having] is not the only thing, but *tenendum* [holding] needful too; and the physician as careful of the regiment [regimen], and fearful of the recidivation [relapse], as of the disease and cure; so divinity is respective to both — both to lay the groundwork surely, *ne corruat,* 'that it shake not' with Esay's *nisi credideritis* [unless you believe (Isa. 7:9; cf. Matt. 7:27, Luke 4:49)]; and to roof it carefully, *ne perpluat,* 'that it rain not through' and rot the principals, with Paul's *si permanseris, alioquin excideris et tu* [if you abide...; otherwise you, too, will be cut off (Rom. 11:22)].

Needful then for religion to call on this virtue; and as for religion to call on, so for our nature to be called on. Wherein, as there is *tenellum quid,* "a tender part" not able to endure the cross, for which we need the virtue of patience; so is there also ἀψίκορόν τι, 'a flitting humor,' not able to endure the tediousness of anything long; for which we no less need the virtue of perseverance. The prophet, in the seventy-eighth Psalm, saith our nature is as a bow, which, when it is bent to his full, except it be followed hard till it be sure and fast, starts back again and is as far off as ever it was [Ps. 78:57]. The Apostle compareth it to "flesh" [Rom. 7:18] as it is, which will *sine sale putrescere* [rot without salt], and if it be not corned, of itself bringeth forth corruption. And to help this our evil inclination forward, there be in all ages dangerous examples to draw us on. The Israelites, after they had passed the Red Sea and all the perils of the desert, and were now come even to the borders of Canaan, even there say, *Bene nobis erat in Ægypto,* "We were better in Egypt" [Num. 11:18]; "let us make a captain and return thither" [Num. 14:4]. The Romans, in the New, at the first so glorious professors that St. Paul saith, "All the world spake of their faith" [Rom. 1:8]; after, when trouble arose and St. Paul was called *coram* [before (a court)] of the same Romans he saith, *Nemo mihi adfuit, sed omnes deseruerunt,* "None stood by me, all shrunk away" [2 Tim. 4:16]. And in these dangerous days of ours, the falling away quite of divers, and some such as have said of themselves with Peter, *Etsi omnes, non ego* [Even if all (fall away), not I (Matt. 26:33)]; and others have said of them, *Etsi omnes, non ille* [Even if all, not he]. The declining of

others, which, as Daniel's image, decay by degrees; from a head of
fine gold fall to a silver breast, and from thence to loins of brass, and
thence to legs of iron, and last to feet of clay [Dan. 2:32–33]; the wavering and amaze of others that stand in the plain with Lot's wife,
looking about, and cannot tell whether to go forward to little Zoar
or back again to the ease of Sodom; show plainly that Lot's wife is
forgotten, and this is a needful *memento,* "Remember Lot's wife." If
then it be ours, and so nearly concern us, let us see, *quantum valent
hæ quinque syllabæ* [how much these five syllables signify].

The Division

I. First, Christ sending our memory to a story past; of the use of
remembering stories in general.

II. Secondly, of this particular of Lot's wife, and the points to be
remembered in it.

III. Thirdly, how to apply those points, that, as St. Augustine saith,
condiant nos, ut sal statuæ sit nobis condimentum vitæ, 'that the salt
of this pillar may be the season of our lives.'[68]

Section I

Christ sending our memory to a story past;
of the use of remembering stories in general

The Prophet Esay doth call us that stand in this place, "the Lord's remembrancers" [Isa. 62:6]; as to God for the people by the office
of prayers, so from God to the people by the office of preaching. In which office of preaching we are employed as much about
recognosce [knowing again/remembering] as about *cognosce* [per-
ceiving]; as much in calling to their minds the things they know and
have forgot, as in teaching them the things they know not, or never
learnt. The things are many we have commission to put men in mind
of. Some touching themselves: for it is many times too true which
the philosopher saith; *Nihil tam longe abest a nobis quam ipsi nos,*
'Nothing is so far from our minds, as we ourselves.' For naturally,
as saith the Apostle, we do παραρρύειν, "leak and run out" [Heb.
2:1]; and when we have looked in the glass, we straight "forget our

fashion again" [James 1:23–24]. Therefore we have in charge to put men in mind of many things, and to call upon them with divers *mementos*. *Memento quia sicut lutum tu*, "remember the baseness of our mold what it is."[69] *Memento quia vita ventus*, "remember the frailness of our life how short it is."[70] *Memento tenebrosi temporis*, "remember the days of darkness are coming," and they be many [Eccles. 11:8]. All which we know well enough, and yet need to be put in mind of them.

But the storehouse, and the very life of memory, is the history of time: and a special charge have we, all along the Scriptures, to call upon men to look to that. For all our wisdom consisting either in experience or memory — experience of our own, or memory of others, our days are so short, that our experience can be but slender; *tantum hesterni sumus* [we are only yesterdays (Job 8:9)], saith Job, and our own time cannot afford us observations enough for so many cases as we need direction in. Needs must we then, as he here adviseth, *interrogare generationem pristinam* [Job 8:8], "ask the former age," what they did in like case; search the records of former times, wherein our cases we shall be able to match, and to pattern them all. Solomon saith excellently, *Quid est quod fuit? Quod futurum est.* "What is that that hath been? That that shall be." And back again, What is that that shall be? That that hath been. *Et nihil novum est sub sole*, "and there is nothing under the sun of which it may be said, it is new but it hath been already in the former generations" [Eccles. 1:9–10]. So that it is but turning the wheel and setting before us some case of antiquity which may sample ours [provide an example for our situation], and either remembering to follow it if it fell out well, or eschew it if the success were thereafter. For example, by Abimelech's story King David reproveth his captains for pursuing the enemy too near the wall, seeing Abimelech miscarried by like adventure [2 Sam. 11:21]; and so maketh use of remembering Abimelech. And by David's example, that in want of all other bread, refused not the show-bread, Christ our Savior defendeth his disciples in like distress [Mark 2:25], and showeth that, upon such extremity, *necessitas* doth even *legem Legi dicere*, 'give a law even to the Law itself.'

Seven several times we are called upon to do it: (1) *Memento dierum antiquorum* [Deut. 32:7, Remember the days of old, saith Moses]; (2) *Recordamini prioris Seculi* — Esay [Isa. 46:9, Recollect (the things) of a former age]; (3) *State super vias antiquas* —

Jeremy [Jer. 6:16, Stand by the ancient roads]; (4) *Investiga patrum memoriam* — Job [Job 8:8, Consult the memory of the ancestors]; (5) *Exemplum sumite Prophetas* — James [James 5:10, Take the prophets as an example]; (6) *Rememoramini dies priscos* — Paul [Heb. 10:32, Recall the former days]; (7) Remember Lot's wife — Christ here; that is to lay our actions to those we find there, and of like doings to look for like ends. So read stories past, as we make not ourselves matter for story to come.

Section II

Of this particular of Lot's wife,
and the points to be remembered in it

Now of and among them all, our Savior Christ after a special manner commendeth unto us this of Lot's wife. Of which thus much we may say, that it is the only one story, which of all the stories of the Old Testament he maketh his choice of, to put in his *memento;* which he would have them which have forgotten to remember, and those that remember never to forget. Oft to repair to this story, and to fetch salt from this pillar: that they lose not what they have done, and so perish in the recidivation of Lot's wife.

Then to descend into the particulars. I find in stories two sorts of *memento:* (1) *Memento et fac,* 'remember to follow'; (2) *Memento et fuge,* 'remember to fly the like.' Mary Magdalene's ointment [Mark 14:39], an example of one; Lot's wife's salt-stone, an example of the other. Or to keep us to this story, Lot looked not back, till he came safe to Zoar; *memento et fac.* Lot's wife did, and died for it; *memento et fuge.*

The verse before showeth why Christ laid the *memento* upon her. Μὴ καταβάτω, μὴ ἐπιστρεψάτω that we should not turn or return back, as she did; that we should not follow her, but when we come at this pillar, turn at it and take another way. That is, we should "remember Lot's wife," but follow Lot; remember her, but follow him.

Now in either of both *mementos,* to follow or to fly, we alway enquire of two points, and so here: (1) *quid fecit,* and (2) *quid passa est;* what they did whose story we read, and how they sped — the fact and the effect. The fact, vice or virtue; the effect, reward or punishment.

Both which concerning this unfortunate woman we find set down in one verse, in the nineteenth of Genesis, what she did; that "she drew back," or "looked back" [Gen. 19:26] — this was her sin. The effect, that she was turned into a salt-stone — this was her punishment. And these two are the two memorandums concerning her to be remembered. First of her fault.

The angel had given charge to Lot and his company, in the seventeenth of that chapter, "Scape for thy life, stay not in the plain, look not once behind thee lest thou perish." "Scape for thy life" — she trifled for all that as if no peril were. "Stay not in the plain," yet stayed she behind. "Look not back lest thou die." She would and did look back, to die for it. So that she did all that she was forbid, and regarded none of the angel's words, but despised the counsel of God against her own soul. This was her sin, the sin of disobedience, but consisteth of sundry degrees by which she fell, needful all to be remembered.

The first was that she did not *severe custodire mandatum Dei*, 'strictly keep her to the angel's charge,' but dallied with it, and regarded it by halves; that is, say what he would, she might use the matter as she would; go or stay, and look about as she list. Such light regard is like enough to have grown of a wandering distrust; lest haply, she had left Sodom in vain, and the angel feared them with that which never should be. The sun rose so clear and it was so goodly a morning, she repented she came away. Reckoning her sons-in-law more wise in staying still, than Lot and herself in so unwisely departing. Which is the sin of unbelief, the bane both of constancy and perseverance. Constancy in the purpose of our mind, and perseverance in the tenor of our life.

From this grew the second, that she began to tire and draw behind, and kept not pace with Lot and the angels. An evil sign. For ever fainting is next step to forsaking; and *sequebatur a longe* [she followed from a distance], a preparative to a giving clean over. *Occasionem quærit*, saith Solomon, *qui vult discedere ab amico*, "he that hath not list to follow, will pick some quarrel or other to be cast behind" [cf. Prov. 18:1].

This tiring, had it grown of weakness or weariness or want of breath, might have been borne with; but it came of another cause, which is the third degree. It was, saith the text, at least to look back, and to cast her eye to the place her soul longed after. Which showeth that the love of Sodom sticked in her still; that though her

feet were come from thence, her heart stayed there behind; and
that in look and thought she returned thither, whither in body she
might not; but possibly would in body too, if as Nineveh did,[71] so
Sodom had still remained.

Looking back might proceed of divers causes: so might this of
hers, but that Christ's application directs us. The verse before saith,
"Somewhat in the house"; something left behind affected her, of
which he giveth us warning. She grew weary of trouble, and of shifting so oft. From Ur to Haran; thence to Canaan; thence to Egypt;
thence to Canaan again; then to Sodom, and now to Zoar; and that,
in her old days, when she would fainest have been at rest. Therefore,
in this wearisome conceit of new trouble now to begin, and withal
remembering the convenient seat she had in Sodom, she even desired to die by her flesh-pots, and to be buried in "the graves of
lust" [Num. 11:34]; wished them at Zoar that would, and herself at
Sodom again, desiring rather to end her life with ease in that stately
city than to remove, and be safe perhaps, and perhaps not, in the
desolate mountains. And this was the sin of restiness of soul, which
affected her eyes and knees, and was the cause of all the former.
When men weary of a good course which long they have holden,
for a little ease or wealth, or I wot not what other secular respect,
fall away in the end; so losing the praise and fruit of their former
perseverance, and relapsing into the danger and destruction, from
which they had so near escaped.

Behold, these were the sins of Lot's wife, a wavering of mind,
slow steps, the convulsion of her neck: all these caused her weariness and fear of new trouble — she preferred Sodom's ease before
Zoar's safety. "Remember Lot's wife."

This was her sin; and this her sin was in her made much more
heinous by a double circumstance, well worth the remembering; as
ever weighty circumstances are matter of special regard, in a story
specially. One, that she fell after she had stood long. The other that
she fell even then, when God by all means offered her safety, and
so "forsook her own mercy" [Jonah 2:9].

Touching the first. These "winter brooks," as Job [6:15] termeth
flitting, desultory, Christians, if they dry; these "summer fruits," as
Amos [8:1–2], if they putrefy; these "morning clouds," as Hosea
[6:4], if they scatter; these "shallow rooted corn" [Matt. 13:5], if they
wither and come to nothing, it is the less grief. No man looked for
other. Pharaoh with his fits, that at every plague sent upon him is

godly on a sudden, and "O pray for me now" [Exod. 8:4, *et passim*]; and when it is gone, as profane as ever he was, beginning nine times, and nine times breaking off again; — he moves not much. To go farther. Saul that for two years [1 Sam. 13:1], Judas that for three, Nero that for five kept well, and then fell away, though it be much yet may it be borne. But this woman had continued now thirty years, for so they reckon from Abraham's going out of Ur to the destruction of Sodom. This, this is the grief: that she should persist all this time, and after all this time fall away. The rather, if we consider yet farther, that not only she continued many years, but sustained many things in her continuance, as being companion of Abraham and Lot in their exile, their travel, and all their affliction. This is the grief, that after all these storms in the broad sea well passed, she should in this pitiful manner be wrecked in the haven. And when she had been in Egypt, and not poisoned with the superstitions of Egypt; when lived in Sodom, and not defiled with the sins of Sodom; not fallen away for the famine of Canaan, nor taken harm by the fullness of the city of the plain; after all this, she should lose the fruit of all this, and do and suffer so many things all in vain — this is the first. Remember it.

The second is no whit inferior; that at that instant she woefully perished, when God's special favor was proffered to preserve her; and that when of all other times she had means and cause to stand, then of all other times she fell away. Many were the mercies she found and felt at God's hand by this very title, that she was Lot's wife. For by it she was incorporated into the house and family, and made partaker of the blessings of the faithful Abraham. It was a mercy to be delivered from the errors of Ur;[72] a mercy, to be kept safe in Egypt; a mercy, to be preserved from the sin of Sodom; a mercy, to be delivered from the captivity of the five kings [Genesis 14]; and this the last and greatest mercy, that she was sought to be delivered from the perishing of the five cities. This no doubt doth mightily aggravate the offense, that, so many ways before remembered by God in trouble, she so coldly remembered him; and that now presently, being offered grace, she knoweth not the day of her visitation; but being brought out of Sodom, and warned of the danger that might ensue, having the angels to go before her, Lot to bear her company, her daughters to attend her, and being now at the entrance of Zoar, the haven of her rest; this very time, place, and presence, she maketh choice of to perish in, and to cast away that which God would have saved; in respect of herself, desperately;

of the angels, contemptuously; of her husband and daughters, scandalously; of God and his favors, unthankfully; "forsaking her own mercy," and perishing in the sin of willful defection.

"Remember Lot's wife," and these two: that she "looked back," after so long time, and so many sufferings. That she "looked back," after so many, so merciful, and so mighty protections. And remember this withal, that she "looked back" only, and went not back; would, it may be, but that it was all on fire. But, whether she would or no, or whether we do or no, this forethinking ourselves we be gone out, this faint proceeding, this staying in the plain, this convulsion of the neck, and writhing of the eyes back; this irresolute wavering, whether we should choose either bodily pleasures in perishing Sodom, or the safety of our souls in little Zoar, was her sin; and this is the sin of so many as stand as she stood, and look as she looked, though they go not back; but if they go back too, they shall justify her, and heap upon themselves a more heavy condemnation. So much for the sin, which we should remember to avoid.

Now for her punishment, which we must remember to escape.

This relapse in this manner, that the world might know it to be a sin highly displeasing his majesty, God hath not only marked it for a sin, but salted it too, that it might never be forgotten.

The wages and punishment of this sin of hers was it, which is "the wages of all sin," that is, "death" [Rom. 6:23]. Death in her sure worthily, that refused life with so easy conditions, as the holding of her head still, and would needs look back and die. ·

The sound of death is fearful, what death soever; yet it is made more fearful four ways, which all be in this of hers.

(1) We desire to die with respite: and sudden death we fear, and pray against. Her death was sudden — back she looked, and never looked forward more. It was her last look.

(2) We desire to have remorse of sin ere we be taken away; and death, in the very act of sin, is most dangerous. Her death was so. She died in the very convulsion; she died with her face to Sodom.

(3) We would die "the common death of mankind, and be visited after the visitation of other men" [Num. 16:29]; and an unusual strange death is full of terror. Hers was so. God's own hand from heaven, by a strange and fearful visitation.

(4) Our wish is to die, and to be buried, and not to remain a spectacle above ground, which nature abhorreth. She so died as she remained a spectacle of God's wrath, and a byword to pos-

terity, and as many as passed by. For until Christ's time, and after, this monument was still extant, and remained undefaced so many hundred years. Josephus, a writer of good account, which lived after this, saith, Ἱστόρηκα αὐτὴν, ἔτι γὰρ καὶ νῦν διαμένει: 'I myself have seen and beholden it, for it stands to be seen to this day.'[73] A reed she was; a pillar she is, which she seemed to be but was not. She was melting water; she is congealed to salt. Thus have we both her fault and punishment. Let us remember both; to shun the fault, that the penalty light not on us.

Section III

How to apply those points, that, as St. Augustine saith,
condiant nos, ut sal statuæ sit nobis condimentum vitæ,
'that the salt of this pillar may be the season of our lives'

Now this pillar was erected, and this verdure given it, for our sakes. For, among the many ways that the wisdom of God useth to dispose of the sin of man, and out of evil to draw good, this is one and a chief one, that he suffereth not their evil examples to vanish as a shadow, but maketh them to stand as pillars for ages to come, with the heathen man's inscription, Ἐς ἐμέ τις ὁρέων εὐσεβὴς ἔστω, 'Look on me, and learn by me to serve God better.'[74]

And an high benefit it is for us, that he not only embalmeth the memory of the just for our imitation, but also powdereth and maketh brine of the evil for our admonition;[75] that as a scent from Mary Magdalene's ointment, so a relish from Lot's wife's pillar, should remain to all posterity.

Profane persons, in their perishing, God could dash to pieces, and root out their remembrance from off the earth. He doth not, but suffereth their quarters, as it were, to be set up in stories, *ut pœnia impii sit eruditio justi,* 'that their punishment may be our advertisement.' Poureth not out their blood, nor casts it away, but saves it for a bath, *ut lavet justus pedes in sanguine peccatoris,* "that the righteous may wash their footsteps in the blood of the ungodly" [Ps. 58:11]; that "all," even the ruin of the wicked, "may cooperate to the good of them that fear God."[76] This woman, in her inconstancy, could he have sunk into the earth, or blown up as saltpeter, that no remembrance should have remained of her. He doth not, but for us and for our sakes he erecteth a pillar: and not a pillar only to point and gaze at, but a "pillar or rock of salt," whence we may and must fetch wherewith to season whatsoever is unsavory in our lives. And this, this, is the life and soul of memory; this is wisdom — the art of extracting salt out of the wicked, triacle [an antidote] out of vipers, our own happiness out of *aliena pericula* [foreign dangers]; and to make those that were unprofitable to themselves, profitable to us. For sure, though Lot's wife were evil, her salt is good. Let us see then how to make her evil our good; see if we can draw any savory thing from this example.

(1) That which we should draw out, is perseverance, *muria virtutum*, as Gregory calleth it, 'the preserver of virtues,' without which, as summer fruits, they will perish and putrefy; the salt of the covenant, without which the flesh of our sacrifice will take wind and corrupt. But St. Augustine better, *regina virtutum*, 'the queen of virtues'; for that, however the rest run and strive and do masteries, yet *perseverantia sola coronatur*, 'perseverance is the only crowned virtue.'[77]

(2) Now perseverance we shall attain, if we can possess our souls with the due care, and rid them of security. Of Lot's wife's security, as of water, was this salt here made. And, if security, as water, do but touch it, it melts away presently. But care will make us fix our eye, and gather up our feet, and "forgetting that which is behind," *tendere in anteriora*, "to follow hard toward the prize of our high calling" [Phil. 3:13–14].

(3) And, to avoid security, and to breed in us due care, St. Bernard saith, 'Fear will do it.' *Vis in timore securus esse? securitatem time;* "the only way to be secure in fear, is to fear security.' St. Paul had given the same counsel before, that to preserve *si permanseris* [if you would continue (Rom. 11:22)], no better advice than *noli altum sapere, sed time* [do not wish to think high, but fear (Rom. 11:20)].

Now, from her story these considerations are yielded, each one as an handful of salt to keep us, and to make us keep.

First, that we see, as of Christ's twelve which he had sorted and selected from the rest, one miscarried: *et illum gregem non timuit lupus intrare*, 'and that the wolf feared not to seize, no, not upon that flock' [cf. John 10:12]; and as of Noah's eight that were saved from the flood, one fell away too [Ham; see Gen. 9:22–25]; so that of Lot's four here, and but four in all, all came not to Zoar — one came short. So that of twelve, of eight, of four; yea, a little after, of two, one is refused [Esau; see Gen. 25:23–34]; that we may remember, few there be that scape from Sodom in the angel's company; and of those, few though they be, all are not safe neither. Who would not fear, if one may perish in the company of angels!

Secondly, that as one miscarrieth, so not every one, but one that had continued so long, and suffered so many things, and after all this continuance, and all these sufferings, falls from her estate, and turns all out and in; and by the inconstancy of one hour maketh void the perseverance of so many years, and as Ezekiel saith, "In the day they turn away to iniquity, all the former righteousness they have done, shall not be remembered" [Ezek. 18:24].

Thirdly, that as she perisheth, so at the same time that Sodom; she by it, and it by her. That one end cometh to the sinner without repentance, and to the just without perseverance. One end to the abomination of Sodom, and to the recidivation of Lot's wife. *Et non egredientes, et egredientes respicientes;* 'they that go not out of her perish, and they that go out of her perish too if they look back.' Lacus Asphaltites[78] is a monument of the one; Lot's wife's salt-stone a memorial of the other.

Lastly, that as one perisheth, and that such an one, so that she perisheth at the gates, even hard at the entry of Zoar; which of all other is most fearful — so near her safety, so hard at the gates of her deliverance; remember, that near to Zoar gates there stands a salt-stone.

These very thoughts, what her case was these four ways, and what ours may be who are no better than she was, will search us like salt, and teach us, that as, if we remember what we have been, we may, saith St. Bernard, *erubescere* [blush]; so if we remember what we may be, we may *contremiscere* [quake]; that we see our beginnings, but see not our ending; we see our *stadium*, not our *dolichum*.[79] And that, as we have great need to pray with the prophet, "Thou hast taught me from my youth up until now — forsake me not in mine old age, now when I am gray-headed" [Ps. 71:18]; so we had need stir up our care of continuing, seeing we see it is nothing to begin except we continue: nor to continue, except we do it to the end.

Remember, we make not light account of the angel's *serva animam tuam* [save your soul (Gen. 19:17)]; blessing ourselves in our hearts, and saying, *non fiet tibi hoc* [This shall not happen to you

(Matt. 16:22)]; we shall come safe, go we never so soft [ever so easily, slowly]; Zoar will not run away.

Remember, we be not weary to go whither God would have us — not to Zoar, though a little one, if our soul may there live; and never buy the ease of our body, with the hazard of our soul, or a few days of vanity with the loss of eternity.

Remember, we slack not our pace, nor stand still on the plain. For if we stand still, by still standing we are meet to be made a pillar, even to stand still, and never to remove.

Remember, we look not back, either with her on the vain delights of Sodom left; or with Peter on St. John behind us, to say, *Domine, quid iste?* [Lord, what about this man? (John 21:20)]. Both will make us forget our following. "None that casteth his eye the other way," is εὔθετος, "meet" as he should be, "meet for the kingdom of God" [Luke 9:62].

But specially remember we leave not our heart behind us, but that we take that with us, when we go out of Sodom; for if that stay, it will stay the feet, and writhe the eye, and neither the one nor the other will do their duty. Remember, that our heart wander not, that our heart long not. This care, if it be fervent, will bring us perseverance.

Now, that we may the better learn somewhat out of her punishment too; let us remember also, that as to her, so to us, God may send some unusual visitation, and take us suddenly away, and in the act of sin too.

Remember the danger and damage; it is no less matter we are about, than *perdet animam* [losing the soul]. Which if we do, we frustrate and forfeit all the fruit of our former well-continued course; all we have done is vain. Yea, all that Christ hath done for us is in vain; whose pains and sufferings we ought specially to tender, knowing that *supra omnem laborem labor irritus*, 'no labor to lost labor'; and Christ then hath lost his labor for us.

Remember the folly; that "beginning in the Spirit" we "end in the flesh" [Gal. 3:3]; turning our backs to Zoar, we turn our face to Sodom; joining to a head of fine gold feet of clay [cf. Daniel 2], and to a precious foundation a covering of thatch.

Remember the disgrace; that we shall lose our credit and account while we live, and shall hear that of Christ, *hic homo;* and that other, *Quid existis in desertum videre?* [What did you go out into the wilderness to see?]: "A reed shaken with the wind" [Matt. 11:7].

Remember the scandal; that, falling ourselves, we shall be a block for to make others fall; a sin no lighter, nor less, nor lighter than a mill-stone [Matt. 18:6].

Remember the infamy; that we shall leave our memory remaining in stories, among Lot's wife, and Job's wife, Demas [cf. 2 Tim. 4:10] and Ecebolius, and the number of relapsed, there to stand to be pointed at, no less than this heap of salt.

Remember the judgment that is upon them after their relapse, though they live, that they do even with her here *obrigescere*, 'wax hard and numb,' and serve others for a *caveat*, wholly unprofitable for themselves.

Remember the difficulty of reclaiming to good — "seven evil spirits" entering instead of one, that their "last state is worse than the first" [Matt. 12:45].

And lastly, remember that we shall justify Sodom by so doing, and her frozen sin shall condemn our melting virtue. For they in the willfulness of their wickedness persisted till fire from heaven consumed them; and they being thus obdurate in sin, ought not she, and we much more, to be constant in virtue? And if the drunkard hold out till he have lost his eyes, the unclean person till he have wasted his loins, the contentious till he have consumed his wealth, *Quis pudor quod infelix populus Dei non habet tantam in bono perseverantiam, quantam mali in malo!* 'What shame is it, that God's unhappy people should not be as constant in virtue as these miscreants have been, and be in vice!'

Each of these by itself, all these put together will make a full *memento*, which if she had remembered, she had been a pillar of light in heaven, not of salt in earth. It is too late for her — we in due time yet may remember it.

And when we have remembered these, remember Christ too that gave the *memento;* that he calleth himself *alpha* and *omega* [Rev. 1:8] — not only *alpha* for his happy beginning, but *omega* for his thrice happy ending. For that he left us not, nor gave over the work of our redemption, till he brought it to *consummatum est* [it is finished]. And that on our part, *summa religionis est imitari quem colis*, 'the highest act of religion, is for the Christian to conform himself, not to Lot's wife, but to Christ, whose name he weareth.' And though *verus amor non sumit vires de spe*, 'true love indeed receiveth no manner strength from hope,' but, though it hope for nothing, loveth nevertheless; yet to quicken our love, which oft is but faint, and for a full *memento*, remember the reward. Remember how Christ will remember us for it; which shall not be the wages of an hireling, or lease-wise for time, and term of years, but αἰῶνες αἰώνων [ages of ages], eternity itself, never to expire, end, or determine, but to last and endure for ever and ever.

But this reward, saith Ezekiel, is for those whose foreheads are marked with *tau* [Ezek. 9:4], which, as *omega* in Greek, is the last letter in the Hebrew alphabet, and the mark of *consummatum est* among them; they only shall escape the wrath to come. And this crown is laid up for them, not of whom it may be said, *currebatis bene*, "ye did run well" [Gal. 5:7]; but for those that can say with St. Paul, *cursum consummavi*, "I have finished my course well" [2 Tim. 4:7].

And, thanks be to God, we have not hitherto wanted this salt, but remembered Lot's wife well. So that this exhortation, because we have prevented and done that which it calleth for, changeth his nature, and becometh a commendation, as all others do. A commendation I say; yet not so much of the people, whose only felicity is to serve and be subject to one that is constant—for otherwise we know how wavering a thing the multitude is — as for the Prince, whose constant standing giveth strength to many a weak knee otherwise. And blessed be God and the Father of our Lord Jesus Christ, that we stand in the presence of such a Prince, who hath ever accounted of perseverance, not only as of *regina virtutum*, 'the queen of virtues,' but as of *virtus reginarum*, 'the virtue of a queen.' Who, like Zerubbabel, first by princely magnanimity laid the corner-stone in a troublesome time; and since, by heroical constancy, through many both alluring proffers and threatening dangers, hath brought forth the head-stone also with the prophet's acclamation, "Grace, grace unto it" [Zech. 4:7] — grace, for so happy a beginning, and grace for so thrice happy an ending. No terrors, no enticement, no care of her safety hath removed her from her steadfastness; but with a fixed eye, with straight steps, with a resolute mind, hath entered herself, and brought us into Zoar. It is a little one, but therein our souls shall live; and we are in safety, all the cities of the plain being in combustion round about us. Of whom it shall be remembered, to her high praise, not only that of the heathen, *illaque virgo viri* [that virgin of manliness], but that of David, that all her days she served God "with a covenant of salt" [2 Chron. 13:5], and with her Israel, from the first day until now. And of this be we persuaded, that "He which began this good work in her, will perform it unto the day of Jesus Christ" [Phil. 1:6], to her everlasting praise, comfort, and joy, and in her to the comfort, joy, and happiness of us all.

Yet it is not needless, but right requisite, that we which are the Lord's remembrancers put you in mind, that as perseverance is the queen of virtues, *quia ea sola coronatur* [for she alone is crowned]; so is it also, *quia Satanas ei soli insidiatur*, 'for that all Satan's malice, and all his practices are against it.'[80] The more careful need we to be, to carry in our eye this example. Which God grant we may, and that our hearts may seriously regard, and our memories carefully keep it, *ut hæc columna fulciat nos, et hic sal condiat nos*, 'that this pillar may prop our weakness, and this salt season our sacrifice,' that it may be remembered, and accepted, and rewarded in the day of the Lord!

Introduction to Nativity Sermon IX

The seventeen Nativity sermons are deservedly the best known of Andrewes's preaching, not because they are uniformly excellent (although some of his most moving writing is found here), but because they give fullest expression to the distinctive note of his theology: wonder and joy at "How much [God] made of us" and "how little He was made for us."[81] Andrewes's vibrant imagination was especially drawn to St. Bernard's paradox of "*Verbum infans*, the Word without a word, the eternal Word not able to speak a word,"[82] and he often dwells upon that wonder:

> "He," that (as in the thirty-eighth of Job he saith) "taketh the vast body of the main sea, turns it to and fro, as a little child, and rolls it about with the swaddling bands of darkness" [Job 38:9] — he comes thus to clouts, himself! . . . There lieth he, the Lord of glory without all glory. Instead of a palace, a poor stable; of a cradle of state, a beast's cratch; no pillow but a lock of hay; no hangings but dust and cobwebs; no attendants, but *in medio animalium* [in the midst of beasts], as the Fathers read the third of Habakkuk [Hab. 3:2]. For if the inn were full, the stable was not empty we may be sure.[83]

Andrewes's thought on the Incarnation develops almost entirely through counterpoint, moving between God and human, birth and death, wrath and love, child and son, shepherds and angels, cratch and cross. Yet always the vibrant images and antitheses are directed to an end that is both theological and pastoral: to bring his hearers to apprehend the paradox of the Incarnation in a way which is "at once sensuous and intellectual"[84] — that is, to bring them to a poetic apprehension that transcends but does not bypass reason. Further, by laying steady emphasis on the practical benefit that the paradox conveys to us, he seeks to elicit the reciprocal devotion that is the appropriate response to God's astonishing love.

This sermon, preached before James at Whitehall Palace, establishes our benefit through elaborate wordplay on "Immanuel." The reader will judge whether the memorable Hebrew-English punning is more effective than infelicitous; in any case, it is not frivolous. The aphorism "His nominals be reals" (a view for which the prophet Isaiah offers much support) expresses the quasi-sacramental significance he assigns to the divine name as a symbol of God's presence with us, now made irrevocable: "He is not, cannot be named without us." The point is crucial to his theology, for Andrewes goes beyond Anselm in seeing salvation in Christ as more than a repurchase of our original condition but rather an improvement upon it, so that God is "with us as never before." As is his practice in the Nativity sermons, Andrewes gives final reinforcement to the verbal symbol by directing his hearers to the Eucharist, the most perfect sign of God's presence with us on earth and the means by which we are prepared for full union in Heaven.

Modern readers will wince at his inference of malice in the Jews' reading *alma* as a "young woman" rather than "virgin" — an interpretation that modern philology supports, though Andrewes's reading is argued, typically, on solid contextual basis and the best scholarship of the time. We are rightly conscious of the prejudice that often underlies the scholarly accusation of malice. Yet Andrewes's indignation stems from the depth of his conviction that the two testaments constitute a unified witness to God's revelation in Jesus Christ. While we cannot assume Andrewes's hermeneutic whole-cloth, it is well to consider the theological loss incurred by the weakening of that conviction in the current interpretive climate. It should also be noted that Andrewes regularly consulted rabbinic sources and often cites them with approval, and his denial that the Jews are responsible for Christ's death (of which the real agent is our sin)[85] compares favorably with much preaching in our own day.

NATIVITY SERMON IX

Preached before the King's Majesty at Whitehall
on December 25, 1614

A part of the chapter read this morning, by order of the Church, for the second lesson.

> Behold, a virgin shall conceive, and bear a son, and she shall call his name Immanuel.
>
> *Ecce virgo concipiet, et pariet filium, et vocabitur nomen ejus Immanuel.*
>
> —ISAIAH 7:14

Of all the writers of the Old Testament, the prophet Esay hath the honor to be the first that is vouched in the New, and of all the places this place the honor to be the first of all, even in the first Evangelist St. Matthew, and in the very first chapter of him. We may well think St. Matthew would be careful to make choice of a very prime and pregnant place, to set it as it were in the front of his Gospel [Matt. 1:23]. This is much honor St. Matthew doth it.

But the angel Gabriel doth it more, who takes this verse as it stands, word for word, and makes it serve for his annunciation or message to the Blessed Virgin without any alteration; not so much as the *ecce* [behold] left out [Luke 1:31].

The tenor of it is all about a child to be born, a child with an *ecce;* in whom, and in whose birth, God should be with us — so with us as never before. On whose so being with us depends all our well or evil being, here and for ever. For better not be at all than be without him; and having him we need nothing else, for *in ipso omnia,* "in him is all" [Col. 1:17].

The Eunuch's question falls fitly in here; "Of whom speaks the prophet this?" [Acts 8:34]. Who is his mother? Who the child? St. Matthew will be as good to us as St. Philip was to him; who, where he enrolls it, tells us who the mother, the Blessed Virgin;

who the child, our blessed Savior. Who else? No virgin ever bare child but she; no child ever *nobiscum Deus* [with us *is* God], and so *Deus*, but he. There is none other to lay claim to it but they.

The Division

Ecce hath in it two powers: one for the ear, to awake it to some matter more than ordinary; another for the eye, to direct it by pointing to some certainty, as here to two certain persons, the mother and the child. And shows us two strange sights in them, *mater virgo*, and *Deus homo*; 'a virgin to become a mother,' 'God to become man.' A virgin to bear; God to be born. In both, and in either of them, three points are offered to us: *ecce concipiet; ecce pariet; ecce vocabit nomen*. Our Savior Christ's first triplicity: the mystery of his holy Incarnation, in *concipiet* [she shall conceive]; his holy Nativity, in *pariet* [she shall bear]; his circumcision, in *vocabit nomen* [she shall call]. And every one of these three makes a several feast. *Ecce concipiet*, the Annunciation; *et pariet*, this feast of the birth of our Lord; *et vocabit nomen*, New Year's Day, when his name was given.

But we apply it to this feast. So doth St. Matthew in his *inspeximus* [we observed (Matt. 2:2)] of it to the birth of Christ. "The birth of Christ," saith he, "was on this fashion" [Matt. 1:18], and then brings in this record out of Esay. As if this *ecce* did in particular point at this day. As in truth we stand not much upon his conceiving now he is born specially as born he is, *ecce pariet* is the point. For then we see him, take him in our arms, then he is "with us" indeed. And when was that? *Ecce pariet* saith the text; *Ecce peperit* [she has borne] saith the day, this very day. This is the chief.

But finding them here all, we will deal with them all: Christ as embryo, in his conception; Christ as ἀρτιγέννητον βρέφος, "a new-born babe," but yet ἀνώνυμος, "without a name"; and Christ with his full Christendom, as named; and named with this name here in the text, the name of "Immanuel."

Of which three, ye may reduce the first two ("conceived" and "born") to his nature; and to make two, to two of the latter make two more, *vocabit* and *nomen*, his name and his vocation — for in his name is his vocation. To bring God to us, to make God with us; him to be with us, that we may be with him for ever. *Nobiscum Deus*, the way; *nos cum Deo* [we *are* with God], the end; which is and so may be the end of the text, and of the day, and of us all. Nothing more worthy our sight than this birth, nor more worth our hearing than this name.

Section I

Ecce virgo

Ecce spreads itself over the whole text — may be repeated at every point of it; but it first points to *ecce virgo*. There we may make a stay, there is a block in our way by the Jews. In no one place doth that of the Apostle's speech appear, that "at the reading of the prophecies of Christ the veil is laid over their hearts" [2 Cor. 3:15]; no where how true the proverb is, that 'malice will even blind a man,' as here in this. This verse so dazzles them, as fain would they turn another way, and not see that they do. They see no virgin here: Esay's word *alma,* say they, is but "a young woman," and not "a virgin" properly. But they say against their own knowledge, in so saying. For first, beside the nature of the word, the very energy gives as much. For it is of *alam,* and that is "to cover"; and so properly is one that is yet covered, and never yet known; opposed to them that have been "uncovered" and "known," after the Hebrew phrase.

And beside, the use of the word for a virgin in other places. Rebecca then a virgin, called by this name [Gen. 24:43]. And Miriam then but six years old, called by it likewise.[86]

And beside their own taking of the word, they themselves, the more ancient of them, so in their Targum[87] — this very word *alamoth* they gloss and paraphrase it by *betuloth,* the proper word for virgins; where it stands this day to be seen.

Besides all this, see whither their malice carrieth them by denying this, even to overturn prophecy, and prophet, and all. For he calls us to see a sign, and that with an *ecce;* and, what is that? If it be but a young woman to conceive, and no virgin, where is the sign? What is become of the *ecce?* It is no sign or wonder, unless it be beside the course of nature; and is it any whit beside the course of nature for a young woman to be with child? Therefore take away *virgo,* and away with the *ecce;* down with the sign. Thus, rather than to bear witness to the truth, sticked they not to expose the word of God, and so God himself to scorn; make the prophet, or, as St. Matthew well saith, "God by the prophet" [Matt. 1:22], to speak idly; give them a sign that is no sign; tell them of a marvel not to be marveled at.

Reject them then, and read confidently as St. Matthew doth, "Behold a virgin" [Matt. 1:23]. With him rest hardly on the skill and integrity of all the seventy,[88] that more than an hundred years before it came to pass turned it παρθένος in Greek, that is "a virgin"; who could skill of their own tongue better than any Kimchi,[89] or Albo,[90] or any Rabbin of them all. This, for *ecce virgo*.

And look, what work we had with the Jew about *ecce virgo*, the like shall we have with the Gentile about *virgo concipiet*. To conceive this conceiving, to join these two, a virgin, and yet conceive or bear; or, conceive and bear, and yet be a virgin. For before the birth, yea before the conceiving come, the virginity is gone. True — in nature; but this is a sign, and so above nature. And in reason so. But this is *nisi credideritis non intelligetis* [Isa. 7:9] "to be believed, otherwise not to be understood," as a little before was said. For what God can do faith can believe, reason cannot comprehend. But this it can; that we do God no great favor as well saith St. Augustine, *Si Deum fatemur, etc.*, 'If we confess God can do somewhat, which we confess our reason cannot reach.'

The Blessed Virgin herself while she stood upon a reason, upon *quia non cognosco virum* [since I have not known a man], asked, "How it might be?" [Luke 1:34] but rested in the angel's resolution, and so let us. Which was of two sorts; first, that the Holy Ghost should be agent in it, and "the power of the Most High bring it to pass" [Luke 1:35]. That which of itself seemeth not credible, put the author to it, put to *ex Spiritu Sancto* [from the Holy Spirit], and it will seem not incredible.

Specially, and that is the second, if we set another by it as unlikely as it, and done though; as this *ecce* of the Virgin's the Angel exemplifies by another *ecce* of Zachary's, in a manner as hard, which yet fell out at the same time. For Elizabeth being barren, first by nature, then by age, and so wanting power to conceive — she was then "gone six months with child" [Luke 1:36]. Now the want of power to conceive is no less material to hinder the conception every way, than want of the soil no less than the want of seed. He that could supply that could also this. He that do it without one, do it without the other. They were cousins, the Blessed Virgin and she; and their signs were so too. One of them made credible by the other.

But I ask St. Paul's question, "Why should it be thought a thing incredible" [Acts 26:8], this to the Gentiles? If, as their religion taught them, they admitted of Minerva's birth,[91] or Pyrrha's progeny,[92] they need not make strange at this. If they say, "The god of nature is not bound to the rules of nature," we say the same. And yet, even in nature, we see it made not altogether incredible. The light passing through a body, the body yet remaining whole – and it is put therefore into the verse to pattern this, *Luce penetratur, etc.* 'The light cometh through the glass, yet the glass is not perished.' No more than the light of heaven passing through breaketh the glass, no more did the God of heaven by his passage violate any whit the virginity of his mother; if we will allow God the maker of the light to do as much as the light he hath made.

But I hold ever best to let every thing rest upon his own base, or bottom; natural upon reason, supernatural upon faith. And this is supernatural; in which *tota ratio facti est in potentiâ facientis,* 'the power of the doer is the reason of the thing done.' God is the doer, *Cujus dicere est facere,* 'to whom it is as easy to do it as to say it.' As the angel concluded, so do I; "With God is nothing impossible" [Luke 1:37]. And that of Christ's, "To faith all things are possible" [Mark 9:23]. And here are both. And where they meet, they make no less a miracle than *mater* and *virgo,* or *Deus* and *homo* – even *fides* [faith] and *ratio* [reason]. And this, for *virgo concipiet.*

Section II

Concipiet

Now to the three particulars; and first, *concipiet.* To make him man, it is well known there wanted not other ways: from the mold,[93] as Adam; from the rib of flesh, as Eve. No need then of *concipiet.* Yes – for he was not to be man only, but to be "the Son of man"; the name in the text, *Filius* [son], and the name that for the most part he giveth himself, and seemeth most to delight in. But Adam was not son to the mold, nor Eve daughter to Adam. And "a son" no way but by *concipiet.* And howsoever of the body of man there may engender that which is not of the same kind, yet by way of conception there cometh of man nothing but man; nothing but of the same nature and substance with that he was conceived of.

This we are to hold; to conceive is more than to receive. It is so to receive as we yield somewhat of our own also. A vessel is not said to conceive the liquor that is put into it. Why? Because it yieldeth nothing from itself. The Blessed Virgin is, and therefore is because she did. She did both give and take. Give of her own substance whereof his body was framed; and take or receive power from the Holy Ghost, whereby was supplied the office and the efficacy of the masculine seed. This is *concipiet*.

And this word is the bane of diverse heresies. That of the Manichee that held he had no true body. That had been, *virgo decipiet*, not *concipiet;* not conceive him, but deceive us. And that of the Valentinian, revived lately in the Anabaptist, that held he had a true body, but made in heaven and sent into her. That had been *recipiet*, but not *concipiet;* received him she had, conceived she had not.

From which his conceiving we may conceive his great love to us-ward. Love, not only condescending to take our nature upon him, but to take it by the same way and after the same manner that we do, by being conceived. That, and no other better beseeming way. The womb of the virgin is surely no such place, but he might well have abhorred it. He did not; *pudorem exordii nostri non recusavit* saith Hilary; 'He refused not that ourselves are ashamed of' [literally, "...the shame of our beginning"];[94] *sed naturæ nostræ contumelias transcurrit*, 'but the very contumelies of our nature (*transcurrit* is too quick a word) he ran through them'; nay he stayed in them, in this first nine months. I say the contumelies of our nature not to be named, they are so mean. So mean indeed as it is verily thought they made those old heretics I named, and others more who yet yielded him to be man, to run into such fancies as they did; only to decline those foul indignities as they took them, for the great God of heaven to undergo.

This therefore, even this, would he have set down in terms terminant [defining terms], of *concipiet* and *pariet*. Trusting we would wisely judge of them, and love him never the less, but the more even for these. Μὴ διὰ τοῦτο ἄτιμος, ὅτι διά σε ταπεινός: 'Honor him nevertheless, because he laid down his honor for thy sake' [Gregory Nazianzen]. No; but *quanto ille minus debita, tanto ego magis debitor;* 'the less due he took on him, the more due from me to him' [Gregory the Great]. In a word, *quanto pro me vilior, tanto mihi charior;* 'the lower for me, the dearer to me' [Bernard]. It brings to mind King David's *vilior adhuc fiam* ["I will be yet more vile than this" (2 Sam. 6:22)], and how God even for that regarded him the more. *Concipiet et pariet,* to conceive and bring forth in us love, honor, and due regard, even for them. It reaches both.

This sure is matter of love; but came there any good to us by it? There did. For our conception being the root as it were, the very groundsill of our nature; that he might go to the root and repair our nature from the very foundation, thither he went; that what had been there defiled and decayed by the first Adam, might by the second be cleansed and set right again. That had our conception been stained, by him therefore, *primum ante omnia* [first before all], to be restored again. He was not idle all the time he was an embryo — all the nine months he was in the womb; but then and there he even eat out of the core of corruption that cleft to our nature and us, and made both us and it an unpleasing object in the sight of God.

And what came of this? We that were abhorred by God, *filii iræ* ["children of wrath" (Eph. 2:3)] was our title, were by this means made beloved in him. He cannot, we may be sure, account evil of that nature, that is now become the nature of his own son — his now no less than ours. Nay farther, given the privilege to the children of such as are in him, though but of one parent believing, that they are not as the seed of two infidels, but "are in a degree holy" [1 Cor. 7:14]; *eo ipso;* and have a farther right to "the laver of regeneration," to sanctify them throughout by "the renewing of the Holy Ghost" [Titus 3:5]. This honor is to us by the dishonor of him; this the good by Christ an embryo.

Section III

Et pariet

Et pariet; and this no more than needs. There may be *concipiet,* and no *pariet* follow. *Venerunt filii ad partus, etc.,* saith the prophet, "The children came to the birth, and no strength to deliver" [Isa. 37:3]. *Pariet* makes all sure.

And *pariet* makes all appear. We could not tell it was *filium* [a son]; knew not what it was, or what it would be. Till he came into the world he was as *thesaurus absconditus* [hidden treasure; cf. Matt. 13:44]; though we had it, we had it not. But when he was born, when come into the world, we see him and handle him; then he was "with us" indeed. "With us" — not as conceived of the same nature with us, but as born and now a person among us. That which was potential in *concipiet*, made actual by *pariet*.

So that this is the θεοφανία, when he came forth "as a bridegroom out of his chamber, or as the sun from his tabernacle to run his race" [Ps. 19:5]. And it was with a *visitavit ab alto* [he visited from on high, cf. Luke 1:78]. Thence an angel cried *ecce*, and sounded it on earth; and a star cried *ecce*, and proclaimed it from heaven. Poets in the West write of it;[95] and wise men in the East saw it, and came a long journey upon it to see him. And what did this *pariet* bring forth? No sooner born, but a multitude of heavenly soldiers[96] sung "Peace to the earth" [Luke 2:13] — belike there had been war before, but "peace" now. Nay, more than peace, εὐδοκία that God had conceived a good liking, was well pleased with men. The same term to men that he useth to Christ himself, "in whom I am well pleased" [Matt. 3:17] — εὐδοκία to both. And what would we more? What lack we now? His name.

And now he is born, might we not leave here, and go no farther? *Rem tenemus* [we have the thing]; what care we for the name? Yes, we must; for *Christus anonymus* will not serve. Therefore Esay, therefore the Angel are careful to bear him to his baptism, to add his name; the Prophet to intimate it, St. Matthew to interpret it. For though we have said much of Christ an embryo, and Christ a newborn nameless babe, yet nothing to that that followeth — to the *ecce* of his name.

This name, if it had been of man's giving, I wot [know] well little heed had been to be taken of it. Men set great titles upon empty boxes. Nay, many times the names given by wise men fall out quite contrary. Solomon called his son Rehoboam, "the enlarger of people"; he enlarged them from ten to two [1 Kings 12]. But his name, St. Matthew tells us, the prophet but brought; it was God that sent it [Matt. 1:22]. And the names of his imposing, there is no surer place in logic than from them. His nominals be reals. As his *dicere, facere* [to say *is* to do], so his *dici, fieri*; "what is said in them comes surely to pass."

Now there were divers names given him at divers times. To express all his perfections, no one name was enough. There was Jacob's name, Shiloh [Gen. 49:10]; that was in respect of his Father, by whom and from whom he was sent. There was Paul's name, Messias, Christ; that was, regard had to the Holy Ghost, by or wherewith he was anointed [cf. Heb. 1:9]. But what were these? *Quid ad nos* [what to us]? We have no part in them. In this we have; and till this came all was *in nubibus* [in clouds], as they say. But in this, Immanuel, *nobiscum Deus* [with us *is* God], here come we in first. For in *Immanu* is *anu* [Hebrew: we], and in *nobiscum, nos* [Latin: we]. And this is the first *nobis*, and the first *cum* we find in any name of his; and therefore of all other we are to make much of it. A virgin to bear, God to be born — matter of wonder, but no benefit at all. But when we hear, it is "with us," and for us, that *ecce* makes us look up to it.

Before I come to it, I would clear a doubt or two of it: one of the name itself; the other of the interpretation, or meaning of the name.

It will be said, this was not his name in the end for all this, but Jesus. True; and St. Matthew knew that well enough, for he sets it down so [Matt. 1:21]. Yet even in that place he sets it so down, presently he vouches this of Esay of Immanuel, as if Immanuel and Jesus both came to one, as indeed they do; one infers the other. Immanuel, "God with us." Why? To what end? To save us from our sins, and from perishing by them. If there be any odds, it is in Immanuel, which is of larger compass. "God with us" to save us, though that be worth all, yet not that way only, but "with us" other ways besides; and all in Immanuel.

"God with us"; why, was he not also with the patriarchs and prophets, and Esay himself, as well as with us? He was; but not as well. Some prerogative we must allow this name, if it be but for this *ecce*. No *ecce* belongs to these. Somewhat more to St. Matthew's gospel than to Esay's prophecy. This name must needs imply a secret antithesis to his former being with us. We say nothing in saying, he is now with us, if he be not so with us now as never before. With them in types and figures of himself; his shadow was with them; but now he himself. With them he was even thus, in this very *Immanu;* but how? In the future tense, *concipiet pariet;* as things to come are made present to hope. But now, *conceptus est, partus est* [he has been conceived/born; cf. Luke 2:11]; *re* [in reality], not in *spe* [hope], all is past and done. So that now *ita nobiscum ut de nobis* [so with us as from us]; nay *ut ipso nos* [as we ourselves], "So 'with us' as even of us now"; of the same substance, nature, flesh and bone that we. "With us" in *concipiet*, conceived as we; "with us" in *pariet*, born as we. Now true as never till now; now so as never so before.

And now, to look into the name. It is compounded, and to be taken in pieces. First, into *Immanu* and *El;* of which, *El* the latter is the more principal by far; for *El* is God. Now, for any thing yet said in *concipiet* and *pariet,* all is but man with us; not "God with us" till now. By the name we take our first notice that this child is God. And this is a great addition, and here, lo, is the wonder. For, as for any child of a woman to "eat butter and honey" [Isa. 7:15], the words that next follow, where is the *ecce?* But for *El,* for God to do it — that is worth an *ecce* indeed.

El is God; and not God every way, but as the force of the word is, God in his full strength and virtue; God, *cum plenitudine potestatis* as we say, 'with all that ever he can do'; and that is enough I am sure.

For the other, *Immanu;* though *El* be the more principal, yet I cannot tell whether it or *Immanu* do more concern us. For as in *El* is might, so in *Immanu* is our right to his might, and to all he hath or is worth. By that word we hold, therefore we to lay hold of it. The very standing of it thus before, thus in the first place, toucheth us somewhat. The first thing ever that we look for is *nos, nobis,* and *noster* [we, (to) us, and our], the possessives; for they do *mittere in possessionem,* 'put us in possession.' We look for it first, and lo, it stands here first; *nobiscum* first, and then *Deus* after.

I shall not need to tell you that in *nobiscum* there is *mecum* [with me]; in *nobiscum* for us all a *mecum* for every one of us. Out of this generality of "with us," in gross, may every one deduce his own particular — with me, and me, and me. For all put together make but *nobiscum.*

The Wise Man out of Immanuel, that is *nobiscum Deus,* doth deduce Ithiel,[97] that is *mecum Deus,* "God with me" — his own private interest. And St. Paul when he had said to the Ephesians of Christ, "Who loved us, and gave himself for us," [Eph. 5:2] might with good right say to the Galatians, "Who loved me and gave himself for me" [Gal. 2:20].

This *Immanu* is a compound again; we may take it in sunder into *nobis* and *cum;* and so then have we three pieces: *El,* the mighty God; and *anu,* we, poor we — poor indeed if we have all the world beside if we have not him to be with us; and *im,* which is *cum,* and that *cum* in the midst between *nobis* and *Deus,* God and us — to couple God and us; thereby to convey the things of the one to the other. Ours to God; alas, they be not worth the speaking of. Chiefly, then, to convey to us the things of God. For that is worth the while; they are indeed worth the conveying.

This *cum* we shall never conceive to purpose, but *carendo* [by deprivation]; the value of "with" no way so well as by without, by stripping of *cum* from *nobis*. And so let *nobis*, "us," stand by ourselves without him, to see what our case is but for this Immanuel; what, if this virgin's child had not this day been born us; *nobiscum* after will be the better esteemed. For if this child be "Immanuel, God with us," then without this child, this Immanuel, we be without God. "Without him in this world," saith the Apostle [Eph. 2:12]; and if without him in this, without him in the next; and if without him there — if it be not *Immanu-el*, it will be *Immanu-hell;* and that and no other place will fall, I fear me, to our share. Without him, this we are. What with him? Why, if we have him, and God by him, we need no more; *Immanu-el* and *Immanu-all*. All that we can desire is for us to be with him, with God, and he to be with us; and we from him, or he from us, never to be parted. We were with him once before, and we were well; and when we left him, and he no longer "with us," then began all our misery. Whensoever we go from him, so shall we be in evil case, and never be well till we be back with him again.

Then, if this be our case that we cannot be without him, no remedy then but to get a *cum* by whose means *nobis* and *Deus* may come together again. And Christ is that *Cum* to bring it to pass. The parties are God and we; and now this day he is both God before eternally, and now today man; and so both, and takes hold of both, and brings both together again. For two natures here are in him. If conceived and born of a woman, then a man; if God with us, then God. So Esay offered his "sign from the height above, or from the depth beneath" [Isa. 7:11]: here it is. "From above," *El;* "from beneath," *anu;* one of us now. And so, his sign from both. And both these natures in the unity of one person, called by one name, even this name Immanuel.

Section IV

Vocabit nomen

I told you, in his name is his vocation or office — to be *cum*, to come between that is, to be a mediator, to make him that was *contra nos* [against us], *nobiscum* [against us, with us] again. "A mediator is not of one, but God is one" [Gal. 3:20]. God and man are two; and they were two, as they say. Were two, and two will be, till he make them one; recapitulate and cast up both into one sum; to knit *anu*, that is "we," and *El*, that is "God," with his *im* [with], into one – one word and one thing, *univoce* again.

So upon the point, in these three pieces there be three persons; so a second kind of Trinity – God, we, and Christ. *El* is God, *anu* we; for Christ nothing left but*im*, that is *cum*, or "with." For it is he that maketh the unity in this Trinity; maketh God with us, and us with God; and both, in and by him, to our eternal comfort and joy.

Thus is he "with us"; and yet all this is but nature still. But the *nobiscum* of his name bodeth yet a farther matter. For indeed the "with us" of his name is more than the "with us" of his nature. If we make a great matter of that, as great it is and very great, behold the *ecce* of his name is far beyond it. "With us" in his nature, that is "with us" as man – that is short. We are more – sinful men; a wretched condition added to a nature corrupt. Will he be "with us" in that too? Else this of nature will smally avail us.

What, in sin? Nay, "in all things, sin only except" [Heb. 4:15]. Yea, that is in being "like us," but not in being "with us." For in being "with us" except sin, and except all; the ridding us of our sin is the only matter, saith Esay after [e.g., Isaiah 24, 40]. Therefore to be with us in all things, sin itself not except. St. John's *caro factum est* [was made flesh (John 1:14)] will not serve. St. Paul's *fuit peccatum* [he became sin (2 Cor. 5:21)] must come too. In "with us" there too. I say it over again: unity of nature is not enough, he is to be "with us" in unity of person likewise. So he was. The debtor and surety make but one person in law. That he was, and then he was *cum*, "with us" throughly, as deep in as we.[98]

And this is the proper *Immanu* of his name. And this the *Immanu* indeed. And till he was thus "with us," no name he had; he was *Christus anonymus*, 'Christ unchristened,' as it were. For his name came not till he became one "with us" in person; not till his circumcision; not, till for us and in our names, he became debtor of the whole law, principal, forfeiture, and all. To "the hand-writing" [Col. 2:14] he then signed with the first-fruits of his blood. And then, name the child, and give him this name, "Immanuel." For thus he was a right "Immanuel," truly "with us." "With us" as men; "with us" as sinful men; "with us" in all things, sin itself not excepted.

May I not add this? It is said in the text, "She shall call" – "she," that is, his mother. Why "she"? To let us understand, that she might give him the name while he undertook this for us. But his Father, till all was discharged and the "hand-writing canceled," till then he suspended, he gave it him not. His mother she did, when he dropped a little blood at the sealing of the bond.[99] But he was fain not to drop blood but to sweat blood, and to shed his blood, every drop of it, ere this "with us" were full answered. And then his Father did it too, *dedit illi nomen super omne nomen* [God gave to him a name above every name (Phil. 2:9)]; then, and not before. His mother now, his Father not till then. But then he had proved himself fully "with us" *per omnia* [through everything], when neither womb nor birth, cratch nor cross, cross nor curse, could pluck him away from us, or make him not to be "with us." Then *vocabit illi nomen* [she shall give him a name], both she and he; mother, Father, and all. "With us" to eat "butter and honey" [Isa. 7:15] seemeth much; and it is so for God. What say ye to drink "vinegar and gall" [Ps. 69:21; cf. Matt. 27:48]? That is much more, I am sure; yet that he did I cannot here say "with us," but for us. Even drunk of the cup with the dregs of the wrath of God, which passed not from him, that it might pass from us and we not drink it.

This, this is the great "with us"; for of this follow all the rest. "With us" once thus, and then "with us" in his oblation on the altar of the temple; "with us" in his sacrifice on the altar of the cross; "with us" in all the virtues and merits of his life; "with us" in the satisfaction and satispassion[100] both of his death; "with us" in his resurrection, to raise us up from the earth; "with us" in his ascension, to exalt us to heaven; "with us," even then, when he seemed to be taken from us — that day by his Spirit, as this day by his flesh. *Et ecce vobiscum* [And behold, I am with you (Matt. 28:20)], and lo, I am true Immanuel "with you" by the love of my manhood; "with you" by the power of my Godhead, still "to the end of the world."

One more yet. He won it, and he wears this name; and in it he wears us. And it is both a comfort to us and a glory that so he wears us. That he is not, cannot be named without us; that when he is named, *et nos una tecum Domine*, 'we are also named with him' [cf. Jer. 14:9]. In *Immanu* is *anu*, and that is "we." This is not it, but this: that he hath set us in the forepart of it; *Immanu* before *El*, *nobiscum* before *Deus*. This note is not out of place in this place, where precedence is made a great matter of; that *Immanu* is before *El*; that is, we first, and God last.

Good manners would in a name compound of him and us, that he should have stood before us, and it have been *Elimmanu* at least — *Deus nobiscum,* and *Deus* before *nobiscum;* not Immanuel, *nobiscum* before *Deus.* He before us; he the priority of the place in all reason. Booz he placed them so,[101] and so should we I dare say, if it had been of our imposing, *Elimmanu.* It had been great arrogancy otherwise. But he giving it himself would have it stand thus; us set before him. There is a meaning in it. And what can it be but this? That in the very name we might read that we are dearer to him than himself; that he so preferred us, and that his own name doth *præ se ferre* [manifest itself] no less, but give out to all the world the *ecce* of St. John's Gospel, *Ecce quomodo dilexit!* [John 11:36]; the *ecce* of his epistle, *Ecce quantam charitatem habuit!* [1 John 3:1], "See, how he loved them!" "Behold, how great love he bare to them!" See it in his very name. We are a part of it; we are the forepart of it; and he the latter; he behind, and we before — before himself, and that by order from himself: he would have it Immanuel. O! whether was greater, humility or charity in him! Hard to say whether, but both unspeakable.

Let us examine this *sine nobis* [without us], a little. How came God from us? Nay, ask not that; but how we came from him. For we went from him, not he from us; we forsook him first. Jonas tell us how; "By following lying vanities, we forsook our own mercy" [cf. Jonah 2:9].

If we went from him first, then should it be in reason *nos cum Deo,* not *nobiscum Deus;* we to him, not he to us. Did we so? No indeed. We sought not him, he was fain to seek us. *Nos cum Deo,* that would not be; it must be *nobiscum Deus* first, or *nos cum Deo* will never be. This second then; that we began the separation — that long of us;[102] but he begins the reconciliation.

Who hath the hurt if God be without us? We, not he. Who gets by *nobiscum?* What gets God by *nobiscum?* Nothing he. What get we? *Multum per omnem modum* [much in every way (Rom. 3:2)]. Why then doth he begin, doth he seek to be with us? No reason but *sic dilexit* [he desired *it* thus], and no reason of that.

But when he sought and offered to be with us, did we regard it? Nor that neither. You see, the Prophet here offers Ahaz a sign, bids him ask it; Ahaz would none [Isa. 7:11–12]. And as he to the sign, so we to the *signatum,* 'the thing signified'; care as little for him or his being "with us," as Ahaz did for his sign. We can be content he in any sort will cease from us, come not at us so long as the world can be with us or we with it; care not for his being with us, till world and all forsake us. How he was fain even to force it on him!

Cast up these then; that he forsakes not, but being forsaken first. That being forsaken, yet he forsakes not though. That he which should be sought to, seeks first, and seeks us by whom he shall get nothing. Yea, when we neglect him so seeking, when Ahaz will no sign, tells him he will give him one, whether he ask or ask not [Isa. 7:14]; that is, will do us good not only without our seeking, but even in a manner against our wills. And tell me, if there be not as much love in *nobiscum*, as in all the rest.

"With us," how we see. Now, "with us" why, or to what end? To more than I have now time to tell you of. Two only I name. One, that of the place — "to save them from their enemies"; as them, so us. Them from Razin and Romely's son [Isa. 7:4; cf. 2 Kgs. 16:1–20]; us from the son of Romely, or Romulus,[103] or whomsoever. If he "with us" on our side, then will he be against them that are against us; and that let us never fear neither our own weakness, nor the enemies' strength. For though we be weak and they be strong, yet Immanuel I am sure that is "with us" is stronger than they.

Our fear most-what [for the most part] groweth, both in sin and in danger, that we look upon ourselves as if it were only *nobis;* as if never a *cum;* or that *cum* were not *El,* "the mighty God." As if with that great *El* all the inferior *els* were not attendant, Micha-el, and Gabri-el; and if he will, "twelve legions of angels" [Matt. 26:53]. Or as if he alone with one word of his mouth, one *Ego sum* [I am he (John 18:5)], could not blow them all down, could not make them all as those in the text, as the tails of a couple of firebrands that have spent themselves, smoke a little, and there is all [Isa. 7:4]. No; if he be "with us," we need not fear what these two, nay not what all the fire-brands in hell can do against us.

And sure strange it is, the saints of God what courage and confidence they have taken, from this very name Immanuel. Go to, saith Esay in the next chapter, "Take your counsel, it shall be brought to naught; pronounce a decree, it shall not stand" [Isa. 8:10]. Why? For Immanuel, "God is with us"; nothing but this name. For as it is a name, so it is a whole proposition, if you will. And after, in the fiftieth chapter, he seeks for enemies; calls them out, "Who will contend with me? Where is my adversary? Let him come near"; [Isa. 50:8] — so little doth he fear them. And these were ghostly [spiritual] enemies; and this was in the point of justification. This for the Prophet.

Now for the Apostle. Never did champion in more courageous manner cast his glove than doth he to his ghostly enemies, to "height," to "depth," to "things present," to "things to come," to all, that none of them "shall be able to sever him" from this *cum*, from his love [Rom. 8:39]. And all in confidence of *si Deus nobiscum* [if God is with us (Rom. 8:31)]; in whom he makes full account to conquer; nay, conquer will not serve — more than conquer he, ὑπερνικῶμεν [we more than conquer (Rom. 8:37)].

The reason is set down, Proverbs 30[:1], where he betakes himself to *Ithiel* first, which is but a slip of Immanuel, *Deus mecum* [God is with me]; and then to *Ithiel* straight joins *Ucal*, "I shall prevail"; not I, but *El* with me. *Ithiel* goeth never alone; *Ucal* attends it still. Get *Ithiel* — if *Ithiel* be with us, *Ucal* will not be away, for *Ithiel* and *Ucal* part not.

Is this all? No; there is another in the very body of the word itself. "With us" — to make us that to God that he was this day made to man. And this indeed was the chief end of his being "with us"; to give us a *posse fieri*, a capacity, "a power to be made the sons of God" [John 1:12], by being "born again of water and of the spirit" [John 3:5]; for *originem quam sumpsit ex utero virginis posuit in fonte baptismatis*, 'the same original that himself took in the womb of the virgin to us-ward, the same hath he placed for us in the fountain of baptism to God-ward.'[104] Well therefore called the womb of the Church σύστοιχον [correspondent] to the virgin's womb, with a power given it of *concipiet et pariet filios* [conceiv(ing) or bear(ing) sons] to God. So his being conceived and born the Son of Man doth conceive and bring forth *(filiatio, filiationem)*, our being born, our being the sons of God. His participation of our human, our participation of his divine nature.

And shall he be "with us" thus many ways, and shall not we be with him — as many I say not, but some, as many as we can? We with him, as he with us? Specially, since upon this issue the prophet puts King Asa, "The Lord is with you, if you be with him" [2 Chron. 15:2] — with you to save you, if you with him to serve him. It holds *reciproce*, in all duties of love, as here was love if ever. "*Immanuel*, God with us," requires *Immelanu*, 'us with God,' again.

He "with us" now I hope, for "where two or three are gathered together in his name, there is he with them" [Matt. 18:20]. But that is in his Godhead. And we are with him; our prayers, our praises are with him; but that is in our spirits whence they come.

These are well, but these are not all we can; and none of these, the proper 'with him' of the day. That hath a special *cum* of itself, peculiar to it. Namely, that we be so with him, as he this day was "with us"; that was in flesh, not in spirit only. That flesh that was conceived and this day born (*Corpus aptasti mihi* [a body you have prepared for me (Heb. 10:5; cf. Ps. 40:7)]), that body that was this day fitted to him. And if we be not with him thus, if this his flesh be not "with us," if we partake it not, which way soever else we be with him, we come short of the *im* of this day. *Im* otherwise it may be, but not that way which is proper to this feast. "Thy land, O Immanuel" [Isa. 8:8], saith the Prophet in the next chapter; and may not I say, this thy feast, O Immanuel? Sure no being with him so kindly, so pleasing to him, so fitting this feast, as to grow into one with him; as upon the same day, so the very same way he did "with us."

This, as it is most proper, so it is the most straight and near that can be — the surest being withal that can be. *Nihil tam nobiscum, tam nostrum, quam alimentum nostrum,* 'nothing so with us, so ours, as that we eat and drink down,' which goeth, and groweth one with us. For *alimentum et alitum* [food and the one fed] do *coalescere in unum,* 'grow into an union'; and that union is inseparable ever after. This then I commend to you, even the being with him in the Sacrament of his body — that body that was conceived and born, as for other ends so for this specially, to be "with you"; and this day, as for other intents, so even for this, for the Holy Eucharist. This, as the kindliest for the time, as the surest for the manner of being with.

And this is the farthest; and this is all we can come to here — here upon earth. But this is not all; there is a farther to come still. For we are not together; we are parted, he and we. He in heaven, and we in earth. But it shall not alway so be. Beside this day Immanuel hath another day, and that day will come; and when it doth come, he will come and take us to himself. That as he hath been our Immanuel upon earth, so he may be our Immanuel in heaven; he with us, and we with him, there for ever.

This of the Sacrament is a preparative to that; will conceive and bring forth the other. For immediately after he had given them the Holy Eucharist, he prayed straight that they that had so been with him in the blessed Sacrament — "Father, my will is," my prayer, my last prayer, "that where I am they may be also" [John 14:3, 17:24].

And he is in heaven, in the joy and glory there; and there he would have us, so *nobiscum Deus in terris* [God *is* with us on earth] brings us to *nos cum Deo in Cœlis* [we *are* with God in heaven], even thither. Thither may it bring us, and thither may we come and there be — he "with us," and we with him for ever! "Immanuel" is the end of the verse; the same be our end, that so we may be happy and blessed without end!

CHAPTER TWO

JOHN DONNE
(1571/72–1631)
"A Sacred Art and Courtship"

> Mary's prerogative was to bear Christ, so
> 'Tis preachers' to convey him, for they do
> As angels out of clouds, from pulpits speak;
> If then th'astronomers, whereas they spy,
> A new-found star, their optics magnify,
> How brave are those, who with their engine, can
> Bring man to heaven, and heaven again to man?

> — "TO MR. TILMAN AFTER HE HAD TAKEN ORDERS"

Donne's literary genius is largely the discovery of our century,[1] and the discovery has been so well publicized that probably only Shakespeare now surpasses him as the most-quoted figure of seventeenth-century English letters. Yet Donne himself would be surprised and almost certainly disappointed to be famed chiefly as a poet; it was his prose, and particularly the sermons, for which he expected to be remembered. Over a period of several years he revised and expanded them for publication, presenting them to his executors several days before his death. And indeed, it is in the 160 extant sermons that the full extent of Donne's artistic as well as theological expression is disclosed. The qualities that make his poetry memorable — audacious imagery, intense personalism, vast emotional range, restless fascination with the world in which he finds himself, combined with moderating humor — these are ever-present in the sermons. There is unmistakable imaginative continuity between the erotic verse of Jack Donne the law student and courtier, and the authoritative but no less impassioned appeals that Dean Donne addressed to cathedral and court audiences.[2] The Holy Sonnets admit us to the religious experience of a mature Donne; in the sermons he bends the force of that experience upon proclamation of the Gospel. But even more than from personal experience, the energy of the sermons derives from the language of Scripture, which Donne reads, uses, and emulates with a poet's awe at the power of words.

The central theme of all Donne's preaching is the mercy of God, recurrent in virtually every sermon. It is an extremely complex notion of mercy that Donne sets forth, encompassing not only comforts and deliverance, but also temptations, sorrows, corrections, and even punishments received as signs of God's "catechistical anger." For God's ways are "medicinal," healing most often by inflicting pain:

> The Lord and only the Lord knows how to wound us out of love; more than that, how to wound us into love; more than all that, to wound us into love not only with him that wounds us, but into love with the wound itself, with the very affliction that he inflicts upon us; the Lord knows how to strike us so, as that we shall lay hold upon that hand that strikes us and kiss that hand that wounds us.... There are natures (there are scarce any other) that dispose not themselves to God but by affliction.[3]

God's mercy wounds us into a wholeness that is finally achieved only in heaven, and all Donne's preaching is an engine trained on that goal, as the verse letter "To Mr. Tilman" suggests. Yet he knows how much we need to be changed in order to enter there. Accordingly, the concept of divine mercy is complemented and clarified by a second theme: mortification, the process of daily death in and to this world, by which we are readied for immortality.

Donne's certainty of heaven frees him to speak with stunning frankness about the present world:

> If there were any other way to be saved and to get to Heaven, than by being born into this life, I would not wish to have come into this world. And now that God hath made this life a Bridge to Heaven, it is but a giddy and a vertiginous thing, to stand long gazing upon so narrow a bridge, and over so deep and roaring waters and desperate whirlpools, as this world abounds with.... Certainly now, now that sin hath made life so miserable, if God should deny us death, he multiplied our misery. (7:359)

Donne's frequent vivid reminders of mortality lay him open to the charge of morbidity, and there is indeed a pronounced note of melancholy in a number of sermons, perhaps unavoidable in a preacher as personally expressive as Donne. But it is well to remember that he preached through plague years in London and military disasters in England's war with France and Spain. Like his listeners, he lived much closer to the reality of death than do many moderns. By the age of 45, two years after his ordination, Donne had lost his young wife and five infant children; within a period of fifteen months (January 1627 to March 1628) at the height of his preaching career, he was badly shaken by the deaths of his eighteen-year-old daughter Lucy and his three most intimate friends. Speaking to audiences familiar with such losses, his frankness about death, which is never separated from the resurrection promise, appears as a responsible, if not gentle proclamation of the Gospel.

Christians lay hold of God's mercy through participation in the life of the Church. The Church is the environment whose sustaining element is mercy:

> The air is not so full of motes, of atoms, as the Church is of mercies; and as we can suck in no part of air, but we take in those motes, those atoms, so here in the congregation we cannot suck in a word from the preacher, we cannot speak, we cannot sign a prayer to God, but that that whole breath and air is made of mercy. (6:170–71)

The offices of the Church are essential in applying the benefits of Christ's work of redemption to the individual soul; only the "true Church," through word and sacraments, "makes the Savior of the world, thy Savior, my Savior" (8:308). Donne balances his personalism with steady emphasis on the established Church as the setting that most safely nurtures the Christian life through its carefully regulated worship and "premeditated" preaching; and the result is a statement of catholic faith rendered with a subjectivity that is peculiarly engaging of the hearer. The temper of the sermons is that of a mature Christian, one who well knows the seductions, sorrows, fascinations, and joys of this world; who has fought many internal battles, both intellectual and spiritual. Above all, the sermons bespeak someone whose own passions and prejudices are not muted but rather qualified by consciousness of membership in the body of Christ and by a governing concern for the "redintegration" of that body.

For Donne, preaching is an active extension to others of the "overflowing mercy" that he has experienced in his own life and to which, according to his reading, Scripture everywhere attests. That conception of the task accounts for two qualities that are pervasively present in the sermons: religious generosity and a particular sympathy with the

dejected. While these may point to aspects of Donne's own temperament, more profoundly they reflect his understanding of God's nature
and serve as the theological cornerstones for his interpretation and
proclamation of the Word.

Donne's unwillingness to exclude anyone from the possibility of salvation distinguishes him from many contemporary preachers, Catholic
as well as Puritan. He cites the misinterpretation and misaffection toward Christ of those "over-pure despisers of others . . . that are loath,
that God should speak so loud as to say, *He would have all men saved*
[1 Tim. 2:4]; and loath that Christ should spread his arms or shed
his blood in such a compass, as might fall upon all" (9:119). Donne's
generosity is entirely different from a philosophical tolerance for different religious positions; that view would gain credence only with John
Locke's writings at the end of the century. Nor does it stem from
any personal respect for his religious opponents, of whom he can be
scathing, although he rarely loses his sense of humor in polemics. But
his reservation on the question of salvation is an important application
of the chief exegetical principle of his favorite theologian, Augustine:
namely, that Scripture must be interpreted in a way consistent with the
rule of charity.[4] The Roman Church's "uncharitableness" regarding the
salvation of the Protestants is in his judgment the clearest indication
that it has evacuated the proper authority of Scripture ("like an ape,
it kills with embracing" [6:252]), which, along with the sacrament of
baptism and the call to a holy life, establishes "the accessibleness, the
communicableness, the sociableness, the affection, (shall I say) the ambition, that God hath, to have us all" (6:160–61). Typically, Donne
does not hesitate to clinch the argument by citing his own case: "I
doubt not of mine own salvation; and in whom can I have so much
occasion of doubt, as in myself? When I come to heaven, shall I be able
to say to any there: Lord! How got you hither? Was any man less likely
to come thither than I?" (8:371).

Donne felt a special pastoral responsibility toward the despairing. He
had himself endured at least one prolonged depression;[5] moreover, he
saw "an extraordinary sadness, a predominant melancholy" to be the
temper of his age, "and therefore I return often to this endeavor of raising your hearts, dilating your hearts with a holy joy, joy in the Holy
Ghost" (7:68–69). While Donne sometimes denounces the presumptuous sinner in terms worthy of the fiercest Puritan, far more often he
offers comfort. There is throughout a buoyant hopefulness, sustained
along with unblinking realism about the difficulties of this life and

grounded in Donne's conviction that God always brings good out of evil, including the evil of our own sin, which is the means by which we are humbled and transformed.

Donne's Life

Donne's was the most restless and ambitious of temperaments, yet the romantic drama of his personal life disqualified him for the political advancement he craved. When in the last sixteen years of his life Donne entered the ministry, at the king's desire and against his own will, his restlessness and ambition were not quelled; they were converted.

He was born in London in 1571 or 1572, probably the worst time in English history for one not inclined to martyrdom to be born into a prominent Catholic family. His mother was related by marriage to Sir Thomas More, and her brother Jasper Heywood headed the Jesuit mission to England, where he was imprisoned and finally exiled in 1584/85. In 1593 Donne's brother Henry, only a year younger than he, died of plague in Newgate Prison, having been arrested for harboring a priest. The impressions, both positive and negative, made by these events remained with Donne for the rest of his life. The Roman Church was the theological adversary he constantly strained to refute; the idea that, within a decade of his death, the Puritans would have the power to behead the king would have seemed to Donne absurd. In light of his family history, there seems to be a personal animus in his particular derision of the Jesuits. Nevertheless, Donne's mind was in large part shaped by his early Catholic tutors, and Aquinas' logic and Augustine's exegetical principles were taken up with increasing frequency as his preaching style matured.

His father, who died in John's early childhood, was a prosperous ironmonger, and for several years John was tutored at home. By the time he enrolled at Hart Hall, Oxford, in 1584, he was already advanced in French and Latin. Two years later he moved to Trinity College, Cambridge, though he took no degree from either university, since as a Catholic he could not swear the oath required of graduates. In 1590 Donne went to London to study law, first at Thavies' Inn and then at Lincoln's Inn. This is the period (until his marriage in 1601) to which most of the secular poems belong; they are evidence that his "enraged curiosity of life" refused to be confined to legal study. Yet Donne remained a diligent student even through his years as a London rake. His earliest biographer and parishioner, Izaak Walton, reports that Donne rose at four "and it was no common business that drew him out of his chamber till past ten: all which time was employed in study; though he took great liberty after it."[6] As the poems and sermons show, he also acquired some proficiency in medicine, science, and foreign literature, and made long tours of Italy and Spain. The desire for money, honor, and escape from what he called "the queasy pain of being beloved and loving" moved him to enlist in two naval expeditions against Spain, and he took part in the battle where the Spanish fleet was destroyed. The experience of war evidently impressed him greatly; it is the source of many images whereby he represents the continual struggle that the Christian faces in this world ("our whole life is a warfare").

Donne's earliest teachers were Jesuits, and it is probable that he had Jesuit contacts at Lincoln's Inn, where his brother was arrested. But his bold use of Catholic themes in the erotic verse (e.g., "Recusancy," "The Canonization") suggests that already as a young man he was claiming freedom from their influence. Certainly his desire for political advancement could not be satisfied as a Roman Catholic. For some years it seems that he had little to do with religious matters, and it was not until several years after his marriage (and in part, as he claimed, due to it) that the latent and angry religiosity of Donne's youth emerged clearly as new faith.

Donne's superb education and facility with languages led to his appointment in 1598 as secretary to Sir Thomas Egerton, Lord Keeper of the Great Seal. Lord Egerton treated his promising secretary as a family member until, in 1601/2, Donne eloped with his favorite niece, seventeen-year-old (and probably pregnant) Anne More. Donne was immediately dismissed from Lord Egerton's service and was for a short time imprisoned. He summed up the effect of the marriage upon his career in a letter to Anne, which concludes, "John Donne, Anne Donne, undone." Travel, study, and a self-indulgent and generous nature had brought him into heavy debt; and Anne's father withheld her dowry for eight years. Meanwhile the couple and their children, whose number increased yearly, lived in semi-poverty by the charity of friends, sometimes severely distressed by illness and depression.

Almost nothing is known about Anne apart from glimpses caught through Donne's letters and poems, which leave no doubt of their mutual devotion: "We had not one another at so cheap a rate, as that we should ever be weary of one another."[7] Walton records that she was "curiously and plentifully educated";[8] and Anne must have been a person of independent spirit and sense as well as charm. Having been orphaned of her mother at 6, she endured an unhappy relationship with her stepmother and ran her uncle's household (after Lady Egerton's death) at 16. Through many years of misfortune and a few of comfort, she held the respect of her brilliant and volatile husband, who chose not to marry again after her death at age 33. Donne seems to reflect upon the nature of the deep attachment between himself and Anne in his interpretation of Genesis 2:18 ("I will make thee a help like thyself"): "not always like in complexion, nor like in years, nor like in fortune, nor like in birth, but like in mind, like in disposition, like in the love of God and of one another, or else there is no helper."[9]

Having by marriage shattered his own rising court-hopes, Donne in the years that followed moved slowly and erratically toward the decision to seek — or better, to accept — holy orders. He moved between the country and London, performing services at court and taking part in James's embassy to France (1612). Around 1603, he must have turned to serious study of the controversies between the churches of Rome and England, especially with regard to the oaths of royal supremacy and allegiance to the sovereign. The first evidence of Donne as a convinced Anglican is his work (between 1605 and 1607) with Thomas Morton, later bishop of Durham, in preparing a series of books arguing against the Catholic position. Morton long urged him to give up politics; and in 1607, when Morton was made dean of Gloucester, he immediately offered Donne his own rich Yorkshire benefice if he would consent to be ordained. Donne refused, after careful consideration, on the grounds that

> some irregularities of my life have been so visible to some men, that though I have, I thank God, made my peace with him by penitential resolutions against them, and by the assistance of his grace banished them from my affections, yet this, which God knows to be so, is not so visible to man as to free me from their censures, and it may be that sacred calling from a dishonor.[10]

Donne's own statement on recusancy, *Pseudo-Martyr*, published in 1610, argues that the Catholics are not true martyrs but rather rebels who may be justly punished for refusing loyalty to their legitimate sovereign. After reading it, James determined to have Donne for a preacher. Donne demurred for several more years, studying Greek and Hebrew even while he wrote poems for wealthy patrons and pressed to become ambassador to Venice. In April 1614 he became Member of Parliament for Taunton, but Donne's last resistance seems to have collapsed when

Parliament was dissolved two months later. He spent the rest of the
year writing his *Essays in Divinity* and was ordained in January 1615.
Although the *Essays* are the work by which Donne prepared himself
for ordination, they mirror his personal experience far less directly than
do the Holy Sonnets and even many of the sermons.[11] They are essentially meditations on Genesis and Exodus, accompanied by prayers. Yet
the concluding prayer is deeply touching in its suggestion that for him
ordination is part of God's on-going and merciful work of conversion:

> Begin in us here in this life an angelical purity, an angelical chastity,
> an angelical integrity to thy service, an angelical acknowledgment that
> we always stand in thy presence and should direct all our actions to
> thy glory. Rebuke us not, O Lord, in thine anger, that we have not
> done so till now; but enable us now to begin that great work; and
> imprint in us an assurance that thou receivest us now graciously, as
> reconciled, though enemies; and fatherly, as children, though prodigals;
> and powerfully, as the God of our salvation, though our own consciences
> testify against us.

Misplaced ambition may well have been one of Donne's flaws; insincerity was not. However reluctantly he accepted divinity as his calling,
there is no reason to doubt the truth of his later statement: "I date my
life from my ministry; for 'I received mercy, as I received the ministry,'
as the Apostle speaks [1 Cor. 4:1]" (7:403).[12] It is, moreover, thoroughly
consonant with his notion of royal authority to see that the king's wish
had led him to follow God's will.

In October 1616, Donne was appointed divinity reader at Lincoln's
Inn, charged to preach fifty sermons per year. The sermons from this
period show him at his most personable; they are frequently humorous,
appealing specifically to the interests of law students and their teachers,
admitting a preference for the Psalms and Paul, even (rarely) telling
a personal anecdote. It is easy to see how engaging must have been
his sympathy and frank humor about the foibles of youth and old age
("Chastity is not chastity in an old man, but a disability to be unchaste"
[2:244]), as well as the accuracy of his moral vision, to an audience
familiar with the preacher's own history in that place. Yet he did not
use charm as a substitute for preparation. Some of Donne's most careful
expositions of Scripture date to this period (e.g., the fine series on Psalm
38). Walton reports that "after his sermon, he never gave his eyes rest,
till he had chosen out a new text, and that night cast his sermon into
a form, and his text into divisions; and the next day betook himself

to consult the Fathers, and so commit his mediations to his memory, which was excellent."[13]

Shortly after Donne became established in this ministry, in August 1617, Anne died following the stillbirth of their twelfth child. The sonnet that he wrote in his grief suggests that he learned not only faithfulness through their marriage but also faith:

> Since she whom I loved hath paid her last debt
> To nature, and to hers, and my good is dead,
> And her soul early into heaven ravished,
> Wholly in heavenly things my mind is set.
> Here the admiring her my mind did whet
> To seek Thee, God; so streams do show the head.... [14]

The sermons bear out the notion that marriage was instrumental in Donne's religious development; very often he speaks as a preacher who is unmistakably a family man (a relatively new phenomenon in the early seventeenth century). He constantly draws upon the practical wisdom gained through a domestic life fortified by love and tried by the strains of sickness, poverty, and his own frustrated ambition. A remarkable instance of this is the first sermon Donne preached before Charles I, within a week of James's death. He chose his text from Psalm 11: "If the foundations be destroyed, what can the righteous do?" The sermon is addressed not so much to the new monarch as to the whole kingdom, rightly fearful that the tense stability maintained under James would erupt into riot.[15] On an occasion when he might have contented himself with currying Charles's favor, Donne speaks as a pastor, calling for a sense of proportion ("Do not call the cracking of a pane of glass, a destroying of foundations" [6:258]), reliance upon the secure foundation of Scripture, and mutual responsibility between sovereign and subjects. Even more notably, he goes beyond matters of church and state to speak at length about maintaining peace in families. The homeliness with which he enjoins the court audience to patience and kindness toward children, servants, and spouse is a striking indication of how he conceives his fundamental pastoral duty even to the heads of state:

> Call not light faults by heavy names ... nor let every light disorder within doors shut thee out of doors, or make thee a stranger in thine own house.... In domestic unkindnesses and discontents, it may be wholesomer to give them a concoction at home in a discreet patience, or to give them a vent at home in a moderate rebuke, than to think to ease them or put them off with false diversions abroad. (6:259)

If marriage to Anne was the first stage of his gradual turning to the work of ministry, the sonnet indicates that her death in a real sense completed that reorientation. It is telling that even his earliest sharp grief found expression in a sermon: his first movement out of the house was to preach at St. Clement Danes Church, where she was buried, on the passage from Jeremiah: "Lo, I am the man that has seen affliction." The preacher's appearance bore out his text, and for some time Donne's friends feared for his health and even his life. But a strong sanity underlay his passion, and gradually Donne recovered his interest in life. The sermons and poems from this time confirm that he was indeed moving through grief to greater religious depths.

In the spring of 1619 he was sent on an embassy to Germany. Despite his reluctance "to leave a scattered flock of wretched children," with his eldest daughter Constance managing the household, the seven months abroad were healing. He returned to preaching at Lincoln's Inn, and there are some excellent sermons from this time; but Donne's manner is less intimate than before, perhaps reflecting the fact that he was once again looking for advancement.

The position James offered the following year seems at last to have contented his ambition; in November 1621, he was elected dean of St. Paul's Cathedral. He now occupied the most distinguished pulpit in the city he so much loved. And there he was loved in turn; for the next nine years, there was no more popular event in London than Dr. Donne's sermons, delivered without notes by a consummate actor in the drama of salvation. People from every level of society came in crowds, and Walton describes what drew them:

> A preacher in earnest, weeping sometimes for his auditory, sometimes with them; always preaching to himself, like an angel from a cloud, but in none; carrying some, as St. Paul was, to heaven in holy raptures, and enticing others by a sacred art and courtship to amend their lives: here picturing a vice so as to make it ugly to those that practiced it; and a virtue so as to make it beloved, even by those who loved it not; and all this with a most particular grace and an inexpressible addition of comeliness.[16]

As dean, Donne was required to preach only three times a year (Christmas, Easter, and Ascension Day), but he did so much more frequently. The position meant that he also oversaw the large staff and the complex business of the cathedral. Long experience of living on a small income proved useful, and he was a careful steward of the cathedral's finances. He was, moreover, conscientious in giving out of his income, now stable for the first time since his marriage. Donne reckoned his alms before his other expenses; perhaps remembering his personal and family history, he showed special concern for prisoners and poor students.[17]

Although Donne kept his resolve not to remarry, the years after Anne's death were not gloomy. He apparently lived contentedly with his children, as well as with his unreformed and ardently papist mother, whom he loved. She lived in the deanery (to the scandal of some parishioners) until her death only three months before her son's. Moreover, Donne derived much pleasure from friendship, which he described as his "second religion."[18] Sociability is one of the chief joys he anticipated in heaven; indeed, in Donne's view God saves us out of desire for our company. His description of St. Matthew making a feast for Jesus shows his own pleasure in company: "Though a Church-man, and an exemplar-man, he was not deprived of a plentiful use of God's creatures, nor of the cheerfulness of conversation" (7:143). As his letters show, he confided deeply in his friends and they in turn were well served by Donne's compassion and common sense: "He was a happy reconciler of many differences in the families of his friends and kindred."[19] In later years, he was particularly close to George Herbert and his mother, Lady Magdalen Danvers. The two poets exchanged verse in Latin and English, and Donne sent Herbert one of the personal seals he had designed for himself: Christ crucified on an anchor, the symbol of hope.

Donne's health, for many years weak, finally broke in 1630, just when it had been decided he should be a bishop. He had wished to die in the pulpit or of his exertions there, and in that he succeeded. After a winter of illness at Constance's home in Essex, goaded by the rumor of his own death, he returned to London to preach his regular sermon before the king on the first Friday in Lent (February 25, 1631). It was said that Dr. Donne had preached his own funeral sermon, which was shortly published under the title *Deaths Duell;* his text was from Psalm 68:20: "To God belong the issues from death." The final move is characteristic; Donne fixes the congregation's gaze on the cross, and thus he bids them farewell:

> There now hangs that sacred body upon the cross, rebaptized in his own tears and sweat, and embalmed in his own blood alive...and as God breathed a soul into the first Adam, so this second Adam breathed his soul into God, into the hands of God. There we leave you in that blessed dependency, to hang upon him that hangs upon the cross, there bathe in his tears, there suck at his wounds, and lie down in peace in his grave, till he vouchsafe you a resurrection, and an ascension into

that Kingdom which he hath purchased for you, with the inestimable price of his incorruptible blood. (10:247–48)

Many years before, Donne had written to a friend that he suspected himself of "an over-earnest desire of the next life,"[20] and his last weeks were spent almost in silence, though he declared himself to be "full of inexpressible joy" in his certainty of God's mercy.

Yet Donne's flair for religious drama did not forsake him at the end. He posed for a life-size portrait, wrapped in his funeral shroud and standing on an urn, "with his eyes shut, and with so much of the sheet turned aside as might show his lean, pale, and death-like face, which was purposely turned towards the east, from whence he expected the second coming of his and our Savior Jesus Christ."[21] This most striking production of Donne's emblematic imagination was set opposite the bed as an object for his own contemplation;[22] it was later copied in white marble for the cathedral. He died on March 31, having "disposed his hands and body into such a posture, as required not the least alteration by those that came to shroud him."[23]

Donne's Preaching

Donne had an exceedingly high view of preaching for one who is usually reckoned an Arminian.[24] The Reformation sensibility, reinforced probably by his poet's devotion to words, is audible in his references to the sacraments as "subsidiary helps" to the word, which was in Christ's time the chief instrument of conversion (10:69; cf. 6:175), and remains indispensable to salvation: "There is no salvation but by faith, nor faith but by hearing, nor hearing but by preaching; ... the proposing of the promises of the Gospel in preaching, is that binding and loosing on earth, which binds and looses in heaven" (7:320). The freeing and transformative power of the sermon is a far more developed aspect of Donne's theology than the efficacy of the sacraments, although he sees the relationship as one of complementarity: "We make the natural body of Christ Jesus appliable to our souls by the words of consecration in the sacrament, and our souls apprehensive, and capable of that body, by the word preached" (3:260).

Yet allied with his high view of preaching is an equally exalted estimation of humankind, which measures Donne's distance from Puritanism. If Calvinist thought stresses the majesty of God, often over against human depravity, Donne (in accord with the Book of Common Prayer) places steady emphasis on the dignity with which a God of unbounded mercy invested us at creation and reinvests us through Christ. He takes up the Renaissance image of the individual as microcosm ("I am a little world") and, by setting it in theological context, greatly magnifies its force:

> Since God is so mindful of him, since God hath set his mind upon him, What is not man? Man is all.... For man is not only a contributary creature, but a total creature; he does not only make one, but he is all; he is not a piece of the world, but the world itself, and next to the glory of God, the reason why there is a world. (6:297–98)

At the heart of Donne's theology of preaching is the conviction that God is as intent upon us as we are upon ourselves. It serves indeed as a structural principle that leads him to break with Protestant conventions of preaching. For Donne gives central significance to the element of *applicatio*, the section of the sermon whose purpose is to demonstrate to the congregation the use of the text in their own lives. According to the most popular preaching manual of the day, the bulk of the sermon is to be devoted to expounding "the sense and understanding" of the text and "to collect a few and profitable points of doctrine out of the natural sense." In a brief conclusion the preacher might "apply (if he have the gift) the doctrines rightly collected, to the life and manners of men in a simple and plain speech."[25] But Donne, refusing to hold sense and use separate,[26] makes the minor and optional element of *applicatio* the test of an adequate interpretation of Scripture:

> This is *exquisita scrutatio*, the true searching of the Scriptures, to find all the histories to be examples to me, all the prophecies to induce a Savior to me, all the Gospel to apply Christ Jesus to me...to search the Scriptures, not as though thou wouldest make a concordance, but an application; as thou wouldest search a wardrobe, not to make an inventory of it, but to find in it something fit for thy wearing. (3:367)

In an important study, Barbara Lewalski argues that Donne, in the later poems and the sermons, contributed vitally to a new literary movement in England that she terms "Protestant poetics."[27] The distinctive character of this religious poetics is its highlighting of the affective dimension of the drama of salvation, for which the Pauline epistles provide the paradigm. Its practitioners, and especially the lyric poets of the seventeenth century, explored their own psychological and emotional states in order to chart the process of regeneration within the individual soul. Thus they developed a language that may be compared in

artfulness and personal intensity to that of the Psalmist and St. Paul —
and it is exactly these qualities that make them Donne's favorite biblical
writers, for both private meditation and preaching.[28]

Yet if his preaching gives unprecedented prominence to personal religious experience, nonetheless Donne's is an "egotism and individualism
still willingly involved in tradition."[29] The most pronounced features
of Donne's style are not in fact new. Dwelling on the words of Scripture, and especially the language of the Psalms; recombining them and
complicating their resonances; concrete and rich imagery; the building momentum that gathers up the whole sweep of human experience
in this world and carries it into a vision of the next — all these are
the marks of a superb religious poet. But more particularly, they reveal Donne as a poet whose habits of mind and view of Scripture are
everywhere informed by the two literary monuments of medieval Christianity: the great poem of the liturgy, and a centuries-long tradition
of commentary on Scripture that is both literary and pastoral in nature. Donne "speaks Scripture"; the Bible is for him, like the church
fathers, not so much a fixed text as a language that remains alive
and fully intelligible only within the Church. The liturgy is at once
basic instruction in the Church's language and also its most perfect
product.

Donne often articulates the Protestant view that the preacher's primary aim is "edification," the teaching of scriptural truth in a way that
is clear and appropriate to both occasion and audience. But if Donne's
end coincides with that of the Puritans, his traditionalist aesthetic dic-
tates means that are diametrically opposite to theirs. At the end of the
sixteenth century, William Perkins established the Puritan program of
preaching, based on principles of logical argumentation set forth by the
French dialectician Peter Ramus.[30] Emphasis is on discovering the one
simple meaning of the text, conceived "as a weaver's web," which is
to be "resolved (or untwisted and unloosed) into sundry doctrines."[31]
Rather than unraveling the biblical text into strands of logical argument, however, Donne weaves its words and images, with their multiple
associations and meanings, into the new tapestry of the sermon. Like
Augustine,[32] he believes that the best preaching is artful as well as
wise: "No man profits by a sermon, that hears with pain, or weariness"
(8:149).

Donne follows Augustine also in finding the best model of eloquence
in the Scriptures themselves: "Whatsoever hath justly delighted any
man in any man's writings, is exceeded in the Scriptures" (2:171). And

the aspect of God's art of discourse which most impresses Donne is the use of metaphor:

> My God, my God, thou art a direct God, may I not say, a literal God, a God that wouldest be understood literally, and according to the plain sense of all that thou saiest? But thou art also (Lord, I intend it to thy glory...) a figurative, a metaphorical God, too: a God in whose words there is such a height of figures, such voyages, such peregrinations to fetch remote and precious metaphors, such extensions, such spreadings, such curtains of allegories, such third heavens of hyperboles, so harmonious elocutions... as all profane authors seem of the seed of the serpent, that creeps; thou art the dove, that flies.[33]

The bold use of metaphor is the most constant and memorable feature of Donne's rhetoric, in the sermons as well as the poems. While the Ramist rhetorician considers figurative language to dilute the pure power of argumentation, for Donne it is essential: metaphor, as the Holy Ghost well knows, is often the best means for applying God's word to the human heart and further, for engendering in us an apprehension of spiritual realities. It is possible to be "too literal" with a book that is meant to make us long for heavenly things (the Revelation to John), as one may be "too allegorical" with a book that teaches about earthly matters (Genesis); and such a narrow literalism "will take from us the consolation of many spiritual happinesses, and bury us in the carnal things of this world" (6:62).

Seeking always to wean his hearers from a suffocating love of this world, Donne holds up the figures of Scripture in order to give them a lively vision and grasp of spiritual realities. Moreover, with the daring ease of one fully at home in the imaginative world into which Scripture opens, he amplifies the biblical metaphors by his own inventions. Particularly, he devises striking images to illustrate the dynamics of redemption from sin. To the soul "sunk even into the jaws of desperation," he offers the Johannine image of the seed of God abiding within (1 John 3:9) and draws the homely inference: "The Holy Ghost hath sat upon that seed, and hatched a new creature in thee, a modest but yet infallible assurance of the mercy of thy God" (4:185). The Holy Ghost is a hen; Christ is "the sewer of all the corruption, of all the sins of this world" (7:55); the three Persons of the Trinity "are so many handles by which we may take hold of God, and so many breasts, by which we may suck such a knowledge of God, as that by it we may grow up into him" (3:263). The images of personal transformation are meant to startle us toward salvation: "Every sin is an incision of the soul,... and then a delight in sin is a going with open veins into a warm bath, and bleeding to death" (9:223). In suffering I am like a mass of dough, "when those afflictions do truly crucify me, and souple [soften, make pliant] me, and mellow me, and knead me, and roll me out to a conformity with Christ" (2:300). "Confession works as vomit... an ease to the spiritual stomach, to the conscience" (9:304); prayer as birdlime whereby we catch the feathery wings of God's mercy (6:170). Occasionally the metaphorical impulse causes Donne to lose his literary balance — as, when considering how preposterous is human enmity toward God, he thinks of the mouse and the elephant and then goes on to extol God as "a multiplied elephant, millions of elephants multiplied into one" (10:135)!

In conformity with Protestant hermeneutics, Donne states the primacy of the literal or plain sense of Scripture, which is "the principal intention of the Holy Ghost, in that place."[34] This is the stable sense of the words, taken in historical and literary context, and distinct from "an emergent, a collateral, an occasional sense" (4:181) — that is, the text as applied to a particular audience. But in fact, Donne attends in detail to the contextual sense only when it serves his own central aim of application, illumining some aspect of the Christian moral life and the human personality as it is engaged with God and directed toward heaven. Particularly clear instances are his treatments of the Psalms and Job, texts to which he is deeply drawn as a poet, but even more so because in them he finds himself mirrored and disclosed. His character, like David's and Job's, is one formed out of struggle. Here Donne's psychological interest makes him resist the allegorical impulse of the medieval commentators to refer the text immediately to Christ. Although he does not hesitate to affirm that ultimately Christ is the "subject of the Word of God, of all the Scriptures" (1:287), he insists that it also be read for the insight it affords into the human situation.

A superb late sermon on Job shows how he sets for his own exposition a middle course between abstract historicism and an equally abstract mysticism, devoid of concern for application:

> Many men have troubled themselves more, how the soul comes into man, than how it goes out....So, many of our expositors upon this Book of Job have spent themselves upon the person, and the place, and the time, who Job was, when Job was, where Job was, and whether there were ever any such person as Job or no; and have passed over too slightly the senses and doctrines of the Book. St. Gregory hath (to good use) given us many "morals"[35] (as he calls them) upon this Book, but truly, not many literals; for, for the most part, he bends all the

sufferings of Job figuratively, mystically upon Christ. Origen, who (except St. Gregory) hath written most of this Book, and yet gone but a little way into the Book neither, doth never pretend much literalness in his expositions.... We must not therefore refuse the assistance of later men, in the exposition of this text, "Not for any injustice in my hands..." [Job 16:17–19]. (9:214)

Donne goes on to explore the confidence, the indignation, and the hope of the godly sufferer. Characteristically, the sermon begins with human anguish and leads to Christ.

Although Donne does not (in contrast to Andrewes) generally work with each passage in its immediate literary context, he is nonetheless a profoundly biblical preacher. His text is usually one verse and never more than three, but in every sermon he brings dozens of other passages to bear on its interpretation. For Donne the relevant context of any passage is the whole of Scripture, conceived as a literary unity that reveals Christ throughout and with progressive clarity. A verse from Hosea is as likely to be illumined by St. John's Apocalypse as by the adjacent verse — indeed, more likely, since heaven is always the horizon of his thinking. Interpreting Scripture is essentially practicing the art of collation, that is, discerning the thematic patterns whereby diverse verses can be meaningfully combined into the great story of salvation: in George Herbert's phrase, "Seeing not only how each verse doth shine, / but all the constellations of the story."

The result is not so much a reasoned exposition of the text as a recollected one; Donne's associative style imitates the activity of the memory and seeks to stimulate it. Like his mentor Augustine, he believes that salvation is a matter of recovering the memory of our real selves, created in the image of God, and of all God's mercies toward us. For all his theatricality and conviction of the importance of his task, Donne is never a presumptuous preacher. Rather, a pronounced humility is evident throughout, for he addresses his audience as though they need not so much to be instructed in Scripture as reminded of it:

Nay, he that hears no sermons, he that reads no Scriptures, hath the Bible without book. He hath a Genesis in his memory; he cannot forget his Creation. He hath an Exodus in his memory; he cannot forget that God hath delivered him, from some kind of Egypt, from some oppression. He hath a Leviticus in his memory; he cannot forget that God hath proposed to him some Law, some rules to be observed.
    ... There may be enough in remembering ourselves, but sometimes, that's the hardest of all; many times we are farthest off from ourselves, most forgetful of ourselves. (2:74)

These words were spoken to a congregation of friends at Lincoln's Inn in the early years of Donne's ministry; but he never lost the self-revealing honesty, the respect for the spiritual stature of others, and the hopefulness expressed here. Those are the qualities that endeared Donne to people of every personal and social condition in seventeenth-century London and make his sermons an enduring model for Anglican pastoral care.[36]

Introduction to "A Wedding Sermon"

This wedding sermon, delivered at the marriage of Margaret Washington and Robert Sands, members of the court circle, may be seen as the consummation of one of Donne's favorite themes, learned from Augustine: that of loving others for God's sake. It is a theme he first took up shortly after his own wife's death,[37] and the fact that this sermon was spoken a few feet from her tomb may have contributed to its remarkable power.

While Donne of course understands the social role of the wife according to seventeenth-century conventions, there is tenderness but also deep respect in his conception of marriage as an alliance of complementary strengths. Christian marriage is a purposeful but not exploitative relationship whereby both parties are preserved "against burning," nurture children in order to populate heaven, and provide "mutual help" toward salvation. In thus stating the purposes of marriage, each accompanied by a blessing, Donne's sermon forms a commentary upon the marriage liturgy, which it would have concluded. It is a fine piece of practical divinity, illustrating the continuity between this world and the next, and revealing the common absurdity of strenuous efforts for our children that do not "leave God in their debt"!

Donne views the secular marriage from a male perspective, but there is a dramatic gender reversal when he treats the eternal marriage between "the Lamb and my soul." Here Donne's theology of surrender (expressed in his best known sonnet, "Batter my heart, three-personed God") demands the feminization of the soul. The scene is one of the most fantastic productions of Donne's "shaping imagination,"[38] as he imagines his tremulous soul vindicated before the congregation of virgins, martyrs, confessors, and patriarchs who would forbid God from "marrying down" so low.

Although Donne, in accordance with the Thirty-Nine Articles, denies that marriage is a sacrament, the whole organization of the sermon argues to the contrary, that secular marriage is "a type of the spiritual, and the spiritual an earnest of that eternal." The sacramental movement from outward to inward, earth to heaven, is typical of Donne. Repeatedly he uses Luther's threefold pattern of redemption in nature, grace, and glory to trace the progress of the soul until its final union with God. Here, drawing out the words of the text into an ascending spiral, he shapes a meditational environment for his hearers, so that this wedding grounds and concretizes their hopes for eternal life.

The sermon is spectacular proof that weddings may provide the occasion for powerful proclamations of the Gospel. Donne notes elsewhere that "the Holy Ghost is amorous in his metaphors; everywhere his Scriptures abound with the notions of love, of spouse, and husband, and marriage songs, and marriage-supper, and marriage-bed" (7:87). This amorous rhetoric is a means whereby the God who is Love offers assurance to fearful Christians, whom Donne believes to be the vast majority. Therefore it must have seemed natural to him to use this celebration among friends to speak with an authority and a breadth of scope that equal the best of the St. Paul's discourses. The sermon is at the same time as intimate as the occasion requires and perhaps the purest example extant of the affective style that Donne learned from Scripture and made the hallmark of his preaching: "True instruction is a making love to the congregation, and to every soul in it (but it is but to the soul).... All our hope of bringing you to love God, is in a loving and hearty manner to propose God's love to you" (9:350–51).

A WEDDING SERMON

Preached at the Marriage of Mistress Margaret Washington
at the Church of St. Clement Danes on May 30, 1621

And I will marry thee unto me forever.
—HOSEA 2:19

The word which is the hinge upon which all this text turns is *Erash*, and *Erash* signifies not only a betrothing, as our later translation[39] hath it, but a marriage; and so it is used by David, "Deliver me my wife Michal whom I married" [2 Sam. 3:14]; and so our former translation[40] had it, and so we accept it, and so shall handle it, "I will marry thee unto me for ever."

The first marriage that was made, God made, and he made it in paradise; and of that marriage I have had the like occasion as this to speak before, in the presence of many honorable persons in this company. The last marriage which shall be made God shall make too, and in paradise too, in the kingdom of heaven; and at that marriage, I hope in him that shall make it, to meet not some, but all this company. The marriage in this text hath relation to both those marriages. It is itself the spiritual and mystical marriage of Christ Jesus to the Church and to every marriageable soul in the Church. And it hath a retrospect — it looks back to the first marriage, for to that the first word carries us, because from thence God takes his metaphor and comparison, *sponsabo*, I will marry. And then it hath a prospect to the last marriage, for to that we are carried in the last word, *in æternum*, I will marry thee unto me for ever. Be pleased therefore to give me leave in this exercise, to shift the scene thrice, and to present to your religious considerations three objects, three subjects: first, a secular marriage in paradise; secondly, a spiritual marriage in the Church; and thirdly, an eternal marriage in heaven. And in each of these three we shall present three circumstances; first the persons, *me* and *tibi*, *I* will marry *thee*; and then the action, *sponsabo*, I *will marry* thee; and lastly the term, *in æternum*, I will marry thee *for ever*.

In the first acceptation then, in the first, the secular marriage in paradise, the persons were Adam and Eve. Ever since they are he and she, man and woman. At first, by reason of necessity, without any such limitation as now; and now without any other limitations than such as are expressed in the law of God. As the Apostles say in the first general council, "We lay nothing upon you but things necessary" [Acts 15:28], so we call nothing *necessary* but that which is commanded by God. If in heaven I may have the place of a man that hath performed the commandments of God, I will not change with him that thinks he hath done more than the commandments of God enjoined him. The rule of marriage for degrees and distance in blood is the law of God; but for conditions of men there is no rule at all given. When God had made Adam and Eve in paradise, though there were four rivers in paradise, God did not place Adam in a monastery on one side and Eve in a nunnery on the other, and so a river between them. They that build walls and cloisters to frustrate God's institution of marriage advance the doctrine of devils in forbidding marriage [cf. 1 Tim. 4:3]. The devil hath advantages enough against us in bringing men and women together. It was a strange and super-devilish invention to give him a new advantage against us by keeping men and women asunder, by forbidding marriage. Between the heresy of the Nicolaitans that induced a community of women (any might take any) and the heresy of the Tatians that forbade all (none might take any), was a fair latitude. Between the opinion of the Manichæan heretics that thought women to be made by the devil, and the Colliridian heretics that sacrificed to a woman as to God, there is a fair distance. Between the denying of them souls, which St. Ambrose is charged to have done, and giving them such souls as that they may be priests, as the Peputian heretics did, is a fair way for a moderate man to walk in. To make them gods is ungodly, and to make them devils is devilish; to make them mistresses is unmanly, and to make them servants is unnoble. To make them as God made them, wives, is godly and manly too. When in the Roman Church they dissolve marriage in natural kindred, in degrees where God forbids it not — when they dissolve marriage upon spiritual kindred, because my grandfather christened that woman's father; when they dissolve marriage upon legal kindred, because my grandfather adopted that woman's father — they separate those whom God hath joined so far as to give them leave to join in lawful marriage. When men have made vows to abstain from marriage, I would they would be content to try a little longer than they do, whether they could keep that vow or no. And when men have consecrated themselves to the service of God in his Church, I would they would be content to try a little farther than they do, whether they could abstain or no. But to dissolve marriage made after such a vow or after Orders is still to separate those whom God hath not separated. The persons are he and she, man and woman; they must be so much: he must be a man, she must be a woman. And they must be no more; not a brother and a sister, not an uncle and a niece. *Adduxit ad eum* [(God) brought to him], was the case between Adam and Eve [Gen. 2:22]; God brought them together; God will not bring me a precontracted person, he will not have me defraud another; nor God will not bring me a misbelieving, a superstitious person; he will not have me drawn from himself. But let them be persons that God hath made, man and woman, and persons that God hath brought together, that is, not put asunder by any law of his, and all such persons are capable of this first, this secular marriage.

In which our second consideration is the action, *sponsabo;* where the active is a kind of passive: I will marry thee is I *will be married unto* thee, for we marry not ourselves. They are somewhat hard driven in the Roman Church when making marriage a sacrament and being pressed by us with this question: If it be a sacrament, who administers it, who is the priest? They are fain [pleased; obliged] to answer the bridegroom and the bride, he and she are the priest in that sacrament. As marriage is a civil contract, it must be done so in public as that it may have the testimony of men. As marriage is a religious contract, it must be so done as that it may have the benediction of the priest. In a marriage without testimony of men they cannot claim any benefit by the law; in a marriage without the benediction of the priest they cannot claim any benefit of the Church. For how matrimonially soever such persons as have married themselves may pretend to love, and live together, yet all that love and all that life is but a regulated adultery; it is not marriage.

Now this institution of marriage had three objects: first, *in ustionem,* it was given for a remedy against burning; and then, *in prolem,* for propagation, for children; and lastly, *in adjutorium,* for mutual help. As we consider it the first way, *in ustionem,* every heating is not a burning; every natural concupiscence does not require a marriage; nay every flaming is not a burning; though a man continue under the flame of carnal temptation, as long as St. Paul did, yet it needs not come presently to a *sponsabo,* I will marry. God gave St. Paul other physic; *gratia mea sufficit* [my grace is sufficient], grace to stand under that temptation [2 Cor. 12:9]. And St. Paul gave himself other physic, *contundo corpus* [I bruise the body], convenient disciplines to tame his body. These will keep a man from burning; for *Vri est desideriis vinci, desideria pati, illustris est, et perfecti.* To be overcome by our concupiscences, that is to burn, but to quench that fire by religious ways, that is a noble, that is a perfect work [Ambrose]. When God at the first institution of marriage had this first use of marriage in his contemplation, that it should be a remedy against burning, God gave man the remedy before he had the disease; for marriage was instituted in the state of innocency when there was no inordinateness in the affections of man, and so no burning. But as God created rhubarb in the world, whose quality is to purge choler, before there was any choler to purge, so God according to his abundant forwardness to do us good, created a remedy before the disease, which he foresaw coming, was come upon us. Let him then that takes his wife in this first and lowest sense, *in medicinam* [for a cure], but as his physic yet make her his cordial physic, take her to his heart and fill his heart with her, let her dwell there, and dwell there alone, and so they will be mutual antidotes and preservatives to one another against all foreign temptations. And with this blessing, bless thou O Lord, these whom thou hast brought hither for this blessing; make all the days of their life like this day unto them; and as "thy mercies... are new every morning" [Lam. 3:22–23], make them so to one another. And if they may not die together, sustain thou the survivor of them in that sad hour with this comfort, that he that died for them both, will bring them together again in his everlastingness.

The second use of marriage was *in prolificationem*, for children. And therefore as St. Augustine puts the case, to contract before, that they will have no children, makes it no marriage but an adultery. To deny themselves to one another, is as much against marriage as to give themselves to another. To hinder it by physic, or another practice – nay to hinder it so far as by a deliberate wish or prayer against children – consists not well with this second use of marriage. And yet in this second use, we do not so much consider generation as regeneration; not so much procreation as education, nor propagation as transplantation of children. For this world might be filled full enough of children, though there were no marriage; but heaven could not be filled, nor the places of the fallen angels supplied, without that care of children's religious education which from parents in lawful marriage they are likeliest to receive. How infinite and how miserable a circle of sin do we make, if as we sinned in our parents' loins before we were born, so we sin in our children's actions when we are dead, by having given them, either example or liberty of sinning. We have a fearful commination [threat] from God upon a good man, upon Eli, for his not restraining the licentiousness of his sons; "I will do a thing in Israel," says God there, "at which every man's ears that hear it shall tingle" [1 Sam. 3:11]. And it was executed; Eli fell down and broke his neck [1 Sam. 4:18]. We have also a promise of consolation to women for children, "She shall be saved in child-bearing" [1 Tim. 2:15], says the Apostle; but as Chrysostom and others of the ancients observe and interpret that place (which interpretation arises out of the very letter) it is, *si permanserint* [if they continue], not if she, but if they, if the children continue in faith, in charity, in holiness, and sobriety. The salvation of the parents hath so much relation to the children's goodness, as that if they be ill by the parent's example or indulgence, the parents are as guilty as the children. Art thou afraid thy child should be stung with a snake, and wilt thou let him play with the old serpent, in opening himself to all temptations? Art thou afraid to let him walk in an ill air, and art thou content to let him stand in that pestilent air that is made of nothing but oaths, and execrations of blasphemous mouths round about him? It is St. Chrysostom's complaint, *Perditionem magno pretio emunt; salutem nec dono accipere volunt* [They buy perdition at a great price; they are not willing to accept salvation as a gift]; we pay dear for our children's damnation, by paying at first for all their childish vanities, and then for their sinful insolencies at any rate; and we might have them saved, and ourselves to the bargain, (which were a frugal way, and a debt well hedged in) for much less than ours, and their damnation stands us in. If you have a desire, says that blessed Father, to leave them certainly rich, *Deum iis relinque debitorem*, do some such thing for God's service, as you may leave God in their debt. He cannot break; his estate is inexhaustible; he will not break promise nor break day; "He will show mercy unto thousands in them that love him and keep his commandments" [Exod. 20:6]. And here also may another shower of his benedictions fall upon them whom he hath prepared and presented here; "Let the wife be as a fruitful vine, and their children like olive plants" [Ps. 128:3]. To thy glory, let the parents express the love of parents, and the children, to thy glory the obedience of children, till they both lose that secular name of parents and children, and meet all alike, in one new name, all saints of thy kingdom, and fellow servants there.

The third and last use in this institution of secular marriage, was, *in adjutorium*, for mutual help. There is no state, no man in any state, that needs not the help of others. Subjects need kings, and if kings do not need their subjects, they need alliances abroad, and they need counsel at home. Even in paradise, where the earth produced all things for life without labor, and the beasts submitted themselves to man so that he had no outward enemy, and in the state of innocency in paradise, where in man all the affections submitted themselves to reason so that he had no inward enemy, yet God in this abundant paradise, and in this secure innocency of paradise, even in the survey of his own works, saw that though all that he had made was good, yet he had not made all good. He found thus much defect in his own work, that man lacked a helper. Every body needs the help of others; and every good body does give some kind of help to others. Even into the ark itself, where God blessed them all with a powerful and an immediate protection, God admitted only such as were fitted to help one another, couples. In the ark, which was the type of our best condition in this life, there was not a single person. Christ saved once one thief at the last gasp, to show that there may be late repentances; but in the ark he saved none but married persons, to show that he eases himself in making them helpers to one another. And therefore when we come to the *posui Deum adjutorium* [I have set the Lord as (my) help; cf. Ps. 16:8], to rely upon God primarily for our help, God comes to the *faciam tibi adjutorium*, I will make thee a help like thyself [Gen. 2:18]: not always like in complexion, nor like in years, nor like in fortune, nor like in birth, but like in mind, like in disposition, like in the love of God and of one another, or else there is no helper. It was no kind of help that David's wife gave him when she spoke by way of counsel, but in truth, in scorn and derision, to draw him from a religious act, as the dancing before the ark at that time was [2 Sam. 6:14–20]. It is no help for any respect, to slacken the husband in his religion. It was but a poor help that Nabal's wife was fain to give him by telling David, "Alas my husband is but a fool, like his name, and what will you look for at a fool's hand?" [1 Sam. 25:25]. It is the worst help of all to raise a husband by dejecting herself, to help her husband forward in this world, by forfeiting sinfully and dishonorably her own interest in the next. The husband is the helper in the nature of a foundation to sustain and uphold all; the wife in the nature of the roof to cover imperfections and weaknesses; the husband in the nature of the head from whence all the sinews flow; the wife in the nature of the hands into which those sinews flow, and enable them to do their offices. The husband helps as legs to her; she moves by his motion. The wife helps as a staff to him; he moves the better by her assistance. And let this mutual help be a part of our present benediction too: In all the ways of fortune let his industry help her, and in all the crosses of fortune let her patience help him; and in all emergent[41] occasions and dangers spiritual, or temporal "O God make speed to save them; O Lord, make haste to help them" [Ps. 70:2].[42]

We have spoken of the persons man and woman, him and her;

and of the action, first as it is physic, but cordial physic; and then for children, but children to be made the children of God; and lastly for help, but true help and mutual help. There remains yet in this secular marriage, the term: how long, for ever, I will marry thee for ever. Now though there be properly no eternity in this secular marriage, nor in any thing in this world (for eternity is only that which never had beginning nor ever shall have end), yet we may consider a kind of eternity, a kind of circle without beginning, without end even in this secular marriage. For first, marriage should have no beginning before marriage; no half-marriage, no lending away of the mind in conditional precontracts before, no lending away of the body in unchaste wantonness before. The body is the temple of the Holy Ghost; and when two bodies by marriage are to be made one temple, the wife is not as the chancel, reserved and shut up, and the man as the walks below, indifferent and at liberty for every passenger. God in his temple looks for first fruits from both; that so on both sides, marriage should have such a degree of eternity as to have had no beginning of marriage before marriage. It should have this degree of eternity too, this quality of a circle to have no interruption, no breaking in the way by unjust suspicions and jealousies. Where there is *spiritus immunditiei*, as St. Paul calls it, a spirit of uncleanness [cf. Rom. 1:24, 6:19 *et passim*], there will necessarily be *spiritus zelotypiæ*, as Moses calls it, a spirit of jealousy [Num. 5:30]. But to raise the devil in the power of the devil, to call up one spirit by another spirit, by the spirit of jealousy and suspicion to induce the spirit of uncleanness where it was not, if a man conjure up a devil so, God knows who shall conjure it down again. As jealousy is a care and not a suspicion, God is not ashamed to protest of himself that he is a jealous God. God commands that no idolatry be committed, "Thou shalt not bow down to a graven image" [Exod. 20:4, 5]; and before he accuses any man to have bowed down to a graven image, before any idolatry was committed, he tells them that he *is a jealous God;* God is jealous before there be any harm done. And God presents it as a curse, when he says, "My jealousy shall depart from thee, and I will be quiet, and no more angry" [Ezek. 16:42]; that is, I will leave thee to thyself and take no more care of thee. Jealousy that implies care, and honor, and counsel, and tenderness, is rooted in God, for God is a jealous God and his servants are jealous servants, as St. Paul professes of himself, "I am jealous over you with a godly jealousy" [2 Cor. 11:2]. But jealousy that implies diffidence, and suspicion, and accusation is rooted in the devil, for he is the "accuser of the brethren" [Rev. 12:10].

So then, this secular marriage should be *in æternum*, eternal, for ever, as to have no beginning before, and so too as to have no jealous interruption by the way; for it is so eternal as that it can have no end in this life. Those whom God hath joined, no man, no devil, can separate, so as that it shall not remain a marriage so far as that if those separated persons will live together again, yet they shall not be new married; so far certainly the band of marriage continues still. The devil makes no marriages; he may have a hand in drawing conveyances, in the temporal conditions there may be practice, but the marriage is made by God in heaven. The devil can break no marriages neither, though he can by sin break of all the good uses and take away all the comforts of marriage. I pronounce not now whether adultery dissolves marriage or no; it is St. Augustine's wisdom to say, where the Scripture is silent, let me be silent too. And I may go lower than he, and say where the Church is silent, let me be silent too; and our Church is so far silent in this, as that it hath not said that adultery dissolves marriage. Perchance then it is not the death of marriage, but surely it is a deadly wound. We have authors in the Roman Church that think *fornicationem non vagam*, that such an incontinent life as is limited to one certain person, is no deadly sin. But there is none even amongst them that diminish the crime of adultery. *Habere quasi non haberes*, is Christ's counsel [1 Cor. 7:29]; to have a wife as though thou hadst none, that is for continency, and temperance, and forbearance and abstinence upon some occasions. But *non habere quasi haberes*, is not so; not to have a wife, and yet have her, to have her that is another's, this is the devil's counsel. Of that salutation of the Angel to the blessed Virgin Mary, "Blessed art thou amongst woman" [Luke 1:28], we may make even this interpretation, not only that she was blessed amongst women, that is, above women, but that she was *benedicta*, blessed amongst women, that all women blessed her, that no woman had occasion to curse her. And this is the eternity of this secular marriage as far as this world admits any eternity; that it should have no beginning before, no interruption of jealousy in the way, no such approach towards dissolution, as that incontinency in all opinions and in all churches is agreed to be. And here also without any scruple of fear, or of suspicion of the contrary, there is place for this benediction upon this couple: Build, O Lord, upon thine own foundations in these two, and establish thy former graces with future; that no person ever complain of either of them, nor either of them of one another, and so he and she are married *in æternum*, for ever.

We are now come in our order proposed at first, to our second part; for all is said that I intended of the secular marriage. And of this second, the spiritual marriage, much needs not to be said. There is another Priest that contracts that, another Preacher that celebrates that, the Spirit of God to our spirit. And for the third marriage, the eternal marriage, it is a boldness to speak anything of a thing so inexpressible as the joys of heaven; it is a diminution of them to go about to heighten them; it is a shadowing of them to go about to lay any colors or lights upon them. But yet your patience may perchance last to a word of each of these three circumstances: the persons, the actions, the term, both in this spiritual, and in the eternal marriage.

First then, as in the former part, the secular marriage, for the persons there we considered first Adam and Eve, and after every man and woman, and this couple in particular; so in this spiritual marriage we consider first Christ and his Church for the persons, but more particularly Christ and my soul. And can these persons meet? In such a distance, and in such a disparagement can these persons meet? The Son of God and the son of man? When I consider Christ to be *germen Jehovæ*, the bud and blossom, the fruit and offspring of Jehovah, Jehovah himself, and myself before he took me in hand, to be not a potter's vessel of earth, but that earth of which the potter might make a vessel if he would, and break it if he would when he had made it [cf. Ps. 2:9; Isa. 30:14; Jer. 18:1–12, 19:10–11]. When I consider Christ to have been from before all beginnings [cf. Col. 1:17], and to be still the image of the Father, the same stamp upon the same metal, and myself a piece of rusty copper, in which those lines of the image of God which were imprinted in me in my creation are defaced and worn, and washed and burnt, and ground away by my many, and many, and many sins; when I consider Christ in his circle, in glory with his Father before he came into this world, establishing a glorious Church when he was in this world, and glorifying that Church with that glory which himself had before, when he went out of this world; and then consider myself in my circle, I came into this world washed in mine own tears, and either out of compunction for myself or compassion for others, I pass through this world as through a valley of tears, where tears settle and swell, and when I pass out of this world I leave their eyes whose hands close mine, full of tears too — can these persons, this image of God, this God himself, this glorious God, and this vessel of earth, this earth itself, this inglorious worm of the earth, meet without disparagement?

They do meet and make a marriage; because I am not a body only, but a body and soul, there is a marriage and Christ marries me. As by the law a man might marry a captive woman in the wars, if he shaved her head and pared her nails and changed her clothes [Deut. 21:12], so my Savior having fought for my soul, fought to blood, to death, to the death of the cross for her, having studied my soul so much as to write all those Epistles which are in the New Testament to my soul, having presented my soul with his own picture that I can see his face in all his temporal blessings, having shaved her head in abating her pride, and pared her nails in contracting her greedy desires, and changed her clothes not to fashion herself after this world, my soul being thus fitted by himself, Christ Jesus hath married my soul, married her to all the three intendments mentioned in the secular marriage: first, *in ustionem*, against burning; that whether I burn myself in the fires of temptation by exposing myself to occasions of temptation, or be reserved to be burnt by others in the fires of persecution and martyrdom, whether the fires of ambition, or envy, or lust, or the everlasting fires of hell offer at me in an apprehension of the judgments of God, yet as the Spirit of God shall wipe all tears from mine eyes, so the tears of Christ Jesus shall extinguish all fires in my heart, and so it is a marriage, *in ustionem*, a remedy against burning.

It is so too, *in prolificationem*, for children: first, *væ soli*, woe unto that single soul that is not married to Christ; that is not come into the way of having issue by him, that is not incorporated in the Christian Church, and in the true Church, but is yet either in the wilderness of idolatry amongst the Gentiles or in the labyrinth of superstition amongst the Papist; *væ soli*, woe unto that single man that is not married to Christ in the sacraments of the Church; and *væ sterili*, woe unto them that are barren after this spiritual marriage, for that is a great curse in the prophet Jeremy, *Scribe virum istum sterilem*: "Write this man childless" [Jer. 22:30], that implied all calamities upon him. And as soon as Christ had laid that curse upon the fig tree, "Let no fruit grow upon thee for ever" [Matt. 21:19], presently the whole tree withered; if no fruit, no leaves neither, nor body left. To be incorporated in the body of Christ Jesus, and bring forth no fruits worthy of that profession, is a woeful state too. *Væ soli:* first, woe unto the Gentiles not married unto Christ; and *væ sterili,* woe unto inconsiderate Christians, that think not upon their calling, that conceive not by Christ; but there is a *væ prægnanti* [Matt. 24:19] too, woe unto them that are with child, and are never delivered; that have sometimes good conceptions, religious dispositions, holy desires to the advancement of God's truth, but for some collateral respects dare not utter them, nor bring them to their birth to any effect. The purpose of his marriage to us is to have children by us; and this is his abundant and his present fecundity, that working now, by me in you, in one instant he hath children in me, and grandchildren by me. He hath married me, *in ustionem,* and *in prolem,* against burning, and for children; but can he have any use of me, *in adjutorium,* for a helper? Surely, if I be able to feed him, and clothe him, and harbor him (and Christ would not condemn men at the last day for not doing these, if man could not do them [cf. Matt. 25:31–46]), I am able to help him too. Great persons can help him over sea, convey the name of Christ where it hath not been preached yet; and they can help him home again, restore his name and his truth where superstition with violence hath diseased him. And they can help him at home, defend his truth there against all machinations to displant and dispossess him. Great men can help him thus; and every man can help him to a better place in his own heart, and his own actions, than he hath had there; and to be so helped in me, and helped by me, to have his glory thereby advanced, Christ hath married my soul. And he hath married it *in æternum,* for ever; which is the third and last circumstance in this spiritual as it was in the secular marriage.

And here the *æternum* is enlarged; in the secular marriage it was an eternity considered only in this life; but this eternity is not begun in this world, but from all eternity in the book of life, in God's eternal decree for my election, there Christ was married to my soul. Christ was never in minority, never under years; there was never any time when he was not as ancient as the Ancient of Days [Dan. 7:9], as old as his Father. But when my soul was in a strange minority, infinite millions of millions of generations, before my soul was a soul, did Christ marry my soul in his eternal decree. So it was eternal, it had no beginning. Neither doth he interrupt this by giving me any occasion of jealousy by the way, but loves my soul as though there were no other soul, and would have done and suffered all that he did for me alone, if there had been no name but mine in the book of life. And as he hath married me to him, in *æternum*, for ever, before all beginnings, and in *æternum*, for ever, without any interruptions, so I know that "whom he loves he loves to the end" [John 13:1], and that he hath given me, not a presumptuous impossibility, but a modest infallibility, that no sin of mine shall divorce or separate me from him [cf. Rom. 8:35–39]; for that which ends the secular marriage ends not the spiritual; not death, for my death does not take me from that husband, but that husband being by his Father preferred to higher titles, and greater glory in another state, I do but go by death where he is become a king, to have my part in that glory and in those additions which he hath received there. And this hath led us to our third and last marriage, our eternal marriage in the triumphant Church.

And in this third marriage, the persons are the Lamb and my soul. "The marriage of the Lamb is come, and blessed are they that are called to the marriage supper of the Lamb," [Rev. 19:7, 9] says St. John, speaking of our state in the general resurrection. That Lamb who was "brought to the slaughter and opened not his mouth" [Isa. 53:7], and I who have opened my mouth and poured out imprecations and curses upon men, and execrations and blasphemies against God upon every occasion. That Lamb who "was slain from the beginning" [Rev. 13:8], and I who was slain by him who "was a murderer from the beginning" [John 8:44]; that "Lamb which took away the sins of the world" [John 1:29], and I who brought more sins into the world than any sacrifice but the blood of this Lamb could take away. This Lamb and I (these are the persons) shall meet and marry; there is the action.

This is not a clandestine marriage, not the private seal of Christ in the obsignation [formal ratification or confirmation] of his Spirit; and yet such a clandestine marriage is a good marriage. Nor it is not such a parish marriage, as when Christ married me to himself at my baptism, in a church here; and yet that marriage of a Christian soul to Christ in that sacrament is a blessed marriage. But this is a marriage in that great and glorious congregation, where all my sins shall be laid open to the eyes of all the world, where all the blessed virgins shall see all my uncleanness, and all the martyrs see all my tergiversations [turnings back], and all the confessors see all my double dealings in God's cause; where Abraham shall see my faithlessness in God's promises, and Job my impatience in God's corrections, and Lazarus my hardness of heart in distributing God's blessings to the poor; and those virgins, and martyrs, and confessors, and Abraham, and Job, and Lazarus, and all that congregation, shall look upon the Lamb and upon me and upon one another, as though they would all forbid those banes [banns], and say to one another, will this Lamb have anything to do with this soul? And yet there and then this Lamb shall marry me, and marry me in *æternum*, for ever, which is our last circumstance.

It is not well done to call it a circumstance, for the eternity is a great part of the essence of that marriage. Consider then how poor and needy a thing all the riches of this world, how flat and tasteless a thing all the pleasures of this world, how pallid and faint and dilute a thing all the honors of this world are, when the very treasure, and joy, and glory of heaven itself were unperfect, if it were not eternal, and my marriage shall be so, in *æternum*, for ever.

The angels were not married so; they incurred an irreparable divorce from God and are separated for ever, and I shall be married to him, in *æternum*, for ever. The angels fell in love, when there was no object presented, before anything was created; when there was nothing but God and themselves, they fell in love with themselves, and neglected God, and so fell in *æternum*, for ever. I shall see all the beauty, and all the glory of all the saints of God, and love them all, and know that the Lamb loves them too, without jealousy on his part, or theirs, or mine, and so be married in *æternum*, for ever, without interruption, or diminution, or change of affections. I shall see the sun black as sackcloth of hair, and the moon become as blood, and the stars fall as a fig tree casts her untimely figs, and the heavens rolled up together as a scroll. I shall see a divorce between princes and their prerogatives, between nature and all her elements, between the spheres and all their intelligences, between matter itself and all her forms, and my marriage shall be, in *æternum*, for ever. I shall see an end of faith, nothing to be believed that I do not know; and an end of hope, nothing to be wished that I do not enjoy; but no end of that love in which I am married to the Lamb for ever. Yea, I shall see an end of some of the offices of the Lamb himself; Christ himself shall be no longer a mediator, an intercessor, an advocate, and yet shall continue a husband to my soul for ever. Where I shall be rich enough without jointure, for my husband cannot die; and wise enough without experience, for no new thing can happen there; and healthy enough without physic, for no sickness can enter; and (which is by much the highest of all) safe enough without grace, for no temptation that needs particular grace can attempt me. There, where the angels, which cannot die, could not live, this very body, which cannot choose but die, shall live, and live as long as that God of life that made it. "Lighten our darkness, we beseech thee, O Lord,"[43] that "in thy light we may see light" [Ps. 36:10]. Illustrate our understandings, kindle our affections, pour oil to our zeal, that we may come to the marriage of this Lamb, and that this Lamb may come quickly to this marriage. And in the meantime bless these thy servants, with making this secular marriage a type of the spiritual, and the spiritual an earnest of that eternal, which they and we, by thy mercy, shall have in the kingdom which thy Son our Savior hath purchased with the inestimable price of his incorruptible blood.

Introduction to "The Fear of the Lord"

Beginning in 1624, Donne served as vicar of St. Dunstan's-in-the-West, a city parish within Temple Bar. Among the parishioners in this fashionable district were the draper Izaak Walton, who became Donne's "convert" and biographer, and John Marriott, his publisher. Although Donne appointed a curate to live in the vicarage, he preached regularly there and took an interest in the furnishings and affairs of the church. The St. Dunstan's sermons show Donne's plainer style of preaching (in comparison to the sermons at St. Paul's and the court) and include some of his clearest statements about the pastor's relation to the congregation.

Among the books of the Old Testament, Donne had a particular love for the Psalms, which provide texts for 34 of the 160 extant sermons.[44] He delighted in the "cheerfulness" of the Psalms, and also for the reliable instruction measured out in their poetry, "because where all the words are numbered, and measured, and weighed, the whole work is the less subject to falsification, either by subtraction or addition" (an argument that, not incidentally, also commends the measured prayer of the established church) (2:50).

The present sermon shows Donne to be an astute pastoral psychologist, who learned his psychology from the Bible. His subject is "the

fear of the Lord," the Hebrew phrase that expresses the basic disposition of the religious person. He begins with a "witty" paradox: this
fear is a courageous virtue. It is not a natural affection but an art form,
which must be learned and practiced. Wisely, Donne does not dismiss
natural fear and the "half-natural" fear of violating custom but rather
shows how holy fear animates and directs our natural fears toward the
purposes of salvation.

Throughout he works to instill confidence in his hearers: we are children of God, and therefore capable of responding to God in love and
standing firm in affliction by "Christian constancy." In the brilliant final
section of the sermon, he appeals to the universal human experience of
love, and reminds us that the fear of loss is always part of love. Thus he
overcomes the Augustinian dichotomy between the "Old Testament of
fear" and the "New Testament of love," drawing a semantic circle that
encompasses both: "The love of God begins in fear, and the fear of God
ends in love; and that love can never end, for God is love."

THE FEAR OF THE LORD

Preached at St. Dunstan's on April 25, 1624

Come ye children, hearken unto me,
I will teach you the fear of the Lord.
— PSALM 34:11

The text does not call children simply, literally, but such men and
women as are willing to come in the simplicity of children; such
children as Christ spoke of, *Except ye become as little children, ye
shall not enter into the kingdom of heaven* [Matt. 18:3]. Come ye
children; come such children. Nor does the text call such as come,
and would fain be gone again; it is come and hearken; not such as
wish themselves away, nor such as wish another man here; but such
as value God's ordinance of preaching, though it be, as the Apostle
says, but *the foolishness of preaching* [1 Cor. 1:21], and such, as
consider the office and not the person, how mean soever. Come ye
children; and when ye are come, hearken; and though it be but I,
hearken unto me, and I will teach you the fear of the Lord; the most
noble, the most courageous, the most magnanimous, not affection,

but virtue, in the world: *Come ye children, hearken unto me, and I will teach you the fear of the Lord.*

To every minister and dispenser of the word of God, and to every congregation belong these words. And therefore we will divide the text between us; to you one, to us appertains the other part. You must come, and you must hearken; we must teach, and teach to edification. There is the *meum et tuum*, your part and our part. From each part, these branches flow out naturally: in yours, first the capacity, as children; then the action, you come; then your disposition here, you hearken; and lastly, your submission to God's ordinance, you hearken even unto me, unto any minister of his sending. In our part, there is first a teaching; for else why should you come, or hearken unto me, or any? It is a teaching, it is not only a praying [entreaty, invitation]. And then there is a catholic doctrine, a circular doctrine, that walks the round, and goes the compass of our whole lives, from our first to our last childhood, when age hath made us children again, and it is the art of arts, the root and fruit of all true wisdom, the true fear of the Lord. Come ye children, hearken unto me, and I will teach you the fear of the Lord.

First then the word, in which, in the first branch of the first part, your capacity is expressed; *filii, pueri,* children, is, from the original, which is *banim*, often accepted in three notions, and so rendered. Three ways, men are called children, out of that word *banim*, in the Scriptures. Either it is *servi*, servants; for they are *filii familiares*, as the master is *pater familias*, father of the family (and that he is, though there be no natural children in the family), the servants are children of the family, and are very often in Scriptures called so: *pueri*, children. Or it is *alumni*, nurse-children, foster-children, *filii mammillares*, children of the breasts; whether we minister to them, temporal or spiritual nourishment, they are children. Or else it is *filii viscerales*, children of our bowels, our natural children. And in all these three capacities, as servants, as sucking children, as sons, are you called upon in this appellation, in this compellation [the act of addressing; accosting], children.

First, as you are servants, you are children; for, without distinction of age, servants are called so, frequently, ordinarily, in the Scriptures, *pueri*. The priest asks David, before he would give him the holy bread, *an vasa puerorum sancta*, whether those children (speaking of David's followers) were clean from women [1 Sam. 25:4]. Here were children that were able to get children. Nay, David's soldiers

are often called so, *pueri*, children. In the first of the Kings, he takes
a muster, *recenset pueros* [1 Kgs. 20:15]; here were children able to
kill men. You are his children (of what age soever), as you are his servants; and in that capacity he calls you. You are *unprofitable servants*
[Luke 17:10]; but it is not an unprofitable service, to serve God. He
can get nothing by you, but you can have nothing without him. The
centurion's servants came when he said come; and was their wages
like yours? Had they their being, their everlasting well-being for their
service? You will scarce receive a servant that is come from another
man without testimony. If you put yourselves out of God's service,
whither will ye go? *In his service, and his only, is perfect freedom.*[45]
And therefore as you love freedom and liberty, be his servants; and
call the freedom of the Gospel the best freedom, and come to the
preaching of that.

He calls you children, as you are servants (*filii familiares*), and he
calls you children, as you are *alumni*, nurse-children; *filii mammillares*, as he requires the humility and simplicity of little children in
you. For, *cum simplicibus sermocinatio ejus* (as the Vulgate reads
that place), God's secret discourse is with the single heart [Prov.
3:32]. The first that ever came to Christ (so as he came to us, in
blood), they that came to him so, before he came so to us, that
died for him, before he died for them, were such sucking children,
those whom Herod slew. As Christ thought himself bound to thank
his Father, for that way of proceeding, *I thank thee, O Father, Lord
of heaven and earth, that thou hast revealed these things unto babes*
[Matt. 11:25]; so Christ himself pursues the same way: *Suffer little
children, and forbid them not to come unto me, for of such is the
kingdom of heaven* [Matt. 19:14]. Of such, not only of those who
were truly, literally children (children in age), but of such as those
(*talium est regnum cœlorum*) [of such is the kingdom of heaven],
such as come in such a disposition, in the humility, in the simplicity, in the singleness of heart, as children do. An habitual sinner
is always in minority, always an infant; an infant to this purpose,
all his acts, all the bands[46] of an infant, are void; all the outward
religious actions, even the band and contract of baptism in an habitual sinner, is void and ineffectual. He that is in the house and
favor of God, though he be a child (a child to this purpose, simple,
supple, tractable, single-hearted), is, as Adam was in the state of innocency, a man the first minute, able to stand upright in the sight
of God. And out of one place of Esay, our expositors have drawn,

conveniently enough, both of these conclusions. *A child shall die 100 years old* [Isa. 65:20], says the prophet; that is (say some), a sinner though he live 100 years, yet he dies a child, in ignorance. And then (say others, and both truly), he that comes willingly, when God calls, though he die a child in age, he hath the wisdom of 100 years upon him. There is not a graver thing than to be such a child; to conform his will to the will of God. Whether you consider temporal or spiritual things, you are God's children. For, for temporal, if God should take off his hand, withdraw his hand of sustentation,[47] all those things which assist us temporally would relapse to the first feeble and childish estate, and come to their first nothing. Armies would be but hospitals, without all strength; council-tables but Bedlams,[48] without all sense; and schools and universities but the wrangling of children, if God and his Spirit did not inanimate our schools, and armies, and councils. His adoption makes us men, therefore, because it makes us his children. But we are his children in this consideration especially, as we are his spiritual children, as he hath nursed us, fed us with his word. In which sense, the apostle speaks of those who had embraced the true religion (in the same words that the prophet had spoken before), *Behold, I, and the children that God hath given me* [Heb. 2:13]. And in the same sense, the same prophet, in the same place, says of them who had fallen away from the true religion, *they please themselves in the children of strangers* [Isa. 2:6], in those men, who have derived their orders and their doctrine from a foreign jurisdiction. In that state where adoptions were so frequent (in old Rome), a plebeian could not adopt a patrician, a yeoman could not adopt a gentleman, nor a young man could not adopt an old. In the new Rome, that endeavors to adopt all in an imaginary filiation, you that have the perfect freedom of God's service, be not adopted into the slavery and bondage of men's traditions; you that are in possession of the ancient religion, of Christ and his apostles, be not adopted into a younger religion. *Religio à religando;* that is, religion that binds; that binds, that is necessary to salvation. That which we affirm, our adversaries deny not; that which we profess, they confess was always necessary to salvation. They will not say that all that they say now was always necessary; that a man could not be saved without believing the Articles of the Council of Trent, a week before that council shut up. You are his children, as children are servants; and *If he be your Lord, where is his fear?* [Mal. 1:6]. You are his children, as he hath nursed you with the milk of his word; and if he be your father so (your foster father), where is his love?

But he is your father otherwise; you are not only *filii familiares*, children because servants, nor only *filii mammillares*, children because nursed by him, but you are also *filii viscerales*, children of his bowels. For we are otherwise allied to Christ, than we can be to any of his instruments, though angels of the Church, prophets, or apostles; and yet, his apostle says, of one whom he loved, of Onesimus, *Receive him, that is mine own bowels; my son*, says he, *whom I have begotten in my bands* [Philem. v. 12]. How much more art thou bound to receive and refresh those bowels from which thou art derived, Christ Jesus himself; receive him, refresh him. Carry that, which the wise man hath said, *miserere animæ tuæ* [Ecclus. 30:23], be merciful to thine own soul, higher then so; and *miserere salvatoris tui*, have mercy upon thine own Savior; *put on the bowels of mercy* [Col. 3:12], and put them on even towards Christ Jesus himself, who needs thy mercy, by being so torn, and mangled, and emboweled, by blasphemous oaths, and execrations. For, beloved, it is not so absurd a prayer as it is conceived, if Luther did say upon his death bed: *Oremus pro Domino nostro Jesu Christo*, Let us pray for our Lord and Savior Jesus Christ. Had we not need pray for him? If he complain that Saul persecutes him, had we not need pray for him? It is a seditious affection in civil things to divide the king and the kingdom; to pray, to fight for the one, and leave out the other, is seditiously done. If the kingdom of Christ need thy prayers and thy assistance, Christ needs it; if the body need it, the head needs it; if thou must pray for his Gospel, thou must pray for him. Nay, thou canst not pray for thyself, but thou must pray for him, for thou art his bowels; when thou in thy forefathers, the first Christians in the primitive Church, wast persecuted, Christ cried out, *why persecutest thou me?* [Acts 9:4]. Christ made thy case his, because thou wast of his bowels. When Christ is diseased, and dispossessed, his truth profligated, and thrown out of a nation that professed it before, when Christ is wounded by the blasphemies of others, and crucified by thee, in thy relapses to repented sins, wilt thou not say to them, to thyself, in the behalf of Christ, why persecute ye me? Wilt thou not make Christ's case thine, as he made thine his? Art not thou the bowels of Christ? If not (and thou art not, if thou have not this sense of his suffering), thou hast no interest in his death by thy baptism, nor in his resurrection by thy feeble half repentances. But in the duty of a child, as thou art a servant, in the simplicity of a child, as thou hast sucked from him, in the interest and inheritance of a child, as thou art the son of his bowels; in all these capacities (and with all these we have done), God calls thee, *come ye children;* and that is our next step: the action, *come.*

Passing thus from the persons to the action, *venite,* come, we must ask first what this coming is? The whole mystery of our redemption is expressed by the Apostle in this word, *venit, that Christ Jesus is come into the world* [1 Tim. 1:15]. All that thou hast to do is to come to, and to meet him. Where is he? At home; in his own house, in the Church. Which is his house; which is his Church? That to thee, in which he hath given thee thy baptism, if that do still afford thee as much as is necessary for thy salvation. Come thither, to the participation of his ordinances, to the exercises of religion there. The gates of heaven shall be opened to you, at last in that word, *venite benedicti,* come ye blessed [Matt. 25:34]; the way to those gates is opened to you now, in the same word, *venite filii,* come ye children, come. Christ can come, and does often, into thy bedchamber, in the visitation of his private Spirit, but here he calls thee out into the congregation, into the communion of saints. And then the Church celebrates Christ's coming in the flesh, a month before he comes, in four Sundays of Advent, before Christmas. When thou comest to meet him in the congregation, come not occasionally, come not casually, not indifferently, not collaterally; come not as to an entertainment, a show, a spectacle, or company; come solemnly, with preparation, with meditation. He shall have the less profit, by the prayer of the congregation, that hath not been at his private prayer before he came. Much of the mystery of our religion lay in the *venturus,* that Christ was to come, all that the law and prophets undertook for, was that *venturus,* that Christ was to come; but the consummation of all, the end of the law and the prophets, is in the *venit;* he is come. Do not clog thy coming with future conditions, and contingencies, thou wilt come, if thou canst wake, if thou canst rise, if thou canst be ready, if thou like the company, the weather, the man. We find one man who was brought in his bed to Christ [Matt. 9:2]; but it was but one. Come, come actually, come earnestly, come early, come often; and come to meet him, Christ Jesus and nobody else. Christ is come into the world, and therefore thou needest not go out of the world to meet him; he doth not call thee from thy calling, but in thy calling. The dove went up and down, from the ark and to the ark, and yet was not disappointed of her olive leaf [Gen. 8:11]; thou mayest come to this place at due times, and mayest do the businesses of the world, in other places too, and still keep thy olive, thy peace of conscience. If no heretical recusancy (thou dost like the doctrine), no schismatical recusancy (thou dost like the discipline), no lazy recusancy (thou forbearest not because thou canst not sit at thine ease), no proud recusancy (that the company is not good enough for thee), if none of these detain thee, thou mayest be here, even when thou art not here; God may accept thy desire; as, in many cases, thou mayest be away, when thou art here; as, in particular thou art, if being here, thou do not hearken to that which is said here; for that is added to the coming, and follows in a third consideration, after the capacity, "children"; and the action, "come"; the disposition, "hearken": *come ye children and hearken.*

Upon those words of David, *conturbata sunt ossa sua* [my bones are troubled (Ps. 6:3)], St. Basil saith well, *habet et anima ossa mea,* the soul hath bones as well as the body. And in this anatomy and dissection of the soul, as the bones of the soul are the constant and strong resolutions thereof, and as the seeing of the soul is understanding — *the eyes of your understanding being opened* [Eph. 1:18] — so the hearing of the soul is hearkening; in these religious exercises, we do not hear except we hearken; for hearkening is the hearing of the soul. Some men draw some reasons, out of some stories of some credit, to imprint a belief of ecstasy and raptures; that, the body remaining upon the floor or in the bed, the soul may be gone out to the contemplation of heavenly things. But it were a strange and a perverse ecstasy, that the body being here, at a religious exercise, and in a religious posture, the soul should be gone out to the contemplation, and pursuit of the pleasures or profits of this world. You come hither but to your own funerals if you bring nothing hither but your bodies; you come but to be interred, to be laid in the earth, if the ends of your coming be earthly respects, praise, and opinion, and observation of men; you come to be canonized, to grow saints, if your souls be here, and by grace here always diffused, grow up to a sanctification. *Bonus es Domine animæ quærenti te,* thou art good, O Lord, to that soul that seeks thee. It is St. Augustine's note that it is put in the singular, *animæ,* to that soul. Though many come, few come to him. A man may thread sermons by half dozens a day, and place his merit in the number; a man may have been all day in the perfume and incense of preaching,[49] and yet have received none of the *savor of life unto life* [2 Cor. 2:16]. Some things an ape can do as well as a man; some things an hypocrite as well as a saint. We cannot see now whether thy soul be here now, or no; but, tomorrow, hereafter, in the course of thy life, they which are near thee and know whether thy former faults be mended or no, know whether thy soul use[50] to be at sermons, as well as thy body uses to go to sermons. *Faith comes by hearing*, saith the Apostle [Rom. 10:17]; but it is by that hearing of the soul, hearkening, considering. And then as the soul is infused by God, but diffused over the whole body and so there is a man, so faith is infused from God, but diffused into our works and so there is a saint. Practice is the incarnation of faith; faith is incorporated and manifested in a body by works; and the way to both is that hearing, which amounts to this hearkening — to a diligent, to a considerate, to a profitable hearing. In which, one essential circumstance is that we be not over-affectionately transported with an opinion of any one person but apply ourselves to the ordinance, *come*, and *hearken unto me*, to any whom God sends with the seal and character of his minister, which is our fourth and last branch in your part.

David doth not determine this in his own person, that you should hearken to him, and none but him, but that you should hearken to him in that capacity and qualification, which is common to him with others, as we are sent by God upon that ministry; that you say to all such, *Blessed art thou that comest in the name of the Lord* [Ps. 118:26]. St. Augustine, and not he alone, interprets this whole Psalm of Christ, that it is a thanksgiving of Christ to his Father, upon some deliverance received in some of his agonies, some of his persecutions; and that Christ calleth us to hearken unto him. To him, so, as he is present with us, in the ministry of his Church. He is a perverse servant that will receive no commandment except he have it immediately from his Master's mouth; so is he too, that pretendeth to rest so wholly in the word of God, the Scriptures, as that he seeks no interpretation, no exposition, no preaching. All is in the Scriptures, but all the Scriptures are not always evident to all understandings. He also is a perverse servant that will receive no commandment by any officer of his masters, except he like the man, or, if his master might, in his opinion, have chosen a fitter man, to serve in that place. And such a perverseness is in those hearers who more respect the man than the ministry, and his manner of delivering it than the message that he delivers. *Let a man so account of us, as of the ministers of Christ, and stewards of the mysteries of God* [1 Cor. 4:1]. That is our *classis*, our rank, our station, what names soever we brought into the world by our extraction from this or that family, what name soever we took in our baptism, and contract between God and us, that name, in which we come to you, is that: *the ministers of Christ, the stewards of the mysteries of God. And so let men account of us*, says the apostle [1 Cor. 4:1]. Invention, and disposition, and art, and eloquence, and expression, and elocution, and reading, and writing, and printing, are secondary things, accessory things, auxiliary, subsidiary things; men may account us, and make account of us, as of orators in the pulpit and of authors in the shop; but if they account of us as of ministers and stewards, they give us our due; that's our name to you. All the Evangelists mention John Baptist and his preaching; but two of the four say never a word of his austerity of life, his locusts, nor his camels hair; and those two that do, Matthew and Mark, they insist first upon his calling, and then upon his actual preaching; how he pursued that calling, and then upon the doctrine that he preached — repentance and sanctification; and after that they come to these secondary and subsidiary things, which added to his estimation and assisted the passage of his doctrine, his good life. Learning, and other good parts, and an exemplar life fall into second places. They have a first place, in their consideration who are to call them, but in you, to whom they are sent, but a second; fix you, in the first place, upon the calling. This calling circumcised Moses' uncircumcised lips [Exod. 6:12]. This made Jeremy able to speak, though he called himself a child [Jer. 1:6]. This is Esay's *coal from the altar... which takes away even his sin, and his iniquity* [Isa. 6:67]. Be therefore content to pass over some infirmities, and rest yourselves upon the calling. And when you have thus taken the simplicity of children (they are the persons, which was our first step), and are come to the congregation (that is your action, and was our second), and have conformed yourselves to hearken (that also is the disposition here, which was our third), and all this with a reverence to the calling before an affection to the man (that is your submission to God's ordinance, and was our fourth and last step), you have then built up our first part in yourselves, and laid together all those pieces which constitute your duty, *Come ye children, and hearken unto me;* and from hence we pass to our duty, *I will teach you the fear of the Lord.*

In this second part, we made two steps; first the manner, *docebo*, I will teach; and then the matter, *timorem Domini*, I will teach you the fear of the Lord. Upon the first, we will stay no longer, but to confess that we are bound to teach, and that this teaching is to preach. And *væ si non*, woe be unto us, if we do not preach. Woe to them, who out of ease or state [high rank] silence themselves. And woe to them too, who by their distemper, and schismatical and seditious manner of preaching, occasion and force others to silence them; and think (and think it out of a profitable and manifold experience) that as forbidden books sell best, so silenced ministers thrive best. It is a duty, *docendum*, we must teach, preach; but a duty that excludes not catechizing; for catechizing seems especially to be intended here, where he calls upon them who are to be taught, by that name, "children." It is a duty that excludes not praying, but praying excludes not it neither. Prayer and preaching may consist [co-exist], nay they must meet in the Church of God. Now he that will teach must have learnt before, many years before. And he that will preach must have thought of it before, many days before. Extemporal ministers, that resolve in a day what they will be, extemporal preachers, that resolve in a minute, what they will say, out-go God's Spirit, and make too much haste. It was Christ's way; he took first disciples to learn, and then out of them he took apostles to teach; and those apostles made more disciples. Though your first consideration be upon the calling, yet our consideration must be for our fitness to that calling. Our prophet David hath put them both together well, *O God, thou hast taught me from my youth* [Ps. 71:17]; (you see what was his university; Moses was his Aristotle; he had studied divinity from his youth). *And hitherto have I declared thy wondrous works*, says he there. Hitherto? How long was that? It follows in the next verse, *Now am I old, and gray headed*, and yet he gave not over. Then God's work goes well forward when they whom God hath taught teach others. He that can say with David *docuisti me*, O God thou hast taught me, may say with him too *docebo vos*, I will teach you. But what? That remains only: I will teach you the fear of the Lord.

There is a fear which needs no teaching, a fear that is naturally imprinted in us. We need not teach men to be sad when a mischief is upon them, nor to fear when it is coming towards them; for fear respects the future, so as sadness does the present; fear looks upon danger, and sadness upon detriment; fear upon a sick friend, and sadness upon a dead. And as these need not be taught us, because they are natural, so, because they are natural, they need not be untaught us; they need not be forbidden, nor dissuaded. Our Savior Christ had them both — fear and sadness; and that man lacks Christian wisdom who is without a provident fear of future dangers, and without Christian charity, who is without a compassionate sadness in present calamities. Now this fear, though but imprinted in nature, is *timor Domini*, the fear of the Lord, because the Lord is the Lord of nature; he is the nature of nature, Lord of all endowments and impressions in nature. And therefore, though for this natural fear you go no farther than nature (for it is born with you, and it lives in you), yet the right use even of this natural fear is from grace. Though in the root it be a fear of nature, yet in the government thereof, in the degrees and practice thereof, it is the fear of the Lord, not only as he is Lord of nature (for so you have the fear itself from the Lord), but as this natural fear produces good or bad effects, as it is regulated and ordered, or as it is deserted and abandoned by the Spirit of the Lord. And therefore you are called hither, come, that you may learn the fear of the Lord; that is, the right use of natural fear, and natural affections, from the law of God. For as it is a wretched condition to be without natural affections, so is it a dangerous dereliction if our natural affections be left to themselves and not regulated, not inanimated by the Spirit of God; for then my sadness will sink into desperation, and my *fear will betray the succors which reason offereth* [Wisd. of Sol. 17:12]. This I gain by letting in the fear of the Lord into my natural fear; that whereas the natural object of my natural fear is *malum*, something that I apprehend *sub ratione mali*, as it is ill; ill for me (for if I did not conceive it to be ill, I would not fear it), yet when I come to thaw this ice, when I come to discusse [dispel] this cloud and attenuate this damp by the light and heat of grace and the illustration [elucidation] of the Spirit of God, breathing in his word, I change my object, or at least I look upon it in another line, in another angle; I look not upon that evil which my natural fear presented me, of an affliction or a calamity, but I look upon the glory that God receives by my Christian constancy in that affliction, and I look upon that everlasting blessedness, which I should have lost if God had not laid that affliction upon me. So that though fear look upon evil (for affliction is *malum pœnæ*, evil as it hath the nature of punishment), yet when the fear of the Lord is entered into my natural fear, my fear is more conversant, more exercised upon the contemplation of good than evil, more upon the glory of God and the joys of heaven than upon the afflictions of this life, how malignant, how manifold soever. And therefore, that this fear and all your natural affections (which seem weaknesses in man, and are so indeed, if they be left to themselves, now in our corrupt and depraved estate), may advance your salvation (which is the end why God hath planted them in you), *come and learn the fear of the Lord.* Learn from the word of God, explicated by his minister, in his ordinance upon occasions leading him thereunto, the limits of this natural fear, and where it may become sin, if it be not regulated and inanimated by a better fear than itself.

There is a fear which grows out of a second nature, custom, and so is half-natural to those men that have it. The custom of the place we live in, or of the times we live in, or of the company we live in. Topical customs of such a place, chronical customs of such an age, personal customs of such a company. The time, or the place, or the persons in power have advanced and drawn into fashion and reputation some vices, and such men as depend on them are afraid not to concur with them in their vices; for amongst persons, and in times and places that are vicious, an honest man is a rebel; he goes against that state and that government which is the kingdom of sin. Amongst drunkards a sober man is a spy upon them; amongst blasphemers a prayer is a libel against them; and amongst dissolute and luxurious persons a chaste man is a Bridewell,[51] his person, his presence is a house of correction. In vicious times and companies a good man is unacceptable, and cannot prosper. And, because as amongst merchants men trade half upon stock and half upon credit, so in all other courses, because men rise according to the opinion and estimation which persons in power have of them, as well as by real goodness, therefore to build up, or to keep up this opinion and estimation in them upon whom they depend, they are afraid to cross the vices of the time, so far, as by being virtuous in their own particular. They are afraid it will be called a singularity and a schismatical and seditious disposition, and taken for a reproach and a rebuke laid upon their betters, if they be not content to be as ill as those their betters are. Now the fear of the Lord brings the *quo warranto* [by what warrant...?] against all these privileged sins and privileged places and persons, and overthrows all these customs and prescriptions. The fear of the Lord is not a topical, not a chronical, not a personal, but a catholic, a canonical, a circular, an universal fear. It goes through all and over all; and when this half-natural fear, this fear grown out of custom, suggest to me that if I be thus tender-conscienced — if I startle at an oath, if I be sick at a health [(drinking) toast], if I cannot conform myself to the vices of my betters — I shall lose my master, my patron, my benefactor. This fear of the Lord enters and presents the infallible loss of a far greater Master, and Patron, and Benefactor, if I comply with the other. And therefore as you were called hither (that is to the explication of the word of God) to learn how to regulate the natural fear, that that fear do not deject you into a diffidence of God's mercy, so come hither to learn the fear of God against this half-natural fear, that is, be guided by the word of God, how far you are to serve the turns of those persons upon whom ye depend, and when to leave their commandments unperformed.

Well; what will this fear of the Lord teach us? Valor, fortitude. Fear teach valor? Yes, and nothing but fear — true fear. As Moses his serpents devoured the false serpents [Exod. 7:12], so doth true fear all false fear. There is nothing so contrary to God as false fear, neither in his own nature, nor in his love to us. Therefore God's first name in the Bible, and the name which he sticks to in all the work of the creation, is his name of power, *Elohim; El* is *fortis Deus,* the God of power, and it is that name in the plural, multiplied power, all power. And what can he fear? God descends to many other human affections; you shall read that God was angry, and sorry, and weary; but *non timuit Deus,* God was never afraid. Neither would God that man should be. So his first blessing upon man [Gen. 1:28–29] was to fill the earth, and to subdue the creatures, and to rule over them, and to eat what he would upon the earth; all acts of power and of confidence. As soon as he had offended God, the first impotency that he found in himself was fear; *I heard thy voice, and I was afraid,* says he [Gen. 3:10]. He had heard the voice of lions and was not afraid. There is not a greater commination [a threat] of a curse than that, *they shall be in a great fear, where no fear is* [Ps. 53:5], which is more vehemently expressed in another place, *I will set my face against you, and you shall fly, when none pursues you* [Lev. 26:17]; *I will send a faintness into their hearts, and the sound of a shaken leaf, shall chase them, as a sword* [Lev. 26:36]. False fear is a fearful curse. To fear that all favors and all preferments will go the wrong way, and that therefore I must clap on a byasse[52] and go that way too — this inordinate fear is the curse of God. David's last counsel to Solomon (but reflecting upon us all) was *be thou strong therefore, and show thyself a man* [1 Kgs. 2:2]. *E culmine corruens, ad gyrum laboris venit,* the devil fell from his place in heaven, and now is put to compass the earth [Gregory the Great]. The fearful man that falls from his moral and his Christian constancy, from the fundamental rules of his religion, falls into labyrinths of incertitudes, and impertinencies, and ambiguities, and anxieties, and irresolutions. *Militia, vita,* our whole life is a warfare.[53] God would not chose cowards; he had rather we were valiant in the fighting of his battles, for battles and exercise of valor we are sure to have. God sent a Cain into the world before an Abel; an enemy before a champion [Gregory the Great]. *Abel non suspicor qui non habet Cain;* we never hear of an Abel but there is a Cain too. And therefore "think it not strange, concerning the fiery trial, as though some strange thing happened unto you" [1 Pet. 4:12]; make account that this world is your scene, your theater, and that God himself sits to see the combat, the wrestling. *Vetuit Deus mortem Job* [Chrysostom]; Job was God's champion, and God forbade Satan the taking away of Job's life; for if he die (says God in the mouth of that Father), *theatrum nobis non amplius plaudetur,* my theater will ring with no more plaudits; I shall be no more glorified in the valor and constancy of my saints, my champions. God delights in the constant and valiant man, and therefore a various,[54] a timorous man frustrates, disappoints God.

My errand then is to teach you valor; and must my way be to intimidate you, to teach you fear? Yes, still there is no other fortitude but the fear of the Lord. We told you before, sadness and fear differ but in the present and future. And as for the present, *nihil aliud triste quam Deum offendere* [Chrysostom], there is no just cause of sadness but to have sinned against God (for sudden sadness arising in a good conscience is a spark of fire in the sea; it must go out), so there is no just cause to fear, but in God's displeasure. *Mens in timore Domini constituta, non invenit extra quod metuat* [Gregory the Great]. God is all; and if I be established in him, what thing can I fear, when there is nothing without him? Nothing, simply; at least nothing that can hurt me; *quæ sunt in mundo non nocent iis qui extra mundum sunt* [those things which are in the world do not hurt those who are beyond the world; Chrysostom], this world cannot hurt him that made it, nor them that are laid up in him. Jonas did but change his vessel, his ship, when he entered the whale; he was not shipwrecked, God was his pilot there, as well as in the ship, and therefore he as confident there. It is meant of Christ, which is spoken in the person of wisdom, *who so hearkeneth unto me, shall dwell safely, and be quiet from the fear of evil* [Prov. 1:33]. And therefore, *when you hear of wars and commotions, be not terrified; these things must come to pass, but the end is not by and by* [Luke 21:9]; imaginations [false beginnings], and temptations, and alienations, and tribulations must come, but this is not the end; the end that God looks for is that by the benefit of his fear we should stand out all these.

So then to teach you the fear of the Lord is to teach you what it doth that you may love it, and what it is that you may know it. That which it doth is that it makes you a constant, a confident, a valiant man; that which God, who is always the same, loves. How doth it that? Thus: as he that is fallen into the king's hand for debt to him is safe from other creditors, so is he that fears the Lord from other fears. He that loves the Lord, loves him with all his love; he that fears the Lord fears him with all his fear too; God takes no half affections. Upon those words, *be not high-minded, but fear* [Rom. 11:20], Clement of Alexandria hath another reading: *super-timé over-fear;* that is, carry thy fear to the highest place; place thy fear there, where it may be above all other fears. *In the multitude of dreams, there are divers vanities, but fear thou the Lord* [Eccles. 5:7]. All fearful things pass away as dreams, as vanities, to him that fears the Lord; they offer at him, but in vain, if he be established with that fear. In Christ there was no bone broken; in him that fears the Lord, no constant purpose is ever shaken. Of Job it is said that he was *perfect and upright* [Job 1:1]. That is a rare wonder, but the wonder is qualified in the addition, *he feared God.* So are they put together in Simeon, *justus et timoratus,* he was a just man [Luke 2:25]; how should he be otherwise? He feared God. Consider your enemies, and be not deceived with an imagination of their power, but see whether they be worthy of your fear, if you fear God. The world is your enemy; *sed vici mundum,* be of good cheer, for I have overcome the world, saith Christ [John 16:33]. If it were not so, yet we are none of it; *ye are not of the world, for I have chosen you out of the world* [John 15:19]. Howsoever, the world would do us no harm, the world would be good enough of itself but that the prince of the world, the devil, is *anima mundi,* the soul of this lower world; he inanimates, he actuates, he exalts the malignity of the world against us and he is our second enemy. It was not the apple but the serpent that tempted; Eve, no doubt, had looked upon the fruit before, and yet did not long. But even this enemy is not so dangerous as he is conceived. In the life of St. Basil we have a story that the devil appeared to a penitent sinner at his prayers and told him, *if you will let me alone, I will let you alone; meddle not with me, and I will not meddle with you.* He found that by this good soul's prayers to God, God had weakened his power, not only upon that man that prayed but upon others too; and therefore he was content to come to a cessation of arms with him, that he might turn his forces another way. Truly he might say to many of us, in a worse sense, *let me alone, and I will let you alone; tempt not me, and I will not tempt you.* Our idleness, our high diet, our wanton discourse, our exposing ourselves to occasion of sin, provoke and call in the devil, when he seeks not us. The devil possesses the world, and we possess the devil. But then, if the fear of the Lord possess us, our own concupiscencies (though they be indeed our greatest enemies, because the war that they maintain is a civil war), shall do us no harm. For as the Septuagint in their translation diminish the power of the devil, in that name Myrmecoleon, a disproportioned creature, made up of a lion and an ant, because as St. Gregory saith upon that place, *formicis leo est, volatilibus formica,* the devil is a lion to ants, dasheth whole hills of them with his paw, that creep under him, but he is but an ant to birds; they prey upon him that fly above him. If we fear the Lord, our concupiscencies, our carnal affections, our selves, may prove our best friends, because as the fire in the furnace did not burn the men [Dan. 3:25] but it burnt off those bands that fettered and manacled them (for they were loose, and walked in the furnace), so our concupiscencies, if we resist them, shall burn off themselves, and file off their own rust, and our salvation shall be surer by occasion of temptations. We may prevent *mortem mortificatione* [Augustine], everlasting death, by a disciplinary life. *Mori, ne moriamur* is his rule, too; to die to the fires of lust here, lest we die in unquenchable fires hereafter; to *die daily* (as St. Paul speaks of himself [1 Cor. 15:31]), lest we die at the last day. To end this, this is the working of the fear of the Lord; it devours all other fears. God will have no half-affections, God will have no partners; he that fears God fears nothing else.

This then is the operation of the fear of the Lord, this is his working; remains only to consider what this fear of the Lord is. And, beloved in him, be not afraid of it, for this fear of God is the love of God. And howsoever there may be some amongst us, whom the height of birth, or of place, or of spirit hath kept from fear, they never feared any thing; yet, I think, there is none that never loved any thing. Obligations of matrimony, or of friendship, or of blood, or of alliance, or of conversation, hath given every one of us, no doubt, some sense in ourselves what it is to love, and to enjoy that which we do love. And the fear of God is the love of God. *The love of the Lord passeth all things* [Ecclus. 25:11], saith the wise man; the love, what is that to fear? It follows, *the fear of the Lord is the beginning of his love.* As they that build arches place centers under the arch to bear up the work till it be dried and settled, but after, all is arch and there is no more center, no more support; so to lie at the Lord's feet a while delivers us into his arms; to accustom ourselves to his fear establishes us in his love. Be content to stop a little, even at the lowest fear, the *fear of hell.* When Saul was upon an expedition, and did not find himself well followed, he took a yoke of oxen and hewed them in pieces, and proclaimed that whosoever came not to the supply, all his oxen should be so served; and upon this (says the text there), *the fear of the Lord fell upon all the people, and they came out, as one man, three hundred and thirty thousand* [1 Sam. 11:7]. If Saul's threatening of their worldly goods wrought so, let God's threatening of thyself — thine inwardest self, thy soul — with hell, make thee to stop even upon thy fear of the Lord, the fear of torment. Stop upon the second fear too, the fear of privation, and loss of the sight of God in heaven; that when all we have disputed with a modest boldness, and wondered with a holy wonder what kind of sight of God we shall have in heaven, then when thou shouldst come to an end and to an answer of all these doubts, in an experimental trial, how he shall be seen (seen thus), thou shalt see then that thou shalt never see him. After thou hast used to hear all thy life blessedness summed up into that one act, *we shall see God,* thou shalt never come nearer to that knowledge; thou shalt never see him. Fear the Lord therefore in this second fear, fear of privation. And fear him in a third fear, the fear of the loss of his grace here in this world, though thou have it now. St. Chrysostom serves himself and us with an ordinary comparison. A tiler is upon the top of the house, but he looks to his footing; he is afraid of falling. A righteous man is in a high place in God's favor, but he may lose that place. Who is higher than Adam, higher than the angels? And whither fell they? Make not thou then thy assurance of standing, out of their arguments that say it is impossible for the righteous to fall, the sins of the righteous are no sins in the sight of God; but build thy assurance upon the testimony of a good conscience, that thou usest all diligence and holy industry that thou mayest continue in God's favor, and fearest to lose it. For he that hath no fear of losing hath no care of keeping. Accustom thyself to these fears, and these fears will flow into a love. As love and jealousy may be the same thing, so the fear and love of God will be all one; for jealousy is but a fear of losing. *Brevissima differentia testamentorum, timor et amor* [there is the slightest difference between the Testaments: fear and love; Augustine]. This distinguishes the two Testaments, the Old is a testament of fear, the New of love; yet in this they grow all one, that we determine [render clear its meaning] the Old Testament in the New, and that we prove the New Testament by the Old. For, but by the Old, we should not know that there was to be a New; nor but for the New that there was an Old. So the two Testaments grow one Bible; so in these two affections, if there were not a jealousy, a fear of losing God, we could not love him; nor can we fear to lose him, except we do love him. Place the affection (by what name soever), upon the right object, God, and I have in some measure done that which this text directed (taught you the fear of the Lord), if I send you away in either disposition, timorous or amorous, possessed with either the fear or the love of God; for this fear is inchoative love, and this love is consummative fear. The love of God begins in fear, and the fear of God ends in love; and that love can never end, for God is love.

CHAPTER THREE

JOSEPH HALL
(1574–1656)
"The Art of Moderation"

I do not more wonder at any man's art than at his who professes to think of nothing, to do nothing. And I do not a little marvel at that man who says he can sleep without a dream. For the mind of man is a restless thing, and though it give the body leave to repose itself as knowing it is a mortal and earthly piece, yet itself, being a spirit and therefore active and indefatigable, is ever in motion. Give me a sea that moves not, a sun that shines not, an open eye that sees not, and I shall yield there may be a reasonable soul that works not.... Since my mind will needs ever be working, it shall be my care that it may always be well-employed.

— "Upon a Man Sleeping"[1]

During the first half of the seventeenth century, Joseph Hall was the most popular preacher in England, active on a scale that is almost unimaginable by present standards. A graduate of a strict Puritan college, he had an orator's training and throughout his life consistently preached three times a week. In the course of more than fifty years of ministry, Hall prepared (for he did not follow the common Puritan practice of extemporaneous preaching) and delivered 7,000 to 8,000 sermons. Hall was a favorite preacher of both James and Charles I, but he preferred the roles of village priest and resident bishop. Indeed, it was in those settings that his most memorable preaching was done. He had charge of the large sees of Exeter and Norwich, at a time when episcopal visitations were eagerly anticipated events; and on a single occasion hundreds or even thousands of people would come to be confirmed by him.

In the sermon preached at his funeral, Hall was honored as the person who had taught the English people "the art of divine meditation." He considered meditation, defined as "a bending of the mind upon

114

some spiritual object . . . until our thoughts come to an issue," as "the very end God hath given our souls for."[2] Hall believed that in his own generation souls had nearly atrophied from disuse; it was "a knowing age," but a cold one. Teaching the skill that enables the practice of true piety was his life's vocation; however, the turbulence of religious politics often interrupted his pursuit of it. Hall's peculiar position as a member of the established Church who respected Puritans and was respected by them meant that he was frequently called upon to serve as ambassador, controversialist, or advisor in matters of conscience. But consistently, throughout his long life, he returned to instruction in the proper use of the soul.

Hall may have fallen short of Andrewes's scholarly depth (though not by much) and Donne's spectacular brilliance, yet he almost certainly exercised a more lasting influence than either on the preaching and prayer of his own and subsequent generations. Hall laid the groundwork for a Protestant discipline of meditation, a counterpart to the Ignatian spirituality widely taught by continental Jesuits. His basic instructional manual, *The Art of Divine Meditation* (1606), went through three editions in as many years. But a better indication of the extent of his influence is the literature produced by the remarkable generation of meditative poets who were his contemporaries: John Donne, George Herbert, Richard Crashaw, Henry Vaughn, Andrew Marvell, Thomas Traherne. Although Hall is today less known than any of them and did not himself write poetry in his mature years, he seems to have exercised at least an indirect influence on them all by fostering among the English people the deep inwardness that is the great vitalizing factor of early seventeenth-century religion. He was the best-known teacher of meditational prayer in England,[3] and thus he educated a reading public for the Protestant lyric poets, whose work reflected its techniques: *viz.*, the use of emblems, ejaculations, and personal applications of salvation history.

Hall's interest for modern preachers lies chiefly in his greatness as an interpreter of biblical narrative. For probing insight into character and motive, his *Contemplations on the Principal Passages of the Holy Story* (Old Testament) and *Contemplations on the Historical Passages of the New Testament* may well be unsurpassed in the history of biblical interpretation. These meditative explorations and amplifications of the biblical narratives were the "wedge of metal" mined from Hall's sermons over some twenty years, and their purpose was to help his fellow clergy and laypeople read the text with profit to their souls. Hall was one of the

early masters of English prose; in their treatment of character and setting the *Contemplations* begin the artistic development that would be
fully achieved in the novel, the prose genre that arose in England sixty
years after his death. But the *Contemplations*, as their name suggests,
are art that comes out of prayer and aims at spiritual transformation.
They were widely read by Hall's contemporaries, especially the clergy,
and continued to have an impact long after his death. By providing
an instrument whereby Anglicans could make serious devotional use of
Scripture, they contributed to the eighteenth-century Evangelical awakening; Hall's meditation on "I thirst" was the text that prompted the
conversion of George Whitefield.

Writing Latin satires in his college years made Hall an acute and un-
sparingly honest observer of human nature, and the reader who comes
to him after reading Donne is struck and may be repelled by his moral
rigor. While Donne preaches always God's mercy to those dejected by
sinfulness, Hall addresses himself chiefly to those who are comfortable
to their own damnation, "not so much as wishing more skill in soul matters, applauding their own safe mediocrity."[4] Like the biblical prophet,
preachers must be trained to deal with evil; their task is to tear down
before building up. Addressing the Lords of the High Court on a solemn
fast day, he asks:

> Who should tell the times of their sins, if we be silent? Pardon me,
> I beseech you, most noble, reverend, and beloved hearers; necessity is
> laid upon me. In this day of our public mourning, I may not be as 'a
> man in whose mouth are no reproofs' [Ps. 38:14]. O let us be thankful
> for our blessings, wherein, through the mercy of God, we outstrip all the
> nations under heaven; but withal, let us bewail our sins, which are so
> much more grievous, because ours. (5:417)

The image of God that Hall upholds is that of the Judge who brings
all human affairs under scrutiny and is most strict with those who have
been most favored (as is the case, he believes, with the English people).
God's justice "will not allow his mercy to be overstrained,"[5] yet this
same God "loves to do all things sweetly" and seeks to turn our hearts
rather than to force obedience. Israel's history teaches us that justice
and mercy work together to prepare us for obedience. Israel in the
wilderness felt God's nearness through provisions of water, meat, bread;
but equally through afflictions of hunger, thirst, and fear of enemies.
Hall points shrewdly to the origin of mistrust in God: "They can think
him absent in their want, and cannot see him absent in their sin: and
yet wickedness, not affliction, argues him gone; yet then is he most

present when he most chastises." The moral stringency in his preaching is best seen as the obverse of the assurance of God's constant presence and minute concern for human well-being, which can be secured only by bringing us to repentance.

Among seventeenth-century preachers, Hall may well have had the sharpest social vision. There is a surprisingly modern note in his sensitivity to systemic oppression, which he ranked with "contempt of God's ministers" and the despoiling and seizure of church property as the crying sins of his time (5:244–45). The late sixteenth and early seventeenth centuries witnessed massive social change and dislocation in England. As the remnants of the feudal system yielded to a free-enterprise economy, some grew rich from coal mining, sea trade, and piracy; but many more were reduced to vagrancy and beggary due to privatization of land, mass unemployment, and rapid inflation.[6] Hall acutely perceives that long enjoyment of material abundance had already declined into "pampered animosity" and asks, "What can follow next, but our miserable indigence and distress?" (5:243–44).

Hall is frequently aggrieved, sometimes acerbic, as he witnesses human violations of justice, yet he does not relinquish charity. Hall is no radical Calvinist and abstains from total condemnations that would defeat the call to repentance: "Every man is as free from an absolute defect as from perfection. I desire not to comprehend, O Lord, teach me to do nothing but wonder."[7] Moreover, along with the characteristic humility that underlies the prayer for wonder, there is throughout Hall's sermons and meditations an unmistakable tone of spiritual contentment. He trusted wholly to God's providence and accepted as generous the terms of its operation. So Hall reflects on King David in old age, betrayed by his son Absalom and received by strangers: "Heaven shall want power and earth means, before any of the household of faith shall want maintenance" (1:487). It would be easy to dismiss his tone as the self-satisfaction engendered by easy circumstances. But when those words were written, Hall and his young family had already lived through some years of poverty. Moreover, when in old age he had, like David, endured heavy personal losses and contemptuous public treatment, he mourned openly, yet without railing. Hall's contentment is itself worthy of trust and may encourage others to "faithful carelessness," for it rests not on particular circumstances but on confidence in God's justice, which prevails always and in minute matters, though worked by roundabout means.

Hall's Life

Joseph Hall was one of twelve children in a family of modest means and strong Puritan leanings. He was born on July 1, 1574, at Ashby-de-la-Zouch in Leicestershire, where his father served as steward to the earl of Huntingdon. The earl was involved in the founding of two Puritan educational institutions, and Joseph — from infancy intended for the ministry — attended both: Ashby Grammar School and Emmanuel College, Cambridge. He was strongly influenced by his mother, Winifride, whom he compared to the mothers of Bernard and Augustine for the intensity of her devotion. Like her son, she had a weak physical constitution "and oft a wounded spirit, the agonies whereof, as [sic] she would oft recount with much passion, professing that the greatest bodily sicknesses were but flea-bites to those scorpions."[8] Hall's spiritual sensitivity, and possibly also his talent for vivid language, may well derive from her, as he notes: "How often have I blessed the memory of those divine passages of experimental [practical] divinity which I have heard from her mouth!" (1:xxi).

Winifride's spiritual counselor was the prominent and extreme Calvinist Anthony Gilby, who also organized the curriculum for the Ashby Grammar School. Hall, though a diligent student, was repelled by Gilby's bitter doctrinal disputations and zeal for presbyterian polity.[9] In 1589, at the age of 15, he went to the new Puritan college at Cambridge. Emmanuel College intended its scholars "to devote themselves to sacred theology and eventually to labor in preaching the Word."[10] The curriculum placed heavy emphasis on the fundaments of biblical study and rhetoric; he studied Hebrew, Latin and Greek composition, and the dichotomous logic of the French Protestant theologian Peter Ramus (1515–72), which had so greatly influenced the shape of the Protestant sermon.[11]

From his university years on, Hall's biography is largely an annotated record of his writings. He claimed to be the first English satirist; whether or not he invented the genre, certainly he refined it and achieved a reputation at age 23 for his dense and riddling poems, which treat sometimes (the "Toothless Satires") minor offenses such as bad poetry and expensive Italian clothes, sometimes (the "Biting Satires") the weighty matters that concerned Hall all his life: greedy landowners who kept tenant-farmers in poverty, adultery, "papistical" religion. There is a continuity of style as well between these early poems and Hall's preaching, for he never lost the satirist's gift of concision and bite in evoking a situation or capturing an intention.

Hall was ordained in December 1600, and a year later became chaplain to Sir Robert Drury of Hawstead in Suffolk. There he began his regimen of preaching three times weekly, in the Great Hall and the village church. In 1603, Hall married Elizabeth Winiffe; the same year, he received his doctorate in divinity and published a long poem to celebrate James's accession to the throne. The poem signals Hall's decision to serve within the established Church, as well as a shift to greater seriousness in his writing, which was henceforth mostly prose.

Hall's own account of his betrothal gives amusing evidence of a temperament that is at the other extreme from Donne's romanticism:

> The uncouth solitariness of my life, and the extreme incommodity of that single housekeeping, drew my thoughts, after two years [at Hawstead], to condescend to the necessity of a married estate, which God no less strangely provided for me. For, walking from the church on Monday in the Whitsun week, with a grave and reverend minister, Mr. Grandidge, I saw a comely and modest gentlewoman standing at the door of that house where we were invited to a wedding-dinner; and, inquiring of that worthy friend whether he knew her, "Yes," quoth he, "I know her well, and have bespoken her for your wife." ... I listened to the motion as sent from God, and at last, upon due prosecution, happily prevailed; enjoying the comfortable society of that meet help for the space of forty-nine years.[12]

Elizabeth bore nine children, all of whom survived to adulthood; the deaths of four of them, and of Elizabeth herself, were the great griefs of Hall's old age. Although there was little of the romantic in Hall, the respect for both women and children expressed in his writings confirms his direct statements that his family life was happy. In one of his extemporary meditations, the sound of a child crying prompts a sensitive reflection upon the fact that children are quick to cry, not always for good reason, but even quicker to seek reconciliation "and offer themselves unto those arms that trespassed. ... It is a great imperfection to want knowledge, but of the two it is better to be a child in understanding than a man in maliciousness."[13] Among the most moving passages of the scriptural *Contemplations* are the internal dialogues of female characters: "Ichabod" (Moses' mother), Jael, Jephthah's daughter, Hannah, Vashti, Bathsheba, and even Jeroboam's wife.

With a woman on the throne and increasing numbers of women owning and managing property, the changing social role of women was a matter for anxiety in the Elizabethan period, especially among the wealthy and aristocratic.[14] Hall followed the Puritan emphasis on the marriage bond and the centrality of the family to God's providential ordering of the world, although in a defense of marriage for clergy, he impatiently asked "if the kingdom of heaven and all religion consisted in nothing but maidenhead or marriage?" (8:481). Hall's views are traditional but hardly reactionary.[15] His contemplation "Jael and Sisera" (printed below) exalts Deborah, wife of Lapidoth, who gave honor to wedlock through public heroism "without regard of her sex."

Marriage and divorce were for Puritan divines pressing concerns of practical divinity. In his later years, Hall wrote extensively on "cases of conscience," devoting much attention to problems in this area. While Protestant preachers did not (contrary to the stereotype) dwell on sex, they were vehement about adultery, and some, Anglican as well as Puritan, proposed that it be treated as a capital crime. Yet Hall, with a pastoral sensitivity and regard for marriage that transcends simplistic idealism, strongly urged the husband of an adulterous wife who sincerely repents to forgive her and restore the marriage bond.[16] Hall also saw that the new legal possibilities for divorce posed a real threat to women, and he argued furiously against his lifelong literary and theological adversary John Milton, who in 1644 published an argument for divorce on the grounds of mental and spiritual incompatibility. Hall objected to what he saw (with some justice) as a man's self-serving rationale for arbitrary dismissal of a displeasing wife. With characteristic opposition to uncompromising religious ideology, Hall asserts that even heresy and infidelity (frequent and sometimes deadly charges in his day) are insufficient cause to separate the wife "from board and bed."[17] Hall reminds his readers that not all virtue is distinctively Christian; piety must not set itself above ordinary compassion and practical necessity.

Hall's young family lived in penury, for at Hawstead he received only £10 per year. During this period, Hall frankly admitted to writing books in order to buy more. The publication of *Meditations and Vows* (1605) opened the door into the happiest period of his life, when he was most productive as preacher and writer. It was one of the first books of meditations in English, and Baron Edward Denny was so impressed that he invited Hall to become his personal chaplain and rector of the abbey church in the populous parish of Waltham, twelve miles from London, where he remained twenty years (1608–28). At this time he also entered the court circle as chaplain to fourteen-year-old Crown Prince Henry, serving one month a year until Henry's sudden death in 1612, and as occasional preacher up until the Civil War (1641). He refused a permanent appointment at court in order to remain at Waltham; and his own favorite work, the *Contemplations*, is based largely on his preaching there.[18]

Diligence was, along with humility, Hall's most pronounced personal characteristic. Indeed, diligence was the form Hall's humility assumed, understanding "humility" in Aquinas' sense of "the patient pursuit of one's own excellence." Thus Hall reported his daily routine to Baron Denny:

> First I desire to awake at those hours, not when I will, but when I must.... My first thoughts are for him, who hath made the night for rest and the day for travel; and as he gives, so blesses both.... While my body is dressing, not with effeminate curiosity, not yet with rude neglect, my mind addresses itself to her ensuing task; bethinking what is to be done, and in what order; and marshaling, as it may, my hours with my work. That done, after some while meditation, I walk up to my masters and companions, my books.[19]

One senses not so much eagerness to please his employer as an acute awareness of responsibility for the use of time and ability that is often expressed in his writings. Hall was not unhealthily addicted to work; as he reassured a concerned friend, his frail body kept him from excessive study. Music, mathematics, and fishing were his preferred forms of recreation, and he liked to meditate while walking out of doors. Nonetheless, work is a central element of his theology; he was one of the principal proponents of a theology of vocation, which is part of the distinctive heritage of English Protestantism. Indeed, it is in this area that seventeenth-century theology has perhaps most significantly shaped modernity, for the "Protestant work ethic" articulated by Hall and others (including Donne and Herbert) has wrought profound changes in the way we all, believers or not, think about the use of time.[20]

The Calvinist concern for calling is the most significant Protestant departure from Roman Catholic asceticism. The theological change accompanied a corresponding shift in the social sphere. The medieval moral hierarchy, in which priests, monks, and feudal lords were preeminent, had been toppled; and the most godly callings were the humble but also economically productive ones of farmer, artisan, tradesman. No one presented the new doctrine of work more engagingly than Hall:

> The homeliest service that we do in an honest calling, though it be but to plow, or dig, if done in obedience, and conscience of God's Com-

mandment, is crowned with an ample reward; whereas the best works for their kind (preaching, praying, offering evangelical sacrifices), if without respect of God's injunction and glory, are loaded with curses. God loveth adverbs; and cares not how good, but how well.[21]

In contrast to Donne, Hall rarely exalts the preacher's role, although he occasionally alludes to the Protestant doctrine that preaching is indispensable for salvation.

Yet Hall was not naive about the harshness of the laborer's life. The particular importance of a theology of work among English Protestants relates to the aggressiveness with which new economic policies were being instituted.[22] And if Hall encouraged ordinary people to see work as a form of the obedient life and thus their own path to sainthood, he was fierce against the hypocrisy that led to exploitation of their labor:

In the country they censure not the oppressing gentleman that tyrannizes over his cottagers, encroaches upon his neighbor's inheritance, encloses commons, depopulates villages, scrouges his tenants to death, but the poor souls that when they are crushed, yield the juice of tears, exhibit bits of complaint, throw open the new thorns, maintain the old wounds; would these men be content to be quietly racked and spoiled, there would be peace.[23]

Even above social oppression, Hall named the desecration and fragmentation of the Church as the chief sin of his time, which he believed was quickly bringing God's judgment upon England. Establishing peace within the Church was the great cause of his life and the subject of almost all his forty-two preserved sermons. In service of this cause he went on two foreign missions, one to Scotland (1616) and two years later to the international Synod of Dort in Holland. The latter especially illustrates the difficulty of holding to a moderate stance in the theological and political climate of the early seventeenth century.

James instructed the delegates to practice their Latin and speak moderately and well; it seems also to have been his hope that they would decisively refute Arminianism and other "hellish doctrines" emanating from the University of Leiden. In a keynote sermon on the text, "Be not righteous overmuch, neither make thyself overwise" (Eccles. 7:16), Hall characteristically spoke against magnifying differences on inessential matters and called for a return to the Bible as the basis for a unified Protestant Church: "We are brothers, Christians, not Remonstrants, Contra-Remonstrants, Calvinists, or Arminians."[24] He must have made a strong impression, for the States General of the Netherlands gave him a gold medal (all the other delegates received silver), which Hall treasured to the end of his life. A serious intestinal infection forced him to leave only two months into the six-month session. The irenic spirit for which he had labored failed; the Arminian "Remonstrants" were banished from Holland and their leader executed.

In the wake of Dort, sensing "that there is a storm coming towards our church," Hall wrote *Via Media: The Way of Peace*. The book is important evidence of his catholicity, for he argued that the central Arminian doctrines (among them election to salvation as synergistically dependent upon humanity as well as God, freedom of the will, and the perseverance of the saints as not being automatic) were not innovative, but rather fundaments on which all Anglicans could agree. In his autobiography, Hall speaks of the book with pride; but James, more interested in scoring points than in reconciliation, forbade its publication.

Probably in part due to James's vacillating favor after Dort, Hall declined to become bishop of Gloucester in 1624, but three years later he accepted from King Charles the large and prosperous see of Exeter. The diocese presented, on a small scale, the dangers of dissension that he saw threatening the Church as a whole; and the unity he achieved there over the next thirteen years is the most convincing proof that personal humility and principled moderation are powerful to overcome deep-rooted animosities. He managed to win the loyalty of almost all the clergy and to settle long-standing disputes within the cathedral chapter, as well as between the cathedral and the city.

In these last years before the English Church ruptured, a bishop of Puritan background was jealously watched by both sides, and Hall had little peace. The Exeter Puritans, who had earlier suffered under Bishop Cotton's (d. 1621) policy of conformity, now felt betrayed from within their own ranks. They were outraged by Hall's statement, published during his first year as bishop, that the Roman Church is "a true visible Church." His response to their indignation shows Hall's reluctance to give up entirely on any part of the body of Christ:

> So as these two may well stand together, a true visible Church, in respect of outward profession of Christianity; and an heretical, apostatical, antichristian synagogue, in respect of doctrine and practice. Grant the Romanists to be but Christians, how corrupt soever, and we cannot deny them the name of a church. Outward visibility gives them no claim either to truth or salvation.[25]

On the other side, Hall made enemies by censuring prominent establishment clergy whom he considered negligent and advancing "those whom I found conscionably forward and painful [painstaking] in their places."[26] In retaliation, they reported him to Archbishop Laud for encouraging "lecturers," nonparochial clergy, often of Calvinist bent, who preached and taught and were financially supported by the people. Three times Hall was on his knees before Charles to defend his loyalty. Yet he and Laud came to respect one another for their shared commitment to a unified catholic Church, a commitment that (ironically, in view of their wide separation on the theological spectrum) brought them both to the Tower of London during the Puritan rebellion.

Although as bishop he mourned the loss of his quiet study at Waltham, Hall continued writing. The most substantial works are those that reflect his commitment to teach the Scriptures: the lengthy *Paraphrase upon the Hard Texts of the Whole Divine Scripture* (1631–32), and the *Contemplations on the Historical Passages of the New Testament* (1633). But increasingly, the drive toward separation, which he viewed as a sin less defensible than "murder or whoredom," forced him to take up controversy: "If truth, oppressed by an erroneous teacher, cry like a ravished virgin for my aid, I betray it if I relieve it not; when I have done, I return gladly to these paths of peace"[27] — that is, to his meditations on Scripture.

His defense of catholic polity, *Episcopacy by Divine Right* (1640), written at Laud's behest, marks Hall's definitive break with the Puritans, who the following year introduced to the House of Commons a bill to extirpate "those fungoid excrescences of Christianity," the bishops. Despite his sincere desire for peace and personal refusal of complacency, Hall's defense of the traditional orders of church and state may well have reinforced the intransigency that issued in civil war. For, though he seems never to have felt the personal admiration for King Charles that he had for James, he argued for the divine rights of kings and bishops, seemingly deaf to the claims of the democratic forces that would eventually alter the political face of Europe. With respect to historical change, Hall was half right and half wrong: "Monarchy was restored and the Church of England re-established, but Parliament was ever to be above the divine right of kings, and 'prelatry,' with its privileges, courts, and pluralities, had to come to an end."[28]

In July 1641, Parliament began impeachment proceedings against twelve bishops, Hall among them. In November, Charles defiantly translated him to the see of Norwich; but on December 30, the twelve bishops were convicted of high treason and sent to the Tower. They were released on bail after five months, and Hall went to settle in Norwich, still hopeful of being effective. He served less than a year before the Act of Sequestration was enacted against him. In April 1643, Hall was ousted from the palace, and the cathedral was desecrated. His autobiography, begun during his imprisonment in the Tower, records his heartbroken witness:

> Lord, what work was here! what clattering of glasses, what beating down of walls! what tearing up of monuments! what pulling down of seats...what a hideous triumph on the market-day before all the country, when, in a kind of sacrilegious and profane procession, all the organ-pipes, vestments, both copes and surplices, together with the leaden cross which had been newly sawn down from over the Greenyard pulpit, and the service-books and singing-books that could be had, were carried to the fire in the public market-place.[29]

With the financial help of their neighbors, the Halls managed to save the library and furnishings; they moved to a small rented house in the village of Heigham, a mile from the bishop's palace. Hall spent the next thirteen years in semiretirement. Until his death he retained the official signature "Josephus Norvicensis"; he preached and even ordained during the interregnum, especially toward the end, as conditions for Anglicans eased. Above all, he wrote, focusing on meditations and "cases of conscience," a branch of theology that was especially important in this time before religious tolerance gained ascendancy, and church attendance and public oaths were obligatory. He weakened only in his eighty-second year and died on September 8, 1656. Following his own request, he was buried without pomp.

Hall's Preaching

Hall demonstrates more clearly than any of his contemporaries the close relation between sermon and meditation that is characteristic of seventeenth-century Anglicans, who often spoke of preaching as "meditation shared with an auditory." Indeed, it is probable that he is largely responsible for establishing that relation, for the Contemplations are the first major literary work in which the two genres are fully fused.[30] They regularly shift from reflection on the human condition into prayer: "Our hearts are but a bare board, till God by his finger engrave his law in them; yea, Lord, we are a rough quarry, hew thou us out, and square us fit for thee to write upon" (1:133–34). Likewise, the sermons themselves invariably conclude with prayer, to which the transition is often imperceptible. The key to the link between sermon and meditation, and what distinguishes them on the one side from the Roman oration and on the other from the Calvinist exposition, is their central concern with application of the text. Their aim is to explore the interaction between the message of the Scriptures and the experience of contemporary Christians and thus to identify patterns of the moral life.

When he became bishop, Hall regretted that he had not devoted more of his earlier preaching energies to catechesis. But one wonders if he was conscious of how much he had in fact achieved. Of the seventeenth-century Anglicans, probably none contributed so much as Hall to the use of Scripture as a guide for practical living. If the *Contemplations* be the best indication of his workaday preaching style, then Hall for decades bent his efforts toward making the biblical text, and especially the Old Testament narratives, intelligible and morally compelling to his hearers.[31] And his success is directly related to his skill as a storyteller. For Hall does not adopt the common ploy of the moralistic preacher: namely, offering a "lesson" and then adducing the text to illustrate it. Rather, he draws his audience into the divine and human drama of the biblical story by rendering the scene with the vividness of a stage set: enter Esau "blowing and sweating for his reward" (1:47); "Jonathan is now at the top of the hill [in the Philistine camp].... The clamor and fear run on, like fire in a train, to the very foremost ranks" (1:361–62). Despite his earnestness, irony keeps Hall's touch light; the building of Babel (printed below) is almost burlesque, as incomprehension turns to anger and finally to disgust with the whole benighted project.

Hall has the natural teacher's gift of giving instruction without condescension. He frequently inserts himself in the scene as close observer, and, like the early novelists, uses the narrator's "I" to give the reader a perspective from which to judge the action. A hard lesson is easier to accept because we seem to be present as Hall himself learns it through observation. From "Of the Deluge":

> Methinks I see those monstrous sons of Lamech coming to Noah, and asking him what he means by that strange work; whether he means to sail upon dry land. To whom when he reports God's purpose and his, they go away laughing at his idleness, and tell one another, in sport, that too much holiness hath made him mad. Yet cannot they all flout Noah out of his faith; he preaches, and builds, and finishes.... Now the day is come, all the guests are entered, the ark is shut, and the windows of heaven open. I doubt not but many of those scoffers, when

they saw the violence of the waves descending and ascending, according
to Noah's prediction, came wading middle deep unto the ark, and importunately craved that admittance which they once denied. But now,
as they formerly rejected God, so are they justly rejected of God. For
ere vengeance begin, repentance is seasonable; but if judgment be once
gone out, we cry too late. While the Gospel solicits us, the doors of the
ark are open; if we neglect the time of grace, in vain shall we seek it
with tears. God holds it no mercy to pity the obstinate. (1:22–23)

Hall's style has been well described as "non-art": "simple and profound, self-knowledgeable, and invariably to the point."[32] There is a
marked contrast with Donne's baroque syntax and extended metaphors
as well as Andrewes's highly concentrated wordplay. Hall's sentences
are often brief and always simply constructed, though the balanced
rhythm is unnoticeably elegant. The *Contemplations* presuppose no special theological or linguistic knowledge; he does not quote from the
fathers, even though his other writings show a special love for Augustine, Bonaventure, and Bernard. The language is concrete, the images
punctilear, often drawn with only a few phrases. Hall uses Anglo-Saxon
roots more frequently than Latin and Greek ones. Sometimes the phras-
ing is colloquial: the Israelites get "quails with a vengeance," Goliath
scorns "the dwarves and shrimps of Israel," Israel's insistence on a king
is a "curious and inconstant newfangleness." Not only in his village
preaching but also in the court, Hall opposed "fine *quelques-choses* of
new and artificial composition" as no less dangerous than innovative
doctrine: "Surely if aught under heaven go down better with us than
the savory viands of Christ and him crucified, of faith and repentance,
and those plainly dressed, without all the lards and sauces of human
devices; to say no worse, our souls are sick and we feel it not."[33]

Hall's contemporaries called him "the English Seneca" for his
brevity, but it is likely that biblical rather than classical authors were
his closest rhetorical models. Especially he seems drawn to the epigrammatic and antithetical style of the Psalms, Proverbs, and Ecclesiastes;
and, like them, his meditations often appeal to the senses and common
human experience to verify spiritual truths. The effect is a fresh address
that is timeless and makes no distinctions of class; Hall's preaching
succeeded with villagers as with the aristocracy, with provincial merchants as with the royal court. Moreover, the plain-spoken yet graceful
style that he pioneered in the early part of the century prevailed among
Anglicans after the Restoration. This commonsense approach restored
the broad base of Christian humanism and thus provided a way to walk

between the enthusiasm of the Puritan extremists, who banned all appeal to reason, and the oversubtle argumentation and "senseless use of concordances" by university-trained Calvinists.[34]

One of the most effective ways that Hall constructs a meditative environment for his hearers is through the use of aphorisms. His preference for short sayings has served as a target for his critics. Milton compared Hall's writing to the breathing of an asthmatic; two centuries later, Coleridge, who preferred the highly ornamented style of Hall's younger contemporary Jeremy Taylor, extended his dislike to the whole person: "I have always considered [Bishop Hall] ... a self-conceited, coarse-minded, persecuting, vulgar Priest, and (by way of anti-climax) one of the first corrupters and *epigrammatizers* of our English Prose Style."[35] The caricature makes it hard to believe that Coleridge had read much of Hall. Nonetheless, he correctly sensed that the prevalence of epigrams is more than a matter of personal taste; rather, it bespeaks Hall's traditional notion of authority, which derives from the Bible.[36]

In his suggestive study of how the Bible operates as an imaginative influence, Northrop Frye distinguishes between two notions of authority as they are represented in different kinds of prose. Socrates and Plato introduced the "democratic authority" of descriptive or continuous prose; "it professes to be a delegate of experiment, evidence, or logic" and invites challenge and questioning.[37] Very different is the traditional authority expressed in the discontinuous prose of the Bible, whose prominent speech forms are the commandment, the prophetic oracle, the proverb, the parable, "in which every sentence is surrounded by silence." Epigrammatic statements invite more than cognitive assent. Hearers are called upon not just to reason but to meditate and render a response out of their whole being. In other words, they are charged to obey, in the true sense (from the Latin *ob-audire*, "listen toward") of disposing oneself fully toward another — the "other" being in some cases a text — in an attitude of listening and then acting in thoughtful response to what one has heard.

Hall does not impose his personal authority on his audience (as Coleridge seems to have thought) but rather confronts them with God's moral demand, using the most subtle and economical of linguistic forms. The reticence of the epigram implies a deep respect for both the judgment of the hearer and the mystery of God, who addresses the single demand for holiness differently to each person. Hall is for modern readers possibly the most quotable of seventeenth-century divines, and one can imagine that his original hearers, simple and sophisticated alike, pondered for days sentences such as these:

> Crosses are not of the nature of those diseases which they say a man can have but once. Their first seizure doth but make way for their reentry. (1:107)

> Satan gives us pleasant entrances into his ways, and reserves the bitterness for the end; God inures us to our worst at first, and sweetens our conclusion with pleasure. (1:98)

> It is rare and hard to commit a single sin. (1:457)

> Strength without counsel is like a blind giant, and counsel without strength is like a quick-sighted cripple. (5:355)

> It were happy if we could be as loath to commit sin as to acknowledge it. (1:256)

Hall correctly believed that the *Contemplations* represent an original approach to the Scriptures. His interest in these retellings of the sacred history is to show "what hath been done, and what should be," that is, to offer moral guidance to those living in a "slippery age."[38] It is a common prejudice of our own age to consider overtly moral concern to be incompatible with great literature.[39] But surely severing the connection between literary excellence and moral guidance belies the whole notion of Sacred Writ, that is, of inspired and carefully crafted text in which each phrase or image is worthy of attention and has potential for nurturing life.

The novel is the literary genre that (in its best exemplars) most subtly and profoundly explores moral themes in relation to human character, and close study of the *Contemplations* suggests that it is more than fortuitous that the first novelists began writing in English only a generation or two after their publication. The claim of direct influence is, of course, speculative; but nonetheless support can be adduced. Daniel Defoe, whose *Robinson Crusoe* (1719) is considered the earliest novel, was educated for the Presbyterian ministry. That fact alone makes it likely that he knew the *Contemplations*, which were widely read by Dissenting clergy as well as by Anglicans. But there is direct evidence to suggest he had read them with some care. Defoe's ironic essay "The Shortest Way with Dissenters" treats the slaying of the Israelites after the golden calf incident in language almost identical to Hall's, although Defoe is ironic where Hall is serious in arguing " 'Twas mercy to the rest to make these be examples."[40]

An important similarity between the early novelists and Hall is their consciousness of creating something new. Hall speaks of the *Contemplations* as "thoughts... I have woven out of myself,"[41] in contrast to the conscientious traditionalism of other Anglicans, including Andrewes and Donne, who "covered" their literary innovations with regular appeals to the authority of the Church and the ancient and medieval expositors. Hall's claim to originality shows something more than personal pride; it represents the beginning of a major cultural shift, evident in phenomena as diverse as Newtonian physics and the philosophy of John Locke. As the seventeenth century advanced, educated English society came to see the test of truth not in conformity to the past, but rather in fresh investigation and willingness to depart from established views.

The best evidence of a connection between the novel and the *Contemplations* lies in the distinctive traits of the new genre. Hall anticipates what is "novel" in the new fiction, namely its realism in depiction of both character and setting. The novel departs from earlier forms of imaginative narration (e.g., epic, allegory) in its realistic individualizing of events: "The plot had to be acted out by particular people in particular circumstances, rather than, as had been common in the past, by general human types against a background primarily determined by the appropriate literary convention."[42] In line with biblical narrative and in contrast to much ancient and medieval exposition, Hall treats the central biblical characters not as static figures of virtue and vice but as real human beings confronted by the demand and promise of God. He regularly goes beyond the Bible itself in giving inside views of their struggles. In the meditation on the sacrifice of Isaac, we hear at length a father's natural anguish at the command to slay a son: "Is it possible that murder should become piety?... Can I not be faithful unless I be unnatural?... Hast thou given me one only son, and must I now slay him? Why did I wait so long for him? Why didst thou give him me? Why didst thou promise me a blessing in him?" (1:35).

Hall's portrayal of emotion is naturalistic, yet his interest is not in emotion as such but rather in the transformation or transcendence of natural feeling which holiness effects. A striking instance is Jephthah's daughter, whom he portrays not as a hapless victim but as a woman whose moral integrity enables her to triumph over the tragic fate to which her father's foolishness and the weakness of her social position (as an unmarried daughter) expose her:

> While Jephthah's daughter was two months in the mountains, she might
> have had good opportunity to escape her father's vow; but as one whom
> her obedience tied as close to her father as his vow tied him to God,
> she returns to take up that burden which she had bewailed to foresee: if
> we be truly dutiful to our Father in heaven, we would not slip our necks
> out of the yoke though we might, nor fly from his commands though
> the door were open. (1:257)

By focusing on her strength of character rather than her social vic-
timization, Hall's meditation exerts a moral demand on the reader. We
are challenged to move beyond our natural responses of outrage at the
father and even beyond sympathy for the daughter and instead contemplate her obedience with admiration, an attitude that has far more
potential than outrage for strengthening our own character.[43]

The connection between Hall's *Contemplations* and the novel il-
lumines the difference between the preaching, which sets forth the
essentially moral concern of Scripture, and a moralistic approach, in
which the interpreter's own view is superimposed on the text and generally renders it mute. Rather, Hall works always from within the biblical
narrative, doing the kind of literary work for which the novel has, because of its suppleness, proven to be the most apt secular genre: namely,
the subtle exploration of how human character is built or torn down
within the murky and shifting medium of time and circumstance.

One of the most engaging features of the *Contemplations* is the
opening sentences. Often they set the moral theme of the meditation: "Before Abraham and Lot grew rich they dwelt together; now
their wealth separates them: their society was a greater good than their
riches" (1:39). Again, Hall guards against misreading by making explicit
the irony subtly present in the biblical narrative: "Israel, that had now
long gone a-whoring from God, hath been punished by the regiment
of the concubine's son [Abimelech], and at last seeks protection from
the son of a harlot [Jephthah]: it is no small misery to be obliged unto
the unworthy" (1:252). Contrast Hebrews 11:32, which misses the irony
and treats Jephthah as a model of faithfulness.

A number of the opening sentences function to set events in a larger
temporal sequence. From "The Golden Calf":

> It was not much above a month since Israel made their covenant with
> God; since they trembled to hear him say, *Thou shalt have no other gods
> but me*; since they saw Moses part from them, and climb up the hill to
> God; and now they say, *Make us gods; we know not what is become of this
> Moses.* (1:122)

By emphasizing the temporal relation between events, he clarifies patterns and tensions that readers of the novel would recognize as the "plot" of biblical history. The novel has been described as the portrayal of "life by time,"[44] and it may well be in tracing the development of character — national as well as individual — and relationships through time that Hall most significantly anticipates the novel.

A comparison with Donne's preaching shows how innovative is Hall's primary interest in the temporal dimension of the Scriptures. Donne follows the ancient and medieval commentators in treating the Bible as a timeless symbolic whole, moving without pause from a verse in Hosea to Genesis, Samuel, Luke, and Revelation, which for him are more illuminative of its literal meaning than is the immediate context. But it is noteworthy that Donne works chiefly with poetic texts, where individual words and images are foregrounded, while Hall prefers narrative, where the interest lies in the consecution of events. There may also be a theological difference at work. Joan Webber has argued that the Puritan stress on conversion and the rapid approach of the time of fulfillment lends greater significance to time and action, in contrast to the view of the "conservative Anglican," which is typically "meditative, anti-historical, obscure and ambiguous, symbolic."[45] It may well be that Puritan theology reinforced the new scientific and philosophical investigations that drew attention to temporal processes in both the natural world and the human mind, while the liturgical base of traditional Anglicanism disposed its adherents to view time as "an aspect of eternity" and thus preserved, for a time at least, the medieval atmosphere of an ever-changing present.

The novelty of Hall's *Contemplations* is that he works with each passage closely within the narrative context of the Hebrew Scriptures. In this he breaks decisively with allegorical exegesis, while yet holding to the Church's ancient conviction that the Old Testament witnesses to Christ. He discovered this witness, not by decoding an ostensible set of references to the Christ story, but rather by probing the deepest moral implications of the narrative at hand. The superb meditation on the death of Absalom (printed below) is an interesting example of his christological reading. Hall reflects upon David's injunction, *Deal gently with the young man Absalom for my sake* (2 Sam. 18:5): "For whose sake must Absalom be pursued, if he must be forborne for thine? He was still courteous to thy followers, affable to suitors, plausible to all Israel; only to thee he is cruel." The very absurdity (not denying its realism) of the king's benevolence toward his rebel son moves the reader to another level of reference. The injurious folly of parental indulgence points to the sublime folly of God's mercy:

> Or whether shall we not rather think this was done in type of that un-measurable mercy of the true King and Redeemer of Israel, who prayed for his persecutors, for his murderers, and even while they were at once scorning and killing him could say, *Father, forgive them, for they know not what they do?* (1:488)

Hall's reputation rightly rests on the *Contemplations*, but his delight-ful extemporal meditations are also valuable to preachers. Because of their brevity (each a paragraph long) and charm, the 140 brief *Occa-sional Meditations* are perhaps the best place to begin reading Hall.[46] Their text is not the Scriptures but what the medieval Church knew as "the Book of the Creatures": the natural elements of sky and earth; plant, animal, and insect life; humankind and its inventions. The pur-pose of the whole is expressed in his meditation on a pair of spectacles: "I look through the glass of the creatures at the power and wisdom of their Maker."[47] The *Occasional Meditations* are an exercise in seeing, following Calvin's dictum that the right way to seek God is not "with presumptuous curiosity" of metaphysical speculation, "but to contem-plate him in his works, in which he approaches and familiarizes, and, in some measure, communicates himself to us."[48]

Hall finds emblems of the divine life and of our own gradual growth in grace in phenomena so common as to be invisible to most people. But the Christian is on pilgrimage through this world, and so, like a traveler in a foreign country, wonders most at what is ordinary.[49] See-ing a man yawn, in involuntary imitation of someone else, reminds him of Christ's extreme sensitivity to the afflictions of the Church. Wasps falling into a trap of sweet liquid prompt the reflection: "Idle and ill-disposed persons are drawn away with every temptation; they have both leisure and will to entertain every sweet allurement to sin and wantonly prosecute their own wicked lusts till they fall into irrecoverable damna-tion."[50] An arm numbed from too long leaning upon it reminds him of the pain and disappointment that inevitably follow from "trusting to an arm of flesh."[51] A left-handed person suggests the need to develop fac-ulties that often languish through disuse. He notes characteristically: "I had rather lack good parts than that good parts should lack me. Not to have great gifts is no fault of mine; it is my fault not to use them."[52]

Each meditation is like a sermon in miniature: beginning with an explication of the phenomenon that is its text; then applying its les-son to the Christian life, and usually to "me," the meditator's own soul;

and concluding often with a prayer. I choose one almost at random to quote in full, for the *Occasional Meditations* are nearly all excellent. "Upon a Spring-water" expresses with particular clarity Hall's marvelously inventive capacity for gratitude:

> How this spring smoketh while other greater channels are frozen up! This water is living while they are dead. All experience teacheth us that well-waters arising from deep springs are hotter in winter than in summer; the outward cold doth keep in and double their inward heat. Such is a true Christian in the evil day; his life of grace gets more vigor by opposition; he had not been so gracious if the times had been better. I will not say he may thank his enemies but I must say he may thank God for his enemies. Oh God, what can put out that heat which is increased with cold? How happy shall I be if I grow so much more in grace as the world in malice!

Hall did not seem to place much value on the *Occasional Meditations* (perhaps they came too easily?), for he never published them himself. But modern readers may find them particularly apt to their own theological needs, for these meditations could serve as a foundation for a devotional practice that takes seriously "the natural world" as the work of God's hands and thus one aspect of divine revelation. Hall's wonder at the creatures is an oblique warning against the danger of viewing the elements of the nonhuman world, including the earth itself, as so many things to be managed for our own ends. "The creatures are half lost if we only employ them, not learn something from them."[53] Writing on the threshold of the scientific age, Hall developed an empirical method of meditation that provides a bridge between religious and scientific apprehensions of the world. Thus it may help this generation with its most important and difficult theological task: discovering the proper place of humanity within the whole created order.

THE TOWER OF BABEL
(Genesis 11)

How soon are men and sins multiplied! Within one hundred years the world is as full of both as if there had been no deluge. Though men could not but see the fearful monuments of the ruin of their ancestors, yet how quickly had they forgotten a flood! Good Noah lived to see the world both populous and wicked again; and doubtless ofttimes repented to have been preserver of some, whom he saw to traduce the vices of the former world to the renewed. It could not but grieve him to see the destroyed giants revive out of his own loins, and to see them of his flesh and blood tyrannize over themselves. In his sight Nimrod, casting off the awe of his holy grandfather, grew imperious and cruel, and made his own kinsmen servants [Gen. 10:8–14]. How easy a thing it is for a great spirit to be the head of a faction, when even brethren will stoop to servitude! And now, when men are combined together, evil and presumptuous motions find encouragement in multitudes; and each man takes a pride in seeming forwardest: we are the cheerfuller in good when we have the assistance of company; much more in sinning, by how much we are more prone to evil than good. It was a proud word, *Come, let us build us a city and a tower, whose top may reach to heaven.*

They were newly come down from the hills unto the plains, and now think of raising up a hill, of building in the plain: when their tents were pitched upon the mountains of Armenia, they were as near to heaven as their tower could make them; but their ambition must needs aspire to a height of their own raising. Pride is ever discontented, and still seeks matter of boasting in her own works.

How fondly do men reckon without God! *Come, let us build;* as if there had been no stop but in their own will; as if both earth and time had been theirs. Still do all natural men build Babel; forecasting their own plots so resolutely, as if there were no power to countermand them. It is just with God that peremptory determinations seldom prosper; whereas those things which are fearfully and modestly undertaken commonly succeed.

Let us build us a city. If they had taken God with them, it had been commendable; establishing of societies is pleasing to him that is the God of order: but a *tower, whose top may reach to heaven,* was a shameful arrogance, an impious presumption. Who could think that we little ants that creep upon the earth should think of climbing up to heaven by multiplying of earth?

Pride ever looks at the highest: the first man would know as God, these would dwell as God; covetousness and ambition know no limits. And what if they had reached up to heaven? Some hills are as high as they could hope to be, and yet are no whit the better; no place alters the condition of nature: an angel is glorious, though he be upon earth; and man is but earth, though he be above the clouds. The nearer they had been to heaven, the more subject should they have been to the violences of heaven, to thunders, lightnings, and those other higher inflammations; what had this been but to thrust themselves into the hands of the revenger of all wicked insolencies? God loves that heaven should be looked at, and affected with all humble desires, with the holy ambitions of faith, not with the proud imaginations of our own achievements.

But wherefore was all this? Not that they loved so much to be neighbors to heaven as to be famous upon earth; it was not commodity that was here sought, not safety, but glory; whither doth not thirst of fame carry men, whether in good or evil! It makes them seek to climb to heaven; it makes them not fear to run down headlong to hell. Even in the best things, desire of praise stands in competition with conscience, and brags to have the more clients. One builds a temple to Diana, in hope of glory, intending it for one of the great wonders of the world; another, in hope of fame, burns it. He is a rare man that hath not some Babel of his own, whereon he bestows pains and cost, only to be talked of. If they had done better things in a vainglorious purpose, their act had been accursed; if they had built houses to God, if they had sacrificed, prayed, lived well; the intent poisons the action; but now, both the act and the purpose are equally vain, and the issue is as vain as either.

God hath a special indignation at pride, above all sins; and will cross our endeavors, not for that they are evil (what hurt could be in laying one brick upon another?), but for that they are proudly undertaken. He could have hindered the laying of the first stone, and might as easily have made a trench for the foundation, the grave of the builders; but he loves to see what wicked men would do, and to let fools run themselves out of breath: what monument should they have had of their own madness, and his powerful interruption, if the walls had risen to no height?

To stop them then in the midst of their course, he meddles not with either their hands or their feet, but their tongues; not by pulling them out, not by loosing their strings, nor by making them say nothing, but by teaching them to say too much: here is nothing varied but the sound of letters; even this frustrates the work, and befools the workmen: how easy it is for God ten thousand ways to correct and forestall the greatest projects of men! He that taught Adam the first words, taught them words that never were. One calls for brick, the other looks him in the face, and wonders what he commands, and how and why he speaks such words as were never heard; and instead thereof brings him mortar, returning him an answer as little understood: each chides with other, expressing his choler, so as he only can understand himself; from heat they fall to quiet entreaties, but still with the same success. At first, every man thinks his fellow mocks him; but now, perceiving this serious confusion, their only answer was silence and ceasing: they could not come together, for no man could call them to be understood; and if they had assembled, nothing could be determined, because one could never attain to the other's purpose: no, they could not have the honor of a general dismission, but each man leaves his trowel and station, more like a fool than he undertook it: so commonly actions begun in glory shut up in shame.

All external actions depend upon the tongue: no man can know another's mind, if this be not the interpreter; hence, as there were many tongues given to stay the building of Babel, so there were as many given to build the New Jerusalem, the evangelical church. How dear hath Babel cost all the world! At the first, when there was but one language, men did spend their time in arts (so was it requisite at the first settling of the world), and so came early to perfection; but now we stay so long of necessity upon the shell of tongues, that we can hardly have time to chew the sweet kernel of knowledge: surely men would have grown too proud, if there had been no Babel! It falls out ofttimes that one sin is a remedy of a greater. Division of tongues must needs slacken any work: multiplicity of language had not been given by the Holy Ghost for a blessing to the church, if the world had not been before possessed with multiplicity of languages for a punishment: hence it is, that the building of our Sion rises no faster, because our tongues are divided; happy were the church of God, if we all spake but one language: while we differ, we can build nothing but Babel; difference of tongues caused their Babel to cease, but it builds ours.

THE ROCK OF REPHIDIM
(Exodus 17)

Before, Israel thirsted and was satisfied; after that, they hungered and were filled; now they thirst again. They have bread and meat, but want drink: it is a marvel if God do not evermore hold us short of something, because he would keep us still in exercise. We should forget at whose cost we live if we wanted nothing. Still God observes a vicissitude of evil and good, and the same evils that we have passed return upon us in their courses. Crosses are not of the nature of those diseases which they say a man can have but once. Their first seizure doth but make way for their reentry. None but our last enemy comes once for all, and I know not if that: for even in living we die daily. So must we take our leaves of all afflictions, that we reserve a lodging for them and expect their return.

All Israel murmured when they wanted bread, meat, water; and yet all Israel departed from the wilderness of Sin to Rephidim at God's command. The very worst men will obey God in something, none but the good in all: he is rarely [unusually] desperate that makes an universal opposition to God. It is an unsound praise that is given a man for one good action. It may be safely said of the very devils themselves, that they do something well, they know and believe and tremble. If we follow God and murmur, it is all one as if we had stayed behind.

Those distrust his providence in their necessity, that are ready to follow his guidance in their welfare. It is an harder matter to endure in extreme want, than to obey an hard commandment. Sufferings are greater trials than actions: how many have we seen jeopard their lives with cheerful resolution, which cannot endure in cold blood to lose a limb with patience! Because God will have his throughly tried, he puts them to both; and if we cannot endure both to follow him from Sin, and to thirst in Rephidim, we are not sound Israelites.

God led them on purpose to this dry Rephidim: he could as well have conducted them to another Elim, to convenient waterings; or he that gives the waters of all their channels, could as well have derived them to meet Israel; but God doth purposely carry them to thirst. It is not for necessity that we fare ill, but out of choice: it were all one with God to give us health as sickness, abundance as poverty. The treasury of his riches hath more store than his creature can be capable of: we could not complain if it were not good for us to want.

This should have been a contentment able to quench any thirst: *God hath led us thither;* if Moses out of ignorance had misguided us, or we chanceably fallen upon these dry deserts, though this were no remedy of our grief, yet it might be some ground of our complaint. But now the counsel of so wise and merciful a God hath drawn us into this want, and shall not he as easily find the way out? *It is the Lord, let him do what he will* [1 Sam. 3:18]. There can be no more forcible motive to patience than the acknowledgment of a divine hand that strikes us. It is fearful to be in the hand of an adversary, but who would not be confident of a father? Yet in our frail humanity, choler may transport a man from remembrance of nature; but when we feel ourselves under the discipline of a wise God, that can temper our afflictions to our strength, to our benefit, who would not rather murmur at himself than he should swerve towards impatience? Yet these sturdy Israelites willfully murmur, and will not have their thirst quenched with faith, but with water. *Give us water.*

I looked to hear when they would have entreated Moses to pray for them; but instead of entreating, they contend; and instead of prayers, I find commands: *Give us water.* If they had gone to God without Moses, I should have praised their faith; but now they go to Moses without God, I hate their stubborn faithlessness. To seek to the second means with neglect of the first is the fruit of a false faith.

The answer of Moses is like himself, mild and sweet: *Why contend you with me? Why tempt ye the Lord?* in the first expostulation condemning them of injustice, since not he but the Lord afflicted them: in the second, of presumption, that since it was God that tempted them by want, they should tempt him by murmuring: in the one, he would have them see their wrong; in the other, their danger. As the act came not from him but from God; so he puts it off to God from himself, *Why tempt ye the Lord?* The opposition which is made to the instruments of God redounds over to his person. He holds himself smitten through the sides of his ministers: so hath God incorporated these respects, that our subtlety cannot divide them.

But what temptation is this? *Is the Lord among us or no?* Infidelity is crafty and yet foolish, crafty in her insinuations, foolish in her conceits. They imply, "If we were sure the Lord were with us, we would not distrust"; they conceive doubts of his presence after such confirmations. What could God do more to make them know him present, unless every moment should have renewed miracles? The plagues of Egypt and the division of the sea were so famous, that the very inns of Jericho rang of them [Josh. 2:10]. Their waters were lately sweetened, the quails were yet in their teeth, the manna was yet in their eye, yea, they saw God in the pillar of the cloud, and yet they say, *Is the Lord amongst us?* No argument is enough to an incredulous heart; not reason, not sense, not experience. How much better was that faith of Thomas, that would believe his eyes and hands, though his ears he would not [John 20:24–25]! O the deep infidelity of these Israelites, that saw and believed not!

And how will they know if God be amongst them? As if he could not be with them, and they be athirst! Either God must humor carnal minds or be distrusted: if they prosper, though it be with wickedness, God is with them: if they be thwarted in their own designs, straight, *Is God with us?* It was the way to put God from them, to distrust and murmur. If he had not been with them, they had not lived; if he had been in them, they had not mutinied. They can think him absent in their want, and cannot see him absent in their sin: and yet wickedness, not affliction, argues him gone; yet then is he most present when he most chastises.

Who would not have looked that this answer of Moses should have appeased their fury? As what can still him that will not be quiet to think he hath God for his adversary? But as if they would willfully war against heaven, they proceed; yet with no less craft than violence; bending their exception to one part of the answer, and smoothly omitting what they could not except against. They will not hear of tempting God; they maintain their strife with Moses, both with words and stones. How malicious, how heady is impatience! The act was God's; they cast it upon Moses, *Wherefore hast thou brought us?* The act of God was merciful; they make it cruel. *To kill us and our children;* as if God and Moses meant nothing but their ruin, who intended nothing but their life and liberty. Foolish men! What needed this journey to death? Were they not as obnoxious to God in Egypt? Could not God by Moses as easily have killed them, in Egypt or in the sea, as their enemies? Impatience is full of misconstruction: if it be possible to find out any gloss to corrupt the text of God's actions, they shall be sure not to escape untainted.

It was no expostulating with an unreasonable multitude: Moses runs straight to him that was able at once to quench their thirst and their fury: *What shall I do to this people?* It is the best way to trust God with his own causes: when men will be intermeddling with his affairs, they undo themselves in vain. We shall find difficulties in all great enterprises: if we be sure we have begun them from God, we may securely cast all events upon his providence, which knows how to dispose and how to end them.

Moses perceived rage, not in the tongues only, but in the hands of the Israelites. *Yet a while longer, and they will stone me.* Even the leader of God's people feared death; and sinned not in fearing. Life is worthy to be dear to all; especially to him whom public charge hath made necessary: mere fear is not sinful: it is impotence and distrust that accompany it which make it evil. How well is that fear bestowed that sends us the more importunately to God! Some man would have thought of flight; Moses flies to his prayers; and that not for revenge, but for help. Who but Moses would not have said, "This twice they have mutinied, and been pardoned; and now again thou seest, O Lord, how madly they rebel; and how bloodily they intend against me; preserve me, I beseech thee, and plague them": I hear none of this; but, imitating the long-suffering of his God, he seeks to God for them, which sought to kill him for the quarrel of God.

Neither is God sooner sought than found: all Israel might see Moses go towards the rock; none but the elders might see him strike it. Their unbelief made them unworthy of this privilege. It is no small favor of God to make us witnesses of his great works; that he crucifies his Son before us, that he fetches the water of life out of the true Rock in our sight, is an high prerogative: if his rigor would have taken it, our infidelity had equally excluded us, whom now his mercy hath received.

Moses must take his rod: God could have done it by his will without a word, or by his word without the rod; but he will do by means that which he can as easily do without. There was no virtue in the rod, none in the stroke; but all in the command of God. Means must be used, and yet their efficacy must be expected out of themselves.

It doth not suffice God to name the rod without a description; *Whereby thou smotest the river:* wherefore, but to strengthen the faith of Moses, that he might well expect this wonder from that which he had tried [previously tested] to be miraculous? How could he but firmly believe, that the same means which turned the waters into blood, and turned the sea into a wall, could as well turn the stone into water? Nothing more raises up the heart in present affiance than the recognition of favors or wonders past. Behold, the same rod that brought plagues to the Egyptians brings deliverances to Israel! By the same means can God save and condemn; like as the same sword defends and kills.

That power which turned the wings of the quails to the wilderness, turned the course of the water through the rock: he might, if he had pleased, have caused a spring to well out of the plain earth; but he will now fetch it out of the stone, to convince and shame their infidelity.

What is more hard and dry than the rock? What more moist and supple than water? That they may be ashamed to think they distrusted lest God could bring them water out of the clouds or springs, the very rock shall yield it.

And now, unless their hearts had been more rocky than this stone, they could not but have resolved into tears for this diffidence.

I wonder to see these Israelites fed with sacraments. Their bread was sacramental, whereof they communicated every day: lest any man should complain of frequence, the Israelites received daily; and now their drink was sacramental, that the ancient Church may give no warrant of a dry communion.

Twice therefore hath the rock yielded them water of refreshing, to signify that the true spiritual rock yields it always. The rock that followed them was Christ [1 Cor. 10:4]: out thy side, O Savior, issued that bloody stream, whereby the thirst of all believers is comfortably quenched: let us but thirst; not with repining, but with faith; this rock of thine shall abundantly flow forth to our souls, and follow us, till this water be changed into that new wine, which we shall drink with thee in thy Father's kingdom [Matt. 26:29].

JAEL AND SISERA
(Judges 4)

It is no wonder if they, who ere fourscore days after the law delivered fell into idolatry alone, now after fourscore years since the law restored, fell to idolatry among the Canaanites. Peace could in a shorter time work looseness in any people. And if forty years after Othniel's deliverance they relapsed, what marvel is it that in twice forty after Ehud they thus miscarried? What are they the better to have killed Eglon the king of Moab, if the idolatry of Moab have killed them? The sin of Moab shall be found a worse tyrant than their Eglon. Israel is for every market: they sold themselves to idolatry, God sells them to the Canaanites: it is no marvel they are slaves if they will be idolaters. After their longest intermission they have now the sorest bondage. None of their tyrants were so potent as Jabin with his nine hundred chariots of iron. The longer the reckoning is deferred, the greater is the sum: God provides on purpose mighty adversaries for his Church, that their humiliation may be the greater in sustaining, and his glory may be greater in deliverance.

I do not find any prophet in Israel during their sin; but so soon as I hear news of their repentance, mention is made of a prophetess and judge of Israel. There is no better sign of God's reconciliation than the sending of his holy messengers to any people: he is not utterly fallen out with those whom he blesses with prophecy. Whom yet do I see raised to this honor? Not any of the princes of Israel, not Barak the captain, not Lapidoth the husband; but a woman, for the honor of her sex; a wife, for the honor of wedlock: Deborah, the wife of Lapidoth.

He that had choice of all the millions of Israel calls out two weak women to deliver his people: Deborah shall judge, Jael shall execute. All the palaces of Israel must yield to the palm tree of Deborah. The weakness of the instruments redounds to the greater honor of the workman. Who shall ask God any reason of his elections but his own pleasure? Deborah was to sentence, not to strike; to command, not to execute: this act is masculine, fit for some captain of Israel. She was the head of Israel; it was meet some other should be the hand. It is an imperfect and titular government where there is a commanding power without correction, without execution. The message of Deborah finds out Barak the son of Abinoam in his obscure secrecy and calls him from a corner of Naphtali to the honor of this exploit. He is sent for, not to get the victory, but to take it; not to overcome, but to kill; to pursue, and not to beat Sisera. Who could not have done this work, whereto not much courage, no skill belonged? Yet even for this will God have an instrument of his own choice: it is most fit that God should serve himself where he list [pleases, chooses] of his own; neither is it to be inquired whom we think meet for any employment, but whom God hath called.

Deborah had been no prophetess if she durst have sent in her own name. Her message is from him that sent herself; *Hath not the Lord God of Israel commanded?* Barak's answer is faithful though conditionate, and doth not so much intend a refusal to go without her, as a necessary bond of her presence with him. Who can blame him that he would have a prophetess in his company? If the man had not been as holy as valiant, he would not have wished such society. How many think it a perpetual bondage to have a prophet of God at their elbow! God had never sent for him so far, if he could have been content to go up without Deborah: he knew that there was both a blessing and encouragement in that presence. It is no putting any trust in the success of those men that neglect the messengers of God.

To prescribe that to others which we draw back from doing ourselves is an argument of hollowness and falsity. Barak shall see that Deborah doth not offer him that cup whereof she dare not begin; without regard to her sex she marches with him to Mount Tabor, and rejoices to be seen of the ten thousand of Israel. With what scorn did Sisera look at these gleanings of Israel! How unequal did this match seem of ten thousand Israelites against his three hundred thousand foot, ten thousand horse, nine hundred chariots of iron! And now in bravery he calls for his troops, and means to kill this handful of Israel with the very sight of his piked chariots, and only feared it would be no victory to cut the throats of so few. The faith of Deborah and Barak was not appalled with this world of adversaries, which from Mount Tabor they saw hiding all the valley below them: they knew whom they had believed, and how little an arm of flesh could do against the God of Hosts.

Barak went down against Sisera, but it was God that destroyed him. The Israelites did not this day wield their own swords, lest they should arrogate any thing. God told them beforehand it should be his own act. I hear not of one stroke that any Canaanite gave in this fight; as if they were called hither only to suffer. And now proud Sisera, after many curses of the heaviness of that iron carriage, is glad to quit his chariot and betake himself to his heels. Who ever yet knew any earthly thing trusted in without disappointment? It is wonder if God make us not at last as weary of whatsoever hath stolen our hearts from him, as ever we were fond.

Yet Sisera hopes to have sped better than his followers in so seasonable a harbor of Jael. If Heber and Jael had not been great persons, there had been no note taken of their tents; there had been no league betwixt king Jabin and them; now their greatness makes them known, their league makes them trusted. The distress of Sisera might have made him importunate; but Jael begins the courtesy and exceeds the desire of her guest: he asks water to drink, she gives him milk; he wishes but shelter, she makes him a bed; he desires the protection of her tent, she covers him with a mantle. And now Sisera pleases himself with his happy change, and thinks how much better it is to be here than in that whirling of chariots, in that horror of flight, amongst those shrieks, those wounds, those carcasses. While he is in these thoughts, his weariness and easy reposal hath brought him asleep. Who would have looked that in this tumult and danger, even betwixt the very jaws of death, Sisera should find time to sleep? How many worldly hearts do so in the midst of their spiritual perils!

Now while he was dreaming doubtless of the clashing of armors, rattling of chariots, neighing of horses, the clamor of the conquered, the furious pursuit of Israel; Jael, seeing his temples lie so fair, as if they invited the nail and hammer, entered into the thought of this noble execution; certainly not without some checks of doubt and pleas of fear: "What if I strike him? And yet who am I that I should dare to think of such an act? Is not this Sisera, the famousest captain of the world, whose name hath wont to be fearful to whole nations? What if my hand should swerve in the stroke? What if he should awake while I am lifting up this instrument of death? What if I should be surprised by some of his followers while the fact is green and yet bleeding? Can the murder of so great a leader be hid or unrevenged? Or if I might hope so, yet can my heart allow me to be secretly treacherous? Is there not peace betwixt my house and him? Did not I invite him to my tent? Doth he not trust to my friendship and hospitality? But what do these weak fears, these idle fancies of civility? If Sisera be in league with us, yet is he not at defiance with God? Is he not a tyrant to Israel? Is it for nothing that God hath brought him into my tent? May I not now find means to repay unto Israel all their kindness to my grandfather Jethro? Doth not God offer me this day the honor to be the rescuer of his people? Hath God bidden me strike, and shall I hold my hand? No, Sisera, sleep now thy last, and take here this fatal reward of all thy cruelty and oppression."

He that put this instinct into her heart did put also strength into her hand: he that guided Sisera to her tent guided the nail through his temples; which hath made a speedy way for his soul through those parts, and now hath fastened his ear so close to the earth, as if the body had been listening what was become of the soul. There lies now the great terror of Israel at the foot of a woman. He that brought so many hundred thousands into the field hath not now one page left, either to avert his death, or to accompany it, or bewail it. He that had vaunted of his iron chariots is slain by one nail of iron; wanting only this one point of his infelicity, that he knows not by whose hand he perished.

NATHAN AND DAVID
(2 Samuel 12)

Yet Bathsheba mourned for the death of that husband whom she had been drawn to dishonor. How could she bestow tears enough upon that funeral whereof her sin was the cause! If she had but a suspicion of the plot of his death, the fountains of her eyes could not yield water enough to wash off her husband's blood. Her sin was more worthy of sorrow than her loss. If this grief had been right placed, the hope of hiding her shame and the ambition to be a queen had not so soon mitigated it; neither had she, upon any terms, been drawn into the bed of her husband's murderer. Every gleam of earthly comfort can dry up the tears of worldly sorrow. Bathsheba hath soon lost her grief at the court. The remembrance of an husband is buried in the jollity and state of a princess.

David securely enjoys his ill-purchased love; and is content to exchange the conscience of his sin for the sense of his pleasure. But the just and holy God will not put it up so [suffer quietly, "put up with" this]. He that hates sin so much the more as the offender is more dear to him, will let David feel the bruise of his fall. If God's best children have been sometimes suffered to sleep in a sin, at last he hath awakened them in a fright.

David was a prophet of God; and yet he hath not only stepped into those foul sins, but sojourns with them. If any profession or state of life could have privileged from sin, the angels had not sinned in heaven, nor man in paradise.

Nathan the prophet is sent to the prophet David for reproof, for conviction. Had it been any other man's case, none could have been more quick-sighted than the princely prophet; in his own, he is so blind, that God is fain [willing, obliged] to lend him others' eyes. Even the physician himself, when he is sick, sends for the counsel of those whom his health did mutually aid with advice. Let no man think himself too good to learn. Teachers themselves may be taught that in their own particular which in a generality they have often taught others. It is not only ignorance that is to be removed, but misaffection.

Who can prescribe a just period to the best man's repentance? About ten months are passed since David's sin, in all which time I find no news of any serious compunction. It could not be but some glances of remorse must needs have passed through his soul long ere this; but a due and solemn contrition was not heard of till Nathan's message, and perhaps had been further adjourned if that monitor had been longer deferred. Alas! What long and dead sleeps may the holiest soul take in fearful sins! Were it not for thy mercy, O God, the best of us should end our spiritual lethargy in sleep of death.

It might have pleased God as easily to have sent Nathan to check David in his first purpose of sinning; so had his eyes been restrained, Bathsheba honest, Uriah alive with honor. Now the wisdom of the Almighty knew how to win more glory by the permission of so foul an evil than by the prevention: yea, he knew how, by the permission of one sin, to prevent millions. How many thousands had sinned, in a vain presumption on their own strength, if David had not thus offended! How many thousands had despaired, in the conscience of their own weaknesses, if these horrible sins had not received forgiveness! It is happy for all times that we have so holy a sinner, so sinful a penitent.

It matters not how bitter the pill is, but how well wrapped. So cunningly hath Nathan conveyed this dose, that it begins to work ere it be tasted. There is no one thing wherein is more use of wisdom than the due contriving of reprehension; which in a discreet delivery helps the disease, in an unwise, destroys nature.

Had not Nathan been used to the possession of David's ear, this complaint had been suspected. It well beseems a king to take information by a prophet.

While wise Nathan was querulously discoursing of the cruel rich man that had forcibly taken away the only lamb of his poor neighbor, how willingly doth David listen to the story! And how sharply, even above law, doth he censure the fact; *As the Lord liveth, the man that hath done this thing shall surely die!* Full little did he think that he had pronounced sentence against himself. It had not been so heavy, if he had known on whom it should have lighted. We have open ears and quick tongues to the vices of others. How severe justices can we be to our very own crimes in others' persons. How flattering parasites to another's crime in ourselves!

The life of doctrine is in application. Nathan might have been long enough in his narration, in his invective, ere David would have been touched with his own guiltiness; but now that the prophet brings the word home to his bosom, he cannot but be affected. We may take pleasure to hear men speak in the clouds; we never take profit, till we find a propriety in the exhortation or reproof.

There was not more cunning in the parable than courage in the application, *Thou are the man.* If David be a king, he may not look not to hear of his faults. God's messages may be no other than impartial. It is a treacherous flattery in divine errands to regard greatness. If prophets must be mannerly in the form, yet in the matter of reproof resolute. The words are not their own: they are but the heralds of the king of heaven; *Thus saith the Lord God of Israel.*

How thunder-stricken do we think David did now stand! How did the change of his color bewray [expose] the confusion in his soul, while his conscience said the same within which the prophet sounded in his ear! And now, lest aught should be wanting to his humiliation, all God's former favors shall be laid before his eyes, by way of exprobration [reproach]. He is worthy to be upbraided with mercies that hath abused mercies unto wantonness. While we do well, God gives, and says nothing; when we do ill, he lays his benefits in our dish, and casts them in our teeth, that our shame may be so much the more by how much our obligations have been greater. The blessings of God, in our unworthy carriage [conduct], prove but the aggravations of sin and additions to judgment.

I see all God's children falling into sin; some of them lying in sin; none of them maintaining their sin. David cannot have the heart or the face to stand out against the message of God; but now, as a man confounded and condemned in himself, he cries out, in the bitterness of a wounded soul, *I have sinned against the Lord.*

It was a short word, but passionate; and such as came from the bottom of a contrite heart. The greatest griefs are not most verbal.

Saul confessed his sin more largely, less effectually. God cares not for phrases, but for affections.

The first piece of our amends to God for sinning is the acknowledgment of sin. He can do little that in a just offense cannot accuse himself. If we cannot be so good as we would, it is reason we should do God so much right as to say how evil we are. And why was not this done sooner? It is strange to see how easily sin gets into the heart, how hardly it gets out of the mouth. Is it because sin, like unto Satan, where it hath got possession is desirous to hold it, and knows that it is fully ejected by a free confession? Or because, in a guiltiness of deformity, it hides itself in the breast where it is once entertained, and hates the light? Or because the tongue is so feed [fed] with self-love, that it is loath to be drawn unto any verdict against the heart or hands? Or is it out of an idle misprision [misconception] of shame, which, while it should be placed in offending, is misplaced in disclosing of our offense? However, sure I am that God hath need even of racks to draw out confessions; and scarce in death itself are we wrought to a discovery of our errors.

There is no one thing wherein our folly shows itself more than in these hurtful concealments. Contrary to the proceedings of human justice, it is with God, *confess, and live.* No sooner can David say, *I have sinned,* than Nathan infers, *the Lord also hath put away thy sin. He that hides his sin shall not prosper; but he that confesseth and forsaketh them shall find mercy.* Who would not accuse himself, to be acquitted of God? O God, who would not tell his wickedness to thee, that knowest it better than his own heart, that his heart may be eased of that wickedness which being not told killeth? Since we have sinned, why should we be niggardly of that action wherein we may at once give glory to thee and relief to our souls?

David had sworn, in a zeal of justice, that the rich oppressor, for but taking his poor neighbor's lamb, should die the death: God, by Nathan, is more favorable to David than to take him at his word; *Thou shalt not die.* O the marvelous power of repentance! Besides adultery, David had shed the blood of innocent Uriah. The strict law was, *eye for eye, tooth for tooth; he that smiteth with the sword shall perish with the sword* [Matt. 26:52; cf. Lev. 24:20]. Yet, as if a penitent confession had dispensed with the rigor of justice, now God says, *Thou shalt not die.* David was the voice of the law, awarding death unto sin; Nathan was the voice of the Gospel, awarding life unto the repentance for sin. Whatsoever the sore be, never any soul applied this remedy and died; never any soul escaped death that applied it not.

David himself shall not die for this fact: but his misbegotten child shall die for him. He that said, *the Lord hath put away thy sin*, yet said also, *the sword shall not depart from thine house*. The same mouth, with one breath, pronounces the sentence both of absolution and death: absolution to the person, death to the issue. Pardon may well stand with temporal afflictions. Where God hath forgiven, though he doth not punish, yet he may chastise, and that unto blood; neither doth he always forbear correction where he remits revenge. So long as he smites us not as an angry judge we may endure to smart from him as a loving father.

Yet even this rod did David deprecate with tears. How fain would he shake off so easy a load! The child is stricken, the father fasts, and prays, and weeps, and lies all night upon the earth, and abhors the noise of comfort. That child, which was the fruit and monument of his odious adultery, whom he could never have looked upon without recognition of his sin, in whose face he could not but have still read the records of his own shame, is thus mourned for, thus sued for. It is easy to observe that good man over-passionately affected to his children. Who would not have thought that David might have held himself well appayd [pleased, satisfied] that his soul escaped an eternal death, his body a violent, though God should punish his sin in that child in whom he sinned? Yet even against this cross he bends his prayers as if nothing had been forgiven him. There is no child that would be scourged if he might escape for crying. No affliction is for the time other than grievous, neither is therefore yielded unto without some kind of reluctation.

Far yet was it from the heart of David to make any opposition to the will of God: he sued, he struggled not. There is no impatience in entreaties. He well knew that the threats of temporal evils ran commonly with a secret condition, and therefore might perhaps be avoided by humble importunity. If any means under heaven can avert judgments, it is our prayers.

God could not choose but like well the boldness of David's faith, who, after the apprehension of so heavy a displeasure, is so far from doubting of the forgiveness of his sin, that he dares become a suitor unto God for his sick child. Sin doth not more make us strange [alienated] than faith confident.

But it is not in the power of the strongest faith to preserve us from all afflictions. After all David's prayers and tears the child must die. The careful servants dare but whisper this sad news. They, who had found their master so averse from the motion of comfort in the sickness of the child, feared him incapable of comfort in his death. Suspicion is quick-witted. Every occasion makes us misdoubt that event which we fear. This secrecy proclaims that which they were so loath to utter. David perceives his child dead, and now he rises up from the earth whereon he lay, and washes himself, and changeth his apparel, and goes first into God's house to worship, and into his own to eat; now he refuses no comfort who before would take none. The issue of things doth more fully show the will of God than the prediction. God never did any thing but what he would. He hath sometimes foretold that for trial which his secret will intended not. He would foretell it: he would not effect it, because he would therefore foretell it that he might not effect it. His predictions of outward evils are not always absolute; his actions are. David well sees by the event what the decree of God was concerning his child, which now he could not strive against without a vain impatience. Till we know the determinations of the Almighty, it is free for us to strive in our prayers; to strive with him, not against him: when once we know them, it is our duty to sit down in a silent contentation [content].

While the child was yet alive, I fasted and wept: for I said, who can tell whether the Lord will be gracious to me, that the child may live? But now he is dead, wherefore should I fast? Can I bring him back again?

The grief that goes before an evil for remedy can hardly be too much; but that which follows an evil past remedy cannot be too little. Even in the saddest accident, death, we may yield something to nature, nothing to impatience. Immoderation of sorrow for losses past hope of recovery is more sullen than useful; our stomach [stubbornness] may be bewrayed by it, not our wisdom.

THE DEATH OF ABSALOM
(2 Samuel 17, 18)

The same God that raised enmity to David from his own loins procured him favor from foreigners; strangers shall relieve him whom his own son persecutes. Here is not a loss, but an exchange of love. Had Absalom been a son of Ammon, and Shobi a son of David, David had found no cause of complaint. If God take with one hand, he gives with another: while that divine bounty serves us in good meat, though not in our own dishes, we have good reason to be thankful. No sooner is David come to Mehanaim, that Barzillai, Machir, and Shobi refresh him with provisions. Who ever saw any child of God left utterly destitute? Whosoever be the messenger of our aid, we know whence he comes. Heaven shall want power and earth means, before any of the household of faith shall want maintenance.

He that formerly was forced to employ his arms for his defense against a tyrannous father-in-law, must now buckle them on against an unnatural son. Now, therefore, he musters his men, and ordains his commanders, and marshals his troops; and since their loyal importunity will not allow the hazard of his person, he at once encourages them by his eye and restrains them with his tongue; *Deal gently with the young man Absalom for my sake.*

How unreasonably favorable are the wars of a father! O holy David, what means this ill-placed love, this unjust mercy, Deal gently with a traitor? But of all traitors with a son? Of all sons, with an Absalom, the graceless darling of so good a father? And all this *for my sake*, whose crown, whose blood, he hunts after? For whose sake should Absalom be pursued, if he must be forborne for thine? He was still courteous to thy followers, affable to suitors, plausible to all Israel; only to thee he is cruel. Wherefore are those arms, if the cause of the quarrel must be a motive of mercy? Yet thou sayest, *Deal gently with the young man Absalom for my sake.* Even in the holiest parents nature may be guilty of an injurious tenderness, of a bloody indulgence.

Or whether shall we not rather think this was done in type of that unmeasurable mercy of the true King and Redeemer of Israel, who prayed for his persecutors, for his murderers; and even while they were at once scorning and killing him could say, *Father, forgive them, for they know not what they do?* If we be sons, we are ungracious, we are rebellious; yet still is our heavenly Father thus compassionately regardful of us. David was not sure of his success. There was great inequality in the number. Absalom's forces were more than double to his. It might have come to the contrary issue, that David should have been forced to say, *Deal gently with the fa-*

ther of Absalom; but in a supposition of that victory which only the goodness of his cause bid him hope for, he saith, *Deal gently with the young man Absalom.* As for us, we are never but under mercy: our God needs no advantages to sweep us from the earth any moment; yet he continues that life and those powers to us whereby we provoke him, and bids his angels deal kindly with us and bear us in their arms, while we lift up our hands and bend our tongues against heaven. O mercy past the comprehension of all finite spirits, and only to be conceived by him whose it is! Never more resembled by any earthly affection than by this of his deputy and type; *Deal gently with the young man Absalom for my sake.*

The battle is joined. David's followers are but a handful to Absalom's. How easily may the fickle multitude be transported to the wrong side! What they wanted in abettors is supplied in the cause. Unnatural ambition draws the sword of Absalom; David's, a necessary and a just defense. They that in simplicity of heart followed Absalom cannot in malice of heart persecute the father of Absalom: with what courage could any Israelite draw his sword against a David? Or, on the other side, who can want courage to fight for a righteous sovereign and father against the conspiracy of a wicked son?

The God of hosts, with whom it is all one to save with many or with few, takes part with justice, and lets Israel feel what it is to bear arms for a traitorous usurper. The sword devours twenty thousand of them, and the wood devours more than the sword. It must needs be a very universal rebellion wherein so many perished. What virtue or merits can assure the hearts of the vulgar, when so gracious a prince finds so many revolters?

Let no man look to prosper by rebellion: the very thickets, and stakes, and pits, and wild beasts of the woods shall conspire to the punishment of traitors. Amongst the rest, see how a fatal oak hath singled out the ringleader of this hateful insurrection, and will at once serve for his hangman and gallows by one of those spreading arms snatching him away to speedy execution.

Absalom was comely, and he knew it well enough. His hair was no small piece of his beauty nor matter of his pride. It was his wont to cut it once a year; not for that it was too long, but too heavy: his heart would have borne it longer if his neck had not complained. And now the justice of God hath plaited a halter of those locks. Those tresses had formerly hanged loosely disheveled on his shoulders; now he hangs by them. He had wont to weigh his hair, and was proud to find it so heavy; now his hair poiseth the weight of his body, and makes his burden his torment. It is no marvel if his own hair turned traitor to him who durst rise up against his father. That part which is misused by man to sin is commonly employed by God to revenge. The revenge that it worketh for God makes amends for the offense whereto it is drawn against God. The very beast whereon Absalom sat, as weary to bear so unnatural a burden, resigns over his load to the tree of justice. There hangs Absalom between heaven and earth, as one that was hated and abandoned both of earth and heaven. As if God meant to prescribe this punishment for traitors, Absalom, Ahithophel, and Judas, die all one death. So let them perish that dare lift up their hand against God's anointed!

The honest soldier sees Absalom hanging in the oak, and dares not touch him: his hands were held with the charge of David, *Beware that none touch the young man Absalom*. Joab upon that intelligence sees him, and smites him with no less than three darts. What the soldier forbore in obedience, the captain doth in zeal; not fearing to prefer his sovereign's safety to his command; and more tendering the life of a king and peace of his country than the weak affection of a father. I dare not sit judge betwixt this zeal and that obedience, betwixt the captain and the soldier: the one was a good subject, the other a good patriot; the one loved the king, the other loved David, and out of love disobeyed; the one meant as well as the other sped [acted expediently].

As if God meant to fulfill the charge of his anointed without any blame of his subjects, it pleased him to execute that immediate revenge upon the rebel which would have despatched him without hand or dart. Only the mule and the oak conspired to this execution; but that death would have required more leisure than it was safe for Israel to give, and still life would give hope of rescue. To cut off all fears, Joab lends the oak three darts to help forward so needful a work of justice.

All Israel did not afford so firm a friend to Absalom as Joab had been. Who but Joab had suborned the witty widow of Tekoah, to sue for the recalling of Absalom from his three years' exile? Who but he went to fetch him from Geshur to Jerusalem? Who but he fetched him from his house at Jerusalem, whereto he had been two years confined, to the face, to the lips of David? Yet now he that was his solicitor for the king's favor is his executioner against the king's charge. With honest hearts all respects either of blood or friendship cease in the case of treason. Well hath Joab forgotten himself to be a friend to him who hath forgotten himself to be a son. Even civilly the king is our common father; our country our common mother: nature hath no private relations which should not gladly give place to these. He is neither father, nor son, nor brother, nor friend, that conspires against the common parent. Well doth he who spake parables for his master's son now speak darts to his king's enemy, and pierces that heart which was false to so great a father. Those darts are seconded by Joab's followers, each man tries his weapon upon so fair a mark.

One death is not enough for Absalom: he is at once hanged, shot, mangled, stoned. Justly was he lift up to the oak who had lift up himself against his father and sovereign; justly is he pierced with darts who had pierced his father's heart with so many sorrows; justly is he mangled who hath dismembered and divided all Israel; justly is he stoned who hath not only cursed, but pursued his own parent [cf. Exod. 21:17, Deut. 21:18–21].

Now Joab sounds the retreat, and calls off his eager troops from execution, however he knew what his rebellious countrymen had deserved in following Absalom. Wise commanders know how to put a difference betwixt the heads of a faction and the misguided multitude, and can pity the one while they take revenge on the other.

So did Absalom esteem himself, that he thought it would be a wrong to the world to want the memorial of so goodly a person. God had denied him sons: how just it was that he should want a son who had robbed his father of a son; who would have robbed himself of a father, his father of a kingdom! It had been pity so poisonous a plant should have been fruitful. His pride shall supply nature: he rears up a stately pillar in the king's dale, and calls it by his own name, that he might live in dead stones who could not survive in living issue: and now behold this curious pile ends in a rude heap, which speaks no language but the shame of that carcass which it covers. Hear this, ye glorious fools, that care not to perpetuate any memory of yourselves to the world but of ill-deserving greatness. The best of this affectation is vanity; the worst, infamy and dishonor: whereas, *the memorial of the just shall be blessed* [Prov. 10:7]; and if his humility shall refuse an epitaph, and choose to hide himself under the bare earth, God himself shall engrave his name upon the pillar of eternity.

There now lies Absalom in the pit, under a thousand gravestones, in every of which is written his everlasting reproach. Well might this heap overlive that pillar; for when that ceased to be a pillar, it began to be a heap; neither will it cease to be a monument of Absalom's shame while there are stones to be found upon earth. Even at this day very pagans and pilgrims that pass that way cast each man a stone unto that heap, and are wont to say, in a solemn execration, "Cursed be the parricide Absalom, and cursed be all unjust persecutors of their parents, for ever." Fasten your eyes upon this woeful spectacle, O all ye rebellious and ungracious children, which rise up against the loins and thighs from which ye fell: and know that it is the least part of your punishment that your carcasses rot in the earth, and your name is ignominy: these do but shadow out those eternal sufferings of your souls for your foul and unnatural disobedience.

Absalom is dead. Who shall report to his father? Surely Joab was not so much afraid of the fact as of the message. There are busy spirits that love to carry news, though thankless, though purposeless; such as Ahimaaz, the son of Zadok, who importunately thrust himself into this service. Wise Joab, who well saw how unwelcome tidings must be the burden of the first post, dissuades him in vain. He knew David too well to employ a friend to that errand. An Ethiopian servant was a fitter bearer of such a message than the son of the priest. The entertainment of the person doth so follow the quality of the news, that David could argue afar off, *He is a good man; he cometh with good tidings.* O how welcome deserve those messengers to be that bring us the glad tidings of salvation; that assure us of the foil of all spiritual enemies; and tell us of nothing but victories and crowns and kingdoms! If we think not their feet beautiful [cf. Isa. 52:7], our hearts are foul with infidelity and secure worldliness.

So wise is Ahimaaz grown by Joab's intimation, that, though he outwent Cushi in his pace, he suffers Cushi to outgo him in his tale; cunningly suppressing that part which he knew must be most necessarily delivered and unpleasingly received.

As our care is wont to be where our love is, David's first word is not, "How fares the host?" but *How fares the young man Absalom?* Like a wise and faithful messenger, Cushi answers by an honest insinuation; *The enemies of my lord the king, and all that rise against thee to do thee hurt, be as that young man is;* implying both what was done, and why David should approve it being done. How is the good king thunderstruck with that word of his blackamoor! Who, as if he were at once bereaved of all comfort, and cared not to live but in the name of Absalom, goes and weeps and cries out, *O my son Absalom, my son, my son Absalom! Would God I had died for thee, O Absalom, my son, my son!* What is this we hear? That he whose life Israel valued at ten thousand of theirs should be exchanged with a traitor's? That a good king whose life was sought should wish to lay it down for the preservation of his murderer? The best men have not wont to be the least passionate. But what shall we say to that love of thine, O Savior, who hast said of us wretched traitors, not, *Would God I had died for you;* but, "I will die; I do die; I have died for you"? O love, like thyself, infinite, incomprehensible; whereat the angels of heaven stand yet amazed, wherewith thy saints are ravished. *Turn away thine eyes from me; for they overcome me. O thou that dwellest in the gardens, the companions hearken to thy voice: cause us to hear it* [Song of Songs 6:5, 8:13]; that we may, in our measure, answer thy love, and enjoy it for ever.

CHAPTER FOUR

FREDERICK W. ROBERTSON
(1816–1853)
"Suggestive Preaching"

> We think of God as a Spirit, infinitely removed from and unlike the creatures he has made. But the truth is ... the mind of God is similar to the mind of man. Love does not mean one thing in man, and another thing in God. Holiness, justice, pity, tenderness — these are in the Eternal the same in kind which they are in the finite being. The present manhood of Christ conveys this deeply important truth, that the Divine heart is human in its sympathies.[1]

In his thirteen years of public life, Frederick Robertson never occupied a prominent pulpit, and only one sermon was published during his lifetime; yet within a few years of his death at the age of 37 he was the best-known preacher in the English-speaking world. His sermons (from Trinity Chapel, Brighton) were published on both sides of the Atlantic and went through eleven editions in twelve years; they were carried on shipboard by sailors and quoted by shopkeepers, as well as studied by theologians, preachers, and poets. Wordsworth and Tennyson considered him the most important religious teacher of the century.

Robertson may be the first Anglican preacher who can truly be called "modern." The contemporary note is struck especially by his psychological interest; his exploration of mental states in relation to the spiritual life in some cases puts him well over a century ahead of his time. Nevertheless, descriptions such as "the father of psychological preaching ... the greatest Victorian pulpit artist of the feelings"[2] are misleading. For Robertson never aims at emotional titillation, nor does he reduce Christian doctrines or genuine experience of God to purely psychological phenomena. The Bible is the primary source and checkpoint for all his psychology; it is by listening first to its voices and observing its characters that he comes to such acute insight into states of consciousness. Then through careful exposition he leads his hearers over the same way he has gone, showing how the Scriptures, and especially the narratives of both Testaments, treat the very problems with which they are struggling — doubt, despair, loneliness, disillusionment with the world — and demonstrating that the truths of Scripture provide the only solid grounding for human life.

It may not be too simple to say that Robertson touched his hearers so deeply because he trusted them. That is to say, he trusted their capacity to recognize and respond to essential truths about God and themselves, the capacity he calls "intuition" or "imagination." And so the hallmark of his preaching is a steady and constantly varied appeal to the spiritual sensitivity with which every person is endowed: women and men; rich or poor; educated or not; in youth, maturity, and old age. He specifically addressed different members of his audience, publicly acknowledging their diverse spiritual gifts and needs and thus bringing them to a better understanding of themselves and one another.

This discriminating attention to the spiritual capacity of each person accounts for the enduring value of Robertson's sermons to subsequent generations of preachers, including our own. For he lived at the beginning of an age when, for the first time in history, that capacity is widely doubted or, worse, devalued. The scientific, industrial, and political revolutions of the mid-nineteenth century wrought irreversible changes not only in society but also in human self-understanding. Robertson had the prescience to see the direction of change and the courage to welcome some of its aspects, including the growing democratization of education and political responsibility. But he also saw the acute threat of an impoverished religious imagination, and it was this threat against which he pitted all his teaching. Through his love of contemporary poetry, Robertson brought into the established church the fresh spirit of Romanticism. His remarkable *Lectures on Poetry*, delivered to an audience of 1,000 people, mostly laborers, in his Brighton parish, are the fullest statement of what he saw as the spiritual need of the age; and they address the sensibility of our own time with startling clarity. He begins by answering the (supposed) objection that modern life demands practical instruction — science, chemistry, mechanics — and not poetry: "But it appears to me that, in this age of mechanics and political economy, when every heart seems 'dry as summer dust,' what we want is, not so much, not half so much, light for the intellect, as dew upon the heart; time and leisure to cultivate the spirit that is within us."[3]

It has been fairly suggested that if one is going to read only one

Anglican preacher, it should be Frederick Robertson. The principles he set forth as the basis of his own teaching could well be the starting point for a study of the particular excellence belonging to Anglican preaching at its best:

First. The establishment of positive truth, instead of the negative destruction of error.

Secondly. That truth is made up of two opposite propositions, and not found in a *via media* between the two.

Thirdly. That spiritual truth is discerned by the spirit, instead of intellectually in propositions; and, therefore, Truth should be taught suggestively, not dogmatically.

Fourthly. That belief in the Human character of Christ's Humanity must be antecedent to belief in His Divine origin.

Fifthly. That Christianity, as its teachers should, works from the inward to the outward, and not *vice versa*.

Sixthly. The soul of goodness in things evil.[4]

Robertson's life and sermons are the demonstration of those principles.

Robertson's Life

Frederick Robertson was born in London on February 3, 1816, the eldest of seven children. His father, a captain in the Royal Artillery, retired to Yorkshire on half-pay in order to attend to his children's education. Frederick studied at home for four years before going to the local grammar school; he later spoke of his parents' careful supervision of his education as a particular blessing of his childhood. He had a year of study at a French seminary while the family was in Tours and at 16 entered the New Academy, Edinburgh, where he was an intense and competitive student, taking top honors in Latin verse, English prose, and French, and a second place in Greek.

His was a happy home life, probably the only extended period of serenity Robertson ever knew; and the dispositions developed then were still evident years later in the preacher. The athletic, adventurous child who played at being a knight and hoped for a military career never lost his passionate desire to redress wrongs. The reflective aspect of his nature showed in a love of animals, and especially birds; he began writing his own illustrated natural history book from his observations. Throughout his life, the capacity to be moved by the beauty of the natural world was one of the strongest elements in Robertson's imagination and, accordingly, in his theology. The family practiced an Evangelical piety and leaned to a moderate Calvinism. His father directed him to ministry, against his own longing for a military career. Robertson never lost his admiration for the soldier's life, which he saw as an emblem of what he valued most in Christianity, "the voluntary sacrifice of one for the sake of many."[5] Although there is no question that Robertson found his vocation in the church, he often chafed at what was for him the onerous discipline of enduring a "watering-place ministry."

He matriculated at Oxford in 1837, where he participated in public debate and took a particular interest in the theological controversy that was the center of attention at the university, coming to a position of studied disagreement with the views of the growing High Church movement. Nonetheless, he listened regularly to Newman's sermons at St. Mary's, and his own preaching eventually came to resemble Newman's in carefulness of thought and simple, elegant style.[6] His memories of Oxford were not happy; he found the "donnishness" of the place chilling and later regretted what he considered to be his own lack of mental concentration. He advised a young friend to follow the wisdom he believed that he had learned too late: "Do not aim at too much."[7] But Robertson may well have gained more from his studies than he recognized, for it cannot be said that he lacked intellectual focus after leaving the university. He had formed a love for a few writers, whose companionship soothed him through the loneliness and the physical pain of later years. He read (by his own estimation) few books; but he chose them with care and studied each until he could have taken an examination on it, "never skimming — never turning aside to merely inviting books; and Plato, Aristotle, Thucydides, Sterne, Jonathan Edwards have passed like the iron atoms of my blood into my mental constitution."[8]

He showed the same passion to internalize the Scriptures. While at Oxford, Robertson memorized the entire New Testament, in both Greek and English, as he shaved and dressed. He later said that the practice had ordered his mind like a concordance, so that any given subject or word called forth a list of passages where it occurs. As a curate, he devoted his study chiefly to Hebrew and biblical criticism; he also memorized Dante's *Inferno*. In his mature years, he read little specifically "religious literature," in part because he was wearied by the current theological controversies between and within the two dominant positions, Evangelical and Tractarian.

Yet in a real sense all his reading was theological, for he believed that the world in its every aspect is "manifested Deity";[9] the wonders and beauty we experience here are meant to induce belief in "the reality of invisible Truth and Beauty."[10] So chemistry, for which Robertson had a special love, increased his awe of God; Shakespeare showed him the full range of human nature and taught him to discern "the soul of good in things evil," which became one of the principles of his preaching.[11] When preparing a series of expository sermons on the books of Samuel, Robertson did not read commentaries but rather studied economics, politics, and cultural history, so that he could better relate the truth of Scripture to the social realities of his own day.

He even digested "light reading" into theology. Robertson's comments on the work of the new women novelists (the Bröntes, Margaret Fuller) show his remarkable intellectual range and ability to forecast a line of development. He believed that women were taking the lead in literature by probing matters of conscience which men had treated too "coarsely," thus raising the question that underlies the chief debates of modern theological ethics: "That great question, how far conventional law is to stifle the workings of inclination, and how far inclination — supposing it be sacred and from our higher nature — is justified in bidding it defiance. . . . It is a perilous question, and opens the door for boundless evil as well as good."[12]

Robertson's consistent reading, as a student and through all the years of his ministry, was poetry. Burns and Shelley are for him "Nilometers" to sound the depths of life's most intense moments; Wordsworth measures the more placid ones; Tennyson's mystical poetry reveals the infinite mystery of the soul. The essential value of poetry is religious, for true poetry (as distinct from "verse") speaks of the invisible truths that are the substance of faith. Poetry is "passion rendered imaginative."[13] It awakens and educates our deepest feelings, and thus renders them truly spiritual; for the refined intuition by which we understand poetry is the same faculty whereby we come to know God. Like the biblical writers, the best poets are "the grand levelers" who appeal to our common humanity and vindicate its sacredness.[14] Robertson's *Lectures on Poetry* are themselves an example of poetry's power to "level up," magnifying the dignity of every person. His addresses to the Working Men's Institute are indistinguishable in tone from the *Lecture on Wordsworth* delivered to members of the Brighton Athenaeum; both bespeak an impartial regard for the intellectual and spiritual integrity of his audience that transcends political rancor. Robertson did not escape accusations of being "a revolutionist and a democrat," but many responded to the trust he showed in them; so that ultimately those who feared one another were united in a common love for their teacher, as the marker on his gravestone in Brighton attests: "He awakened the holiest feelings in poor and rich, in ignorant and learned. Therefore is he lamented, as their guide and comforter...."

Almost all of the published sermons and lectures date to his six years in Brighton, where he was incumbent at Trinity Chapel, Brighton, but he previously served in three other parishes. In 1840, following his ordination, he moved as curate into a poor parish in Winchester, where he and the rector immediately faced the gentry's opposition to their plan to build a new church and establish parochial schools. Within a few months, however, he reported that "many of the common people hear us gladly, and some of the upper classes are beginning to manifest curiosity and interest."[15] He devoted much time to training teachers for the Sunday schools, and his method could still provide a model for both clergy and lay leadership: on Sunday he gave them questions on the Epistle for the following week, and then met with them during the week to discuss the answers they had worked out for themselves. He practiced a rigorous rule of life, studying hard, giving all the income he could spare to the poor, and denying himself food and sleep, a discipline that he later came to see as unnatural. As he matured, he understood that personal weakness, like false doctrine, should not be crushed but rather countered by a higher truth or a positive attachment to what is good; he had learned to fight evil, "as Perseus fought with the sea-monster — from above."[16]

After only a year his health broke, due perhaps to the rigors of his asceticism and the death of a much-loved sister. Nonetheless, he looked back on his first curacy as the best time of his ministry: "I am conscious of having developed my mind and character more truly, and with more fidelity, at Winchester than anywhere."[17] To recover, he took a walking trip through the Rhineland and Switzerland; at Geneva he met and shortly thereafter married the Englishwoman Helen Denys. Robertson almost never mentions his wife in his many letters — a curious omission, since he otherwise discloses so much of himself. It is probable that a sense of propriety forbade deep discussion of his experience of marriage. But the paucity of even casual references, as well as some direct comments (in the sermons) about disillusionment, suggest that he and his wife had no real kinship of souls, despite (or because of?) the highly romantic view of women he retained to the end of his life. By contrast, his experience of fatherhood seems to have been rich. Two of his children, Charlie and Ida, lived to adulthood. His letters make frequent mention of his work with his son, whom he educated at home, as his own father had done with him. Moreover, the sermons (especially "Jacob's Wrestling," "The Loneliness of Christ," "The Illusiveness of Life") show a respectful understanding of children's emotional life and spiritual development.

In the summer of 1842, Robertson began a new job in Cheltenham, a moderately fashionable town where the superficiality of social contacts repelled him. He felt that his sermons were unintelligible and his ministry a failure; yet his diary shows long lists of the poor and sick visited, as well as payments made to clear debts for laborers. His happiest times seem to have been two summer holidays spent in rural parishes, which were nearly empty when he came but rapidly filled with farmers and laborers as word of his preaching spread. Despite his own sense of failure, it was in Cheltenham that Robertson became a distinctive preacher. Under the influence of the rector, Archibald Boyd, he prepared carefully, beginning his study on Thursday morning instead of Saturday, as had been his practice at Winchester. He was no longer content with doctrinal discourses or impassioned speeches on the love of God; now he began to do the close exegetical work that provided a foundation for practical instruction on the whole scope of Christian life.

The change in his preaching was the beginning of a move away from Evangelical Christianity. One of Cheltenham's fashions was religious controversy, and Robertson was horrified by the violent agitations of the extreme Evangelicals, who seemed to him to rely on sentiment instead of principle. An extract from a letter written during his first year in Cheltenham indicates his objection to a narrowly Calvinist interpretation of the Gospel:

> The fact is, we have one thing, and only one to do here on earth — to win the character of heaven before we die. This is practical, and simple to understand ... what madness is it to spend our time in speculating about our election! ... As a topic of preaching, I desire to make it very subordinate to the end toward which it converges, the restoration of sinners to the heavenly purity which they have lost.[18]

As this statement suggests, Robertson's principles were those of catholic Christianity as mediated through the English Reformers: the universal efficacy of baptism and the church's absolution of penitents, the essential goodness of the world and the sacredness of ordinary life, the capacity of every person to recognize the fundamental spiritual truths as they are evidenced in Scripture. These principles would seem to have set him at the center of the established church, but the center was not an easy place to occupy in the mid-nineteenth century, and Robertson described himself as "a theological Ishmael," despised by the Tractarians and increasingly suspect to the Evangelicals.[19] The agony of final separation from the Evangelicals came after five years in Cheltenham. Typically for Robertson, it resulted not only from doctrinal difference but also from disappointment in persons: "After finding littleness where I expected nobleness, and impurity where I thought there was spotlessness, again and again I despaired of the reality of goodness."[20] Robertson relied greatly upon his few friends, and the sudden loss of a relationship he had taken to be permanent precipitated a second breakdown in health and the great faith crisis of his life.

A second time he looked to walking and beauty to heal him. In September 1846, he left for the Continent, where he spent six weeks hiking alone in the Tyrol, then another two months in Heidelberg, studying Goethe and Schiller and serving in a local parish. The weeks of radical doubt in the Tyrol had changed him, bringing him to a trust in God "no longer traditional, but of his own."[21] Yet Robertson never put the experience of doubt so far behind him that he could not draw upon it for the sake of others. It gave him a particular sensitivity to the spiritual pain of those who crave certainty of something beyond themselves and this life but are not able to lay hold of it. His sermon "The Doubt of Thomas" is a brilliant example of the encouragement he offered to those struggling to believe: "The honest doubt of Thomas craves a sign as much as the cold doubt of the Sadducee. And a sign shall be mercifully given to the doubt of love which is refused to the doubt of indifference."[22]

Robertson returned to England eager to have his own parish, and he wrote to Bishop Wilberforce of Oxford, who offered him St. Ebbe's, the Evangelical parish he had attended as a student. The position seemed ideally suited to him, with a congregation of students and town-residents, both middle-class and poor. However, difficulties arose in housing his family on the small stipend; and at the same time he was offered the well-paid incumbency of Trinity Chapel, Brighton. He was unwilling to make a decision based largely on finances, nor did he wish to serve in a resort-town; but Wilberforce recommended that he go, and after two months he left Oxford with regret: "So grand an opening for important, but not glittering usefulness, I shall probably never have again."[23]

Brighton was in fact more than a resort-town; it was a microcosm of Victorian England: an intellectual center where social, political, and theological issues were publicly debated; where not only the several religious parties were represented, but also opposition to religion, in the forms of both silent contempt from the wealthy and open rejection by the laborers. Robertson set to work with fervor, determined to spend the few years he rightly believed he had left attempting to realize his vision of the church: a society based upon the practical principles of love as revealed by the Gospel, namely, *sacrifice* for the benefit of others, and *duty*, "to make [one's] brethren free inwardly and outwardly."[24] He understood that full development of the inward life — which is the essence of Christianity — can be achieved only through the convergence of self-rule over the passions and freedom from political oppression.

The European revolutions of 1848 coincided with Robertson's first year in Brighton. Unlike most Anglican clergy, he saw these upheavals as full of hope, showing the relevance of the Bible's own teachings about the just limits of authority and the rights of common people. Accordingly, he chose the book of Samuel for a new series of expository lectures on Sunday afternoons and spent an entire year on a study of Israel's monarchy. An anonymous protest against his "political" sermons forced Robertson to defend himself to the bishop. He concluded his letter thus: "I feel that in dealing with God's truth, a minister of Christ is clear from the charges of presumption if he speak strongly, yet affectionately, of evil or faults in his social superiors. It brings no pleasure with it.... An earnest searching ministry among the rich is very, very saddening work. The rest of my life will be consecrated to the poor."[25] The laborers of Brighton recognized that he had their interests at heart, and at their request he became involved in founding the Workingmen's Institute, which provided regular educational opportunities through lectures, a library, and a reading room.

Robertson could not simply join the ranks of Christian Socialists, for he believed that socialism erred fundamentally in seeking to bind people together on grounds of interest rather than sacrifice. He felt himself to be a misfit in politics as well as theology: "My tastes are with the aristocrat, my principles with the mob."[26] He believed that the discord between a "recoil from vulgarity" and sympathy with the poor marred his usefulness in taking a principled stand on public issues, but it is doubtful if he really appreciated the importance of his own role as mediator. The sermons and lectures reveal Robertson to be a consistent witness to the Gospel message, which neither promises nor demands that class distinctions be erased, but rather asserts the spiritual dignity of every human being, consisting in the capacity to transcend self through love of God. Thus Robertson showed how members of different classes might rise above natural resentments and make complementary contributions to the common life.

Robertson worked quietly and steadily in Brighton. He devoted much time to teaching, holding weekly Bible studies in his home or in the vestry, and preparing confirmands with care. Both the letters and the sermons show him to be a gifted teacher of children, whose method was to guide them patiently while they worked out an idea for themselves. Although his congregation was composed largely of the business class, he kept his vow to the bishop. He regularly visited the poor and showed a special concern for the "invisible" members of Brighton society: prostitutes, prisoners, shopkeepers' assistants who had to work late at night. All these he saw as in different ways victims of a social system that protected the convenience and covered the sins of the wealthy at the expense of the poor.

Preaching was the core of Robertson's ministry, and he gave two sermons each Sunday. The morning sermon was on a passage he chose, rarely from the lectionary. Often he used the case method, analyzing a biblical character, examining the mind of Paul or the Psalmist in order to treat the central matters of faith and doctrine: inspiration, baptism, atonement, doubt, worldliness, and so on. In the afternoon addresses, he worked his way through whole books, choosing those that seemed to match the spiritual and intellectual temper of the age and his particular congregation. After completing Samuel, he moved on to Genesis. The *Notes on Genesis* are a fine example of how Robertson fulfilled his intellectual responsibility as a pastor by dealing honestly with the challenge to faith represented by the brewing crisis over "Bible and biology." He begins by noting the *kind* of truth the text conveys: "Moses had not a scientific message to deliver; but the marvel is this, that there is not one spiritual fact that can be overturned."[27] The spiritual truths he discovers prove to be not only compatible with but indeed reinforced by the new science: for example, that the world reflects a single Intelligence; that it was made good; that the universe as it exists now is different from what it once was; that God works by gradation, "with steady and increasing energy," and by order, "evolving harmony from discord." The crisis over biblical "higher criticism" was far less acute in England than on the Continent, but it is nonetheless interesting to note the lack of trauma with which Robertson adumbrates a rudimentary form of the "documentary hypothesis" that Wellhausen would develop fully a generation after his death. Robertson's good literary sense and close attention to the text led him to note differences of style and discrepancies in detail between the two creation accounts, although he still saw Moses as their compiler. Moreover, his discussion of the complementarity of the different accounts is an excellent example of what contemporary scholars call "a canonical approach" to the final form of the text.[28] He then turned more directly to the problems of congregational life, producing sermon series on Acts and Corinthians; his sermon on Paul's farewell discourse to the Corinthians was almost the last he preached.

Trinity Chapel became crowded on Sundays, and Robertson's fame began to spread through England; but he refused to become a traveling celebrity preacher. While still a student, he had reflected in a letter to his mother that the great danger of popular preaching was its failure to observe "the difference between deeply affecting the feelings and permanently changing the heart."[29] He was rarely convinced that even his preaching at home had more than passing effect. Indeed, he compared the pulpit to the ballroom, French literature, and "irregular life" for exciting an unproductive craving for stimulus on the part of both preacher and audience: "I can only defend it on that which I believe to be the great law of our being, sacrifice — sacrifice for others. You can have little idea of the gloomy thoughts with which I have to struggle on many Sunday evenings."[30]

Robertson took little rest in his few years of mature life, and the letters indicate that he struggled often with depression, a subject he treats with refreshing frankness in the sermons.[31] He did not cultivate melancholy and sought to relieve it with long walks, good reading, and letters in which he poured out his honest feelings; nonetheless, his was not a disposition that lent itself readily to happiness. He was, as he described the Apostle Paul, "all his life a suppressed volcano."[32] Despite his warm affections and strong loyalties, he seems not to have found deep comfort in companionship: "No soul touches another soul except at one or two points; and those chiefly external. . . . In the central deeps of our being we are alone."[33] His own loneliness gave him keen sympathy with the misery of others. A constant theme of the sermons is the Christian duty to do the little we can do for those who are suffering, and especially suffering the anguish of their own sin: namely, represent to them by kind words and actions "God's sympathy and God's pardon," which is the whole message of the Gospel.[34]

But Robertson's sympathy was tempered by his soldier's view of life. He had little patience with those who wallowed in pain rather than learned from it. One story illustrates the bluntness of his pastoral style.

A woman who had recently joined the congregation gave him the account of her sufferings and asked if he had ever heard of a case such as hers. He responded, "Yes, numbers; it is the case of all. Suffering is very common, and so is disappointment"; and further, "I suppose it would not have been very good for you to have had it all your own way." "Then do you think I am better for this blighting succession of griefs?" "I do not know, but I know you ought to be." At that point, he referred her to Wordsworth's poetry.[35]

During the years in Brighton, Robertson's thinking went deep into the mystery of pain, and certainly part of his genius as a theologian was to see the necessary relation between suffering and the invisible Beauty he longed for. He recognized that only a lasting sensitivity to spiritual pain renders us capable of fundamental moral change, that is, able to receive the goodness that comes from God instead of continually projecting outward our own false feelings: "Goodness is better than happiness; and if pain be the minister of goodness, I can see that it is a proof of Love to debar happiness.... I know that the heart, like a wound, must bleed till the wound has cleansed itself by its own blood."[36]

The final year of Robertson's life was dominated by physical pain. He suffered from a disease that caused shooting head pains[37] so severe that he could do little but prepare and preach his sermons. He died on August 15, 1853, the sixth anniversary of his coming to Brighton. The great breach within his religious life seems to have been healed at his deathbed, where he was attended by the incumbent of St. Margaret's Chapel, Brighton, a clergyman noted for his fervent Evangelical piety. It is reported that Robertson's final conversation was about the Atonement. He had sometimes been critical almost to the point of caricature of the Evangelical emphasis on the blood of Christ rather than the moral act of sacrifice. But at the end he seems to have transcended theological controversy with a vision of Truth. Almost his last words were: "I see it all. It is Christ, and only Christ."

Robertson's death fulfilled the prayer he had written in his diary while still a curate at Cheltenham, which expresses the spirit of sacrifice that governed and sanctified his brief, intense ministry:

Bring into captivity every thought to the obedience of Christ. Take what I cannot give: my heart, body, thoughts, time, abilities, money, health, strength, nights, days, youth, age, and spend them in Thy service, O my crucified Master, Redeemer, God. Oh, let not these be mere words! Whom have I in heaven but Thee? and there is none upon earth that I desire in comparison of Thee. My heart is athirst for God, for the living God. When shall I come and appear before God?[38]

Robertson's Preaching

Robertson's ninety-three extant sermons diverge sharply from the topical preaching typical of the Victorian pulpit, its form "artificial as an epic," consisting of proposition and proof based on common experience, often making unabashed appeal to the emotions.[39] By contrast, Robertson begins invariably with the biblical text. His method is the reverse of the practice, as common then as now, of using Scripture *illustratively*, to support an argument derived from external sources. Rather, he reads the text *suggestively*, searching for the basic statements about our humanity implicit or explicit in the text, dwelling on the historical form in which those fundaments are presented in order to anchor contemporary religious experience. The Bible's stories, promises, and mandates, the characters it delineates, and above all the spirit of Christ, toward whom "all the lines of Scripture converge"[40] — from these are derived the hermeneutical principles by which the Christian's experiences are to be interpreted, and the moral principles by which actions are to be judged.

Much of the force of his preaching is in the simplicity and naturalness of the style, which was the perfect vehicle for Robertson's intense earnestness. He spent several days each week bringing his thoughts into a clear order and then preached extemporaneously,[41] usually with no more than a few words on a slip of paper, which he crumpled as his energy rose. His voice was low and penetrating, thrilling "not so much from feeling as from the repression of feeling."[42] The effect was tremendous: a Brighton shoemaker said, "His words haunted you for days and days" — in contrast to the evaporating influence of another contemporary preacher who "would be twenty minutes in finding fine pegs to hang his words on."[43] His words haunted because, unlike the studied rhetoric of the propositional preacher, they set forth simple truths that called imagination into action; but always Robertson left it up to his hearers to determine the appropriate form of their action. He inadvertently described the effect of his sermons in speaking of the books from which he himself most benefited,

> from those that can kindle life within us, and set us thinking, and call conscience into action — not from those that exhaust a subject and

leave it threadbare, but from those that make us feel there is a vast deal more in that subject yet, and send us, as Eli sent Samuel, into the infinite dark to listen for ourselves.[44]

Years after Robertson's death, there were people in Brighton who could quote at length from sermons that had never been published. The sermons could be held in memory because of their tight logical coherence: each develops a single line of thought from first to last, and that line proceeds clearly from the biblical text. The introductions frame the subject with great care, usually in two divisions: the loneliness of Christ and the temper of his solitude, the greatness of God and the greatness of humanity, perversion of great gifts and perversion of the conscience.

Unity and clarity of thought create a building momentum through the sermons, and the conclusions are especially telling examples of the suggestive style. They are never dazzling flights of rhetoric, like Donne's finales; the tone is generally terse, subdued. Sometimes he ends with a question: "And will you dare to say that prayer is no boon at all unless you can reverse the spirit of your Master's prayer, and say, 'Not as Thou wilt, but as I will?' "[45] Sometimes there is a specific charge: "Plant your foot upon reality,"[46] "Get the habit — a glorious one — of referring all to Christ. How did He feel? think? act? So then must I feel, and think, and act."[47] Sometimes it is a simple statement, but not an obvious one: "There is no wretchedness like the wretchedness caused by an undetermined will to those who serve under it."[48] In every case, he offers a challenge that leaves the audience encouraged, yet always with a sober sense of their own responsibility before God. Robertson brings to preaching the wisdom he learned from observing the military life: the way to ennoble ordinary people is, first, show them their duty, and then trust them to do it. This, as he knew, is the same means by which Christ wins the hearts of the redeemed.[49]

Perhaps the single most important factor in Robertson's power is his broad and profound knowledge of the Bible. He is able to find the truth in any one passage and present it simply because he looks at it from a perspective informed by all the Scriptures. Moreover, he is remarkably even-handed in his selection of passages to preach, drawing widely from both testaments. His affinity for Paul was probably nurtured in childhood, and it may be from him that Robertson learned to look for principles: "It is a peculiarity of St. Paul's mind that he never can speak of an act as an isolated thing."[50] The Lectures on the Epistles to the Corinthians could well stand as a model for preaching those texts. Yet

Robertson reached far beyond the "reduced Paulinism" of the typical Evangelical canon.[51] He preached more broadly because his theology was broader, deeply grounded in Creation and Incarnation, in contrast to the Evangelical tendency to a one-sided stress on the Atonement as effecting salvation *from* this world.

Robertson recognized the chief theological problem of the modern age as waning belief in the divinity of Christ and believed that the only solution was not to assert lifeless dogma but to begin as the Gospels do,

> with Christ the Son of Man . . . God's character revealed under the limitations of humanity. . . . Enter into His childhood. Feel with Him when he looked round about Him in anger, when he vindicated the crushed woman from the powerless venom of her ferocious accusers; when He stood alone in the solitary Majesty of Truth in Pilate's judgment-hall; when the light of the Roman soldier's torches flashed on Kedron in the dark night, and He knew that watching was too late; when His heartstrings gave way upon the Cross.[52]

"The Sympathy of Christ" and "The Loneliness of Christ" surely rank among the greatest treatments of the Incarnation in the history of Christian preaching. But Robertson's way is not, like Lancelot Andrewes's, to paint a scene; rather, he "works from the inward to the outward," beginning with the essential traits of the divinely human nature. Of particular interest, from the standpoint of modern theology, is his observation that the heart of Christ "had in it the blended qualities of both sexes." Indeed, "the one great novelty of the Christian revelation" is to show in him the divine nature of "gentleness, and lovingness, and virgin purity," along with — and even exalted above — power and wisdom, which all religions have held to be divine. He saw the recent revival in England of adoration of the Virgin Mother as an attempt (albeit misguided) to correct the long neglect within Christianity of this uniquely revealed truth:

> But so long as the male was looked upon as the only type of God, and the masculine virtues as the only glory of his character, so long the truth was yet unrevealed. This was the state of heathenism. And so long as Christ was only felt as the Divine Man, and not the Divine Humanity, so long the world had only a one-sided truth.[53]

Robertson is a superb narrative preacher because he knows how to work theologically with the two main elements of narrative: character and temporality. His brilliant analysis of character brings something genuinely new, not only to the Gospels but also to the interpretation of Hebrew Scripture: Elijah is a study in religious despondency, Eli "a shy, solitary, amiable ecclesiastic and recluse,"[54] Balaam shows "how a man may be going on uttering fine words, orthodox truths, and yet be rotten at the heart."[55] An acute consciousness of time and the stages of human life enhances the study of character: the story of Eli and Samuel is a story of friendship between childhood and old age; Joseph's forgiveness of his brothers is the spiritual fruit of many years of experience and trial; Ecclesiastes, "the saddest book in the Bible," shows the weariness that comes at the end of a life whose chief aim is pleasure. One of his recurrent themes is the proper use of time, "the solemn inheritance to which every man is born heir, who has a life-rent in this world — a little section cut out of eternity and given us to do our work in."[56] He calls upon his hearers to look at the faces of the elderly and read how they have occupied themselves, well or ill. It is striking how often he turns directly to the youth and urges them to pay attention to their present, irrecoverable opportunities for learning: "Oh! remember every period of human life has its own lesson, and you cannot learn that lesson in the next period."[57]

Robertson takes the innocence of childhood seriously, as a necessary stage in spiritual growth; children "*ought* to see nothing yet but Heaven, and angels ascending and descending."[58] But he is unsentimental about its passing. He has the spiritual guide's gift for making incisive distinctions in fundamental matters; and so he distinguishes between innocence (ignorance of evil) and saintliness, which "is to know evil and good, and prefer good.... We will not mourn over the loss of simplicity, if we have got instead souls indurated [made firm] by experience, disciplined, even by fall, to refuse the evil and choose the good."[59] Self-knowledge is essential, yet Robertson recognizes the corrosive effects of unabsolved guilt and asserts that the church's most essential function is to proclaim God's pardon and make it felt by sinners. "The Restoration of the Erring" and "The Irreparable Past" are probing explorations of the difference between a tormented consciousness of guilt and a healthy one.

"I know the Bible and have lived in it"[60] — Robertson interpreted all events of his own time in light of the biblical story, and therefore he was a severe and accurate critic, with the rare ability to see through the religious caviling that preoccupied so many of his contemporaries. An important example of his ability to bring the language and thought of the Scriptures to bear on a present issue is "The Syndenham Palace, and the Religious Non-Observance of the Sabbath" (one of the few sermons with which he ever expressed satisfaction). Robertson, who had once been a strict Sabbatarian, was now the only Brighton clergyman to oppose the closing of a local entertainment palace on Sunday, for he had come to see that such "observance" penalized the poor. He meets the Sabbatarians on the biblical ground they have chosen, but with a firm grasp of basic principles he turns the argument against them:

> It may be that God has a controversy with this people. It may be, as they say, that our Father will chasten us by the sword of the foreigner. But if He does, and if judgments are in store for our country, they will fall — not because the correspondence of the country is carried on upon the sabbath-day; nor because Sunday trains are not arrested by the legislature; nor because a public permission is given to the working classes for a few hours' recreation on the day of rest — but because we are selfish men; and because we prefer pleasure to duty, and traffic to honor; and because we love our party more than our Church, and our Church more than our Christianity; and our Christianity more than truth, and ourselves more than all. These are the things that defile a nation; but the labor and the recreation of its poor, these are not the things that defile a nation.[61]

Although Robertson lived in a time of religious controversy almost as fierce as that of the seventeenth century, there is surprisingly little polemic in his preaching. Rather than exhausting himself with defense or attack, he aimed exclusively at establishing a clear view of the truth. When he once expressed surprise that he was "so long unmolested, in spite of great grumbling, dissatisfaction, and almost personal hatred," a member of the congregation suggested to him the reason:

> You preach positively instead of negatively; you state truths which they cannot deny...; they can only say it is dangerous, they dare not say it is false...; you set up your truth, and they are dismayed to find, if *that* be true, their view is knocked down, but you did not knock it down.[62]

One of the strong impressions made by Robertson's sermons is confidence in the greatness of God's truth. It is not so fragile that it must be fearfully defended, so small that it can be contained within any theological system. Robertson's sermons on baptism are perhaps the best example of his view that spiritual truth is never a compromise between two positions, but rather comprehends both in order to unite them at a higher level. Thus the view of baptism held by the Church of England and supported by Scripture reconciles the opposing views of the Roman church and modern Calvinism. The Romans correctly maintain that the benefit of baptism belongs to all, against the Calvinist view that it is efficacious only for the elect, and that discerning election is a matter of right feeling or opinion. But they are wrong to say that it *makes* the baptized a child of God. Rather, the sacrament proclaims a fact that already obtains but is effectual only when recognized and lived out. It is a doctrine of baptism that "sanctifies materialism."[63] Against the gnostic spirituality common in his day and recurrent throughout the history of the church, Robertson asserts that the opposite of spirituality is not commitment to the well-being of the material world and love of its beauty, but rather sin.

Truth in its fullness is without bounds; nonetheless, what we need to know of it is within our reach, and the humble heart arrives at truth more readily than does the reason. Robertson's view of the truth shows him to be a wise and encouraging spiritual counselor, who observed the traditional Anglican distinction between essential and nonessential matters of faith:

> If there be any truths which are only appreciable by the acute under-standing, we may be sure at once that these do not constitute the soul's life, nor error in these the soul's death.... Remember how much is certain.... Be assured that there is little to be known here; much to be borne; something to be done.[64]

Robertson offers proof that there is no fundamental dichotomy be-tween the aesthetic and ethical interests of preaching, between appeals to the love of beauty and the desire for justice.[65] When preaching is at its best, the two operate together: the ethical focus providing the firm ground for aesthetics, the aesthetic element not only enlivening ethical discourse but immeasurably heightening our sense of the good, until de-sire attaches to its highest goal, "to see the King in His beauty." A sense of earthly beauty rightly leads to love of what is infinite, opening us to the eternal precisely because even the greatest temporal beauty cannot satisfy, but leaves us still craving and seeking.[66] Robertson's subtle the-ology is in its entirety an exposition of "the illusiveness of life"[67] — of how God inexorably wounds our affections, disappoints our natural an-ticipations and noble ambitions, and only in this way makes us long for the kingdom of heaven, indeed forms it in our souls. His own history offers an illustration: the young man who longed to make bold sacri-fices on the battlefield or in unremitting service to the poor was called instead to the nonheroic life of "the Brighton preacher," yet ultimately found his sainthood in the unpromising circumstances of a middle-class ministry.

Introduction to "Elijah"

In this superb character study, Robertson's acute psychological insight leads him to recognize in bold, energetic Elijah a type of religious despondency. The careful analysis of the causes of despondency and God's treatment of it shows the practical aspect of his pastoral sensitivity: ministry to the dispirited often begins with the simple helps of food and rest. Moreover, he recognizes, doubtless from his own experience, that despondency can be relieved, but probably not eradicated. Indeed, despondency may even be viewed as a spiritual gift, for it makes God necessary. In one of the most striking moves of the sermon, Robertson suggests that the depression born of inactivity is "one of the signatures of man's immortality." It points to the high destiny God intends for each of us; the pressure of that destiny is felt even by those who betray it. Robertson engenders mutual sympathy in his audience by showing that the miserable condition of "having nothing to do" is widespread, proceeding from accidents of widowhood and the single life, affecting the poor and, even more frequently in our "artificial civilization," the rich, who are rather to be pitied than envied.

A distinctive element of Robertson's thought is that God uses nature to soothe the agitated mind. He takes a sacramental view of nature: "The visible universe is the thought of the Eternal, uttered in a word or form in order that it might be intelligible to man."[68] Moreover, the "utterance" of the natural world sometimes speaks for humankind, interpreting our souls more eloquently than we can ever interpret nature, and in that process exalting them. The description of Elijah's spirit rising "with the spirit of the storm" mirrors Robertson's account of his own experience while hiking in the Tyrol, where his depression was healed:

> I wish I could describe one scene, which is passing before my memory this moment, when I found myself alone in a solitary valley of the Alps, without a guide, and a thunderstorm coming on...: the slow, wild wreathing of the vapors round the peaks, concealing their summits, and imparting in semblance their own motion, till each dark mountain form seemed to be mysterious and alive; ... the rising of the flock of choughs, which I had surprised at their feast on carrion, with their red beaks and legs, and their wild, shrill cries, startling the solitude and silence, till the blue lightning streamed at last, and the shattering thunder crashed as if the mountains must give way; and then came the feelings, which in their fullness man can feel but once in life — mingled sensations of awe and triumph, and defiance of danger, pride, rapture, contempt of pain, humbleness, and intense repose, as if all the strife and struggle of

the elements were only uttering the unrest of man's bosom; so that in all such scenes there is a feeling of relief, and he is tempted to cry out exultingly, There! there! all this was in my heart, and it was never said out till now![69]

There is a frank statement of one of Robertson's recurrent themes: "For the most part life is disappointment." Yet he offers genuine encouragement to his audience, as God offered it to Elijah, in the reminder that finally there is no failure for those who act, not out of the expectation of personal success, but out of earnest desire to do the tasks that have been given them. Robertson understood that the only assured result of noble action is the attainment of noble character; and further (a point in which he anticipates modern psychology) that the most effective influence on others is exercised unconsciously, as "the aggregate result of our whole character."

ELIJAH

Preached at Trinity Chapel, Brighton, on October 13, 1850

But he himself went a day's journey into the wilderness, and came and sat down under a juniper-tree; and he requested for himself that he might die; and said, It is enough; now, O Lord, take away my life; for I am not better than my fathers.

— 1 KINGS 19:4

It has been observed of the holy men of Scripture that their most signal failures took place in those points of character for which they were remarkable in excellence. Moses was the meekest of men, but it was Moses who "spake unadvisedly with his lips" [Ps. 106:33]. St. John was the apostle of charity; yet he is the very type to us of religious intolerance, in his desire to call down fire from heaven [Luke 9:54]. St. Peter is proverbially the apostle of impetuous intrepidity, yet twice he proved a craven. If there were anything for which Elijah is remarkable, we should say it was superiority to human weakness. Like the Baptist, he dared to arraign and rebuke his sovereign: like the commander who cuts down the bridge behind him, leaving himself no alternative but death or victory, he taunted his adversaries the priests of Baal, on Mount Carmel, making them gnash their teeth and cut themselves with knives, but at the same time insuring for himself a terrible end, in case of failure, from his exasperated foes. And again, in his last hour, when he was on his way to a strange and unprecedented departure from this world — when the whirlwind and flame-chariot were ready, he asked for no human companionship. The bravest men are pardoned if one lingering feeling of human weakness clings to them at the last, and they desire a human eye resting on them — a human hand in theirs — a human presence with them. But Elijah would have rejected all. In harmony with the rest of his lonely severe character, he desired to meet his Creator alone. Now it was this man — so stern, so iron, so independent, so above all human weakness — of whom it was recorded that in his trial-hour he gave way to a fit of petulance and querulous despondency to which there is scarcely found a parallel. Religious despondency, therefore, is our subject.

I. The Causes of Elijah's Despondency

1. Relaxation of Physical Strength

On the reception of Jezebel's message, Elijah flies for his life — toils on the whole day — sits down under a juniper-tree, faint, hungry, and travel-worn; the gale of an Oriental evening, damp and heavy with languid sweetness, breathing on his face. The prophet and the man give way. He longs to die: you cannot mistake the presence of causes in part purely physical.

We are fearfully and wonderfully made [cf. Ps. 139:14]. Of that constitution, which in our ignorance we call union of soul and body, we know little respecting what is cause and what is effect. We would fain believe that the mind has power over the body, but it is just as true that the body rules the mind. Causes apparently the most trivial: a heated room — want of exercise — a sunless day — a northern aspect — will make all the difference between happiness and unhappiness, between faith and doubt, between courage and indecision. To our fancy there is something humiliating in being thus at the mercy of our animal organism. We would fain find nobler causes for our emotions. We talk of the hiding of God's countenance, and the fiery darts of Satan. But the picture given here is true. The body is the channel of our noblest emotions as well as our sublimest sorrows.

Two practical results follow. First, instead of vilifying the body, complaining that our nobler part is chained down to a base partner, it is worth recollecting that the body too is the gift of God, in its way divine — "the temple of the Holy Ghost"; and that to keep the body in temperance, soberness, and chastity, to guard it from pernicious influence, and to obey the laws of health, are just as much religious as they are moral duties; just as much obligatory on the Christian as they are on a member of a Sanitary Committee. Next, there are persons melancholy by constitution, in whom the tendency is incurable; you cannot exorcise the phantom of despondency. But it is something to know that it is a phantom, and not to treat it as a reality — something taught by Elijah's history, if we only learn from it to be patient, and wait humbly the time and good pleasure of God.

2. Want of Sympathy

"I, even I only, am left." Lay the stress on *only*. The loneliness of his position was shocking to Elijah. Surprising this: for Elijah wanted no sympathy in a far harder trial on Mount Carmel. It was in a tone of triumph that he proclaimed that he was the single, solitary prophet of the Lord, while Baal's prophets were four hundred and fifty men.

Observe, however, the difference. There was in that case an opposition which could be grappled with: here there was nothing against which mere manhood was availing. The excitement was past, the chivalrous look of the thing gone. To die as a martyr, yes, that were easy, in grand failure; but to die as a felon — to be hunted, caught, taken back to an ignominious death — flesh and blood recoiled from that.

And Elijah began to feel that popularity is not love. The world will support you when you have constrained its votes by a manifestation of power, and shrink from you when power and greatness are no longer on your side. "I, even I only, am left."

This trial is most distinctly realized by men of Elijah's stamp and placed under Elijah's circumstances. It is the penalty paid by superior mental and moral qualities, that such men must make up their minds to live without sympathy. Their feelings will be misunderstood, and their projects uncomprehended. They must be content to live alone. It is sad to hear such appeal from the present to the judgment of the future. Poor consolation! Elijah has been judged at that bar. We are his posterity: our reverence this day is the judgment of posterity on him. But to Elijah what is that now? Elijah is in that quiet country where the voice of praise and the voice of blame are alike unheard. Elijah lived and died alone; once only the bitterness of it found expression. But what is posthumous justice to the heart that ached *then*? What greater minds like Elijah's have felt intensely, all we have felt in our own degree. Not one of us but what has felt his heart aching for want of sympathy. We have had our lonely hours, our days of disappointment, and our moments of hopelessness – times when our highest feelings have been misunderstood, and our purest met with ridicule. Days when our heavy secret was lying unshared, like ice upon the heart. And then the spirit gives way: we have wished that all were over – that we could lie down tired, and rest like the children, from life – that the hour was come when we could put down the extinguisher on the lamp, and feel the last grand rush of darkness on the spirit.

Now, the final cause of this capacity for depression, the reason for which it is granted us, is that it may make God necessary. In such moments it is felt that sympathy beyond human is needful. Alone, the world against him, Elijah turns to God. "It is enough: now, *O Lord.*"

3. Want of Occupation

As long as Elijah had a prophet's work to do, severe as that work was, all went on healthily; but his occupation was gone. Tomorrow and the day after, what has he left on earth to do? The misery of having nothing to do proceeds from causes voluntary or involuntary in their nature. Multitudes of our race, by circumstances over which they have no control – in single life or widowhood – in straitened circumstances – are compelled to endure lonely days, and still more lonely nights and evenings. They who have felt the hours hang so heavy can comprehend part of Elijah's sadness.

This misery, however, is sometimes voluntarily incurred. In artificial civilization certain persons exempt themselves from the necessity of work. They eat the bread which has been procured by the sweat of the brow of others – they skim the surface of the thought which has been ploughed by the sweat of the brain of others. They are reckoned the favored ones of fortune, and envied. Are they blessed? The law of life is, in the sweat of thy brow thou shalt eat bread. No man can evade that law with impunity. Like all God's laws, it is its own executioner. It has strange penalties annexed to it: would you know them? Go to the park, or the esplanade, or the solitude after the night of dissipation, and read the penalties of being useless, in the sad, jaded, listless countenances — nay, in the very trifles which must be contrived to create excitement artificially. Yet these very eyes could, dull as they are, beam with intelligence: on many of those brows is stamped the mark of possible nobility. The fact is, that the capacity of ennui is one of the signatures of man's immortality. It is his very greatness which makes inaction misery. If God had made us only to be insects, with no nobler care incumbent on us than the preservation of our lives, or the pursuit of happiness, we might be content to flutter from sweetness to sweetness, and from bud to flower. But if men with souls live only to eat and drink and be amused, is it any wonder if life be darkened with despondency?

4. Disappointment in the Expectation of Success

On Carmel the great object for which Elijah had lived seemed on the point of being realized. Baal's prophets were slain — Jehovah acknowledged with one voice — false worship put down. Elijah's life-aim, the transformation of Israel into a kingdom of God, was all but accomplished. In a single day all this bright picture was annihilated.

Man is to desire success, but success rarely comes. The wisest has written upon life its sad epitaph — "All is vanity," that is, nothingness.

The tradesman sees the noble fortune for which he lived, every coin of which is the representative of so much time and labor spent, squandered by a spendthrift son. The purest statesmen find themselves at last neglected, and rewarded by defeat. Almost never can a man look back on life and say that its anticipations have been realized. For the most part life is disappointment, and the moments in which this is keenly realized are moments like this of Elijah's.

II. God's Treatment of It

1. First he recruited his servant's exhausted strength. Read the history. Miraculous meals are given — then Elijah sleeps, wakes, and eats: on the strength of that goes forty days' journey. In other words, like a wise physician, God administers food, rest, and exercise, and then, and not till then, proceeds to expostulate; for before, Elijah's mind was unfit for reasoning. Persons come to the ministers of God in seasons of despondency; they pervert with marvelous ingenuity all the consolation which is given them, turning wholesome food into poison. Then we begin to perceive the wisdom of God's simple homely treatment of Elijah, and discover that there are spiritual cases which are cases for the physician rather than the divine.

2. **Next Jehovah calmed his stormy mind by the healing influences of nature.** He commanded the hurricane to sweep the sky, and the earthquake to shake the ground. He lighted up the heavens till they were one mass of fire. All this expressed and reflected Elijah's feelings. The mode in which nature soothes us is by finding meeter and nobler utterance for our feelings than we can find in words — by expressing and exalting them. In expression there is relief. Elijah's spirit rose with the spirit of the storm. Stern, wild defiance — strange joy — all by turns were imaged there. Observe, "God was not in the wind," nor in the fire, nor in the earthquake. It was Elijah's stormy self reflected in the moods of the tempest, and giving them their character.

Then came a calmer hour. Elijah rose in reverence — felt tenderer sensations in his bosom. He opened his heart to gentler influences, till at last out of the manifold voices of nature there seemed to speak, not the stormy passions of the man, but the "still small voice" of the harmony and the peace of God.

There are some spirits which must go through a discipline analogous to that sustained by Elijah. The storm-struggle must precede the still small voice. There are minds which must be convulsed with doubt before they can repose in faith. There are hearts which must be broken with disappointment before they can rise into hope. There are dispositions which, like Job, must have all things taken from them before they can find all things again in God. Blessed is the man who, when the tempest has spent its fury, recognizes his Father's voice in its under-tone, and bares his head and bows his knee, as Elijah did. To such spirits, generally those of a stern rugged cast, it seems as if God had said, "In the still sunshine and ordinary ways of life you cannot meet me, but like Job, in the desolation of the tempest, you shall see my form, and hear my voice, and know that your Redeemer liveth."

3. Besides, God made him feel the earnestness of life. What *doest* thou here, Elijah? Life is for doing. A prophet's life for nobler doing — and the prophet was not doing, but moaning.

Such a voice repeats itself to all of us, rousing us from our lethargy, or our despondency, or our protracted leisure, "What doest thou here?" here in this short life. There is work to be done — evil put down — God's Church purified — good men encouraged — doubting men directed — a country to be saved — time going — life a dream — eternity long — one chance, and but one forever. What *doest thou* here?

Then he went on farther: "Arise, go on thy way." That speaks to us: on thy way. Be up and doing; fill up every hour, leaving no crevice or craving for a remorse, or a repentance to creep through afterwards. Let not the mind brood on self; save it from speculation, from those stagnant moments in which the awful teachings of the spirit grope into the unfathomable unknown, and the heart torments itself with questions which are insoluble except to an active life. For the awful future becomes intelligible only in the light of a felt and active present. Go, return on thy way if thou art desponding — *on thy way;* health of spirit will return.

4. He completed the cure by the assurance of victory; "Yet have I left me seven thousand in Israel who have not bowed the knee to Baal." So, then, Elijah's life had been no failure after all. Seven thousand at least in Israel had been braced and encouraged by his example, and silently blessed him, perhaps, for the courage which they felt. In God's world for those that are in earnest there is no failure. No work truly done — no word earnestly spoken — no sacrifice freely made, was ever made in vain. Never did the cup of cold water given for Christ's sake lose its reward.

We turn naturally from this scene to a still darker hour and more august agony. If ever failure seemed to rest on a noble life, it was when the Son of Man, deserted by his friends, heard the cry which proclaimed that the Pharisees had successfully drawn the net round their divine victim. Yet from that very hour of defeat and death there went forth the world's life — from that very moment of apparent failure there proceeded forth into the ages the spirit of the conquering cross. Surely if the cross says anything, it says that apparent defeat is real victory, and that there is a heaven for those who have *nobly and truly* failed on earth.

Distinguish, therefore, between the real and the apparent. Elijah's apparent success was in the shouts of Mount Carmel. His real success was in the unostentatious, unsurmised obedience of the seven thousand who had taken his God for their God.

This is a lesson for all: for teachers who lay their heads down at night sickening over their thankless task. Remember the power of *indirect* influences: those which distill from a life, not from a sudden, brilliant effort. The former never fail, the latter often. There is good done of which we can never predicate the when or where. Not in the flushing of a pupil's cheek, or the glistening of an attentive eye; not in the shining results of an examination does your real success lie. It lies in that invisible influence on character which he alone can read who counted the seven thousand nameless ones in Israel.

For ministers, again — what is ministerial success? Crowded churches — full aisles — attentive congregations — the approval of the religious world — much impression produced? Elijah thought so; and when he found out his mistake, and discovered that the applause on Carmel subsided into hideous stillness, his heart well-nigh broke with disappointment. Ministerial success lies in altered lives and obedient humble hearts: unseen work recognized in the judgment-day.

What is a public man's success? That which can be measured by feast-days and the number of journals which espouse his cause? Deeper, deeper far must he work who works for eternity. In the eye of that, nothing stands but gold — real work: all else perishes.

Get below appearances, below glitter and show. Plant your foot upon reality. Not in the jubilee of the myriads on Carmel, but in the humble silence of the hearts of the seven thousand, lay the proof that Elijah had not lived in vain.

Introduction to
"The Message of the Church to Men of Wealth"

Robertson preached this sermon as a guest preacher in a London series addressed to the working classes. It brought him unwanted notoriety: the press accused him of preaching "democratic principles" and associated him with the Christian Socialist movement of F. D. Maurice and Charles Kingsley. Robertson, in fact, opposed popular socialism on the grounds that it glossed over the real Christian challenge, namely for the transformation of human nature:

> Whether the soil of the country and its capital shall remain the property of the rich, or become more available for the poor, the rich and the poor remaining as selfish as before — whether the selfish rich shall be able to keep, or the selfish poor to take, is a matter, religiously speaking, of profound indifference.[70]

The sermon on David and Nabal is a fine example of Robertson's sophisticated social analysis, which proceeds from his understanding of the biblical text; indeed, he supports his observations so firmly with biblical exposition that the offensive theme must be heard. The innovative aspect of his exegesis is that David, traditionally the type of the pious person or the righteous monarch, is here treated as a laborer — not an ideal figure, but one who demonstrates both the inherent dignity of that class and the temptation to violence which the present social system fosters. Robertson's sympathy with the working classes stemmed from his focus on the earthly life of Christ, who was born to labor. His sermons are complementary to Dickens's novels in portraying, sympathetically but without romance, the difficulties of working-class life: "It is sorrow to be looking for employment; it is sorrow, often and often it is sorrow, to be doing it, sick or well, languid or vigorously fresh; when the head is aching and the heart is sick, still the laboring man must be up and doing."[71] Yet he also asserts that there is a blessing in labor, a health of body and mind often lacking in the "luxurious, pampered few" who escape its rigor. This blessing itself confers upon the working classes a spiritual strength and responsibility toward others, even the rich, corresponding to the obligations conferred upon the wealthy by their education and material privilege.

THE MESSAGE OF THE CHURCH
TO MEN OF WEALTH

Preached at St. John's Church, Fitzroy Square, London,
on June 15, 1851

And Nabal answered David's servants, and said, Who is David? and who is the son of Jesse? There be many servants nowadays that break away every man from his master. Shall I then take my bread, and my water, and my flesh that I have killed for my shearers, and give it unto men, whom I know not whence they be?

                    —1 SAMUEL 25:10, 11

I have selected this passage for our subject this evening, because it is one of the earliest cases recorded in the Bible in which the interests of the employer and the employed, the man of wealth and the man of work, stood, or seemed to stand, in antagonism to each other.

It was a period in which an old system of things was breaking up, and the new one was not yet established. The patriarchal relationship of tutelage and dependence was gone, and monarchy was not yet in firm existence. Saul was on the throne but his rule was irregular and disputed. Many things were slowly growing up into custom which had not yet the force of law; and the first steps by which custom passes into law from precedent to precedent are often steps at every one of which struggle and resistance must take place.

The history of the chapter is briefly this: Nabal, the wealthy sheep-master, fed his flocks in the pastures of Carmel. David was leader of a band of men who got their living by the sword on the same hills: outlaws, whose excesses he in some degree restrained, and over whom he retained a leader's influence. A rude irregular honor was not unknown among those fierce men. They honorably abstained from injuring Nabal's flocks. They did more: they protected them from all harm against the marauders of the neighborhood. By the confession of Nabal's own herdsmen, "they were a wall unto them both by night and day, all the time they were with them keeping their flocks."

And thus a kind of right grew up: irregular enough, but sufficient to establish a claim on Nabal for remuneration of these services; a new claim, not admitted by him: reckoned by him an exaction, which could be enforced by no law: only by that law which is above all statute-law, deciding according to emergencies — an indefinable instinctive sense of fairness and justice. But as there was no law, and each man was to himself a law, and the sole arbiter of his own rights, what help was there but that disputes should rise between the wealthy proprietors and their self-constituted champions, with exaction and tyranny on the one side, churlishness and parsimony on the other? Hence a fruitful and ever-fresh source of struggle: the one class struggling to take as much, and the other to give as little as possible. In modern language, the Rights of Labor were in conflict with the Rights of Property.

The story proceeds thus: David presented a demand, moderate and courteous enough (vs. 6, 7, 8). It was refused by Nabal, and added to the refusal were those insulting taunts of low birth and outcast condition which are worse than injury, and sting, making men's blood run fire. One court of appeal was left. There remained nothing but the trial by force. "Gird ye on," said David, "every man his sword."

Now observe the fearful, hopeless character of this struggle. The question had come to this: whether David, with his ferocious and needy six hundred mountaineers, united by the sense of wrong, or Nabal, with his well-fed and trained hirelings, bound by interest and not by love to his cause, were stronger? Which was the more powerful — want whetted by insult, or selfishness pampered by abundance; they who wished to keep by force, or they who wished to take? An awful and uncertain spectacle, but the spectacle which is exhibited in every country where rights are keenly felt, and duties lightly regarded — where insolent demand is met by insulting defiance. Wherever classes are held apart by rivalry and selfishness, instead of drawn together by the law of love — wherever there has not been established a kingdom of heaven, but only a kingdom of the world — there exist the forces of inevitable collision.

I. The Causes of This False Social State

Ia. False Basis on Which Social Superiority Was Held to Rest

Throughout Nabal's conduct was built upon the assumption of his own superiority. He was a man of wealth. David was dependent on his own daily efforts. Was not that enough to settle the question of superiority and inferiority? It was enough on both sides for a long time, till the falsehood of the assumption became palpable and intolerable. But palpable and intolerable it did become at last.

A social falsehood will be borne long, even with considerable inconvenience, until it forces itself obtrusively on men's attention, and can be endured no longer. The exact point at which *this* social falsehood, that wealth constitutes superiority, and has a right to the subordination of inferiors, becomes intolerable, varies according to several circumstances. The evils of poverty are comparative – they depend on climate. In warm climates, where little food, no fuel, and scanty shelter are required, the sting is scarcely felt till poverty becomes starvation. They depend on contrast. Far above the point where poverty becomes actual famine, it may become unbearable if contrasted strongly with the unnecessary luxury and abundance enjoyed by the classes above. Where all suffer equally, as men and officers suffer in an Arctic voyage, men bear hardship with cheerfulness: but where the suffering weighs heavily on some, and the luxury of enjoyment is out of all proportion monopolized by a few, the point of reaction is reached long before penury has become actual want: or again, when wealth or rank assumes an insulting, domineering character – when contemptuous names for the poor are invented, and become current among the more unfeeling of a wealthy class – then the falsehood of superiority can be tolerated no longer: for we do not envy honors which are meekly borne, nor wealth which is unostentatious.

Now it was this which brought matters to a crisis. David had borne poverty long – nay, he and his men had long endured the contrast between their own cavern-homes and beds upon the rock, and Nabal's comforts. But when Nabal added to this those pungent biting sneers which sink into poor men's hearts and rankle – which are not forgotten, but come out fresh in the day of retribution – "Who is David? and who is the son of Jesse? There be many servants nowadays that break away every man from his master," then David began to measure himself with Nabal; not a wiser man – nor a better – nor even a stronger. Who is this Nabal? Intellectually, a fool; morally, a profligate, drowning reason in excess of wine at the annual sheep-shearing; a tyrant over his slaves – overbearing to men who only ask of him their rights. Then rose the question which Nabal had better not have forced men to answer for themselves. By what right does this possessor of wealth lord it over men who are inferior in no one particular?

Now observe two things.

1. An apparent inconsistency in David's conduct. David had received injury after injury from Saul, and had only forgiven. One injury from Nabal, and David is striding over the hills to revenge his

wrong with naked steel. How came this reverence and irreverence
to mix together?

We reply. Saul had a claim of authority on David's allegiance;
Nabal only one of rank. Between these the Bible makes a vast difference. It says, The *powers* which be are ordained of God. But
upper and *lower*, as belonging to difference in property, are fictitious terms: true, if character corresponds with titular superiority;
false if it does not. And such was the difference manifested in the
life of the Son of God. To lawful authority, whether Roman, Jewish,
or even priestly, he paid deference; but to the titled mark of conventional distinction, none. "Rabbi, Rabbi," was no divine authority
[cf. Matt. 23:78]. It was not power, a delegated attribute of God —
it was only a name. In Saul, therefore, David reverenced one his
superior in authority; but in Nabal he only had before him one surpassing him in wealth. And David refused, somewhat too rudely, to
acknowledge the bad, great man as his superior: would pay him
no reverence, respect, or allegiance whatever. Let us mark that distinction well, so often confused — kings, masters, parents: here is
a power ordained of God. Honor it. But wealth, name, title, distinctions, always fictitious, often false and vicious, if you can claim
homage for these separate from worth, you confound two things
essentially different. Try that by the test of his life. Name the text
where Christ claimed reverence for wealth or rank. On the Mount
did the Son of Man bow the knee to the majesty of wealth and
wrong, or was his sonship shown in this, that he would not bow
down to that as if of God?

2. This great falsehood respecting superior and inferior rested on
a truth. There had been a superiority in the wealthy class once. In
the patriarchal system wealth and rule had gone together. The father
of the family and tribe was the one in whom proprietorship was cen-
tered; but the patriarchal system had passed away. Men like Nabal
succeeded to the patriarch's wealth, and expected the subordination which had been yielded to patriarchal character and position;
and this when every particular of relationship was altered. Once the
patriarch was the protector of his dependents. Now David's class
was independent, and the protectors, rather than the protected:
at all events, able to defend themselves. Once the rich man was
ruler in virtue of paternal relationship. Now wealth was severed from
rule and relationship: a man might be rich, yet neither a ruler, not
a protector, nor a kinsman. And the fallacy of Nabal's expectation

consisted in this, that he demanded for wealth that reverence which had once been due to men who happened to be wealthy.

It is a fallacy in which we are perpetually entangled. We expect reverence for that which was once a symbol of what was reverenced, but is reverenced no longer. Here in England it is common to complain that there is no longer any respect of inferiors towards superiors — that servants were once devoted and grateful, tenants submissive, subjects enthusiastically loyal. But we forget that servants were once protected by their masters, and tenants safe from wrong only through the guardianship of their powerful lords; that thence a personal gratitude grew up; that now they are protected by the law from wrong by a different social system altogether; and that the individual bond of gratitude subsists no longer. We expect that to masters and employers the same reverence and devotedness shall be rendered which were due to them under other circumstances, and for different reasons; as if wealth and rank had ever been the claim to reverence, and not merely the accidents and accompaniments of the claim — as if anything less sacred than holy ties could purchase sacred feelings — as if the homage of free manhood could be due to gold and name — as if to the mere Nabal-fool who is labeled as worth so much, and whose signature carries with it so much coin, the holiest and most ennobling sensations of the soul, reverence and loyalty, were due by God's appointment.

No. That patriarchal system has passed forever. No sentimental wailings for the past, no fond regrets for the virtues of a by-gone age, no melancholy, poetical, retrospective antiquarianism can restore it. In church and state the past *is* past: and you can no more bring back the blind reverence, than the rude virtues of those days. The day has come in which, if feudal loyalty or patriarchal reverence are to be commanded, they must be won by patriarchal virtues or feudal real superiorities.

Ib. Cause of This Unhealthy Social State: A False Conception Respecting Rights

It would be unjust to Nabal to represent this as an act of willful oppression and conscious injustice. He did what appeared to him fair between man and man. He paid his laborers. Why should he pay anything beyond stipulated wages?

David's demand appeared an extravagant and insolent one, provoking unfeigned astonishment and indignation. It was an invasion of his rights. It was a dictation with respect to the employment of that which was his own. "Shall I then take my bread, and my water, and my flesh that I have killed for my shearers, and give it unto men whom I know not whence they be?"

Recollect, too, there was something to be said for Nabal. This view of the irresponsible right of property was not *his* invention. It was the view probably entertained by all his class. It had descended to him from his parents. They were prescriptive and admitted rights on which he stood. And however false or unjust a prescriptive right may be, however baseless when examined, there is much excuse for those who have inherited and not invented it; for it is hard to see through the falsehood of any system by which we profit, and which is upheld by general consent, especially when good men too uphold it. Rare indeed is that pure-heartedness which sees with eagle glance through conventionalisms. This is a wrong, and I and my own class are the doers of it.

On the other hand, David and his needy followers were not slow to perceive that they had their rights over that property of Nabal's.

Men on whom wrongs press are the first to feel them, and their cries of pain and indignation are the appointed means of God to direct to their wrongs the attention of society. Very often the fierce and maddened shriek of suffering is the first intimation that a wrong exists at all.

There was no law in Israel to establish David's claims. This guardianship of Nabal's flocks was partly a self-constituted thing. No bargain had been made, no sum of reward expressly stipulated. But there is a law besides and above all written law, which gives to written laws their authority, and from which so often as they diverge, it is woe to the framers of the law: for their law must perish, and the eternal law unseen will get itself acknowledged as a truth from heaven or a truth from hell — a truth begirt with fire and sword, if they will not read it except so.

In point of fact, David had a right to a share of Nabal's profits. The harvest was in part David's harvest, for without David it never could have been reaped. The sheep were in part David's sheep, for without David not a sheep would have been spared by the marauders of the hills. Not a sheaf of corn was carried to Nabal's barn, nor a night passed in repose by Nabal's shepherds, but what told of the share of David in the saving of that sheaf, and the procurement of that repose (not the less real because it was past and unseen). The right which the soldier has by law to his pay was the right which David had by unwritten law — a right resting on the fact that his services were indispensable for the harvest.

Here, then, is one of the earliest instances of the rights of labor coming into collision with the rights of property: rights shadowy, undefined, perpetually shifting their boundaries, varying with every case, altering with every age, incapable of being adjusted except rudely by law, and leaving always something which the most subtle and elaborate law can not define, and which in any moment may grow up into a wrong.

Now when it comes to this, rights against rights, there is no determination of the question but by overwhelming numbers or blood. David's remedy was a short, sharp, decisive one. "Gird ye on every man his sword." And it is difficult, for the sake of humanity, to say to which side in such a quarrel we should wish well. If the rich man succeed in civil war, he will bind the chain of degradation more severely and more surely for years, or ages, on the crushed serf. If the champions of popular rights succeed by the sword, you may then await in awe the reign of tyranny, licentiousness, and lawlessness. For the victory of the lawless, with the memory of past wrongs to avenge, is almost more sanguinary than the victory of those who have had power long, and whose power had been defied.

We find another cause in circumstances. Want and unjust exclusion precipitated David and his men into this rebellion. It is common enough to lay too much weight on circumstances. Nothing can be more false than the popular theory that ameliorated outward condition is the panacea for the evils of society. The Gospel principle begins from within, and works outward.

The world's principle begins with the outward condition, and expects to influence inwardly. To expect that by changing the world without, in order to suit the world within, by taking away all difficulties and removing all temptations, instead of hardening the man within against the force of outward temptation — to adapt the lot to the man, instead of molding the spirit to the lot, is to reverse the Gospel method of procedure. Nevertheless, even that favorite speculation of theorists, that perfect circumstances will produce perfect character, contains a truth. Circumstances of outward condition are not the sole efficients in the production of character, but they are efficients which must not be ignored. Favorable condition will not produce excellence, but the want of it often hinders excellence. It is true that vice leads to poverty: all the moralizers tell us that, but it is also true that poverty leads to vice.

There are some in this world to whom, speaking humanly, social injustice and social inequalities have made goodness impossible. Take, for instance, the case of these bandits on Mount Carmel. Some of them were outlawed by their own crimes, but others doubtless by debts not willfully contracted — one at least, David, by a most unjust and unrighteous persecution. And these men, excluded, needy, exasperated by a sense of wrong, untaught outcasts, could you gravely expect from them obedience, patience, meekness, religious resignation? Yes, my brethren, that is exactly the marvelous impossibility people do most inconsistently expect; and there are no bounds to their astonishment if they do not get what they expect: superhuman honesty from starving men, to whom life by hopelessness has become a gambler's desperate chance! chivalrous loyalty and high forbearance from creatures to whom the order of society has presented itself only as an unjust system of partiality! We forget that forbearance and obedience are the very last and highest lessons learned by the spirit in its most careful training. By those unhallowed conventionalisms through which we, like heathens, and not like Christians, crush the small offender and court the great one — that damnable cowardice by which we banish the seduced and half admire the seducer — by which, in defiance of all manliness and all generosity, we punish the weak and tempted, and let the tempter go free — by all these we make men and women outcasts, and then expect from them the sublimest graces of reverence and resignation!

II. The Message of the Church to the Man of Wealth

The message of the Church contains those principles of life which, carried out, would, and hereafter will, realize the divine order of society. The revealed message does not create the facts of our humanity — it simply makes them known. The Gospel did not make God our Father, it authoritatively reveals that he is so. It did not create a new duty of loving one another, it revealed the old duty which existed from eternity, and must exist as long as humanity is humanity. It was no "new commandment," but an old commandment which had been heard from the beginning.

The Church of God is that living body of men who are called by him out of the world, not to be the inventors of a new social system, but to exhibit in the world by word and life, chiefly by life, what humanity is, was, and will be, in the idea of God. Now so far as the social economy is concerned, the revelations of the Church will coincide with the discoveries of a scientific political economy. Political economy discovers slowly the facts of the immutable laws of social well-being. But the living principles of those laws, which cause them to be obeyed, Christianity has revealed to loving hearts long before. The Spirit discovers them to the spirit. For instance, political economy, gazing on such a fact, as this of civil war, would arrive at the same principles which the Church arrives at. She too would say: Not selfishness, but love. Only that she arrives at these principles by experience, not intuition — by terrible lessons, not revelation — by revolutions, wars, and famines, not by spiritual impulses of charity.

And so because these principles were eternally true in humanity, we find in the conduct of Abigail towards David in this early age, not explicitly, but implicitly, the very principles which the church of Christ has given to the world; and more — the very principles which a sound political economy would sanction. In her reply to David we have the anticipation by a loving heart of those duties which selfish prudence must have taught at last.

The spiritual dignity of man as man. Recollect David was the poor man, but Abigail, the high-born lady, admits his worth: "The Lord will certainly make my lord a sure house; because my lord fighteth the battles of the Lord, and evil hath not been found in thee all thy days." Here is a truth revealed to that age. Nabal's day, and the day of such as Nabal, is past; another power is rising above the horizon. David's cause is God's cause. Worth does not mean what a man is worth — you must find some better definition than that.

Now this is the very truth revealed in the Incarnation. David, Israel's model king, the king by the grace of God, not by the conventional rules of human choice — is a shepherd's son. Christ, the King who is to reign over our regenerated humanity, is humbly born — the poor woman's son. That is the Church's message to the man of wealth, and a message which it seems has to be learned afresh in every age. It was new to Nabal. It was new to the men of the age of Christ. In his day they were offended in him, because he was humbly born. "Is not this the carpenter's son?" [Matt. 13:55]. It is the offense now. They who retain those superstitious ideas of the eternal superiority of rank and wealth have the first principles of the Gospel yet to learn. How can they believe in the son of Mary? They may honor him with the lip, they deny him in his brethren. Whoever helps to keep alive that ancient lie of upper and lower, resting the distinction not on official authority or personal worth, but on wealth and title, is doing his part to hinder the establishment of the Redeemer's kingdom.

Now the church of Christ proclaims that truth in baptism. She speaks of a kingdom here in which all are, as spirits, equal. She reveals a fact. She does not affect to create the fact. She says — not hypothetically, "This child *may* be the child of God if prevenient grace has taken place, or if hereafter he shall have certain feelings and experiences"; nor, "Hereby I create this child magically by supernatural power in one moment what it was not a moment before": but she says, authoritatively, "I pronounce this child the child of God: the brother of Christ the first-born — the son of him who has taught us by his son to call him *our* father, not *my* father. Whatever that child may become hereafter in fact, he is now, by right of creation and redemption, the child of God. Rich or poor, titled or untitled, he shares the spiritual nature of the second Adam — the Lord from heaven."

The second truth expressed by Abigail was the law of sacrifice. She did not heal the grievance with smooth words. Starving men are not to be pacified by professions of good will. She brought her two hundred loaves, and her two skins of wine, her five sheep ready dressed, etc. A princely provision!

You might have said this was waste — half would have been enough. But the truth is, liberality is a most real economy. She could not stand there calculating the smallest possible expense at which the affront might be wiped out. True economy is to pay liberally and fairly for faithful service. The largest charity is the best economy. Nabal had had a faithful servant. He should have counted no expense too great to retain his services, instead of cheapening and depreciating them. But we wrong Abigail if we call this economy or calculation. In fact, had it been done on economical principles, it would have failed. Ten times this sum from Nabal would not have arrested revenge. For Nabal it was too late. Concessions extracted by fear only provoke exaction further. The poor know well what is given because it must be given, and what is conceded from a sense of justice. They *feel* only what is real. David's men and David felt that these were not the gifts of a sordid calculation, but the offerings of a generous heart. And it won them — their gratitude — their enthusiasm — their unfeigned homage.

This is the attractive power of that great law, whose highest expression was the cross. "I, if I be lifted up, will draw all men unto me." Say what you will, it is not interest, but the sight of noble qualities and true sacrifice, which commands the devotion of the world. Yea, even the bandit and the outcast will bend before that as before a divine thing. In one form or another, it draws all men, it commands all men.

Now this the Church proclaims as part of its special message to the rich. It says that the divine death was a sacrifice. It declares that death to be the law of every life which is to be like his. It says that the law, which alone can interpret the mystery of life, is the self-sacrifice of Christ. It proclaims the law of his life to have been this: "For their sakes I devote (sanctify) myself, that they also may be devoted through the truth."

In other words, the self-sacrifice of the Redeemer was to be the living principle and law of the self-devotion of his people. It asserts that to be the principle which alone can make any human life a true life. "I fill up that which is behind of the afflictions of Christ in my flesh, for his body's sake, which is the Church." We have petrified *that* sacrifice into a dead theological dogma, about the exact efficacy of which we dispute metaphysically, and charge each other with heresy. That atonement will become a living fact only when we humbly recognize in it the eternal fact that sacrifice is the law of life. The very mockers at the crucifixion unwittingly declared the principle: "He saved others; himself he cannot save" [Matt. 27:42, Mark 15:31]. Of course — how could he save himself who had to save others? You can only save others when you have ceased to think of saving your own soul; you can only truly bless when you have done with the pursuit of personal happiness. Did you ever hear of a soldier who saved his country by making it his chief work to secure himself? And was the captain of our salvation to become the Savior by contravening that universal law of sacrifice, or by obeying it?

Brother men, the early Church gave expression to that principle of sacrifice in a very touching way. They had all things in common. "Neither said any of them that aught of the things which he possessed was his own" [Acts 4:32]. They failed, not because they declared that, but because men began to think that the duty of sharing was compulsory. They proclaimed principles which were unnatural, inasmuch as they set aside all personal feelings, which are part of our nature too. They virtually compelled private property to cease, because he who retained private property when all were giving up was degraded, and hence became a hypocrite and liar, like Ananias.

But let us not lose the truth which they expressed in an exaggerated way: "Neither said any of them that aught of the things which he possessed was his own." Property is sacred. It is *private* property; if it were not, it could not be sacrificed. If it were to be shared equally by the idle and the industrious, there could be no love in giving. Property is the rich man's own. Nabal is right in saying, My bread — my water — my flesh. But there is a higher right which says, It is not yours. And that voice speaks to every rich man in one way or another, according as he is selfish or unselfish: coming as a voice of terror or a voice of blessing. It came to Nabal with a double curse, turning his heart into stone with the vision of the danger and the armed ranks of David's avengers, and laying on David's soul the sin of intended murder. It came to the heart of Abigail with a double blessing: blessing her who gave and him who took.

To the spirit of the cross alone we look as the remedy for social evils. When the people of this great country, especially the rich, shall have been touched with the spirit of the cross to a largeness of sacrifice of which they have not dreamed as yet, there will be an atonement between the rights of labor and the rights of property.

The last part of the Church's message to the man of wealth touches the matter of rightful influence. Very remarkable is the demeanor of David towards Nabal, as contrasted with his demeanor towards Abigail. In the one case, defiance, and a haughty self-assertion of equality; in the other, deference, respect, and the most eloquent benediction. It was not therefore against the wealthy class, but against individuals of the class, that the wrath of these men burned.

See, then, the folly and the falsehood of the sentimental regret that there is no longer any reverence felt towards superiors. There *is* reverence to superiors, if only it can be shown that they are superiors. Reverence is deeply rooted in the heart of humanity — you cannot tear it out. Civilization — science — progress — only change its direction: they do not weaken its force. If it no longer bows before crucifixes and candles, priests and relics, it is not extinguished towards what is truly sacred and what is priestly in man. The fiercest revolt against false authority is only a step towards submission to rightful authority. Emancipation from false lords only sets the heart free to honor true ones. The freeborn David will not do homage to Nabal. Well, now go and mourn over the degenerate age which no longer feels respect for that which is above it. But behold — David has found a something nobler than himself. Feminine charity — sacrifice and justice — and in gratitude and profoundest respect he bows to that. The state of society which is coming is not one of protection and dependence, nor one of mysterious authority, and blind obedience to it, nor one in which any class shall be privileged by divine right, and another remain in perpetual tutelage; but it is one in which unselfish services and personal qualities will command, by divine right, gratitude and admiration, and secure a true and spiritual leadership.

Oh, let not the rich misread the signs of the times, or mistake their brethren: they have less and less respect for titles and riches, for vestments and ecclesiastical pretensions, but they have a real respect for superior knowledge and superior goodness: they listen like children to those whom they believe to know a subject better than themselves. Let those who know it say whether there is not something inexpressibly touching and even humbling in the large, hearty, manly, English reverence and love which the working-men show towards those who love and serve them truly, and save them from themselves and from doing wrong. See how David's feelings gush forth: "Blessed be the Lord God of Israel which sent thee this day to meet me: and blessed be thy advice, and blessed be thou which hast kept me this day from coming to shed blood, and from avenging myself with mine own hand."

The rich and the great may have that love if they will.

To conclude. Doubtless David was wrong: he had no right even to redress wrongs thus; patience was his divinely appointed duty; and doubtless in such circumstances we should be very ready to preach submission and to blame David. Alas! We, the clergy of the Church of England, have been only too ready to do this: for three long centuries we have taught submission to the powers that be, as if that were the only text in Scripture bearing on the relations between the ruler and the ruled. Rarely have we dared to demand of the powers that be, justice; of the wealthy man and the titled, duties. We have produced folios of slavish flattery upon the divine right of power. Shame on us! We have not denounced the wrongs done to weakness: and yet for one text in the Bible which requires submission and patience from the poor, you will find a hundred which denounce the vices of the rich — in the writings of the noble old Jewish prophets, *that*, and almost that only — *that*, in the Old Testament, with a deep roll of words that sound like Sinai thunders: and *that* in the New Testament in words less impassioned and more calmly terrible from the apostles and their master: and woe to us in the great day of God, if we have been the sycophants of the rich instead of the redressers of the poor man's wrongs — woe to us if we have been tutoring David into respect to his superior, Nabal, and forgotten that David's cause, not Nabal's, is the cause of God.

CHAPTER FIVE

HENRY PARRY LIDDON
(1829–1890)
"The Responsibility of Revealed Religion"

We *can* believe, if we are not predisposed morally against belief. This is one reason why faith is made so much of in the New Testament; it is a test of our moral fidelity to natural light. For nothing are we more responsible than for the duty of preparing the way of the Lord in the soul by making a clean sweep of all those dispositions which indispose us to receive Him.[1]

Henry Parry Liddon belonged to two worlds: the university at Oxford and the metropolis of London. Coming to Oxford the year following Newman's departure to enter the Church of Rome, he was impressed by John Keble's preaching and profoundly changed by a personal relationship with Edward Pusey which was to be the dominant influence of his adult life. Liddon spent more than fifty years as student and teacher at Oxford, where he drew large crowds to lectures on biblical topics and aligned himself firmly, with Pusey, against the "destructive criticism" of the Bible coming from the Continent. Yet Liddon's heart was first of all in preaching rather than the scholarly work his mentor encouraged.

As spiritual guide, Liddon exercised an influence over young men at Oxford comparable to that of Newman a generation before; probably no other preacher addressed so clearly the deep tension between the life of faith and the modern intellectual climate. But for all his intellectual acumen, Liddon had a breadth of scope and a common touch that his great predecessor lacked, and his most important role was as preacher for the new phenomenon of the metropolis. During the last twenty years of his life, Liddon spent three months each year resident at No. 3 Amen Court in St. Paul's Cathedral Close. As senior canon, he was instrumental in bringing the cathedral back from near dereliction and establishing it as the preaching center of the English Church, thus inaugurating the worldwide renewal of cathedral worship. Liddon attracted as many as 4,000 listeners to hear closely argued sermons more than an hour in length. It is a graceful irony that this doctrinal conservative, a professor tinged with sacerdotalism, should yet have been so alive to the cultural currents of modernism that he was able to speak powerfully to the multitudes who felt the difficulty of upholding the apostolic faith against that stream.

His genius lay in using the language of the Bible to identify plainly the moral and spiritual dimensions of the problems his listeners faced. Liddon's contemporaries often remarked on the "loftiness" of his preaching. But it was not the loftiness of one oblivious to the concerns of ordinary people; Liddon was able to treat great themes because Scripture had lifted him high enough to gain an accurate perspective on the moral life. The extraordinary vividness of his sermons stems from the conviction that our world is in all essential respects continuous with that of the Bible, and that its revelation is intended for our practical benefit. Accordingly, despite his rigorous logic, he made no attempt to translate the thought of the Bible into the categories of modern rationalism. Rather, he clarified the language and concepts of the Bible for those whose scope was dangerously narrowed by the excessive claims of rationalism, which hindered them in reckoning with the moral realities Scripture treats. In an age of fashionable skepticism, Liddon argued against the illogic of confining eternal truth within the limits of human experience and rational proof.

In 1877, the young priest Francis Paget, later bishop of Oxford, presented an afternoon sermon at St. Paul's. He recounts that Liddon's only comment was across the door of the cab as they parted: " 'Good night,' he said, in the quiet penetrating voice which his friends can never forget — 'Good night: I dare say you will come in time to know what people really need.' "[2] Liddon's own preaching proceeded entirely from his conviction that what people really need is careful, practical exposition of Christian dogma as it is revealed through Scripture, so that they may be strengthened against the hours of temptation and of death. The history of the Church in the last century has shown the prescience of his consistent message: when the Church ceases to assert the claims of revealed religion, far from gaining credence, it merely forfeits its capacity for effective action.

Liddon's Life

Henry Parry Liddon was born on August 20, 1829, the eldest surviving child of ten; the family home was in Devonshire. His father Matthew, a captain in the Royal Navy, had served as second-in-command to Commo. Edward Parry in the 1819 attempt to discover the Northwest Passage, although the voyage so injured Captain Liddon's health that he gave up active service. Liddon's mother Ann was a voracious reader, well versed in English, French, and Italian literature, who held a strong Evangelical faith. The other strong adult influence on the boy came from his aunt and godmother, Louisa Liddon. She, too, was highly intelligent and deeply religious, and Henry later named her as the person who had loved him most and whom he had most loved in his life. He never married, and all his life he remained close to his family, especially his sisters; with one of them, Mrs. Ambrose, he shared his London home for twenty years.

Although as a young man Liddon was offered a military commission, he seems never to have intended any work but the ministry. He began composing sermons at the age of 14, under the influence of the virulently anti-Roman local vicar, on such standard Evangelical topics as "Reading the Scriptures" and "Preparation for Judgment." In 1844, he began to attend King's College School, London. A schoolmate later recalled of him:

> As a schoolboy I always thought he looked just what he did as a priest. There was the same expression of sweet, somewhat fatherly, somewhat melancholy interest. He would reprove, exhort, advise boys just as a young priest does in his own congregation. We expected it of him, and it never seemed to us to be in any way stepping out of his own business when he gave one of us a lecture or a sharp rebuke. . . . He was entirely a priest among boys.[3]

In October 1846, Liddon went to Oxford and became resident at Christ Church, where he would retain his status as Student (resident scholar) for the rest of his life. He was a good, but not outstanding, student in classics; in his leisure he enjoyed music, conversation, and long walks with friends. Shortly after coming to Oxford, Liddon was drawn toward the High Church movement. Moved by Keble's sermons, he soon made Pusey's acquaintance and became a regular visitor in his home. Rumors circulated among the students about candlelit Compline services in Liddon's room.

Whether or not the rumors were true (Oxford was highly suspicious of "papal aggression" in the aftermath of Newman's departure), Liddon was never an ardent ritualist. Rather, what he admired in Pusey, and learned from him, was devotion to the language of Scripture. Pusey's reverent philological work contrasted with the growing ranks of those for whom biblical scholarship was an end in itself, as though "God had become Incarnate in order to aid the sale of their grammars and dictionaries."[4] In a memorial address given after nearly forty years of friendship, Liddon observed that to visit him was "to move out of the world into another atmosphere, where the language of the Bible was translated into reality . . . where the unseen was reckoned for more than the seen; and where all persons and events were looked at from a distant and higher point of view."[5] Inadvertently, Pusey was a great force in Liddon's formation as a preacher, for he taught him the theological importance of language: "Language is the original gift of the soul, projected into the world of sound. . . . In it may be studied the minute anatomy of the soul's life — that inner world in which thought takes shape and conscience speaks, and the eternal issues are raised and developed in their final form."[6]

After completing his studies, Liddon had to wait two years to be ordained; during that time he read theology, worked as a tutor, and traveled to Scotland and the Continent. The highlight of the trip was three weeks spent in Rome, where he had an audience with Pius IX and was pressed hard by a monsignor to join the Roman Church. The monsignor's inference of infidelity distressed him, but it also served to clarify his allegiance to the English Church. Although some years later he acknowledged that "there are many features in the Roman Catholic Church which are much more in harmony with my mind and soul than the corresponding features of our own Church," he was unable to accept the doctrine of papal infallibility. The position to which Newman had moved — "Rome or nothing" — seemed to him unwarranted by the facts of history, and further, designed to "drive more men of our time into sheer unbelief than we can contemplate without a shudder."[7]

In December 1852, Liddon was ordained deacon and began a curacy at Wantage. Soon he began preaching extempore, following the excellent advice of Pusey: "Know accurately what you should say; pray for God's Holy Spirit; say nothing about which you doubt, nothing rashly. Labor for accurate thought altogether, that you may not overstate anything."[8] But Liddon was never physically strong, and within a few months his health broke under the strain of hard study combined with the demands of parish life.

In August 1854, he was appointed vice-principal of the new theological college that Bishop Wilberforce had built on his palace grounds at the village of Cuddesdon, six miles from Oxford. Liddon's high-church tendencies aroused immediate panic in the diocese; even before the appointment had been fixed, he was required to write the bishop a lengthy assurance that he would not indiscriminately commend private confession to the students. But Wilberforce's hope in founding the college was to correct "the want of clerical tone, and of religious habits" he saw among university-educated clergy; and for this job he had chosen well. Liddon's academic lectures may have gone over the heads of many students, but his chapel addresses and spiritual guidance were singularly effective in promoting "earnestness of life," especially among the unsophisticated. The firmly regulated devotional system, based on the Eucharist, the Daily Office, and meditation, is still in place today.

It is likely that Liddon was effective in preparing young men for ministry because his own devotional life was both disciplined and completely without affectation. All his life he was rigorous in saying the Daily Office and often used the Lesser Hours; when he speaks of prayer, one senses that it was indeed for him "not an effort but an atmosphere."[9] The essence of religion is "the establishment and maintenance of a real bond" between the soul and God.[10] In "The Priest in His Inner Life," an essay addressed chiefly to young clergy, Liddon speaks perceptively about the burdensome incompatibility they must feel between their own souls and the language of the Prayer Book. The means for eliminating this incompatibility is meditation, by which the soul comes "to feel at home" with the language of Scripture and especially the devotional language of the Psalms. Liddon outlines the procedure for "systematic meditation upon dogmatic truth" in a few pages that may be among the best brief practical guides for meditation ever written. Liddon's own failed curacy made him fully realistic about the unprecedented demands the modern world places on clergy; he speaks to those who must measure out their prayer time in minutes rather than hours. Meditation draws upon every faculty — memory, imagination, intellect, and affection — in bringing the soul to apprehend the most important truth about human life, namely that "man was made for God."[11] The fruit of meditation is "collectedness," which extends the atmosphere of prayer so that every facet of the priest's ministry — pastoral visits, celebration of the Eucharist, spontaneous prayer and speech, and even the time normally wasted on train platforms and going from one house to the next — may be consecrated to God's purposes.

During four years at Cuddesdon, Liddon managed to keep a number of wavering students from joining the Roman Church. With his usual practicality and bluntness, he advised one to go home, study five hours a day, pray resolutely, and avoid indulging in "that sickly feeling." He also weathered opposition from visiting bishops who decried the chapel's "gaudy" appearance, with its cross over the altar, white and green altar cloths, and painted murals. Liddon agreed to make the changes the bishops required and even gave up celebrating before the altar (rather than at one end), although he regarded this as a concession on a point of doctrine. But the final storm came when, in December 1858, a student precipitately left to be received into the Roman Church. Diocesan clergy demanded Liddon's resignation, which Wilberforce reluctantly accepted, after failing to win Liddon to his view on the proper training of ordinands: "He pressed me on *the* point of Eucharistic Adoration."[12] Years later, Liddon referred to leaving Cuddesdon as "the only great disappointment of my life."[13]

The following year, as vice-principal at St. Edmund Hall, Liddon began working with undergraduates. He began an open series of Sunday evening lectures. Seven men attended his first lecture on the Epistle to Hebrews, but steadily he had to find larger rooms to accommodate the crowd, until finally he was lecturing to 400 at Christ Church Hall. He had hoped that the position would give him time to work on the commentary on the Pastoral Epistles which he had undertaken as a battle waged on two fronts: against the "Negative Criticism" coming from Germany and also against the narrow interpretation of catholic faith afforded by popular evangelism. But a diary entry from 1860 reveals that Liddon regularly subordinated scholarly work to his chief vocation of the priestly cure of souls. He set forth the following questions for self-examination:

1. Do I endeavor to teach my pupils the Religion of our Lord more earnestly and constantly than anything else?
2. Do I walk and talk with them as often as possible with this view?
3. Do I conscientiously prepare my Lectures?
4. Do I allow the work of the Hall to interfere with
   (1) The Commentary.
   (2) Midday prayer.
   (3) Sympathy for old Cuddesdon men.
   (4) Spiritual reading.[14]

In this period, Liddon's reputation as a preacher also grew. Wilberforce regularly assigned him a place in the Lenten sermon series in Oxford; in 1860, he gave forty-two sermons in different places throughout England, in addition to preaching at the Hall Chapel. Two serious attacks of illness made him resign from the Hall in November 1862; he moved into the rooms at Christ Church College which he would retain until his death. Life remained full with sermons (his diary records occasions when 2,000 were present), theological research for the bishop of Oxford, and service as examining chaplain to the bishop of Salisbury; but now he had plenty of time for study and for conversation with undergraduates.

The same year he listed his "motives for exerting myself at Oxford to save souls and in the Commentary"; most telling are "the Day of Judgment — account of time" and "the weakness of the Church cause."[15] The sense of urgency that informs all Liddon's writings is perhaps one trace of his Evangelical upbringing, but it also reflects his accurate perception of how drastically theology and the spiritual life of ordinary people were affected by the changing intellectual atmosphere of modern Europe. He saw that theological scholarship was largely moving away from the task of providing practical moral guidance that had occupied it for eighteen centuries. His reaction against "negative criticism" of the Bible was undoubtedly too vehement; he did not distinguish with sufficient care between discussion of literary history and the challenges to the Bible's essential truth claims. So, for example, he failed to see that accepting a Hellenistic date for the book of Daniel does not necessitate the conclusion that it is "not merely an uninspired book, but a dishonest one." Yet, a century after the nearly universal triumph of historical criticism in the academy, it appears that Liddon was right in his observation that "theology . . . may be so handled as to lose altogether its grace and purpose. It may be resolved into the arid study of ancient texts, or into an almost mechanical play upon a set of propositions, while He, Whose living presence alone gives life and animation to all, is really lost sight of."[16]

He noted sadly the prominence of "commercial considerations" and the concomitant loss of genuine intellectual leadership within the university: "Oxford is more and more a great shop, trading on the tastes of the British public, abandoning to public prejudices its own best traditions, but in turn feeling that it cannot trifle with the general tastes of its customer."[17] Perceiving a subtle but mounting hostility to religion, he wished to see theological study separated out altogether, so that the Church's colleges could do their work without compromise.

Yet despite his distaste for "Oxford Liberal calculations," Liddon never withdrew from the life of the university, as Newman had done even while still preaching weekly at St. Mary. Membership in the Dante Society was one of Liddon's greatest pleasures; he took a personal interest in the undergraduates and often met with them for informal chats over coffee. He was a marvelous storyteller; one fellow-Student recalled that "he was for many of us the life of the Christ Church Common Room."[18] But the world outside the university also interested him profoundly. He loved music, architecture, and painting; he understood children and played hard at their games; he regarded natural beauty as "sacramental" and on seaside holidays would wedge himself into the rocks to say his prayers, sometimes shouting out psalms and chants against a storm.

Of Liddon's written work, the only piece of sustained theological argument is *The Divinity of Our Lord*, delivered as the Bampton Divinity Lecture Sermons of 1866. The eight lectures were designed as an extension of Liddon's pulpit ministry, for they develop at length the point he takes up again and again in the sermons: namely, that revealed truth is essential to the moral life. He sought to counter the newly fashionable view "that there is some sort of necessary opposition between dogma and goodness."[19] Liddon struck a responsive chord; the lectures were delivered to huge crowds and subsequently went through numerous printed editions. Liddon's last work, completed just a month before his death, was to write the preface to the fourteenth edition.

In 1868 Liddon declined the presidency of the new undergraduate college founded in memory of John Keble, believing that he lacked the command of history and philosophy necessary to lead the battle against secular humanism. Two years later, he finally accepted official responsibilities exactly suited to his gifts. In 1870, he was appointed both senior canon at St. Paul's and Ireland Professor of Exegesis. He lived in Oxford during the academic year and spent the summer months — late April through August — in London. The beginning of a new era at St. Paul's was marked by two changes: restoration of daily Eucharist and moving the evening preaching service from the choir to the nave. The beautiful building was not designed for preaching, and Liddon had to shout at the top of his voice to be heard. Nonetheless, people came in crowds drawn across a broad theological spectrum, from all strata of society, from every part of the city, and even (in large numbers) from the suburbs. A colleague later described Liddon's preaching as

> the personal factor by which the claim of St. Paul's to become once more a wide spiritual home for London could make itself heard and felt over the hearts of large multitudes. . . . No one could suppose the changes in the Services and Ritual at St. Paul's were superficial, or formal, or of small account, so long as that voice rang on, like a trumpet, telling of righteousness and temperance and judgment, preaching ever and always, with personal passion of belief, Jesus Christ and Him crucified.[20]

Liddon was proud of St. Paul's, and frequently he spent Saturday afternoons leading parties of tourists through it. He developed a particular concern for the choir boys, in both their spiritual and physical welfare. He tried to teach them reverence and spoke to them honestly about the deficiencies he perceived in his own devotion. Many of the children boarded away from home in unsupervised situations and earned their living by singing in music halls; Liddon was instrumental in building a choir house to provide the protection and education they needed.

Crises over ritual recurred periodically, especially during his early years at St. Paul's. The first was the most doctrinally serious. In 1871, when Archbishop Tait proposed that use of the Athanasian Creed be discontinued, Liddon threatened to retire from the Church of England and made a rare address to a public meeting (with 3,000 in attendance!) in order to argue his position. After more than a year of controversy, the creed was allowed to stand, unaltered, in the Book of Common Prayer. But the troubles with Tait were not over. In 1874, when Disraeli became prime minister, he introduced the antiritualist Public Worship Regulation Bill to Parliament. It passed, and a number of priests were persecuted and even served lengthy jail sentences for such infractions as celebrating from an eastward position with lighted candles, mixing water with the wine, and making the sign of the cross. Although Liddon was not personally threatened, he grieved deeply for the suffering clergy; again, he addressed a large public meeting on their behalf. During another outbreak of "popular Puritanism" in 1877, the Privy Council declared vestments to be illegal, but by this time Liddon was more sanguine: "I cannot think that in the long run this violent contempt for history and language will really succeed."[21]

In an 1872 sermon at St. Mary's, Oxford, Liddon articulated the view of controversy that enabled him to engage in so many battles in defense of orthodoxy without succumbing to crankiness:

The controversies of our day may do us lasting harm, if they lead us to adhere to our own opinions only because they are our own...and weaken by dividing moral forces which, when united, are none too strong to cope successfully with the energies of evil around us. But, if we should have received in any degree the high and rare grace of an intrepid loyalty to know truth allied to a really unselfish spirit, we too may "take up serpents, and if we drink any deadly thing it shall not hurt" us [Mark 16:18]. Nay, more — to be forced back upon the central realities of the faith which we profess; to learn to know and feel, better than ever before, what are the convictions which we dare not surrender at any cost; to renew the freshness of an early faith, which affirms within us, clearly and irresistibly, that the one thing worth thinking of, worth living for, if need were, worth dying for, is the unmutilated faith of Jesus Christ our Lord — these may be the results of inevitable differences, and, if they are, they are blessings indeed.[22]

Despite Liddon's conservatism on dogmatic issues, the London press often described him as a Liberal. While he rejected many implications of that term, it is true that Liddon's breadth of scope was in some ways better suited to the city than to the rarefied atmosphere of the university. He was not afraid to preach on political subjects and joined a number of Dissenting clergy in opposition to England's support for the Turks in the Bulgarian uprising of 1875–76. He wisely treated the situation as a problem of justice rather than religious conflict. With respect to the question of Disestablishment, which became more vexed after the Irish Church was disestablished in 1868, he openly acknowledged that he saw some advantage to it, for "our real danger lies in the direction of attempts to save the Church from Disestablishment and Disendowment by 'Liberalizing' — that is, destroying — what it has of fixed doctrine and discipline."[23] In the last year of his life he followed with painful interest the London dockworkers' strike and contributed eagerly to their strike fund.

Moreover, Liddon was a natural ecumenist, genuinely interested in the religious views of others, both Christians and non-Christians. During a two-month tour of Russia with C. L. Dodgson (Lewis Carroll) in 1867, he had been impressed by the exuberant devotion of the people and saw the Eastern Church as a force "to which I believe there is no moral parallel in the West."[24] During the Bulgarian uprising he went to Eastern Europe to offer succor but also to explore the possibility of reunion with the Eastern Church. His friends in England included rabbis, Dissenters, Roman Catholics, and (perhaps most remarkable) Anglicans whose views departed almost entirely from his own (for example,

Dean Stanley of Westminster). Liddon's patience with difference is to be distinguished from the easy relativism that has no concept of absolute truth, for it was based on confidence that God's purpose would be achieved: "The Church is Catholic enough to make us sure that she will one day be literally more so; holy enough, to satisfy us that Christ is in the midst of her. These 'notes' will be completed one day, and meanwhile we wait, in patience."[25]

The year 1882 saw great change: Pusey died in September, and Liddon resigned his professorship in order to write his mentor's biography. Only apprehension of Pusey's displeasure had restrained him from retiring long before, for he felt that he was no longer able to exercise significant influence. He had lost his seat on the university's Hebdomadal Council in 1873; and his lectures, formerly addressed to a full hall, now attracted a handful of students. But Liddon was far too punctilious to serve as biographer, and probably too personally involved. He assembled more than 100 bound volumes of letters and papers, many of which he recopied from his mentor's nearly illegible hand, as well as another fifty volumes of letters received, and bundles of reference material. Much time was devoted to writing lengthy analyses of early sermons and other works. Some felt that Pusey's *Life* hastened Liddon's death; the biography was published posthumously, in four volumes.

The time devoted to the *Life* is perhaps the signal instance of Liddon's unusual freedom to choose his work without regard for institutional constraints. For all his gifts, he never held a position of foremost responsibility in either church or university. Although several times promoted for bishop (including the See of London),[26] he was never offered a position he felt he could accept. Even as professor he chose his lecture topics freely and did not have to prepare students for general examinations. Yet in one way this enviable freedom may have worked to his detriment. As a friend of many decades observed, he "escaped the discipline of insuperable difficulties and of dependence upon others which, while it brings indeed its own temptations, is none the less a safeguard of the exercise of judgment."[27] One can imagine that closer confinement within institutional life might have moderated Liddon's tendency to extrapolate along a single line of logic in defense of first principles and perhaps saved him from the increasing intellectual isolation that saddened his final years.

In 1885 Liddon began to suffer disabling head pain, in addition to his normal rheumatism. His doctors prevailed on him to spend the winter and spring in Egypt and the Holy Land.[28] Liddon has been described as "a tourist *sub specie aeternitatis*" — the ideal traveler, for whom culti-vated associations only increase childlike wonder. In the diary he kept from schooldays on, he carefully recorded notes about history, scenery, geography, and geology, as well as anecdotes and conversations, which he would later dramatize for friends and students. Liddon's sermons on Old Testament texts in particular show that the language and scenery of the Bible had long had special vividness for him, but his enthusiasm increased yet more:

> Our Lord seems to have sanctioned the aesthetic principle by deigning to choose so beautiful a neighborhood for some of the great scenes of His life on earth. . . . I wonder how I can have let so many years pass by without making a great effort to see spots, compared with which the interest of all else on earth is tame indeed.[29]

He was a devout but far from gullible tourist. Based on his reckonings about the locations of Jerusalem's walls at the time of Jesus, he astutely reckoned that the newly touted "Garden Tomb" was indeed a fake — as archaeologists agree today. Liddon made a point of meeting with Or-thodox leaders in Cairo and Jerusalem, and these interviews made him critical of England's "missionary" efforts in the Levant. He saw the van-ity of the Church Missionary Society's profession of Christian unity, at the same time that it ignored Muslims and attempted to win Christians over from the Eastern Church. The appointment of an English bishop to Jerusalem he regarded as presumptuous and insulting.

The last year of his life was embittered by the controversy surround-ing publication (in November 1889) of *Lux Mundi*, a collection of essays by Oxford scholars whose aim was "to put the Catholic faith into its right relation to modern intellectual and moral problems."[30] Especially distressing to Liddon was the essay by Charles Gore, "The Holy Spirit and Inspiration." Gore acknowledges "a considerable idealizing element in the Old Testament history" as well as the gradual growth of the Mo-saic law; at these and other points where Gore accepts "the sure results" of historical study, Liddon saw "practically a capitulation at the feet of the young Rationalistic Professors."[31] Reconciliation between the two friends came at Liddon's deathbed, where Gore was shortly to be one of the most frequent visitors.

On Whit Sunday 1890, Liddon preached at St. Mary's his first Ox-ford sermon in six years. By June he was very ill with neuralgia, suffering agonizing head pains. The last doctor who attended him could find no sufficient physical cause for the seriousness of his illness; his clos-est friend said "he had lost all heart about the Church." Newman's death in August was a severe blow. In his last days, he was moved to be near the sea he so much loved. The final shock was a letter telling him of the death of his godson, received on Monday, September 8; death came to him the following morning, suddenly and gently. St. Paul's was crowded for the burial service, which was conducted with the greatest simplicity possible. The final hymn was his favorite, "When Morning Gilds the Skies." Its refrain sums up the aim of all Liddon's work: "Let Jesus Christ be praised!"

Liddon's Preaching

After Newman left Oxford and the English Church, Liddon was the public voice of the Oxford movement, for he expressed more fully than anyone else its central element — which was not, as is commonly thought, ritualism, but rather a conviction that Scripture *in all its parts* holds spiritual meaning for every age and that underlying the literal sense of the Old Testament is a spiritual sense which throughout bears witness to Jesus Christ.[32] The Tractarians had learned from the church fathers and the monastic theologians of the Middle Ages that Scripture, like the world itself, appears differently to the natural mind than it does to the mind awakened by faith, which does not violate ordinary reason but rather deepens its perceptions. At the heart of Liddon's preaching is the "doctrine of the second sense." In one of his last sermons, preached at St. Paul's three months after the publication of *Lux Mundi*, Liddon affirms that "the Bible is indeed the most interesting book in the world; to the poet, to the historian, to the philosopher, to the student of human nature, to the lover of the picturesque and of the marvelous, to the archaeologist, to the man of letters, to the man of affairs." But to dwell solely on that is like coming into the cathedral and noting no more than the skill and cost of its construction and the beauty of the liturgy, thus missing its purpose: namely, to bring souls into communion with God.[33]

Frequently, and almost consistently in his Oxford sermons, Liddon worked to show his listeners the resistance that inevitably arises in the natural mind when it is confronted with revealed truth. He wisely perceived that "intellectual opposition to Revelation...does not usually seek us Christians in the open field" but rather "take[s] refuge on some natural heights, or behind some artificial earthworks," confining itself to the realm of natural reason and — with apparent modesty but in fact, irrational pride — refusing to engage questions of spiritual truth.[34] Liddon presented a major challenge to the university community in "The Conflict of Faith with Undue Exaltation of Intellect," preached in the Oxford Lenten Series of 1865. With a barrage of questions that might take its inspiration from the divine speeches in Job, he presses them to recognize that honest scientific investigation must end in confession of a mystery:

> Look at those...forces with which you seem to be so much at home, and which you term attraction and gravitation. What do you really know about them? You name them: perhaps you can repeat a mathematical expression which measures their action. But after all you have named and described an effect; you have not accounted for, you have not penetrated into, you have not unveiled its cause. Why, I ask, in the nature of things, should such laws reign around us? They do reign, but why? what is the power which determines gravitation? where does it reside? how is it to be seized, apprehended, touched, examined? There it is: but there, inaccessible to your keenest study, it remains veiled and buried. You would gladly capture and subdue and understand it; but, as it is, you are forced to confess the presence of something which you cannot even approach.[35]

The passage is a good example of the "conscientious intensity" that one journalist described as the most prominent characteristic of his pulpit style. Liddon's language is graceful but plain; "as if he were too busy, too much in earnest, to stop for ornament."[36] Nothing blunts the force of his argument, which proceeds always directly from a biblical text and often achieves technical perfection as he makes clear logical progression through a field of thought, anticipating carefully every line of objection and revealing its underlying presupposition. There is a strict simplicity of focus; each sermon aims at illumining a single biblical concept or aspect of moral character. Yet it is viewed ultimately within the framework of the whole scope of Revealed Truth, which is not a commonplace book of edifying notions but an organic whole, whose every element is dependent upon all others, so that "a believer passes from one truth to another, not by a fresh intellectual jerk or effort, but in obedience to a sense of sequence which he cannot resist."[37]

Above all, there is a quality of selflessness, which is the great virtue of Liddon's theology even more than of his personality. An observation from the brilliant Ascension Day sermon speaks to our own contemporary theological climate perhaps even more strongly than to that of Liddon's day: "Selfishness is never less attractive than when it would leave its imprint on the sacred structure of theology. Yet we are not infrequently confronted by systems in which the assurance, or satisfaction, or consciousness of the believer is made the center of a theological panorama, while the revealed Nature or economies of God are banished to its circumference." Liddon everywhere reads Scripture with a view to how we should order our moral lives, but even that is not an end in itself. The final aim of the Christian life is not to accrue virtue to ourselves, or even to secure the temporal happiness of others, but rather to rejoice in beholding God's nature and divine life. Liddon was more sensitive than most preachers of his time to what the modern Church would recognize as justice issues: racial prejudice, systemic oppression of the poor, abuse of children. But the Ascension Day sermon opens up a "vertical dimension" of the concept of justice that is generally eclipsed: namely, what justice means *within the life of God.* Ironically, this is the very aspect which, from the perspective of traditional theology, is most fundamental. The Ascension of Christ to God's right hand affords a vision of glory in which the claims of self may even be forgotten, as "the soul beholds a solemn act of reparation for the suffering life which had preceded it, and rejoices with a joy which belongs to the highest sense of satisfied justice."[38]

If the university sermons are characterized by intellectual intensity, in the St. Paul's sermons Liddon became expansive, drawing upon the full range of his interests and imagination in order to engage his diverse metropolitan audience. There is no loss of precision; if anything he was more conscious of ordering his argument and eliminating unnecessary rhetorical flourishes. Most of Liddon's early sermons were carefully thought out, then preached from spare notes, although as soon as possible afterward he would write a close analysis of the sermon. But at St. Paul's, he found that the momentous physical effort required to be audible made spontaneous speech difficult, and he began preaching from manuscript.

In these sermons we see Liddon's gifts as a teacher; among modern preachers, perhaps no one more successfully refutes the common notion that the overtly instructive sermon cannot be compelling. The key to Liddon's success as a popular preacher is the unfailing respect he shows his listeners. He assumes nothing but the intrinsic interest of the text for inquiring minds. Everything is explained, so that one could come to his sermons with virtually no prior knowledge of the Bible. Many of the preserved sermons from St. Paul's treat Old Testament subjects; typically he begins by establishing a context — liturgical, literary, cultural, historical — for treating the passage at hand so as to clear up a confusion or highlight its chief points. "The Overthrow of Egypt" opens with the observation that the history of the Exodus is always read in connection with Easter. In "David Preparing for the Temple," he explains that "the Books of Kings are a civil history which cannot leave the Church out of sight; the Books of Chronicles are a church history which cannot ignore the civil power."[39] "Ahab at Naboth's Vineyard" begins with an explanation that Deuteronomic law requires the forfeiture of a traitor's family property. "The True Confidence" (on the Rabshakeh's speech in 2 Kings 18) offers a brief review of the Assyrian conquest of southwest Asia.

The most inviting and instructive openings are those in which Liddon evokes a narrative scene. The call of Elisha becomes vivid as the details of the biblical narrative are explored to reveal the enduring significance of this event, which is "an astonishing instance of the power of a religious influence." The twelve yoke of oxen show that Elisha was a man of substance, but the moment that Elijah cast his mantle, without a word of persuasion or a moment of pause,

> Elisha ran after the prophet who was already vanishing from his sight. ...Up to that moment his farm on the banks of the Jordan had been his all, as, in a later age, their boats and nets had been everything to the fishermen on the Sea of Galilee, who were predestined to the apostolate of the world. Elisha does not linger to drop regrets over this cherished past. He forthwith slays the oxen with which he had just been ploughing: he takes the plough-tackling for fuel, that he may boil their flesh; he gives one parting entertainment to his acquaintances and the neighborhood, that they may have no doubt either of his goodwill towards themselves, or of his lofty resolution: and then he leaves the scene of his labors, his field, his home, his all, to become the servant of Elijah.[40]

Liddon's love of landscape is evident in vivid geographical descriptions, especially in sermons preached after his trip to the Holy Land. "The Death of Aaron" opens with a picture of a windstorm in the Arabah, and rising out of it is Mount Hor, "a dark, red, bare rock, with two striking summits, which are seen, like the Malverns — only with a much sharper outline — far and near."[41] Geography is for Liddon suggestive of both historical and spiritual events. As Aaron takes a last look at the world he is soon to leave:

> Away to the east were the hills of Seir, through which the Edomites had refused a passage to Israel; and on the south, the wide and seemingly

boundless expanse of the desert of the wanderings; and on the west, the line of hills that formed the southern boundary of Canaan, through which Israel had vainly endeavored to force its way; and to the north, the Dead Sea, and the downs and bays and cliffs on its western bank, which one day were to mean so much for Judah. And no doubt his conscience lay spread out like a landscape before that inward gaze, only less clearly than beneath the Eye of his God. A deathbed is like a mountain top for the survey of life, and the deserts through which we have wandered, and the barriers which have checked our progress, and the hopes, bright or dim, which have cheered us on, and the feebleness, and fear of man, and self-seeking, and petty vanity — if nothing more — which have spoiled so much that God meant for Himself, stand out in clear outline above the haze of the distant past.[42]

Liddon often compares biblical scenes to those familiar to his audience. Jerusalem is surrounded by deep ravines, like Durham or Luxembourg; the valley of Achor is a highland valley like Glencoe, and in both places natural beauty has made a tragic history memorable. Nineveh is about the size of Berlin or St. Petersburg, Jerusalem smaller than the London parish of Islington. Reading the sermons, one begins to feel like an experienced traveler in the ancient world, as formerly strange places acquire a set of associations stretching across centuries and, with that, a moral character. Nineveh was dreaded as "the home of rapacity, injustice, violence, cruelty, conducted on a truly imperial scale."[43] Conversely, Egypt exerted a perpetual attraction for the Israelites; its seductions and abiding dangers were beauty, cultural refinement, easy living, and also a religion "not wholly corrupt and false, but cleverly lowered down and adapted to the average instincts of human nature."[44]

Upon Jerusalem he lavishes attention, as does the Bible itself: for its beauty, its religious and political centrality, and its "unworldliness," which made it influential far beyond its obvious importance. Love of Jerusalem is surely one of the most consistently expressed passions of the Old Testament, yet rarely do Christians take sufficient note even to wonder at that passion. In articulating the modern insensibility, Liddon draws his hearers into the spirit of the Bible and invites them to be pilgrims:

No city in the world has so profoundly influenced the highest life of millions of the human race as has Jerusalem. London, New York, Paris are magnificent in their way...but in all that touches the highest thoughts and the deepest motives to action known to us men, they are insignificant indeed by comparison with that little highland town in a remote province of the empire of Turkey....We quiet Englishmen, surveying our

own metropolis, are not tempted to indulge in the transcendental rhap-
sodies which Victor Hugo has lavished upon Paris; we read his effusions
in cold blood; perhaps we smile at them as somewhat unsuited to an age
of common sense. But if we are wise, we do not smile at the ecstasies
of prophets and psalmists before that holier though much smaller city in
the East. For the measurements of the realm of matter afford no clue
whatever to the measurements of the realm of spirit; and elect souls will
go on crying to the end of time, with an ever-deepening meaning in
their words: "Our feet shall stand in thy gates, O Jerusalem."[45]

Above all, the vividness and instructiveness of his sermons stem
from his acute perceptivity about human character. By means of brilliant analogies he shows that the biblical characters are stock figures in
moral dramas, recurrent in every age. Samuel stands to Eli as a cathedral chorister does to the archbishop; and, for all Eli's weakness, it is
a remarkable sign of his humility that he can accept the word of his
own downfall from the child. The old prophet of Bethel (1 Kings 13)
who deceives the young prophet is like a cynical old "religious adven-
turer" who discourages young clergy from striving for the high ideals
he himself has forsaken. Naaman the leper, outraged by Elijah's simple
command to bathe in the Jordan, "represents human nature, anxious
to be blessed by God's Revelation of Himself, yet unwilling to take the
blessing except on its own terms."[46] Saul is "the cool-headed man of the
world," who, despite many natural virtues, is indifferent to the will of
God. Nonetheless,

> the world likes his mixture of generosity and haughtiness, and his jaunty
> carelessness about all that points to the mystery and the responsibility
> of human life.... It is better to have our part with David than with
> Saul; with a loyalty to God that is not always consistent, rather than an
> outward propriety, if so it be, that is never really loyal.[47]

Liddon was sometimes criticized as lacking elegance, for he mixed
the words of Scripture freely with secular allusions and even the jar-
gon of the newspapers he read nearly as regularly as his prayers. But
in using common language to express spiritual truths he resembled the
biblical writers themselves and thus reinforced the central message of
all his preaching: that the deepest mysteries of God's Revelation are addressed to us in our most ordinary capacities and fundamental needs.
In a sermon at St. Paul's the Sunday following Liddon's death, Canon
Scott Holland honored his colleague as the "single-hearted preacher of
the Revelation of God":

As the words of Scripture rang from his lips (and who could ever make Scripture ring as he did?), their original force seemed to reach and touch us across all the dividing years. No insincerity withheld it. . . . Can there be a better test of the spiritual sincerity of a man than this — that we feel no shock when he speaks to us the Bible language? . . . As we listened, that inner world that lies before the spiritual eye was once more felt to be laid bare.[48]

Introduction to "The Young Man in Dothan"

This sermon is a superb example of Liddon's practical divinity, in which he sets forth the nature of spiritual sight and examines "as through a microscope" the process by which faith is acquired. He draws careful distinctions and connections between faith and imagination, faith and natural reason, and faith and trust. The absolute difference between faith and the *natural* imagination which he sets forth here is in some contrast with his earlier discussion on the role of the imagination in the practice of meditation, where he acknowledges that natural faculties can be directed to supernatural ends. Liddon amplifies Augustine's notion of the Trinity of the Mind (memory, understanding, and will) with the suggestion that imagination joins these three in effecting the "interpenetration of the soul by the atmosphere of Revealed Truth," specifically in moving us "to gaze in perpetual fascination on His surpassing Beauty."[49]

The notion that faith is a test of our moral nature is central to Liddon's thinking; and here he offers a succinct statement of the nature of that test, upon which it would be difficult to improve: "A man believes upon adequate although not absolutely compulsory evidence, in obedience to the promptings of his heart and will." Faith comes to us as God's gift, but not usually one that is spontaneously granted. The Church provides the atmosphere in which we may both ask for faith and prepare ourselves to receive it — that is, the ground is prepared through both self-knowledge and accurate knowledge of God. Liddon's view of the Church as "a world-embracing mixed society," whose members include the angels and "the spirits of the blessed dead," is a valuable reminder to our own age, when "inclusivity" and "diversity" are the watchwords of ecclesiology, of the full dimensions of the mystical reality that is the Body of Christ.

It is characteristic of Liddon to conclude by using the language of Scripture to confront us with the vision of God; and here the *Te Deum,* familiar from the Morning Prayer service, is shown to be an extension of Elisha's simple prayer, "Lord, open mine eyes, that I may see." In a final pastoral move, he shows his congregation how to make that prayer their own.

THE YOUNG MAN IN DOTHAN

Preached at St. Paul's on August 25, 1872

And Elisha prayed, and said, Lord, I pray thee, open his eyes, that he may see. And the Lord opened the eyes of the young man; and he saw: and, behold, the mountain was full of horses and chariots of fire round about Elisha.

—2 KINGS 6:17

Those of us who read our Bibles least carefully must have observed the remarkable number and character of the miracles which cluster round the lives of Elijah and Elisha. There is nothing like it in the case of any other prophet, if perhaps we except Daniel. And the reason is not difficult to see. Great outbursts of the miraculous, attesting God's energetic presence at particular times and places, appear to recur in sacred history in cycles—when truth has to be announced, promulgated afresh, or saved from extinction. One such there was in the days of Moses, when Israel was delivered from Egypt, and the faith of Sinai proclaimed; another in those of Joshua, when the Promised Land was taken possession of; another in the time we are considering, the time of Elijah and Elisha, when the belief and law of Sinai were threatened with extinction by the apostasy of the court of Israel and the attacks of the powerful Syrian monarchy; another during the Babylonish Captivity, when Israel sat down and wept over the memories of Sion by the waters of the heathen exile. A last great display of miraculous power was in the days of the incarnate son of God, Jesus Christ, and his apostles—the days in which God, who had "at sundry times and in divers manners spoken in times past unto the fathers by the prophets," spoke finally and fully in his son [Heb. 1:1, 2]—the epoch of his largest and last unveiling of his nature and will to us, the intelligent and moral creatures of his hand.

The miracles belonging to these different periods are unlike each other up to a certain point. Each period has, so to express it, its own characteristic miracles. But, on the other hand, there is likeness between them, arising from their common object and purpose, which cannot be mistaken. Not to go beyond our text, this miracle of Elisha's is peculiarly evangelical: it is just such a miracle as befits the drift and purpose of the Gospel, considered as an unveiling of a higher world to man. It especially anticipates such miracles of our Lord's as that by which he healed the man born blind [John 9:1–38], in which at one and the same time he gave the gift of natural sight and the higher gift of spiritual sight — the lower gift being at once a type and earnest of the higher.

I

Let us briefly recall the circumstances under which this miracle was worked.

Elisha was on good terms with Jehoram, then king of Israel; and Jehoram was at war, as his father and grandfather had been before him, with the Syrians of Damascus, the inveterate enemies of the kingdom of Israel. The Syrians, at this later period, seem to have carried on the war by a system of predatory incursions into the territory of Israel; and on several occasions Elisha warned King Jehoram of the place which the Syrians intended to surround, and by thus putting him on his guard, enabled him to escape, or at any rate to defeat the measures of the enemy. The king of Syria suspected that a failure which occurred so often must be due to some treachery on the part of his own officers, but on his making inquiry they told him that the prophet Elisha possessed such powers as to be able to keep the king of Israel informed of the Syrian king's most secret plans: "The prophet that is in Israel telleth the king of Israel the words that thou speakest in thy bedchamber" [2 Kgs. 6:12]. The Syrian king hereupon resolved to capture the prophet, if possible, and with this view sent a large body of troops by night to surround Dothan, a small town some twelve Roman miles north of Samaria, where Elisha was then residing. When Elisha's servant went out in the morning, and found that the town was completely invested by the Syrians, he returned to his master in despair. Escape seemed impossible. "Alas, my lord! What shall we do?" [v. 15]. Elisha quieted him by saying that he should not fear, since "those that are with us are more than those that are with them" [v. 16]. This statement must have at first seemed absurd to the servant, who compared the few Israelites shut up in the small town with the numerous Syrian army outside it. But Elisha prayed the Lord to open his servant's eyes, that he might see something more than the world of sense – the world above, around, beyond it. The servant accordingly beheld a repetition of Jacob's vision, who, when threatened with danger from Esau, had seen a double army of angels encamped around himself [Gen. 32:1, 2]. "The Lord opened the eyes of the young man; and he saw: and, behold, the mountain was full of horses and chariots of fire round about Elisha" [2 Kgs. 6:17].

What is meant by "the opening of the eyes of the young man"? It was not the gift of natural sight, since he saw the Syrian host round Dothan, and was terrified. It was a higher gift, analogous probably to clairvoyance – a supernatural ecstasy which laid open to him for the time being, as to St. John in Patmos, the world of spirits under such form as his intelligence could bear. The same thing had occurred in an earlier age to Balaam. His eyes, we are told, were opened, and he saw an angel stopping his path, an angel whom his natural eye had not seen [Num. 22:31]. It was the gift of a new and more piercing sense reaching into a sphere of being previously out of reach. It was like a natural discovery by the aid of a powerful telescope: the discovery of a planet unseen before, but of the existence of which an astronomer is certain by calculations which cannot fail him. Elisha's servant knew full well, as a truth of his religion, that there were such beings as angels. God, at Elisha's prayer, gave him a new power of spiritual sight; and he saw them.

What did he see? "He saw, and, behold, chariots of fire and horses of fire round about Elisha." The chariots and horses are not here, as in the account of the ascent of Elijah, vehicles for a glorious passage to heaven, but symbols of the divine power and protection. But in both passages the highest intelligences take a shape, like the forms in Ezekiel, which imply that their true nobility is service. The immaterial spirits become cognisable by the servant of Elisha, under forms of active power best calculated to reassure him. Fire is the symbol of the Godhead, as being the most ethereal of the earthly elements: the gift of Pentecost sat as tongues of fire on the apostles [Acts 2:3, 4]; God is a consuming fire [Heb. 12:29]; the seraph is properly the "burning spirit"; the horses and chariots mean warlike force. Still, what the servant sees is not a material, but a spiritual reality — taking a form which assured him of God's sure protection through the agency of those ministers of his who do his pleasure [Ps. 103:21], when all is dark to the ordinary eye. "The angel of the Lord tarrieth round about them that fear him, and delivereth them" [Ps. 34:8].

II

Here then we may study, as it were through a microscope, the act or process of faith in the human soul. What is faith? It is, says the apostle, "the substance of things hoped for, the evidence of things not seen" [Heb. 11:1]. It is the faculty which reaches to an object beyond sense, yet which apprehends that object with a certainty equal at least to the certainty of things of sense. Let us pause to consider rather more at length what faith is, and what it is not.

Faith, then, first of all, is not an act of the natural imagination. It is necessary to say this, because a great many persons constantly allude to it in terms which imply that it is. They speak of "a person of great faith," meaning that he is very imaginative; that he has an unusual share of that privileged and versatile faculty which does, indeed, achieve so much for society and for literature, which is the well-spring of poetry, the soul and genius of constructive art, but which is less welcome in the sphere of religion, because its highest efforts result in surrounding us with the unreal while investing it with the attributes of reality.

No. Faith is not another word for a vivid imagination. Imagination deals with that which is not, faith with that which is; imagination with fiction, faith with fact. The objects of faith and the objects of imagination may have this in common, that they are both beyond the reach of the natural sight. But there is this difference: that the objects of faith, being real, may become visible to a higher sight than that of the bodily eye, while the objects of imagination can never be thus visible to the soul; being fictions, however pleasing, they occur to it as fictions — as fictions of its own creation — not as realities.

When men speak of faith as a vivid and energetic form of imagination, they mean to deny this, without saying that they do so. They mean to imply that just as Virgil projected a picture of the nether world out of the wealth of his fancy, so evangelists and apostles have traced their own beautiful pictures of heaven and their awful descriptions of hell and of judgment in the pages of our Testaments by the aid of an extraordinary variety of the religious imagination. The evangelists and apostles were not poets, whatever else they were; they were eminently prosaic, and the remark of Rousseau, that the inventor of the Gospel history must have been not less wonderful than its hero, is at least a satisfactory reply to this theory of faith doing the work of imagination. The apostles say with St. Peter, "We have not followed cunningly devised fables" [2 Pet. 1:16] and with St. John, "That which we have seen and heard, declare we unto you" [1 John 1:3]. Among ordinary Christians, is it not a matter of daily experience that the most earnest and practical believers are constantly persons who are strikingly wanting in the faculty of imagination, and who look at all the concerns of life in a matter-of-fact way which forbids the idea of their ever, under any circumstances, giving the reins to fancy?

In the case before us, Elisha's servant did not create by an act of imagination a splendid picture in the air, after the manner of a Milton or a Rubens — a picture of fiery beings circling round the form of his beloved and imperiled master. It was psychologically impossible. He had his eye upon the hard and menacing fact before him: upon the lines of the Syrian troops who were sent to capture the prophet, his master. He could see nothing beyond the sphere of sense, and was terrified at what he saw, until Elisha prayed that he might see further — into another sphere. Then he saw the world of spirits. But the world of spirits was a thing utterly independent of his imagination. It would have been none the less real if he had never seen it, just as the Syrian troops would have been none the less real if Elisha's servant had been born blind and had never seen them. His new power of seeing the chariots and horses of fire round about Elisha did not create these spiritual forms and beings. There they were, whether he and others saw them or not, just as the more remote planets were certainly revolving in their orbits during the centuries when our science had not yet reached them by her reckonings and her telescopes. Elisha had been just as much encompassed by the spirit-world the moment before his servant saw that this was the case as he was the moment afterwards. The man's new sight could not create, as his blindness could not have destroyed, the reality.

I hear it whispered, "Yes; but there is a common sense, based on our ordinary experience, which resists these notions of an invisible world actually around and about us." But what is the real worth of this "common sense"? When the comet of 1858 appeared, a lecturer made a tour of some country villages in Devonshire, with a view to telling the country people some facts about the beautiful object which night by night attracted so much attention; and among other points he touched upon the calculations which astronomers had made as to the enormous length of this comet's tail. I recollect hearing a countryman who treated this part of his lecture with contemptuous incredulity. "I saw the comet myself," said the peasant to a sympathizing crowd of villagers, "and its tail was just four feet long; and how are we to believe this man, who tells us that it was many millions of miles long?" That was the "common sense" of ordinary sight pitted against the common sense of that higher insight into nature which is won by scientific investigation. But science, too, can sometimes be guilty of an appeal to common sense of this sort against the assertions of a still higher insight into the supersensuous realities than her own — against the assertions of faith. The astronomer, with Lord Rosse's telescope at his disposal, sees — he does not imagine — heavenly bodies utterly out of the reach of your ordinary sight or mine; and the servant of Elisha, when the eyes of his spirit were opened, saw, by the aid of a new spiritual faculty, what he would not have imagined — the world of spirits floating in all its power and beauty round his imperiled master.

Nor is faith only the conclusion, the final act, of a process of natural reasoning. If this were the case, it would necessarily follow that all people with good understandings must necessarily be believers in Christianity. We know that this is not the case. We know that many persons of great natural abilities, such as Voltaire, have been unbelievers; and this alone would show that something besides natural intelligence is implied in an act of faith. No man whose mind is not impaired can go through a proposition of Euclid and refuse to assent to the conclusion, but many people do read Paley's *Evidences*,[50] or what St. Paul says about the resurrection, and yet do not admit St. Paul's and Paley's conclusion, that Christianity is certainly from God. If believing in Christianity were simply an affair of the natural understanding, this could not be — it would be just as inevitable to believe St. Paul as to believe Euclid.

Why is this so? Why is acceptance of religious truth not as imperative upon the human understanding as the acceptance of mathematical truth? Because the act of faith is not merely an act of the intelligence. It is an act of the whole inward nature of the affections and the will, as well as of the understanding. "With the heart," says St. Paul, "man believeth unto righteousness" [Rom. 10:10]. The affections and the will have a great deal to say to an act of faith. The understanding cannot compel it. The evidence at the disposal of the understanding is less than absolutely mathematical, and it does not convince unless the moral nature is in such a condition as to wish that it should be convincing. The evidence of religion at our disposal is designedly less than strictly irresistible; in order that there may be room for the play of our moral nature – so that the act of faith may be a test, not of the goodness of our natural understandings, but of the state of our hearts and dispositions. If faith were merely an assent of the understanding to a conclusion warranted by sufficient evidence, it is plain that St. Paul could never speak of it as he does when writing to the Romans and the Galatians, as that which justifies before God. Goodness of understanding could be no more a reason for our acceptance with God than strength of limbs or retentiveness of memory.

Faith is indeed spoken of as it is in the New Testament, because it is a test of the moral nature; because a man believes upon adequate although not absolutely compulsory evidence, in obedience to the promptings of his heart and will. A man who has made the most of natural light will desire the light of revelation; will be looking out for it; will believe that the author of the law of right and wrong within him is likely to unfold something more about Himself. But then what is it which at the decisive moment makes the desire of the heart on the one side, and the evidence at the disposal of the understanding on the other, result in an act of faith? What is it which strikes the sacred spark, which combines the action of the understanding and the yearnings of the heart into a single act, which supersedes while it combines both of them?

"The Lord opened the eyes of the young man; and he saw: and, behold, horses of fire and chariots of fire round about Elisha." Faith is, in the last resort, the fire lighted in the soul by a ray of grace: a gift from God – a fresh gift which nature can neither rival nor anticipate. Elisha might have insisted upon many considerations which ought, in reason, to have satisfied the young man, that God and his holy ones were near at hand, and that the near presence of the Syrians did not amount to any real reason for despair. Had God not helped the patriarch Jacob thus? Had he not delivered Israel in the wilderness, and David from the wild beasts and from the hand of Saul, and Elijah quite recently from all the power of Ahab and Jezebel? Was it to be supposed that he would desert his prophet now? Or that, happen what might, he was unconcerned or powerless? Elisha did not argue: he prayed. He prayed that the Lord would open the eyes of the young man to see things as they are — to see not merely the world of sense, but the world of spirit. And his prayer was granted.

This exactly agrees with what we learn about faith in the New Testament. Faith is represented as a new spiritual sense — an endowment or gift bestowed upon the soul of man by the Holy Ghost. It is contrasted with natural sight: "we walk by faith, and not by sight," says St. Paul [2 Cor. 5:7]. It is contrasted with natural reason: since "the natural man receiveth not the things of the spirit of God, neither can he know them, because they are spiritually discerned" [1 Cor. 2:14]. It is a higher reason than nature gives; it is a higher and more perfect sight, which God gives to nature, which nature cannot, if she would, herself achieve. "Faith," says St. Paul again, "is not of yourselves: it is the gift of God" [Eph. 2:8]. Thus it happened that when the Lord had opened the heart of Lydia, she believed the things that were spoken by Paul [Acts 16:14]. Thus St. Paul prays that the Ephesians may know what is the hope of their calling, and what the riches of the glory of His inheritance among the saints. He does not expect them to know this by nature, but only when "the eyes of their understanding are enlightened," that is, as a consequence of faith [Eph. 1:17, 18].

Do I say that natural reason has no office whatever to discharge in the work of establishing our religious convictions? Far from it. If this were so, not merely the evidential theology of the Church but much of the language of the Bible itself would be a vast mistake. Reason can do much for faith. Reason stands to faith as did the Baptist to Christ our Lord; she is the messenger which makes ready the way of faith in the soul. Reason can explain, infer, combine, reduce difficulties to their true proportions, make the most of considerations which show what is to be expected. But she cannot do the work of God's grace: she cannot open the eyes of the young man, and make him see. If this last triumph is to be achieved, it must be by grace, given in answer to prayer. Too often men do not believe, not because belief is impossible for reasonable men, but because they imagine it to be simply the result of a natural form of mental exercise instead of a heavenly gift, for which indeed natural reason may and should prepare the way, but which is given in answer to prayer. Brethren, would you believe, pray, and sooner or later you will believe.

Faith is not the same thing as trust. Certainly men speak loosely nowadays of having faith in a person or an institution, meaning that they trust the man's character or the efficiency of the institution. If we cannot profess this faith we do not therefore cease to believe that the man or institution exists, but only that certain qualities are wanting which command our confidence. In this popular way of speaking we are really making the word "faith" do the work of another word besides itself — the word "trust." But, properly speaking, faith precedes trust: trust is based on faith. In order to trust a person you must know from authority, if you do not know by experience, that he is a person whom it is well to trust; and when this knowledge is received on authority it is, properly speaking, faith. Much of the faith shown towards our Lord in the Gospel was trust as well as faith, just as it was obedience as well as faith. But faith was the basis of trust, as it was the basis of obedience, and to trust Jesus Christ is as distinct a thing from believing in him as obeying him is.

The act by which Elisha's servant saw the world of spirits round about his master was not an act of trust. No doubt it led on to such an act: it was meant to do so. Elisha, to whom the spirit-world lay open, prayed that what he saw might be seen by his servant; that his servant might have confidence in God's power to save them from the Syrians. But the act of apprehension of that which had been before hidden from the natural sight was a totally distinct thing from the confidence to which it was intended to lead. It was the illuminated soul gazing with open eyes at realities beyond the sphere of sense; it was practically a consummate act of faith.

III

Let us see in this history.

1. A remedy against despondency, such as good Christians often feel on contemplating the state of the world at particular periods. All seems to be going against the cause of right, of truth, of God. "The enemy crieth so, and the ungodly cometh on so fast, for they

are minded to do me some mischief, so maliciously are they set against me" [Ps. 55:4]. The Psalmist's cry is echoed by the Church, kneeling at the foot of the throne of Christ, throughout the centuries; intellectual assailants, political adversaries, all the passions, all the prejudices, all the misapprehensions of unregenerate humanity, come down and besiege the prophet in Dothan. All might seem lost again and again, if the eyes of the spirit could not be opened to perceive that "they which are with us are more than they which are with them" [2 Kgs. 6:16]. Courage! The unseen is greater than the seen; the eternal will outlive the things of time. An act of faith may cross the threshold, and may at once correct the apparent preponderance of evil by a vision of the throne and of the resources of the All-Good.

2. See, too, in this history our patent of nobility. It has been a common saying, quoted in order to explain and justify many changes on the Continent within the last ten years, that it is better to be citizens of a great state than of a small one. It is better for many reasons; for this among the rest. There is an inspiration which comes from the sense of wide and noble fellowship, of high and distinguished associates and guardians, which is denied to those who have it not. And in his kingdom God has provided us with this. All the races of the world furnish their contributions to the universal Church, but the frontier of sense is not the frontier of the Church; it embraces both worlds — the unseen as well as the visible. "Ye are come," says the apostle, writing to Christian converts, "unto Mount Sion, and unto the city of the living God, the heavenly Jerusalem, and to an innumerable company of angels, to the general assembly of the Church of the first-born, whose names are written in heaven, and to God the judge of all, and to the spirits of just men made perfect, and to Jesus, the mediator of the new covenant" [Heb. 12:24]. The Church is, according to the apostle, a world-embracing mixed society, consisting here of the faithful, there of the blessed angels and the spirits of the blessed dead; united in the bonds of indissoluble communion, and all ranged beneath the throne of thrones — the throne of God, of Jesus.

Does this lofty conviction, think you, inspire no hatred of sin, no longing for a higher life, no wish to live as the companion of beings who constitute the household of God and are our predestined fellow-citizens? The Syrian host may press us hard — the host of temptations, of bad thoughts, of bad acquaintances, of haunting memories — but when, at the prayer of the Church, or our own, our eyes open upon the realities around and above us, we may remember that we have a great destiny before us, and means at hand to prepare for it. "To have no sense of the invisible," said a great writer, "is the ruin of art." To have no sense of the invisible, it may be most certainly added, is the ruin of virtue.

Lastly, see here the real secret of effective prayer and praise. Why is prayer, particularly public prayer, in so many cases a cold and heartless form? For two reasons, especially. Men enter on it without having any true knowledge of themselves — of their sins and wants, as well as of their hopes and fears; of their real state before God, as well as of their reputed character in the eyes of men — in a word, they have no true knowledge of that for which prayer wins a remedy. Thus they have no personal interests to import into the public language of the Church; they do not know enough about themselves to say with perfect sincerity that they "have erred and strayed from [God's] ways like lost sheep,"[51] or that there are things which, for their unworthiness, they dare not, and for their blindness they cannot ask.[52] But secondly, and chiefly, prayer is so cold and heartless a form because men have no true sight of God, of Jesus, of his majesty, his beauty, his glory, such as is possible to our finite and purblind gaze — of the everlasting worship which surrounds him, of the courtiers around his throne, those ministers of his that do his pleasure. Until this is the case, at least in some degree, what a torrent of unmeaning verbiage is the public language of the Church! Take that glorious hymn in which the Morning Prayer service culminates, the *Te Deum*. If the soul sees nothing beyond the veil, what must be meant when the lips repeat such verses as

> To thee all angels cry aloud: the heavens, and all the powers therein,
> To thee cherubim, and seraphim continually do cry,
> Holy, holy, holy, Lord God of Sabaoth;
> Heaven and earth are full of the majesty of thy glory!

or when, after this first ascent towards the throne of the thrice-holy, there follows a second

> The glorious company of the apostles praise thee;
> The goodly fellowship of the prophets praise thee;
> The noble army of martyrs praise thee;
> The Father, of an infinite majesty;
> Thine honorable, true, and only son;
> Also the Holy Ghost, the comforter!

or when all is finally concentrated on Jesus Christ — as "the king of glory," as "the everlasting son of the Father," with whom we may plead for help, because "when he took upon him to deliver man, he did not abhor the virgin's womb" — because "when he had overcome the sharpness of death he opened the kingdom of heaven to all believers!" How unutterably piteous for us, if when such words are sung, we are relieving the weariness of mental contact with vacancy, by dwelling on the triumphs of great composers, or on the skill of trained choirs, or on the associations of an historical building, or, it is possible enough, by thinking of something which ought to have been dropped out of our minds when we entered the church door! There are few better prayers on entering a church than Elisha's, " 'Lord, open mine eyes, that I may see.' I do not wish to mock thee by lip-service; I do not wish to pile my ordinary business thoughts, or thoughts of pleasure, on the very steps of thy throne. Open mine eyes that I may see thee in thy beauty, and in thy glorious presence may lose my relish for all that only belongs to time." Believe me, it is when the soul struggles thus with God in spiritual agony, that it is emancipated from the tyranny of sense, and, like the dying Stephen, really sees the heavens opened, and Jesus standing at the right hand of God [Acts 7:55, 56].

Introduction to
"Elisha at the Assumption of Elijah"

Over a period of more than fifteen years, Liddon preached what amounts to a series of excellent sermons on the Elijah–Elisha stories, which were appointed as readings during the summer season (Sundays after Trinity), when he was resident at St. Paul's. The freshness of his treatment stems largely from the decision to tell the story of the two contrasting characters, master and disciple, from the disciple's perspective. The sermon may well reflect Liddon's own reflections upon the death of his master two years before the sermon was preached; for in Liddon's eyes Pusey was, like Elijah, a powerful upholder of "unpopular truth" in the struggle against "fashionable evil."

Liddon was on holiday on the Continent when Pusey became ill; and, to his great grief, the old man died before his disciple could reach

England. His own loss may lend force to his presentation of the view, strong in Victorian society and nearly eclipsed in our own day, that to attend the deathbed of a Christian is more than a duty and a sad burden; it is a privilege. For at that moment the moral quality of a person's life comes at last wholly into view (cf. "The Death of Aaron," cited above p. 215), and thus it affords the final and even perhaps the most significant moment of witness to God's "invigorating grace" and faith in God's mercy.

Yet, with a fine pastoral touch, Liddon also acknowledges that death often provides an occasion for pettiness and degrading rivalries, as evidenced in the "ill-natured question" posed by the prophetic bands at Bethel and Jericho: "Knowest thou that the Lord will take away thy master from thy head today?" The terse exchange between Elisha and the other young men is brilliantly illumined by Liddon's comparison of the taunters to members of university theological colleges who are contemptuous of those who lack that distinction and jealous of any recognition they may obtain.

Although the subject of the sermon is one that touches everyone closely, the preacher included, there is no trace of sentimentality in his treatment, no more than in the biblical narrative itself. Indeed, there is a strong note of encouragement in his observation: "No single death could be to Christendom what Elijah's death was to the religion of Israel." Typically, Liddon grounds that encouragement not only in his personal faith experience but in the reality of the Church, where the Holy Spirit is perpetually active to repair our losses and supply our lack, and "where the greatest and humblest of his servants are equally dependent for all that they have and are."

ELISHA AT THE ASSUMPTION OF ELIJAH

Preached at St. Paul's on August 31, 1884

And it came to pass, when the Lord would take up Elijah into heaven by a whirlwind, that Elijah went with Elisha from Gilgal.

—2 KINGS 2:1

The translation or assumption of Elijah probably interests more people, and more powerfully, than any event, with at most two or

three exceptions, in the Old Testament. Elijah himself is always interesting. He interests us as children, on account of the variety and
splendor of his adventures; and he interests us still more as men,
on account of his unique place in sacred history, and his value as a
study of character. Of the two great figures which the wild highland
race of Gilead contributed to the history of Israel — Jephthah and Elijah — Elijah is incomparably the more commanding. Great in himself,
he was made greater by the circumstances with which he was in
almost perpetual conflict. To the settled communities of Judah and
Ephraim he must have worn almost as strange a look as he would
present could he appear in Regent Street or Ludgate Hill, with his
long thick hair hanging down his back, with his skin girdle round his
waist, and his cape of sheepskin, or mantle, as it is called, thrown
loosely across his shoulders. When, from time to time, Elijah appeared, no one could exactly say whence, it was felt that something
evil had been done, or that something tragical was impending. He
was emphatically a prophet of judgment. His life was a long struggle against the utter apostasy from the moral law and worship of
the Lord God of Israel to which the court of Israel was committed.
This it was which led him to proclaim the penal drought of three
years' duration to Ahab; to confront Ahab when, with Obadiah, he
was making a survey of the impoverished land; to bid him summon
the eight hundred and fifty prophets of Baal and Ashtoreth to their
judgment and doom on Carmel; to denounce to Ahab the penal visitations of God in the garden of the murdered Naboth, outside the
royal city of Jezreel; to foretell to Ahaziah his approaching death,
when he had sent to the heathen oracle of Ekron to ascertain the
issue of his illness; to call down fire upon the companies of soldiers
which were sent to take him in his hermitage on Mount Carmel;
and even to send a letter to the apostatizing king of Judah, Jehoram,
announcing his approaching end. And it was this struggle against
fashionable evil which forced Elijah, again and again, to seek safety
by betaking himself to some remote hiding-place; at one time in the
torrent-bed of the Cherith, which ran like a deep fissure through his
native hills of Gilead; at another, strangely enough, in the very heart
of the country of his enemies, with a widow woman at Zarephath,
between Tyre and Sidon; at another in the territory of Judah at Beer-
sheba; at another amid the rocky precipices of Horeb, the scene
of his greatest vision; at another in caves on the slopes of Carmel.
His life was by turns that of a statesman whose strong will swayed

the fall and rise of kingdoms, and that of a hermit whose long vigils and prayers were unwitnessed by any human eye. And now this life, so active and so passive, so strong and so yielding, so courageous and at times so verging on despair, has come to its close. The prophet is at Gilgal—the village, we can hardly doubt, of that name in Samaria — when he is told that the time of his departure is at hand. "And it came to pass that when the Lord would take up Elijah into heaven by a whirlwind, that Elijah went with Elisha from Gilgal."

The verse before us directs attention to a point which evidently has a first place in the sacred writer's mind, and indeed governs his narrative. It is that at this supreme moment of his life Elijah was not alone: he went with Elisha from Gilgal. The narrative which follows is not more an account of Elijah's passing away into another world than of Elisha's relation to him at the time: and we shall perhaps consider it most usefully if we place ourselves at the point of view of the servant rather than that of the master, and accompany Elisha from Gilgal to the closing scene beyond the Jordan. There are characters and subjects which, like the orb of the sun at noonday, cannot be gazed at directly; they are best understood if we stand aside to look at them, or try to measure their import by tracing its effect on the conduct and destiny of others.

I

And here we note, first, the strong overmastering affection which bound Elisha to Elijah. Ever since Elisha's call at Abel-meholah he had been generally in Elijah's company, on the footing at once of a trusted younger companion and a confidential servant. The same sort of relation had existed between Moses and Joshua, as a preparation for the duties to which Joshua would be called after the great lawgiver's death. It was a relationship, on one side of fatherly affection, on the other of devoted service and reverence. Elisha's title of honor in later years was, "The son of Shaphat, who poured water on the hands of Elijah" [2 Kgs. 3:2]. The phrase was vivid: it implied that the solitary, stern, reserved prophet admitted his younger friend to the high honor of intimacy and service, and that this permission had been gratefully accepted. And so they moved through life, the wisdom of years and of commanding inspiration leaning, as it might seem, on the active enthusiasm of generous youth, and deepening mutual attachment by the interchange of what each had to give: strong grasp of truth, patient thought, wise counsel on one side, and all the varied attentions of loving service on the other.

But now Elijah had been warned that the end was near; and he would rather be alone. Much was before him which no one would fully understand but he; scenes to which the language of sympathy is inadequate, and amid which anything that it could attempt would be almost an impertinence. Elijah would be alone. Solitude was never unwelcome to Elijah: it never is unwelcome to those who have a constant sense of the presence of God, and who find in communion with him, and in discovering more and more of their own condition with respect of his will, more than enough to occupy them. They only are entirely dependent upon the society of their fellow-creatures who live on the surface of their existence, and who have no true experience of what lies beneath. A great soul, too, like Elijah has its appropriate and inevitable reserve. While shallower natures talk glibly of all that passes within them, and find a satisfaction in taking the world into confidence, more solid characters shrink from this exposure; just as a deep volume of water rolls on in silence towards the sea, while a shallow brook ripples chatteringly over its rocky bed, and proclaims to all the world how small are its resources. Nor does the love of solitude at certain times in life imply lack of sympathy: since true sympathy has other and better ways of expressing itself than incessant talking.

> Oft when we pine, afar from those we love,
> More close are knit the spirits' sympathies
> By mutual prayer; distance itself doth prove
> A greater nearness; with such stronger ties
> Spirit with spirit talks, that when our eyes
> Behold each other, something sinks within,
> Mocked by the touch of life's realities.[53]

Nor in desiring to be alone was Elijah thinking only of himself. No doubt he wished to spare his faithful companion the pain of parting. If Elisha would only remain at Gilgal, he would hear somewhere, and at some time, that his beloved master had disappeared. There would be no picture of a scene, never to be blotted out from memory, to haunt Elisha's later life. There would only be the contrast — the great contrast — between visible presence and felt absence; all the connecting links would belong to imagination and conjecture. So out of affection for Elisha, no less than from personal feeling and preference, Elijah would have said unto Elisha, "Tarry here, I pray thee, for the Lord hath sent me to Bethel" [2 Kgs. 2:2].

But affection like Elisha's does not always enter into the motives which would have ruled Elijah. It takes no thought of self: it would rather suffer from being close to its object, than escape suffering by distance. And it is too impetuous, not unfrequently, to be entirely considerate; like those warm-hearted foreigners, who, thinking only of the immediate satisfaction of the sentiment of attachment, clasp some reserved English friend to their arms in the public streets. Elisha did not care for the pain which the sight of the departing Elijah might cause him: and he could not stop to understand the yearning for solitude which, in those solemn moments, the great prophet would feel. Hence the exclamation, "As the Lord liveth, and thy soul liveth, I will not leave thee" [2 Kgs. 2:2]. At Bethel, and again at Jericho, Elijah renewed the request that Elisha would remain behind; and at Bethel and at Jericho — in the same terms — Elisha refused [2 Kgs. 2:4, 6]. He would cling to his great master to the last, no matter what he might have to endure in doing so. They should be parted, if at all, by a higher than any human judgment. And each time, it is remarkable, Elijah gave way.

That iron will, before which kings and captains quailed in terror, bent with obedient sympathy to the reiterated protestation of an affectionate servant. They were together through the whole of that last journey — at Gilgal, at Bethel, at Jericho, and at last beyond the Jordan.

We may have seen something of the same kind in a last illness — an illness extended like Elijah's last journey — over three or more stages before the end is reached. There is the first stage, when it is understood that things are looking very serious — the stage from Gilgal to Bethel; and then there is a halt, and we think that recovery is even probable. Then comes a second stage — from Bethel to Jericho — when a new advance is made in the downward course, and the gravest apprehensions are entertained. But there comes another halt at Jericho: again hope — always buoyant and optimizing — flickers up into a belief that convalescence is possible, until the illness takes a fatal turn, and the patient sets out to cross that dark river which is never repassed.

Few of us are like the saintly solitary of ancient Israel, so plunged in the sense of the encompassing presence of God, as to desire no created sympathy to supplement that satisfaction which is drawn from felt contact with the Uncreated and the Infinite. Few can lie down to die, like that great figure of the Middle Ages, at Salerno, with the exclamation, "I have loved righteousness and hated iniquity; therefore I die in exile."[54]

Most of us yearn, at that solemn time, for human words of love and pity, and human faces, and human hands, which soften, if they cannot delay, the stern approach of death; and human friends who should accompany us to the gate, if there they must leave us and can pass no further.

But a long illness, with its three or more stages — continued week after week, month after month — is a trial even to devoted affection. Affection is sometimes keen between Gilgal and Bethel; cooler between Bethel and Jericho; scarcely better than a mechanical service in the later stage. To be tended by the love of an Elisha is a great blessing: to be an Elisha to some solitary soul, which in its isolation scarcely dares reveal itself to any human heart, is perhaps a greater. Such experiences, such duties, come to most of us sooner or later in life: but Elisha little thought when he first set eyes on Elijah in the field of Abel-meholah, that he would be the witness of his last hours between Gilgal and the Jordan.

II

Next we may notice the vexations and annoyances to which Elisha's devotion to his master exposed him during the last hours of Elijah's life. At Bethel and Jericho, there were schools of the prophets, institutions which dated from the days of Samuel. In these establishments, young men who had, or were thought likely to possess, the prophetical gift, were taught the meaning, especially the moral meaning, of the sacred law, and the whole body of truth which the prophetical order had gradually learnt from the more eminent of its inspired members. These schools of the prophets were more like diocesan colleges for training young men for holy orders than any other institutions among us: they were centers of religious information and religious influence — houses in which the spirit of the order of prophets was carefully fostered and strengthened, and from which issued men who profoundly influenced the religious convictions and conduct of their contemporaries. Such schools or colleges there were at Ramah, at Bethel, at Jericho, at Gilgal, and elsewhere.

Some of them were very numerously attended: and all of them were of real importance to the religious life of the country.

Elijah's lofty character and conspicuous services would have won the hearts and kindled the imaginations of the young men who attended the prophetical colleges: and it is possible that in making his way towards the Jordan, the frontier of his native Gilead, where he hoped to die, he so shaped his course as to be able to take solemn leave of these great communities settled in Bethel and Jericho. From Gilgal the travelers arrived first of all at Bethel; and here the members of the prophetical college showed what we must at least think a great want of consideration for Elisha. Somehow or other, whether through a revelation conveyed to some other prophet, or through a report of what Elijah had been saying at Gilgal, and possibly elsewhere, the rumor was in circulation at Bethel that Elijah would soon be leaving the world. The school of the prophets at Bethel do not seem to have looked upon Elisha with very favorable eyes. They probably regarded him as an inferior sort of person, who had arrived at an eminence which he did not really deserve, through his association with the great Elijah. Elisha, it is probable, had never had any connection with these prophetical schools, and their members may have been disposed to regard him much as some clergymen who have had an university education, are said to regard other clergymen who have never been at the university. Men are really to be valued, not by their antecedents or decorations, or the accidents of their education, but by what they are in themselves, by what God's wonder-working grace has made them, by their intellectual and moral endowments, by their place and work in the Church of God. But human nature is much the same in its leading characteristics from age to age, and the members of the prophetical college at Bethel reflected with some satisfaction that when Elijah was withdrawn, Elisha would find his level. It was not disagreeable to them to tell Elisha what was coming, and to observe the effect that the news would have upon him. "And the sons of the prophets that were at Bethel came forth to Elisha, and said unto him, Knowest thou that the Lord will take away thy master from thy head today? And he said, Yea, I know it; hold ye your peace" [2 Kgs. 2:3]. The same ill-natured question was put to Elisha by the members of the college of prophets at Jericho, and it elicited the same reply [v. 5]. There was plainly a common understanding — a feeling running throughout the prophetic order, to which the question gave expression; and the strength of the feeling may be measured by the fact that even the presence of Elijah did not silence the questioners. Their jealousy of Elisha was too keen to allow them to understand what was due to the last hours of the prophet who was so soon to leave them.

It has been within the experience of many of us, I suppose, that the pettinesses of human nature are by no means always awed into silence by the presence of death. Nothing is more melancholy in the history of royalty than the undercurrent of selfish intrigue and gossip which so often surrounds the dying moments of a sovereign. The scramble for place and power is with difficulty, if at all, delayed until the last breath of the dying ruler has been drawn. The rivalries which have hitherto been repressed by an instinct of prudence, will break out, even prematurely, into most unlovely forms of activity: and display, on a pathetic scale, the hollowness of the life whose outward mien has been that of a perfectly sincere and easy courtesy. Nor need we have recourse to memoirs of court life to illustrate this insensibility of selfish passion to all that is implied in the presence of death. In very humble families a death is often discounted long before it has actually taken place. Keen eyes picture to themselves the altered circumstances of the family; the new social center of gravity; the new distribution of income; the putting down the influential from their seat, and the exalting those who wish to take their place; the new domestic order which will unfold itself when the will has been read, and its probable disappointments and surprises have been duly appreciated. You know, my brethren, whether I am exaggerating. But Elisha's questioners are often asking their questions under new circumstances: "Knowest thou that the Lord will take away thy master from thy head today?" And wherever the solemnity of death is understood, the profanity of intruding these topics is understood too; and the answer of every reverent and healthy soul is Elisha's: "Yea, I know it; hold ye your peace."

III

Lastly, there was the solemn interchange of confidences between the departing prophet and his successor. If the last hours of a friend's life often make heavy demands on affection, if the sick-room has sometimes its trials, and even its degradations, it also not seldom has blessings that are all its own.

Elisha had resisted Elijah's last minute injunction to stay at Jericho, and he had turned a deaf ear to the question addressed to him by the local college of prophets. Elijah and Elisha had walked across the plain, in full view of the associated prophets who were gathered to watch them from the rocky heights behind the town of Jericho: and then Elijah had smitten with his mantle the waters of the Jordan: and they had passed to its eastern side – the side of Elijah's native Gilead.

And now the closing scene was imminent. But before it took place the departing prophet, as if recognizing the devoted affection of the man who, in spite of himself, had followed him from Gilgal, wished to give a token of his interest and gratitude. "Ask what I shall do for thee, before I be taken away from thee" [2 Kgs. 2:9]. It is the language of one who knows that he has power with God, and is too sincere to disguise it. Prayer moves the will that rules the world; and those who have been, for long years, living near the Almighty, may speak of answers to prayer with a humble confidence which would be folly or irreverence in other men.

"Ask what I shall do for thee, before I be taken away from thee." What should Elisha answer? He is on his trial, as was Solomon in the vision or dream at Gibeon; he is balancing perhaps between matter and spirit, between earthly ambition or gain and the generous promptings of disinterested service. "Ask what I shall do for thee." What should Elisha ask? Should it be a long life, or great wealth, or the humiliation of personal rivals? Solomon had not asked for these things; he had asked for nothing material, nothing selfish or base; but for a spirit of practical wisdom that would enable him to rule his people [1 Kgs. 3:9]. Elisha will ask for that which in a prophet would answer to the royal gift of wisdom – a double portion of the spirit of his master [2 Kgs. 2:9]. This has been often understood to mean a prophetical gift twice as great in its range and intensity as that entrusted to Elijah. If that were the meaning of the phrase, Elisha's prayer was not granted. It cannot be said that Elisha – startling as were his miracles – occupies so great a place in sacred history as did Elijah. He is, indeed, as a type of our Lord, greater than the type of our Lord's forerunner. But in their whole manner of life and conduct the two prophets differ too widely to admit properly of being compared. Elijah was a recluse, leading a life, for the most part, remote from the haunts of men: Elisha, a dweller in cities, on familiar terms with his fellow-men, sharing their habits and influencing their lives by constant contact. Elijah belonged to the desert: Elisha to civilization. Elijah's work was destructive — the sworn enemy of all persons and institutions which interfered with the honor of the Lord God of Israel: Elisha's career was constructive and conciliatory. His relations with Naaman the Syrian are inconceivable in Elijah. He was the friend and adviser of influential persons: he was even welcome at the court: a king mourned by the side of his dying bed. In Elijah's case, the miracles were but illustrations of character; in Elisha's, character only forms a thin link between successive miracles. In short, the whole temper and career of the two prophets differ so, that the specific spirit of Elijah, instead of being doubled in Elisha, was scarcely reproduced in him at all. The phrase points to the general prophetical gift; and Elisha asks that he might receive not twice as great a gift as his master, but, as the Hebrew term implies, the double portion of an eldest son; twice as much as that of any other prophet. But Elijah hesitates: "Elisha," he says, "has asked a hard thing" [v. 10]. Elijah may be able, by his intercession, to procure this boon, but also he may fail. If Elisha sees him at the moment of his departure, the prayer will have been granted: but only if he does see him.

Elisha's motive for such a request will seem clear, if we put ourselves in his place. The fortunes of the true religion in Israel were still at a very low ebb, and in losing Elijah, it seemed that good men — the remnant that had not bowed the knee to Baal — were losing everything. What a blank, what a hopeless, desolate prospect lay before them, when the great prophet should have gone! Who would then uphold unpopular truth? Who would then withstand powerful idolatry, inspire the evil with apprehension, and encourage and strengthen hearts that failed? It was not for himself — it was that he might be able still to do something for others — that Elisha asked for a double portion of the prophetical spirit.

In the Church of Christ the individual counts for less than in the Jewish church, just as in Judaism he counted for less than in paganism. No single death could be to Christendom what Elijah's death was to the religion of Israel. Christians know that the greatness of a Paul or an Augustine is the work of the Holy Spirit, and that what he has done once, he may do again. The individual, too, whose value is so great in an imperfect and local religious system, seems insignificant when confronted with the majesty of the universal Church: and when, in Christendom, men speak as though this and that loss were irreparable, they know not what spirit they are of. No loss is irreparable in his kingdom who perpetually makes all things new [Rev. 21:5], and where the greatest or humblest of his servants are equally dependent for all that they have and are.

To most of us Elisha's prayer would be safely paraphrased, without reference to what may have been given to or withheld from others. The most essential feature of the prophetical spirit is shed abroad in Christian hearts by the Holy Ghost which is given us. It is the sense of the love of God:

> I ask not wealth, I ask not length of days,
> Nor joys which home and rural scenes bestow,
> Nor honor among men, nor poet's praise,
> Nor friendship, nor the light of love to know,
> Which with its own warm sun bathes all below:
> Nor that the seed I sow should harvest prove;
> I ask not health, nor spirit's gladdening flow,
> Nor an assured pledge of rest above,
> If only Thou wilt give a heart to know Thy love.[55]

But the value to Elisha, in after life, of that parting scene was independent of and higher than the gift which it won for him — the last solemn communications; the reply; the answer; and then no more, but the chariots of fire and the horses of fire, and the rapture into the Unseen. The elevation of the scene was beyond language; but Elisha could not refrain from the cry, "My father, my father! The chariot of Israel, and the horsemen thereof" [2 Kgs. 2:12]. There is nothing quite like it in sacred history. It is far above the silent removal of Enoch from earth, and far below the calm majesty of the Ascension, when no chariots of fire were needed to sweep the risen body of the Redeemer from the earth; when, as they beheld, he was taken up, and a cloud received him out of their sight [Acts 1:9]. At the moment of death heaven has at times been opened to the humblest Christians, and he who makes the flames of fire his ministers, has displayed himself, as to Stephen [Acts 7:55–56], ere the soul has parted from the body.

Yet in any case the outward accompaniments of the departure from this world of a great and saintly soul are far less important than the fact itself. Some who hear me may have been present at deathbeds which they will never forget. Some, very probably, will some day be present at them, and may remember what is now said to them. Few events in life are of such vital bearing on our eternal state as these high experiences. To be at the bedside of a dying Christian, to listen to his last words and join in his last prayers, to partake, it may be, in his last Communion, is to know something of Elisha's feelings beyond the Jordan, nay, something of the mind of the Apostles on the mount of the Transfiguration or on the mount of the Ascension. In such scenes Calvary and Tabor are often strangely blended: the physical suffering with the lofty and transcendental calm — the visible break-up of the poor human framework with the spiritual illumination of the chariots of fire and horses of fire, that are already on their way from paradise. For if so much was possible under the old law — a shadow from first to last of good things to come [Heb. 10:1] — what may not be, what has not been, possible for Christians with whom our Lord and Savior, incarnate, crucified, interceding, is present, ready "to save to the uttermost them that come unto God by him" [Heb. 7:25]? To witness a Christian deathbed is to witness not a triumph of human energy, or composure, or fortitude; but a display of his invigorating grace — the mercy and the majesty of the Redeemer, rendered visible in the peace and joy of the redeemed. Faith does not now see the chariots of fire and horses of fire; but she listens for words which, since the consecration they received on Calvary, mean infinitely more — "Into thy hands I commend my spirit, for thou hast redeemed me, O Lord, thou God of truth" [Ps. 31:6; Luke 23:46].

CHAPTER SIX

HOLY PREACHING
Ethical Interpretation and the Exegetical Imagination

He often tells them that sermons are dangerous things, that none goes out of church as he came in, but either better, or worse; that none is careless before his Judge, and that the word of God shall judge us. By these and other means the Parson procures attention; but the character of his sermon is holiness; he is not witty, or learned, or eloquent, but holy. A character that... is gained, first, by choosing texts of devotion, not controversy, moving and ravishing texts, whereof the Scriptures are full. Secondly, by dipping and seasoning all our words and sentences in our hearts, before they come into our mouths, truly affecting, and cordially expressing all that we say, so that the auditors may plainly perceive that every word is heart-deep.

— GEORGE HERBERT, "THE PARSON PREACHING"

Joan of Arc: "I hear voices telling me what to do. They come from God."
Capt. Robert de Baudricourt: "They come from your imagination."
Joan: "Of course. That is how the messages of God come to us."

— GEORGE BERNARD SHAW, *St. Joan*

In seventeenth-century England, preaching was the most popular form of public entertainment and sermons the most widely read literature. The great London preachers dazzled theologically sophisticated audiences, but they also drew the common people in crowds, for religious controversy was the daily news. And like all national celebrities, they had their less talented imitators in the provinces. When George Herbert asserted that the character of the Country Parson's sermon is holiness, he meant that preachers should stop trying to impress their people and instead move them to repentance and an all-involving commitment to the Christian life. The purpose of this chapter is to present a view of biblical preaching that is coherent within the contemporary context[1] and, further, to commend a style of poetic preaching that is capable of motivating such a commitment.

Specifically, I maintain that holy preaching is explicitly oriented toward the biblical text and is characterized by a willingness to acquire new habits of thought in order to read it with comprehension. Such a willingness to think in new ways is the disposition necessary for ethical interpretation of the Scriptures; it is also the essence of the biblical concept of repentance. These two — ethical interpretation and repentance — are closely linked. I use the term "ethical interpretation" to designate an approach to the text which evidences curiosity about the unknown, the strange, the other-than-ourselves — curiosity acute enough to open us to the possibility of personal change in response to what we learn. And profound personal change, motivated by fresh thinking, is what the Bible means by "repentance." The concept includes more than contrition for specific sins; it entails a radical reorientation of self (cf. Hebrew *teshuvah*, from *shuv*, "turn"), a reordering of mental habits (cf. Greek *metanoia*, "change of mind"). Here I shall argue that the preacher's chief task is to establish and maintain within the worshipping community the conditions that make it possible to hear the Scriptures as the Word of God, that is, as an invitation and challenge to change.

This argument is integrally related to the strand of biblical preaching that has been traced in this book; for the idea that there is a connection between reading the Scriptures with comprehension and moral transformation was central to the English Reformation. Thomas Cranmer draws that connection in "A Fruitful Exhortation to the Reading and Knowledge of Holy Scripture," the first of the homilies distributed for general usage in reformed English churches:

> And in reading of God's word, he most profiteth not always that is most ready in turning of the book, or in saying of it without the book; but he that is most turned into it, that is most inspired with the Holy Ghost, most in his heart and life altered and changed into that thing which he readeth; he that is daily less and less proud, less wrathful, less covetous, and less desirous of worldly and vain pleasures; he that daily (forsaking his old vicious life) increaseth in virtue more and more.[2]

Reading the Scriptures *as the Word of God* is the basic identifying activity of the Christian community. The essential form of the common life is in the broadest sense a conversation, in which members of the community explore and debate their meaning, and find ways to live together in obedience to what they have read. In what follows I stress the need for openness in conversation, so that many voices may be heard: the different voices within the biblical text, within the community, and also the voices of outsiders. Maintaining openness requires both curiosity and trust — among the members of the community and even more in the text which they have gathered to hear. This curiosity and trust express themselves in a conviction that, no matter how strange or unappealing a given passage may be, there must be something in it for us, something to be gained from the work of painstaking, acute listening which is the fundamental act of obedience (cf. Latin ob-audire). While the interpretive conversation is open-ended with respect to the form that a faithful response may take in the present situation, it is nonetheless grounded by conviction of the necessity and, finally, the safety of listening to the text.

If the interpretive conversation is open-ended, it is not infinitely so. Walter Brueggemann suggests that the biblical text delineates "a few basic options for the faithful life."[3] The implications of this are perhaps obvious but worth noting: namely, there is more than one way to pursue the faithful life; but in any given situation, there are not many choices that can be validated on the basis of the vision, the promise, and the demand of the biblical text. In order to clarify the following discussion, I state briefly what I consider to be the essential content of the Christian faith, that is, what constitutes the theological framework in which the interpretive discussion about Scripture takes place. For the trust required to maintain openness must be based initially on certain common commitments. The faith commitments shared by all Christians are those made in baptism and nurtured through participation in the liturgy: profession of faith in a Triune God, traditionally (though not exclusively) known by the names of Father, Son, and Holy Spirit; in the incarnation of God in Jesus Christ; in the redemptive value for all humankind of his suffering, death, and resurrection, in which we share through baptism; in the presence and power of the Holy Spirit animating the Church. These basic commitments must obtain within the community of faith if its readings of Scripture are to be in continuity with the theological understandings of Christian communities in other places and times, which is one criterion for the valid exercise of the interpretive imagination.

I agree with the view taken by many "conservatives" that strong factors in the present cultural and theological climate militate against a clear profession of baptismal faith.[4] But I believe also that liberals and conservatives often become entrenched in opposing theological positions — about inclusive language, homosexuality, evangelization, justice versus salvation as the central concern of the Gospel — which pre-scind on either side from a wide-ranging, deeply curious investigation of the biblical text. The great challenge to contemporary preachers, what-ever their positions on these issues and others that threaten to divide parishes, denominations, or the Church as a whole, is to develop a rich, flexible, biblically based language of public discourse. The fundamental challenge is exactly the same as that which was faced and met, in the two great periods of Anglican preaching, by the five men whose work is presented here; very likely it is the abiding challenge to preachers of every age.

But the specific form of the challenge must be re-identified with some precision by each generation. It has been a basic premise of this study that one's preaching style always reflects a certain way of under-standing the Bible, and so the question might be posed: what kind of preaching does the current state of biblical studies require?[5] Note that this is not the same as asking, what kind of preaching does it presently encourage? I do not believe that, on the whole, contemporary biblical scholarship is encouraging of or even particularly interested in preach-ing. Indeed, it may be one important task of great preachers to call biblical scholars back to the service of the Church by reminding them of the real nature of the text they are accustomed to handle in brisk professional fashion. At the dawn of historical criticism, H. P. Liddon's Oxford sermons issued such a call; and we must hope that it can still be articulated and heard in our own day. In my judgment, it is the responsibility of preachers to use the insights of contemporary biblical scholarship yet not to assume its preoccupations uncritically. Compe-tent and diligent biblical preachers do not know the text less well than their counterparts in biblical studies; they know it differently. There-fore the appropriate relationship between homiletics and biblical studies should be one of complementarity and, invariably, mutual correction. In my judgment, the current state of biblical studies invites correction from preaching in two directions: namely, hermeneutics and ethics.

The hermeneutical correction required is to set forth the text in a way that transcends simple rationalism, while yet respecting historical consciousness and the workings of reason. In a series of seminal lectures on the role of imagination in preaching, theologian Joseph Sittler speaks of the urgent problem of hermeneutics posed by the profound unfold-ing of the matrix out of which the biblical witness was fashioned and further, the reconstruction of theological method in "open disengage-ment from all previous alliances." The drastic difference in vocabulary and worldview between the Bible and our own time, but more particularly between the Bible and modern biblical studies, forces preachers and theologians to do "fresh foundational work":

> For engagement, then, with the powers of irrelevance, incomprehension, denial, and of sheer emptiness, a new work of the imagination is required both of the theologian and the preacher. When an age matures to a point where it displays a radical transference of interest, and when its very language reveals that what former times felt as fact are [sic] no longer so felt, then the central task is clearly exposed. Demythologization as a biblical program inevitably begets symbolization as a theological program. When, that is to say, it becomes the effort of biblical theology to penetrate to the divine realities, forms, and intentions that have temporally invested in reportorial forms available to the moment, it becomes the principal effort of systematic theology to interpret the biblical story in amplest symbolic dimensions. When myth is the term for story, symbol is its vocabulary.[6]

The ethical challenge is to represent accurately the essentially moral vision of Scripture and to address the moral concerns of the faith community, without resorting to either simplistic moralisms or amoral sentimentality. Meeting that challenge in the work of preaching involves a profound vulnerability, first on the part of the preacher and then from the auditors; and that very vulnerability is the mark of authenticity that distinguishes ethical proclamation of the Gospel from moralistic prating. The nature of the vulnerability that ethical preaching requires is suggested by Paul Holmer, in his exposition of Kierkegaard's view of the ethical life: "Ethicality is not a matter of searching for conceptual truth; it is rather a matter of seeking to become the truth.... Ethicality does not produce objective truths — it transforms the subject."[7]

Biblical speech forms themselves offer models for a style of preaching which seeks to transform its subjects without being "preachy." Nathan does not harangue David on violations of the sixth, seventh, and tenth commandments (2 Samuel 12); he uses a story, which the king may or may not have taken as fictional, that enables David to see the moral contours of the situation and render an accurate judgment on himself.[8] Isaiah sings a love-song about a vineyard (Isa. 5:17); Lady Wisdom (Prov. 1:20–33, 8:1–9:18) freely mixes prophetic summons, accusations, and promises with the reasonable appeal of a teacher and also womanly allure in order to win the *ingénu* to the right path. In every case, the preachers within the Bible appeal to the heart, which would seem to be what Herbert intended when he commended "ravishing" rather than controversial texts to the Country Parson; it is the heart ravished by just guilt and wholesome desire that is the best moral instructor.

These examples of biblical preaching all demonstrate a quality too little evident even in contemporary preaching that claims to take direct inspiration from the Bible, namely preaching with an explicit social agenda that is sometimes termed "prophetic." The quality that marks the preaching of the genuine biblical prophets is irony. Homiletician Charles Rice points to something fundamental in biblical preaching when he suggests that we need a more ironic and less heroic mode of discourse.[9] Ironic speaking implies a certain voluntary marginalization, a willingness to remain outside the power structure and articulate a vision without a program attached, to speak fearlessly to the present situation and yet admit with all humility that the future remains obscure. The signal instance of the contrast between ironic and heroic preaching is Jeremiah's "Amen" to the vainglorious assertions of Hananiah that the Lord is breaking the yoke of the king of Babylon (Jer. 28:1–11). The situation is the ultimate marginalization, exile, which Jeremiah accepts as sufficient — that is, as providing at least the minimal conditions for Israel to maintain its faithfulness to God (cf. chap. 29) — and Hananiah and the other lying prophets do not. On this occasion Jeremiah, having no word from the Lord, goes his way in silence; both prophet and people must be content with his "uninspired" reminder of the long history of prophets telling (truly) of "war and evil and plague." Much that goes by the name of "prophetic preaching" is in fact heroic. Like Hananiah, it invokes God's word to endorse our own programs rather than to call their premises into question. In Dietrich Bonhoeffer's terms, it is reading Scripture for ourselves rather than against ourselves.[10]

The hermeneutical and the ethical challenges dovetail in the imperative for a style of preaching that takes seriously the imaginative character of biblical language as the chief means by which the Scriptures exercise what has traditionally been called their "authority." It is not despite but just because of their strong appeal to the imagination that virtually all Christians in ages previous to our own have looked to them — if not always honored them in practice — as "primary and decisive... in matters of faith and morals."[11] The biblical writers understood far better than we generally do that the chief faculty of moral discernment is a rich critical imagination. Garrett Green has argued well that the biblical term "heart," whose thoughts and intentions the Word of God probes (Heb. 4:12), is the functional equivalent of what he calls "the paradigmatic imagination," by which we form, with the aid of the Scriptures, accurate ideas about God and the world. "Both heart and imagination are at once the seat of intellectual as well as emotional faculties"; both are susceptible to deception and capable of deceit as well as of truthfulness.[12]

Drawing the connection between my use of the word "imagination" and the biblical "heart" is a step toward meeting what may be the most obvious objection to the approach to the Scriptures commended here. For many people feel that imagination is a special intellectual endowment, like a pronounced gift for music or foreign languages, which they and most others lack. But of course everyone has "heart," and so each of us is equally charged to lift to God a discerning and responsive imagination. The biblical preacher understands that the imagination becomes capable of faithfulness as it is filled with scriptural stories, images, prayers, and exhortations. The preachers treated here strive in various ways to deepen the impress of those biblical speech forms on an imagination shaped by participation in the catholic tradition reaching from ancient times to the present. In what follows I offer a contemporary understanding of the character of the biblical witness which, I believe, provides for proper exercise of the imagination in the Church's interpretation and proclamation of Scripture.

A Perspectival Witness

As I stated at the outset, the stimulus for this book is a problem: namely, that there is little serious wrestling with the biblical message in mainline churches. In my judgment, that lack is due chiefly to a neglected and atrophied Christian imagination, to which the language of the Bible is largely unintelligible. I think it is safe to say that the Scriptures are less accessible to the average believer today than before the Reformation, even if most churchgoers own a personal copy in semi-idiomatic English. They are inaccessible, not because we lack historical information about the biblical world (indeed, we have more of it than any previous generation), but because we do not have the imaginative skills to probe the subject matter of the Bible: love and forgiveness, suffering, redemption, the persistence of evil and the birth of boundless hope. For the most part, secular education and the mass media have left us ill-equipped to deal with those nonmolecular facts of human existence which can be verified but not predicted; proclaimed, probed, understood both with reason and deep in the bones, but yet not fully explained in terms of logical concepts and a chronological sequence of events.

The only language adequate to express and draw connections among such more-than-logical phenomena is the poetic language of symbol: myth, metaphor, proverb, parable, even (and not least) of legal code, as Mary Douglas's brilliant work on Leviticus has demonstrated.[13] The function of symbolic language is, in Paul Ricoeur's terms, to "redescribe" reality and thus "disclose a world" richer in meaning than the one we had previously inhabited.[14] It is just the biblical writers' fluency in the language of symbol that constitutes the gap between their epistemological presuppositions and our own. For modern technological culture is perhaps unparalleled among the "high cultures" of history for its impatience and ineptitude with the subtleties of verbal expression, as anyone who has read computer manuals knows. Toward the end of the last century, Cardinal Newman wrote a prescient reflection on the imaginative impoverishment that plagues modernity: "I consider...that it is not reason that is against us, but imagination. The mind, after having, to the utter neglect of the Gospels, lived in science, experiences, on coming back to Scripture, an utter strangeness in what it reads."[15]

I propose that the preacher's first and most important responsibility is to educate the imaginations of her hearers so that they have the linguistic skills to enter into the world which Scripture discloses, and may thus make a genuine choice about whether to live there. The biblical preacher is a sort of elementary language teacher, not a translator, as we most frequently (if unconsciously) assume. For whether or not preachers have read or remember Bultmann, they often engage in a program of demythologizing the Bible, that is, translating it into the terms of modern rationalism. Thus, as I recently heard, John's version of the miracle of the loaves and fishes becomes a display of impressive generosity in a child who shared his lunch, moving others in the crowd to do likewise; and we also should emulate him in our own context.

The attraction of such an approach is obvious: it makes Scripture conformable to our accustomed categories of thought and supports socially valuable behavior. This combination of effects is what is usually meant by "making the Bible relevant." But the problem is that ready applicability has been purchased at the price of what the Bible actually says. While there might be some moral force to a story of public sharing of scant resources, the one that John tells is quite different; he says that Jesus made more food on the spot. Thus he invites us to contemplate a world where offering up all the little we have inexplicably yields more, in bewildering abundance. Responding to that invitation requires that we do something both more difficult and more ethically significant than sharing our lunch: namely, that we think in fundamentally new ways about the presence and power of God. As I have noted, the New Testament word for taking on new mental habits is *metanoia*, "a change of mind," commonly rendered "repentance." The preacher who invites the congregation to contemplate the multiplication of the loaves and fishes or the parting of the Red Sea *without translating away the wonder*, calls upon the congregation to repent.

It is evident that offering a conceptual translation is far easier for both preacher and hearer than sustaining attention to the particularities of a text whose thought categories are so foreign to us. As anyone who has ever engaged in language study knows, success requires a certain dogged patience with the strange which is perhaps the essence of intellectual generosity. The reward for learning to listen to the Bible on its own terms is that a more spacious world opens to us. And there we see exposed the terrible limitations that we previously accepted as givens of the human condition; further, we see those limitations overcome: in the faithfulness of God kept in the face of Israel's faithlessness; in the suffering psalmists' utter trust in God, expressed equally in wild hope and bitter accusation; in the incarnation, death, and resurrection of Jesus Christ. The relevance of the Scriptures is that they disclose a vision of reality that takes account of my needs, my longing, and my despair, not that they endorse my thinking and lifestyle as presently constituted.

The miracle stories are parade examples of what is in fact the Bible's regular rhetorical strategy of using imaginative language to jostle us into radically new ways of looking at the world and ourselves. But it is more customary for Christians to speak of the Scriptures as being "inspired" than "imaginative." While Anglicans have generally been reluctant to define too closely the nature of the Holy Spirit's inspiration, it seems valid to consider inspired utterance as a special category of imaginative speech, which greatly exceeds even the author's own capacity for conceptualization. T. S. Eliot, speaking of secular as well as religious poetry, suggests that "if the word 'inspiration' is to have any meaning, it must mean just this, that the speaker or writer is uttering something which he does not wholly understand — or which he may even misinterpret when the inspiration has departed from him."[16] Certainly the images that Scripture itself uses to describe the Word of God suggest that it can be neither contained nor controlled: a hammer beating within a body until the blows resound in words, a fire raging inside, a baby bursting from the womb.

If inspired speech may confound even the one who utters it, this is rather due to its vast capacity for meaning than to vagueness. The Scriptures are a treasure-room out of which the scribe trained for the kingdom of heaven brings what is new and what is old (Matt. 13:52). Yet, as all the preachers represented here recognize, there is a reticence inherent in symbolic language that is not separable from its richness; that is to say, it begs and begets interpretation. The peculiar susceptibility to interpretation that characterizes imaginative speech, and is developed to the highest degree in the Scriptures, would seem to be the quality that makes them the source of continually renewed life in the Church and, at the same time, of perpetual disagreement. Bonhoeffer's image beautifully expresses the dual character of reticence and richness: "The Bible is that book in which God's word is stored until the end of all things."[17] The reference to the end-time is notable as it bears upon the need for both humility and charity in interpretation. All the preachers represented here have a heightened awareness of the Scripture's inexhaustible fruitfulness for interpretation. At the same time, they share a strong eschatological sense, now rare in mainstream Protestant preaching. If the full truth of revelation cannot be known until "Christ is all in all" (Col. 3:11), then we waste our powers and perhaps even do harm by overpreaching the mysteries of God and pretending to a certainty that has not been granted.[18]

In his "attempt to construct some account of scriptural inspiration from first principles," Austin Farrer focuses on the fact that the supernatural mystery that is the heart of Christ's teaching is expressed in certain "tremendous images" — for example, Christ as the Son of Man, the true Adam; the supper as the symbol "of sacrifice and communion, of expiation and covenant" — without which "the teaching would not be supernatural revelation, but instruction in piety and morals. . . . The great images interpreted the events of Christ's ministry, death and resurrection, and the events interpreted the images; the interplay of the two is revelation." He describes how this process of reflection on images continued in the mind of the apostles "with an inexpressible creative force. The several distinct images grew together into fresh unities, opened out in new detail, attracted to themselves and assimilated further image-material. . . . This is the way inspiration worked. The stuff of inspiration is living images."[19] Following from this view of inspiration, "theology is the analysis and criticism of the revealed images"; it tests and determines their sense.[20]

Farrer's view that it is the centrality of images that makes the Scriptures something more than a moral treatise contributes to an understanding of the nature of ethical preaching. Although he does not treat the distinct role of the preacher, it is consistent with his view of apostolic inspiration to say that the preacher holds forth the biblical images, articulates them so that they may continue to inspire reflection and action through the whole worshipping community. Her task, then, is the very opposite of translating the images into the univocal language of modern rationalism. In probing the complexity of the images, she only makes them more problematic, more resistant to translation into a series of handy moral lessons, and thus ultimately a more fruitful resource for the Church in confronting the intractably difficult moral questions that trouble it in every age.

The strangeness of Scripture is no small part of its moral value — strangeness not only in the view of reality it expresses but also in its very manner of address. The language of the Bible is designed to arouse curiosity in the heart that is disposed to be faithful. Curiosity is much underrated as an ethical as well as intellectual virtue; for it is the basis of the ethical stance. The primary ethical question is how we relate to those who differ from ourselves; and curiosity is fundamentally an interest in the character and perspective of the other, a willingness to give them a hearing and grant them, initially at least, coherence.[21] The Scriptures themselves are for the Christian community the paradigmatic "other"; there can be no ethical preaching that does not take respectful account of how deeply alien to us is this written witness to the Word of God.[22]

Curiosity is a virtue that is cultivated and bears fruit in the imagination, which is itself the interpretive faculty by which we relate to that which is strange, not fully known, or not immediately present to us. And, of course, that is most of reality, past, present, and future. Hence, constant exercise of the imagination is a practical necessity for every healthy human being, and not only the science fiction writer or the religious mystic (if "mystic" be taken in the narrow sense of one with a special receptivity to visionary or auditory experience). We use it in composing a letter or a sermon (to be received some time in the future in circumstances at which we can now only guess), designing a garden or an investment portfolio, figuring out why a teenager is sulking. A healthy, flexible imagination is the "coping mechanism" by which, moment by moment, we make the small extrapolations that give us a history (the past) and a world (the present) and enable us to envision a future or at least trust that there is one.

Although the imaginative capacity is universal and is employed in countless quotidian situations, it does indeed have a mystical dimension, in the sense of involving us, to a greater or lesser extent, in an apprehension of the totality of life, which is essentially mysterious. As Richard Kroner has argued in a foundational study of imagination as an aspect of religious knowledge, "an image of ultimate truth is included in every practical situation, and . . . this image is truly religious, or, if not, then it is pseudo-religious and superstitious."[23]

For the spiritual life, the most important use of imagination is in coming to know God. The fact that we know God imaginatively is congruent with the way we know all other persons and also ourselves. We do not form a theory about our intimates. Theorizing about persons, as a substitute for knowing them, is otherwise known as prejudice; and it is the basis of oppression and hatred, not intimacy. Rather we form an *image* of those whom we love: a picture, based on the limited data of our experience, which is whole yet nevertheless always incomplete, subject to constant revision and addition. Similarly, when we want to know about a stranger, we ask someone close to them for an approximation of their character: "What is he like? Tell me about him." We intuitively know not to ask for an objective measure of the person — "Who *is* she?" — but rather for an impressionistic evaluation of what she is *like*. The qualifier "like" lends modesty to all assertions; it acknowledges the perspectival character of personal testimony.[24]

The biblical witness to the nature of God is likewise impressionistic and perspectival. Rigor in maintaining the modesty of our assertions would seem to be what underlies the prohibition against graven images. We must not try to show God directly; we can do no more than indicate what God is like. With respect to observing the proper limits on the witness of faith, there is an instructive contrast between idolatrous Israel proclaiming over the golden calf, "These are your gods, O Israel" (Exod. 32:4), and the prophet Ezekiel. The first chapter of the book of Ezekiel is the least dogmatical text imaginable. Ezekiel's report of his vision of God by the river Chebar is so full of qualifying particles that the Hebrew is almost untranslatable:

> There was something like a throne, resembling sapphire; and up above the likeness of a throne was what resembled a human form. And above what resembled his loins I saw the like of gleaming amber, having the

semblance of fire enclosing it all around, and below what resembled his loins I saw the semblance of fire, and there was flashing about him. The semblance of the bow in the midst of clouds on a rainy day — such was the appearance of the flashing all about. This was the appearance of the image of the glory of the LORD. (Ezek. 1:26–28a; translation my own)

The prophet, who had a reputation as a great lyrical stylist (Ezek. 33:32), here willingly trips over his own tongue lest his description of God be taken as objective representation.

The work of interpretation is greatly complicated, and its interest incalculably increased, by the diversity of perspectives with which the biblical witness presents us. There is an essential coherence, traditionally called "unity," to the Scriptures, which historical criticism has tended to obscure with its isolating emphasis on the (presumed) conditions and process of production lying behind a given text. Their unity derives from the fact that it is one God who is made known to us, through Israel's varied witness. God's character is revealed as having integrity but not predictability; we worship not a stone idol of unchanging demeanor but a living God of whom certain basic traits are repeatedly affirmed: "merciful and gracious, slow to anger and abounding in steadfast love" (Ps. 145:8, cf. Exod. 34:6 et passim). God's character discloses, reinforces, and complicates itself through two Testaments. It is the partiality and volatility of personal relationship, as well as the gradual maturing of the relationship between God and Israel, which accounts for the extraordinary diversity of the Scriptures.

The aim of all the Scriptures is to give us an inside view of committed relationship with the God of Israel, based upon the testimony of those most deeply experienced in it. Yet this acknowledgment of the perspectival character of the biblical witness is to be distinguished from relativism, for it rests on the claim that the Scriptures have an essential, mystical unity. When the Church affirms in worship that the Bible is, in its entirety, the Word of God, it means that the Scriptures are not a miscellany of opinions or even facts about God. Rather, they reveal God. More precisely, the carefully crafted written word, reshaped and transmitted by many hands, is the ambiguous medium through which God chooses to be known to us. However obliquely, dimly ("through a glass darkly"), nonetheless it is very God who is thus known to us, by the inspiration of the Holy Spirit.

It follows from this that the chief homiletical task is not to pronounce "the Truth," although a knowledge of truth will emerge, however falteringly, when the partnership of mutual speaking and listening is faithfully maintained between pastor and people. Indeed, attempts to expound "the (single, immutable) meaning" of the Scriptures are inherently unethical, for they fail to respect the character of this "other" that is the *living* word of God. Rather the preacher is to articulate, over weeks and years, the text's multiple voices, so that those voices may form the background against which the voices within the community are heard — and alongside them, the threats, accusations, and skepticism of outsiders, which are not wholly unjust. When the character of the sermon is holiness, listeners are invited into a wide-ranging but disciplined conversation, ongoing through the ages and advanced, with each generation of faith and unfaith, into new areas of concern. That conversation enhances the coping skills of the participants, which is to say, it helps them stand in responsible relation to the whole of the created world. The responsibility is real, though it be assumed through an imaginative effort, guided by the Scriptures. In practical terms, for the ordinary North American Christian, taking that responsibility means relating one's present activity and belief to a larger individual and family history, to the Apostles' Creed and the domestic and foreign policies of the current government administration, to the disobedience in the Garden and the fall of Jerusalem, the AIDS crisis and drug wars, the crucifixion on Golgotha, and destruction of the rain forests.

As the biblical witness is itself ineluctably personal (though not private), so the preacher who would be faithful to it must become personally involved in a process akin to the interpretation of poetry, a process to which intellect, emotion, memory, conscience, and will all contribute, and by which over a lifetime all are transformed. For "sermons are dangerous things"; no one comes out of the interpretive process as she went in, least of all the preacher. Wherever anyone succeeds in doing so, the scriptural inspiration that animates the community of faith has been temporarily eclipsed.

Preaching that acknowledges the character of the Scriptures as a personal and imaginative witness to faith is genuinely inclusive, in two senses. First, it recognizes that in many, perhaps most cases, people may in good faith genuinely disagree about the correct interpretation of the facts and the right course of action. Through conversation we maintain the common life, which provides the only basis for serious and (relatively) safe exploration of the few options that conduce to faithful living. Second, such an acknowledgment facilitates conversation with outsiders and makes room for their voices to be heard within the community of faith, without disguising — indeed, while foregrounding — the personal commitment that obtains there. But respectful attention to others who do not share our own views and commitments should not be confused with the too-common error of liberalism in treating the Christian story (including Israel's history) as a matter of private and elective interest to believers. In a time when the dominant culture categorically denies the public relevance of revealed religion and asserts that the search for truth is self-authenticating, the Church is especially pressed within the context of its own shared life to test and criticize interpretations of the multifaceted truth to which the Scriptures attest. In the next section I shall argue that exegetical preaching is essential to this process of testing interpretations.

Conversation in Community

The preachers I have treated in this book were chosen for their skill as exegetical preachers; all of them derive meaning from the text by attending closely to its words and specific form. Their style of preaching contrasts with the thematic preaching that, in my experience, is dominant in pulpits, in which it is not so much the text itself that is explored but rather a doctrinal or moral principle abstracted from the text. I hope that I have established the case — rather, that these five preachers have established it for me — that exegetical preaching is not inherently boring or "irrelevant," as many preachers fear. On the contrary, wrestling with the peculiarities and difficulties of the text is the surest way to maintain the liveliness of the interpretive conversation by perpetuating within the community of faith an openness toward the other, including and above all the other that is Scripture itself. The problem with thematic preaching, practiced as a norm, is the tendency to reinforce an established viewpoint; whereas the aim of preaching is, or should be, fundamental change. In his lectures on homiletics to the Confessing Church seminary at Finkenwalde, Dietrich Bonhoeffer comments perceptively: "Thematic preaching carries the danger that only the proposed problem and the suggested answer will be remembered; apologetic comes to the fore and the text is ignored."[25] The best argument for exegetical preaching is that it allows the text to function as what it is: inspired speech, potent to introduce to the community of faith new directions for movement and also new problems, more fruitful than the ones advanced by our own agendas. For not all problems are of equal ethical value, no more than all solutions; and it is crucial for the health of the community to identify accurately and dwell upon the problems which Scripture invites us to ponder. The divine "answer" to Job (Job 38 — 41) and Jesus' conversations with both disciples (e.g, Mark 8:14–21, 10:35–45) and religious leaders (Mark 12:13–27) are key instances of God's regular strategy of orienting us to the truth by setting aside the problems that had previously occupied us and posing questions that lead us, if we allow them to do so, more deeply into the mysteries that hold our life.

The inspiration of the Scriptures becomes an operative ethical force when not just the preacher but the whole community is concerned and competent to give close attention to their words and images. Surprising metaphors challenge our ready categorizations: "Love is strong as death, passion fierce as Sheol" (Song of Songs 8:6). The simile leads the preacher of a wedding sermon to consider that love may be more like death than (as we generally think) its polar opposite. Their likeness in strength and fierceness suggests that love is the only thing that consumes us as fully as does death; love teaches us to give ourselves wholly and freely, and thus it is the best preparation for death, to which the whole Christian life is directed. Consonant with the Gospel and directly contrary to our cultural assumptions, death does not defeat what love has built but rather completes it.

Serious, ongoing exegetical preaching, aimed at identifying patterns of faithful relationship with God and neighbor, exposes the inadequacy of narrowly issue-oriented resort to the text. In considering a building program, it may be less effective for a congregation to study the account of Solomon's Temple construction than to discuss the achievements and failures of the seven churches in the Revelation to John. Again, the teaching about homosexuality in Leviticus should be studied in the context of the larger vision of holiness which that book sets forth, and further in light of Jesus' understandings of purity and community. There may not be a "right answer" to the questions that most deeply trouble us; but such an approach helpfully confounds the self-serving tendency to proof-texting on both sides and opens up the possibility of genuinely new insight.

To a very great extent, then, the Church's life is its interpretive conversation. The Roman Catholic theologian Nicholas Lash has suggested that the proper business of the Church is to be "an academy of word-care," a guild of (mostly amateur) philologists, skilled lovers of the Word of God.[26] This business is carried on in worship and private prayer, in vestry meetings, hospitals, and classrooms, as well as in the pulpit. In those settings and countless others, scriptural language is probed, its sense tested in light of all that we experience and know from other sources. Conversely (and crucial to the accuracy of our interpretation), our experience is scrutinized in light of the revealing images; the words of the Scriptures provide a measure against which the coherence of our thought and action is to be tested. Over the course of years, the disciplined care of words challenges the identity and commitments of every participant.

The idea that the meaning of Scripture is known through this interpretive conversation has implications for our understanding of scriptural authority. The model I propose is that the Bible functions in decision-making something like a healthy family ethos; it is less like a set of rules to be applied than a verbal tradition in which Christians mature as individuals and as a community. Every family shapes behavior and gives criteria for moral judgment through the stories it tells, the instructions it gives, the customs it institutes and observes, through explicit prohibitions and demands, as well as indirect statements of expectation, aspiration, and also fear.[27] Following this model, the preacher's responsibility is to promote a detailed and accurate understanding of the Church's Scripture-based ethos which has traditionally been known as the Rule of Faith. Thus she provides for the continuance of that ethos, yet not with a view to immutability, for without regular change, every heritage must die. If Scripture is truly the focus of the Church's attention, then it will inevitably beget new interpretations, sometimes as a result of new historical or philological knowledge. But much more significantly, we often and legitimately depart from the interpretations of our predecessors, or our own earlier understandings, because Scripture addresses us as the living Word of God; and therefore it does not speak in identical fashion on every occasion. Freshened by the Holy Spirit, it is at each reading a new utterance, directed personally but not privately to each hearer and generation of faith.

Indeed, as in a healthy family, the very integrity Scripture has bred in us may lead us at points to make thoughtful departures from its judgments. In considering the range of interpretive freedom that Scripture not only grants but encourages, it is useful to reflect on the fact that, generations of redaction notwithstanding, the final form of the Scriptures does not ameliorate its internal tensions: for example, the Deuteronomic slave legislation (Deut. 15:12–18) is set forth alongside the earlier regulations in the Covenant Code (Exod. 21:2–11), with no indication of how Israel is to adjudicate between them. In a number of cases, tensions are even underscored. The Israelite sages juxtapose contradictory sayings (Prov. 26:4–5), and Qohelet makes a science of reversing himself (Eccles. 2:2 and 8:15, 7:3 and 7:9, 5:17 and 7:2, and so on). The account of the rise of the monarchy (1 Samuel 8–12) is a tangle of "pro" and "con" views whose origin is uncertain; but the effect is to imply that from the outset kingship was a very mixed blessing for Israel, about which opposite conclusions can legitimately be drawn. The prophets give drastically different moral assessments of even the primordial images of wilderness wandering (contrast Jer. 2:2 and Hos. 2:16–17 with Ezek. 20:13), the patriarch Jacob (contrast Hos. 12:3– 15 and Mal. 1:2), and the Jerusalem Temple (contrast Isaiah 6 and Ezekiel 8). The diversity within the biblical tradition suggests that disagreement and reinterpretation is itself part of the inspiration of the Holy Spirit animating the community of faith.

Opposite to this kind of open-ended, many sided conversation about the Scriptures, which I set forth as the process of ethical interpretation, is moralism. If the ethical stance is characterized by respectful curiosity about what is strange, moralism insists that one's own view is incontrovertible and stands in no need of supplementation. The Bible has throughout the history of the Church often been wielded as a weapon in battles both internal and external, and what I have said about the Scriptures' address to the imagination offers one way of understanding why such usage is unethical in its treatment not only of persons but also of the text. It ignores the call, which the Bible addresses continually to all its readers, to enter into relation with what is strange to us; theoretical positions, not texts, are treated as canon, that is, as the measure of faithfulness.

Instances may be cited of the contemporary Church's moralistic exclusion from the interpretive conversation of certain positions or persons who might legitimately be heard. However, I believe that the current critical climate evidences even more strongly a different kind of moralizing about whose dangers liberal churches and seminaries in particular tend to be naive. Specifically, I mean a moralism that is directed against the Bible and denies the authority of those portions that we take to represent moral insight inferior to our own. This variety of moralism is ancient; it was the first heresy identified by the Church, in the form of Marcion's attempted exclusion of the entire Old Testament. The best safeguards against this heresy, I believe, are two: first, making the fullest possible use of the knowledge and methodological sophistication that, by the grace of God, is presently available to the Church, and second, taking care that the insights of the past are not lost but are brought into conversation with present concerns. Therefore, in our own time, ethical interpretation requires that the preacher make regular use of both historical critical methods (bearing in mind also the critiques of that method which come from feminist and liberation perspectives) and the Church's tradition of scriptural interpretation, including and especially the liturgy.

I hope it is clear from what I have already said that an imaginative approach to Scripture does not invalidate historical criticism, but rather directs it toward the end of repentance, that is, toward a change of heart or mind that produces new moral vigor. Neither does the agenda of ethical interpretation mandate the investigation of only those texts or fields of study that are of obvious pastoral or spiritual relevance. The exegetical imagination is enriched by any study, however technical, that draws us into deeper consideration of the words and form and images of the text, that is, study that forces and enables us to read the text with care, rather than tempting us to talk around or "get behind" it in order to reconstruct social settings or literary layers for which there is no direct evidence. Thus, study that is practical for ministry includes advanced Hebrew syntax and poetic structure as well as ancient Near Eastern agricultural and funerary practice.

With respect to the problem of moralizing against the Bible, the most important function of historical study is to keep us from imposing our cultural assumptions upon a world we do not readily comprehend. The work of Carol Meyers, drawing on archaeology and social anthropology, challenges the view that the social role of women in early Israel was oppressively restricted, as she shows how economic balance is maintained in a society where the home is the primary production unit.[28] In so doing, she reminds us (obliquely) that the consumer-oriented system in which virtually all North Americans, men and women alike, participate is very far from the ideal for settlement of the Promised Land. Again, an accurate historical perspective could challenge a sense of moral superiority to the vengeful composer of Psalm 137, who longs to see Babylonian babies bashed against the rock. For the decision-making elements in our society (which include the writer and probably all readers of this book) are in terms of power more readily compared to the Babylonian tormentors than to the defeated Israelites to whom we would counsel mercy, and an educated imagination might well consider who could legitimately wish that our empire not last through another generation.

The second counter to moralizing against the biblical text, the tradition of premodern interpretation, seems to sort oddly with historical criticism. But it should be noted that "premodern" is not identical to "precritical" interpretation. The ancient and medieval commentators were not naive about the complexity of meaning, however their hermeneutics might differ from our own; the early Reformers reckoned seriously with the human and historical character of the text, even though the Holy Spirit remained for them the real author. But, unlike almost all modern biblical scholars, they were essentially unconcerned about the problem of historical distance between the biblical world and their own. They saw (correctly, I believe) that the real problem is the moral distance between the world the text calls us to inhabit and the one in which we are too content to stay. Liturgical usage often provides valuable clues to traditional understandings that call into question the sophistication and adequacy of contemporary readings. For preachers whose lectionary reflects ancient tradition (as the Anglican lectionaries do in part), previously "unpreachable" texts may well be opened up by consideration of the moral purpose a given text is meant to serve at a particular time in the Church year. This is true, because ancient tradition is generally more sensitive to the symbolic potential of the text.

Psalm 149 appears at first especially ill-chosen for the Feast of All Saints, perpetuating the unhappy stereotype of the serious religious person as a ruthless fanatic:

> Let the high praises of God be in their throats
> and two-edged swords in their hands,
> to execute vengeance on the nations
> and punishment on the peoples,
> to bind their kings with fetters
> and their nobles with chains of iron,
> to execute on them the judgment decreed.
> This is glory for all his faithful ones.
> Praise the LORD! (vv. 6–9)

The psalm might be dismissed as expressing "the spirit of the O.T., not of the N.T.";[29] yet many overtly irenic psalms were passed over in favor of this one to celebrate the glory of the saints. There must be something in the disconcerting conjunction between violence and praise that offers a key to the nature of sainthood. In fact, a regular pattern is discernible in the lives of the saints: fighting the evil within (contrition) prepares the way for contending with evil in the world. Considered in this light, the psalm points, in the highly condensed and suggestive language of poetry, to the fact that the self-inflicted violence of penitence, turned against our own private empire-building, clears the way for God's praise.

An attitude of moral superiority to the biblical text may be a sign that one is reading too literally. The interpretation suggested here takes the two-edged sword as a metaphor for the word of God that "is able to judge the thoughts and intentions of the heart" (Heb. 4:12; cf. Eph. 6:17, Rev. 1:16). There is more modern utility than is perhaps first evident for Augustine's principle regarding figurative interpretation, "that what is read should be subjected to diligent scrutiny until an interpretation contributing to the reign of charity is produced. If this result appears literally in the text, the expression being considered is not figurative."[30]

The search for an interpretation that conduces to charity does not mean whitewashing the Scriptures to remove all signs of Israel's idolatry and vituperation. I do not believe it can be maintained that the writers of either Testament were at all times successful in upholding the mystery and radical grace of God's presence, while determining concrete ways to live with their fears and their enemies. But in this case and many others, a figurative interpretation is on several counts preferable to writing off the text as further evidence of the primitive warlike spirit of ancient Israel. First, it has the support of the explicit New Testament reading and amplification of the metaphor of the two-edged sword. Second, a figurative interpretation does not depend on a historical assumption for which there is no evidence, namely, that the Israelites were more primitive than ourselves in either humanitarian concern or literary usage. Third (and most important), it respects the psalm as a witness to faith that can provide guidance for the Christian life, which is what the Church has always affirmed by its use of the term "Old Testament." Our modern awareness of the historical character of the biblical witness makes impossible any simple repristination of allegorical interpretation; we cannot decode the Hebrew Scriptures as a timeless system of references to Christ. John Howard Yoder's suggestion that they are to be read "directionally," as a story of promise and fulfillment,[31] better accords with their historical character as well as their function in the moral formation of readers.

Augustine's principle of charity might be seen as one element of a hermeneutics of humility, which is surely no less necessary either to the

full comprehension of the text or to our own dignity, than is a hermeneutics of suspicion, now widely recognized as a fundament of feminist
biblical interpretation.[32] The two hermeneutics may indeed be complementary. If women must clearly name the fact that the biblical texts do
not generally show as full an awareness of their experience as of men's,
neither can they afford to be naive about their own participation in sin.
The first several chapters of the Bible point to the truth (which has
frequently been underplayed on one side or the other) that women and
men share equally in the tendency to assert their own desires and perceived needs against God, and at the expense of one another. Rather
than refusing to read certain parts of the biblical text which are "identified as sexist or patriarchal,"[33] it is essential that we listen to every
scriptural text together if the Church is to achieve spiritual health as
a community in which men and women are free to acknowledge their
sinfulness to one another, to seek and offer forgiveness. At the very
least, we must listen because all those texts are part of our common
heritage, which, as modern psychology has taught us, can do permanent harm only if we ignore it. But the potential is much greater than
merely exposing the evil in a given text and thereby avoiding harm. For
if, having moved beyond naivete, we can trust the Scriptures enough
to affirm that, spoken in the ongoing life of the Church, they are indeed the living Word of God, addressed to and thereby dignifying every
member, then we must believe that they hold the key to our full per-
sonhood in Christ. Inevitably, men and women, old and young, poor
and rich, joyous and suffering, will hear different messages and find different stumbling blocks. Yet nonetheless we are pressed to exercise our
imagination in order to discover the perspective in which every part of
Scripture may be heard as the Word of God, that is, to discover how it
calls us to repentance.

To call the Bible "the Word of the Lord" is to confess our vulnerability to the Word that is foreign to us, our willingness to think in radically
new ways in order to receive it as gift and promise, "Thanks be to God."
The most important pastoral problem for the preacher is how to create
an environment in which the congregation can safely sustain an appropriate vulnerability to the Bible as God's Word. To refuse that effort
is what the Bible calls "hardness of heart," which Paul treats as the
antonym of "repentance" (Rom. 2:4–5; cf. Mark 6:52, Exod. 7:13, 22
et passim). Yet to accept it is difficult and painful, and so the preacher
must convey the assurance that listening to the text will never mean
giving up one's own right to a questioning, critical voice in the inter-

pretive conversation. The notion of "appropriate vulnerability" suggests a kind of responsiveness to the text somewhat different from that implied in Erich Auerbach's famous dictum that the Bible's claim to truth is "tyrannical" and its stories (in contrast to Homer's) "seek to subject us, and if we refuse to be subjected we are rebels."[34] While it is true that the Scriptures confound us far more often than they flatter or enchant, nonetheless their final aim is not subjugation but rather "edification" (a word much used in seventeenth-century homiletics). They upbuild the community of faith by seizing and stretching its imagination to entertain new possibilities for human life.

A New Homiletic

"The new homiletic" is a phrase that appears frequently now in the literature about preaching.[35] It is widely agreed that the preaching task is presently being reformulated, perhaps more drastically than at any time since the Reformation. Reliance on deductive method and the language of the lecture hall is repeatedly targeted for criticism, as symptomatic of a scientific approach in which the preacher seeks to present a persuasive statement of the truth, using the Bible as a sourcebook of objective propositions. In this older model of preaching as the art of sacred rhetoric, the audience is addressed with a view to intellectual persuasion, although ideally they are dazzled in the process. The newer literature tends to speak less of persuasion than imagination, and of engaging the audience in a creative process.[36] It reckons with scriptural forms along with their contents, and often aims at a sermon style that emulates the biblical writers in their use of story and metaphor. Thus Thomas Troeger summarizes the shift: "Homiletics, which began as the discipline of sacred rhetoric, is becoming the discipline of imaginative theology."[37]

The new sensibility about preaching that is emerging would seem to have an affinity with the style of poetic preaching represented by the sermons in this volume. It is probably no coincidence that a new appreciation of the symbolic capacity of religious language is reasserting itself in the present age, when, as in both the seventeenth and the nineteenth centuries, one of the chief facts of life confronting the preacher is the general collapse of what Joseph Sittler calls the "mental, emotional, and image context of the past."[38] These poet-preachers of the past offer modern preachers resources to contend with the forces and consequences of our own rapid cultural erosion: loss of personal security on a massive scale, a technological society that does not provide intellectual and emotional nourishment or even prepare people to receive it, a future that threatens more than it invites.

From them we may begin to learn how to "speak Scripture," the language not only of the biblical writers but also of the ancient and medieval commentators and theologians, as well as the poets who through centuries composed the prayers and hymns of the liturgy. They initiate us into the art of Christian conversation, the long and deep conversation about what God is "like." Each of them reads the great pattern in Scripture from his distinctive perspective; yet their readings are complementary and yield a picture that is multifaceted but coherent: God is humble (Andrewes) and abounding in mercy (Donne); the world bespeaks God's just providence (Hall), beauty (Robertson), and miraculous truth (Liddon).[39]

If much of the sickness of our age is cultural amnesia — living as though we came from nowhere and are under no obligation to head anywhere in particular — then participation in that millennia-long conversation may be seen as a way of healing our public memory. "The art of salvation is but the art of memory";[40] regaining fluency in the language of the Scriptures and the long tradition of their interpretation can enrich the depleted memory of the Church. For that language of story and symbol is the key to a store of memories that belong to us solely as we claim our identity as God's people and hear ourselves personally addressed by God's word. Those memories stretch all the way back to our creation in God's image; they enable us to participate in Israel's redemption and covenant and to see that those paradigmatic experiences give order and meaning to our own histories. By thus giving us a directed past, they have the power to draw us beyond the fearful and unimaginative absorption in the present that is such a strong element in our spiritual malaise.

Active, skillful involvement in that conversation also helps heal our internal conflicts, or at least enables us to live better with them. The political significance of exegetical conversation within the body of Christ should not be underestimated. These preachers lived in times when Europeans were slaughtering each other for their religious opinions — and they are doing so again even as this book goes to press. In their various situations, the preachers' resolute focus on Scripture, as well as their wide-ranging appeal to authorities from every age, was a hedge against empty religious polemic and pointed a way forward, beyond compromise, to a deeper engagement with the truth. The diversity of the tradition stands as a reminder of the limitations of any single historical vantage-point and a caution against dogmatic pronouncements on all but the few essential matters of faith. I would suggest that one area in which the contemporary Church might take particular encouragement and instruction from this strain of poetic preaching is the current struggle over inclusive language, especially in speaking about the Godhead. The great metaphorical preachers Donne and Andrewes show the remarkable freedom that the exegetical preacher can legitimately claim in speaking about what God is like, when the Scriptures serve, not as a constraint, but as a warrant and guide for our imaginations.

Simone Weil asked the question that weighs even more heavily now, fifty years after her death: "Where will a renewal come to us, to us who have spoiled and devastated the whole earthly globe?"; and answers, "Only from the past, if we love it."[41] Because words always come freighted with history, it is in large part the work of the poet, the true philologist, to teach us to love the past, and in that love to find curiosity and even confidence about the future. These five preachers can help us understand and accept our own poetic obligation: not to be versifiers, but to dwell on words, and thus to mediate between past and future. The preacher who loves the words of the text is in the deepest sense evangelical, out of memory bringing forth the promises that enable us to move forward responsibly and with hope.

NOTES

Introduction

1. "The Parson Preaching," *A Priest to the Temple or, the Country Parson: His Character and Rule of Holy Life* in *The Works of George Herbert* (Oxford: Clarendon, 1941), 233.

2. Thomas Birch, *The Life of the Most Reverend Dr. John Tillotson* (1752), cited by Charles Smyth, *The Art of Preaching: A Practical Survey of Preaching in the Church of England 747–1939* (London: SPCK, 1953), 106.

3. *Self-Consuming Artifacts: The Experience of Seventeenth-Century Literature* (Berkeley: University of California Press, 1972), 380.

4. Thomas Sprat, *The History of the Royal-Society of London, for the Improving of Natural Knowledge* (1667), quoted by Smyth, *Art of Preaching*, 135.

5. Cf. *Three Restoration Divines: Barrow, South, Tillotson*, ed. Irène Simon (Paris: Société d'Edition "Les Belles Lettres," 1967), 276.

6. Cf. the masterful study by Horton Davies, *Like Angels from a Cloud: The English Metaphysical Preachers, 1588–1645* (San Marino, Calif.: Huntington Library, 1986).

7. Cf. David Schlafer, "Preaching in the Shape of the Liturgy," *Amen!* (a publication of the Liturgical Commission of the Diocese of New York, n.d.), 8–12.

8. *The Sermons of John Donne*, ed. George Potter and Evelyn Simpson, 10 vols. (Berkeley: University of California Press, 1953–62), 2:73.

9. Reginald H. Fuller, *What Is Liturgical Preaching?* (London: SCM Press, 1957), 21–22.

10. *The Primacy of Faith* (New York: Macmillan, 1943), 138.

11. This apt phrase is taken from Benedicta Ward's brief discussion of the preaching of Mark Frank (1613–64) in Richard Southern et al., *The Beauty of Holiness: An Introduction to Six Seventeenth-Century Anglican Writers* (Oxford: SLG Press, 1976), 16.

Chapter One. LANCELOT ANDREWES

1. Of the Sending of the Holy Ghost no. 14, 1621; in *Ninety-six Sermons by the Right Honourable and Reverend Father in God, Lancelot Andrewes, Sometime Lord Bishop of Winchester* (Oxford and London: James Parker, 1878; rpt., New York: AMS Press, 1967), 3:372. The text is James 1:16–17: "Every good and

perfect gift is from above." All sermon citations are from this edition, noted by volume and page.

2. The official account of the supposed plot against James' life by the Scottish Earl of Gowrie and his brother is full of inconsistencies; Cf. Paul A. Welsby, *Lancelot Andrewes: 1555–1626* (London: SPCK, 1958), 141–42.

3. Bishop Buckeridge's Funeral Sermon for Andrewes, printed with the *Ninety-Six Sermons* (5:303).

4. *A Priest to the Temple*, in *The Works of George Herbert*, 233.

5. Of the Sending of the Holy Ghost no. 4, 1611 (3:173).

6. Ash Wednesday no. 7, 1623 (1:430–31).

7. T. S. Eliot treats Andrewes as "one of the community of the born spiritual" in his famous essay, *For Lancelot Andrewes* (Garden City, N.Y.: Doubleday, Doran, 1929), 10. Cf. Nicholas Lossky, *Lancelot Andrewes the Preacher (1555–1626): The Origins of the Mystical Theology of the Church of England* (Oxford: Clarendon Press, 1991), 335–36.

8. Nativity no. 3, 1607 (1:41).

9. The thought appears in the works of several Greek theologians (e.g., Irenaeus, *Adversus Haereses*, 3.10.2; Athanasius, *De Incarnatione*) and also Augustine (Sermon 13, *In Nativitate*).

10. Nativity no. 7, 1612 (1:117).

11. Of the Passion no. 2, 1604 (2:158).

12. *De Trinitate* 4.2; translation by Edmund Hill, *The Works of St. Augustine: A Translation for the Twenty-first Century* (Brooklyn, N.Y.: New City Press, 1990).

13. Jean LeClercq, *The Love of Learning and the Desire for God: A Study of Monastic Culture* (New York: Fordham University Press, 1982), 28. The resemblance between Gregory and Andrewes may be drawn on several points: their fundamental orientation toward prayer and practical mysticism, frequent use of vivid, homely images, and the exegetical practice of "following [a subject] hard," as Andrewes describes Gregory; cited by Joan Webber, "Celebration of Word and World in Andrewes's Style," *Journal of English and Germanic Philology* 64 (1965): 268.

14. Henry Isaacson, "The Life and Death of the Late Reverend and Worthy Prelate Lancelot Andrewes, Late Bishop of Winchester," in *The Works of Lancelot Andrewes*, vol. 11 (Oxford: John Henry Parker, 1854; rpt., New York: AMS Press, 1967), iii.

15. Frequently cited is Andrewes's formula: "For us, one Canon recorded by God in writing, Two testaments, Three Symbols, the first Four Councils, Five Centuries, and the series of Fathers in them...fix the rule of our Religion" (from a Latin sermon of 1613, cited by Lossky, *Lancelot Andrewes*, 337). In view of Andrewes's very frequent appeal to the authority of later councils and commentators, Lossky is perceptive in his suggestion that "the celebrated formula was perhaps less a limitation than a sort of lowest common denominator proposed for the partisans of a moderate Reform."

16. In the late sixteenth century, both universities were strongly influ-

enced by Calvinist theology and practice, and Andrewes belonged to several study groups that included Puritans. It is likely that his exposure to Reformed theology dated to childhood: while the religious sympathies of his family are unknown, the merchant class to which they belonged leaned heavily toward Protestantism.

17. Of the Sending of the Holy Ghost no. 15, 1623 (3:390). The text is 1 Cor. 12:47: "Now there are diversities of gifts, but the same Spirit."

18. Isaacson, "Life and Death," xxv.

19. Bishop Buckeridge's Funeral Sermon (5:304).

20. Cf. Helen C. White's sensitive discussion in *English Devotional Literature (Prose), 1600–1640* (Madison: University of Wisconsin, 1931), 248–52.

21. R. L. Ottley, *Lancelot Andrewes* (Boston: Houghton, Mifflin, 1894), 185.

22. Bishop John Hacket, cited by Isaacson, "Life and Death," xvii n.

23. Nativity no. 13, 1619 (3:229).

24. David Lloyd, *State Worthies* (1766), 347; cited by G. M. Story, *Lancelot Andrewes: Sermons* (Oxford: Clarendon Press, 1967), xxiii.

25. This seems to be the view of Andrewes's biographer Paul Welsby, who comments that "there is no evidence that James ever took Andrewes's advice upon anything that really mattered" (*Lancelot Andrewes*, 208).

26. Alexander Whyte, *Lancelot Andrewes and His Private Devotions*, 2d ed. (Edinburgh: Oliphant Anderson and Ferrier, 1896), 12.

27. The Gunpowder Plot and Gowrie Conspiracy sermons often express a delight in vengeance worthy of the Psalmist: "Nay, would they make men's bowels fly up and down the air? Out with those bowels; what should they do in, that have not in them that, that bowels should have [compassion]. Would they do it by fire? Into the fire with their bowels, before their faces" (Gunpowder no. 7, 1615 [4:339]).

28. Kenneth Fincham, *Prelate as Pastor: The Episcopate of James I* (Oxford: Clarendon Press, 1990), 45, 49.

29. "A Sermon Preached at Chiswick in the Time of Pestilence," 1603 (5:235).

30. Criticism is most frequently leveled at his role in promoting the Essex divorce so that the king's favorite Rochester could marry Lady Essex (Frances Howard). Florence Higham, in *Lancelot Andrewes* (London: SCM, 1952), 63–73, has argued, to my mind persuasively, that it was not servility but rather sympathy (it was a young, unconsummated marriage followed by years of separation) and ignorance of the full circumstances of the intrigue that led Andrewes to accede to the king's wishes.

31. Of the Resurrection no. 6, 1611 (2:292).

32. See Fincham, *Prelate as Pastor*, 20, 302.

33. Ash Wednesday no. 7, 1623 (1:428–29).

34. Bishop Buckeridge's Funeral Sermon (5:302).

35. See "A Sermon Preached at Chiswick" (5:235).

36. Lent no. 4, 1594 (2:64; this volume, p. 27).

37. His fullest instruction on prayer is offered in the "Nineteen Sermons upon Prayer in General, and the Lord's Prayer in Particular," printed with the *Ninety-Six Sermons* (5:309–489).

38. A letter of John Chamberlain, cited by Welsby, *Lancelot Andrewes*, 253.

39. Bishop Buckeridge's Funeral Sermon (5:304).

40. *The Private Devotions of Lancelot Andrewes*, ed. Thomas Kepler (Cleveland: World Publishing, 1956), 139–40.

41. Horton Davies provides a good overview of seventeenth-century English preaching in *Worship and Theology in England, 1603–1690* (Princeton: Princeton University Press, 1975), 2:133–84.

42. Joseph Glanvill, *An Essay Concerning Preaching* (1678; 2d ed., 1703), 71, cited by W. Fraser Mitchell, *English Pulpit Oratory from Andrewes to Tillotson: A Study of Its Literary Aspects* (London: SPCK, 1932), 6; italics mine.

43. Mitchell, *English Pulpit Oratory*, 159.

44. Nativity no. 3, 1607 (1:38).

45. Eliot, *For Lancelot Andrewes*, 17.

46. Lent no. 4, 1594 (see below, p. 27).

47. Nativity no. 15, 1622 (1:258). Cf. Eliot:

> A cold coming we had of it,
> Just the worst time of the year
> For a journey, and such a long journey:
> The ways deep and the weather sharp,
> The very dead of winter.

48. Ibid., 1:259.

49. Nativity no. 14, 1620 (1:239).

50. Ibid. The significance of Bethlehem's littleness is developed at much greater length in Nativity Sermon no. 10, 1615 (1:157–62).

51. Nativity no. 3, 1607 (1:37).

52. Nativity no. 7, 1612 (1:116).

53. This is the text of Nativity Sermon no. 3, 1607 (1:32–44).

54. Nativity no. 12, 1618 (1:201).

55. Davies, *Like Angels from a Cloud*, 37.

56. Cited by Lossky, *Lancelot Andrewes*, 46n.

57. Ash Wednesday no. 4, 1619 (1:362).

58. *Ethics* (New York: Macmillan, 1965), 131.

59. Cited by Fincham, *Prelate as Pastor*, 279.

60. Cf. Lossky's observation: "If [Andrewes] is little involved in the religious quarrels of his own time, it is not from flight into another time, but because in his theological vision most of these problems are bypassed by the rediscovery of a theological language that will not let itself be shut up in the more or less rationalizing impasses of the conflict between Reform and Counter-Reform" (*Lancelot Andrewes*, 350). In his Good Friday sermon of 1604 (treated below), Andrewes explores the fine line between overpreaching the

mysteries and a silence that shrinks back "with derogation to [God's] love" (2:148).

61. Nativity no. 3, 1607 (1:35).

62. E.g., Of the Passion no. 2, 1604 (2:139–41); Easter no. 6, 1611 (2:274); Of the Sending of the Holy Ghost no. 7, 1614 (3:225–227).

63. Of the Passion no. 2, 1604 (2:141–42).

64. "The Parson Preaching," 235.

65. Birch, Life of Tillotson; cf. Smyth, Art of Preaching, 103–7.

Remember Lot's Wife

66. This sermon picks up the imagery of Mary's ointment box from the Lenten sermon preached before Elizabeth the previous year, on Mark 14:46 (3:37–60). Mary is a central figure in the sermons on the Resurrection; see particularly the sympathetic and admiring treatment of Mary weeping at the sepulcher (Resurrection no. 14, 1620; 3:323).

67. Cf. John Booty, "Wisdom in All Her Ways," Sewanee Theological Review 34, no. 4 (1991): 108. By contrast, Jacobean preachers chose the political festivals of Guy Fawkes Day and the anniversary of the Gowrie Conspiracy, rather than Lent, for this reminder.

68. Augustine, On the Psalms, Psalm 75 (Eng. 76), v. 12.

69. The Latin is in the second person ("Remember what clay you are"), recalling the Ash Wednesday liturgy; cf. Gen. 3:19.

70. Latin: "Remember what a (puff of) wind is life"; cf. Job 7:7.

71. Nineveh represents the acme of evil in a city; of the story of Jonah and the war poem of Nahum.

72. According to rabbinic legend, with which Andrewes was familiar, Abraham and Lot came from a family of idol-makers in Ur.

73. Josephus Flavius, Jewish Antiquities, bk. 1, chap. 11.

74. Herodotus, History of the Persian War, bk. 2, chap. 141.

75. As Moses did with the Golden Calf; cf. Exod. 32:20.

76. Cf. Rom. 8:28; the Greek text reads "those who love God."

77. St. Bernard; Letter 32, near the end; and Letter 109, in the middle.

78. Asphalt Lakes; referring to the mineral pools at the southern end of the Dead Sea, where Sodom is traditionally located.

79. The contrast is between short- and long-distance racing tracks.

80. St. Bernard, Letter 32, near the end.

Nativity Sermon IX

81. Nativity no. 12, 1618 (1:208).

82. The primary meaning of Latin infans is "speechless"; derivatively, it denotes a small child.

83. Nativity no. 12, 1618, 1:204.

84. Lossky, Lancelot Andrewes, 41.

85. Of the Passion no. 1, 1597 (2:127), Cf. Of the Passion no. 2, 1604 (2:151–52).

86. Cf. Exod. 2:8; Andrewes follows the common assumption that the sister of Moses to which this story refers is Miriam. Andrewes accepts rabbinic tradition about her age, which the Bible does not mention.

87. The Aramaic translation of the Hebrew Bible; the place referred to is Song of Songs 1:3.

88. The legendary seventy translators of the Hebrew Bible into Greek (the Septuagint).

89. David Kimchi of Provence (1160?–1235?), an eminent Jewish commentator and grammarian.

90. Joseph Albo of Aragon (1380–1444), a rabbinic philosopher.

91. Minerva (Athena) sprang forth full-grown and fully armored from the head of Jupiter (Zeus).

92. In Greek mythology, Pyrrha and her husband Deucalion correspond to Noah and his wife. The only humans to survive the Deluge, they produced a hardy new race by casting stones on the ground, which took human form.

93. "The earth," from which Adam was molded.

94. Hilary (Bishop of Poitiers, d. 367), Liber Contra Arianos vel Auxentium.

95. Virgil's Fourth Eclogue was regarded as a pagan witness to Christ.

96. Andrewes plays at greater length on the military sense of "heavenly hosts" in the twelfth Nativity sermon (1618; Sermons 1:210–11).

97. Prov. 30:1; Andrewes plays with the meaning of the Hebrew name.

98. The Christmas sermon preached to the same audience five years before comments with more precision on Paul's phrase, "Him that knew no sin, he made sin" (2 Cor. 5:21): "that is, made him to be handled as a sinner" (Nativity no. 4, 1609 [1:56]).

99. That is, at Jesus' circumcision (Luke 2:21).

100. Literally, "suffering enough." The coinage seems to be Andrewes's own. The complementarity of satisfaction ("doing enough") and satispassion is illumined by his statement in the fourth Nativity sermon (1609): "The one half of the Law, that is, the directive part — he was made under that, and satisfied it by the innocency of his life, without breaking so much as one jot or tittle of the Law; and so answered that part as it might be the principal. The other half of the Law, which is the penalty — he was under that part also, and satisfied it by suffering a wrongful death, no way deserved, or due by him; and so answered that, as it may be the forfeiture" (Sermons 1:55–56).

101. The reference is to Boaz' greeting to the harvesters, "The Lord be with you" (Ruth 2:4).

102. That is, we have been about it (the separation) for a long time.

103. The founder of the city of Rome, here referring to the pope. Andrewes plays on the similarity of names between Romulus and (Pekah) son of Remaliah, king of Israel.

104. Leo the Great (pope, d. 461), Sermon on the Festival of the Nativity 5.5.

Chapter Two. JOHN DONNE

1. Edward Le Comte traces the awakening of interest in Donne's work in *Grace to a Witty Sinner: A Life of Donne* (New York: Walker and Co., 1965), 225–47.

2. That there is close continuity between Donne's poems and the prose is the theme of John Carey's *John Donne: Life, Mind and Art* (London: Faber and Faber, 1990). While the book is extremely valuable in "tracing the distinctive structures of Donne's imagination," Carey does not perceive the centrality of Donne's emphasis on God's mercy and therefore seriously misrepresents the rhetoric of the sermons as "a final and fully adequate expression of his power lust" (108).

3. *Sermons of John Donne*, ed. Potter and Simpson, 6:212–13. All quotations are from this edition, cited by volume and page.

4. Thus Augustine states his method for distinguishing between literal and figurative passages in Scripture: "that whatever appears in the divine Word that does not literally pertain to virtuous behavior or to the truth of faith you must take to be figurative. Virtuous behavior pertains to the love of God and of one's neighbor; the truth of faith pertains to knowledge of God and of one's neighbor.... Therefore in the consideration of figurative expressions a rule such as this will serve, that what is read should be subjected to diligent scrutiny until an interpretation contributing to the reign of charity is produced. If this result appears literally in the text, the expression being considered is not figurative" (*On Christian Doctrine* 3:10, 15).

5. *Biathanatos*, Donne's treatise on suicide, probably comes from the time when his fortunes were at their lowest ebb. Evelyn Simpson dates it no earlier than 1606, and not long before *Pseudo-Martyr*, completed in 1609 the year that Sir George More at last granted Anne Donne her dowry. See *A Study of the Prose Works of John Donne* (Oxford: Clarendon Press, 1948), 157.

6. *The Life of John Donne, D.D., Late Dean of St. Paul's Church, London* (London: H. K. Causton, n.d.), 120.

7. From a letter written by Donne to his brother-in-law, Sir Robert More, August 10, 1614 (quoted in Walton's *Life*, 74n).

8. *Life*, 35.

9. 3:247 (cf. below, 87).

10. Quoted by Walton, *Life*, 41–42. Evelyn Simpson points out that the wording is not true to Donne and probably represents Walton's paraphrase of Donne's conversations (*Prose Works of John Donne*, 23).

11. The *Essays* were published posthumously (1651) by the author's son John.

12. I have corrected Potter and Simpson's text reference.

13. Walton, *Life*, 119.

14. Holy Sonnet XVII.

15. The sermon was published, at Charles' command, shortly after its delivery (April 3, 1625).

16. Walton, *Life*, 69.

17. Ibid., 128–33.

18. *Letters* (1651), 85; cited by Simpson, *Prose Works of John Donne*, 291.

19. Walton, *Life*, 129.

20. Walton, *Life*, 46.

21. Quoted by Walton, *Life*, 141.

22. This aspect of Donne's imagination is treated by Joan Webber in her superb study, *Contrary Music: The Prose Style of John Donne* (Madison: University of Wisconsin Press, 1963), and again by Barbara Lewalski, *Protestant Poetics and the Seventeenth-Century Religious Lyric* (Princeton: Princeton University Press, 1979), 253–82.

23. Walton, *Life*, 147.

24. Like Andrewes, he simply identified himself as a member of the one true and catholic Church. In this formative period of the English Church, drawing party lines is difficult and of limited use. Donne speaks admiringly of Calvin and often follows his interpretations, but he clearly departs from Calvinist theology in his frequent insistence on human cooperation with God's grace, on the possibility of salvation for all, and on the fundamental and finally ineradicable goodness of humanity, stamped in the divine image. C. Fitzsimons Allison argues that Donne is not an Arminian but "an eloquent advocate for orthodox Anglicanism before it became corrupted by moralistic innovations"; and remarks aptly, "He preached justification; he did not preach *about* justification. He eloquently evoked the qualities and properties of sanctification, but he did not preach *about* sanctification" (*The Rise of Moralism* [Wilton, Conn.: Morehouse Barlow, 1966], 210, 188).

25. William Perkins, *The Art of Prophesying*, quoted by Mitchell, *English Pulpit Oratory*, 99–100. The dedicatory epistle of *The Art* is dated 1592; it was in print at the time of Donne's death.

26. Donne resembles Lancelot Andrewes in his insistence on the practical utility of the sense of the text, although he is much freer in developing the application than the rigorously exegetical Andrewes.

27. Lewalski, *Protestant Poetics*, 253–82.

28. As one of many references, see the introduction to the series on Psalm 38 (2:49–50).

29. Webber, *Contrary Music*, 116.

30. Cf. John S. Chamberlin's discussion of Ramist logic in *Increase and Multiply: Arts-of-Discourse Procedure in the Preaching of John Donne* (Chapel Hill: University of North Carolina Press, 1976), 76–83.

31. "The Art of Prophesying," cited by Chamberlin, in ibid., 81.

32. *De Doctrina Christiana*, bk. 4.

33. "Expostulation 19," *Devotions upon Emergent Occasions*, ed. Anthony Raspa (Montreal: McGill-Queen's University Press, 1975), 99.

34. 6:62. The authorities upon whom Donne relies in assessing the interpretive possibilities are chiefly the Fathers and a judicious selection of contemporary commentators, both Reformed and Catholic. Although he him-

self is not bound by a tradition of interpretation, Donne would have regarded as license for chaos the Puritan poet John Milton's principle: "Every believer has a right to interpret the Scriptures for himself, inasmuch as he has the Spirit for his Guide, and the mind of Christ in him" (*De Doctrina Christiana* I:xxx, in *The Works of John Milton* [New York: Columbia University Press, 1934], 16:265).

35. Gregory the Great's massive *Moralia* was the most widely read medieval commentary on Job and for centuries the vehicle by which Christians knew the Book.

36. Cf. William Petersen's discussion of Donne and Herbert as setting the early pattern for Anglican pastoral care, in James E. Griffiss, *Anglican Theology and Pastoral Care* (Wilton, Conn.: Morehouse Barlow, 1985), 11–22.

A Wedding Sermon

37. See the moving sermon on Prov. 8:17, "I love them that love me" (1:236–51).

38. See Simpson's fine discussion of this sermon in the introduction to the third volume of Donne's *Sermons* (3:21–26).

39. The Authorized ("King James") Version of 1611.

40. The Geneva Bible of 1560.

41. Having the character of an emergency.

42. The invocation to Evening Prayer, *The Book of Common Prayer.*

43. Collect for Aid against Perils, belonging to the service for Evening Prayer, *The Book of Common Prayer.*

The Fear of the Lord

44. Several of the best Cathedral sermons on the Psalms are available (in somewhat abbreviated form) in the recent volume, *Selections from the Divine Poems, Sermons, Devotions, and Prayers: John Donne,* ed. John Booty, Classics of Western Spirituality (New York: Paulist Press, 1990).

45. From "A Collect for Peace," in the Morning Prayer service of *The Book of Common Prayer.*

46. Promises or contractual obligations; bonds.

47. Maintaining a person (or thing) in being; divine support.

48. The hospital of St. Mary of Bethlehem in Lambeth, London; used as an asylum for the insane.

49. Donne refers to the practice, fashionable among Londoners, of "sermon tasting," that is, going from one church to another to hear renowned preachers.

50. Follow a practice; be accustomed to...

51. A London prison, so-named for St. Bride's (Bridget's) well nearby.

52. The phrase "clap on a byasse [bias]" seems to derive from the game of bowls and to denote setting the bowl on an oblique course.

53. Cf. Job 7:1; "Does not humanity have hard service upon earth...?" Donne is playing upon the Hebrew word *tsaba'*, which denotes any kind of compulsory service, most frequently military service.

54. Turning in different directions; vacillating.

Chapter Three. JOSEPH HALL

1. Occasional Meditation No. 107; the texts of the *Occasional Meditations* and *The Art of Divine Meditation* have been edited, along with a very helpful introductory essay, by Frank Livingstone Huntley, *Bishop Joseph Hall and Protestant Meditation in Seventeenth-Century England: A Study with the Texts of* The Art of Divine Meditation *and* Occasional Meditations (Binghamton, N.Y.: Center for Medieval and Early Renaissance Studies, 1981).

2. *The Art of Divine Meditation*, chap. 2.

3. There is a debate about the relation between Hall and the Counter-Reformation tradition of meditation stemming from Ignatius of Loyola and Francis de Sales. Louis Martz, in *The Poetry of Meditation: A Study in English Religious Literature of the Seventeenth Century*, 2d ed. (New Haven: Yale University Press, 1962), argues that Hall is an important mediator of this tradition and notes especially the influence of the Ignatian exercises in the vivid representation of a biblical scene, often with oneself in it, which is pronounced in Hall's meditations. Barbara Lewalski presents the counterthesis that the Protestant poets and preachers "undermined" the Jesuits' manuals by drawing their inspiration directly from the Bible and also from the fifteenth-century *Devotio Moderna* movement in the Low Countries. But claims of deliberate undermining seem no more susceptible of proof than those of conscious mediation. There are indeed large differences between Hall's method and the Jesuits'. True to his Calvinist training, Hall draws on a much wider range of biblical texts, while the Ignatian exercises focus largely on a personal apprehension of Jesus' Passion and the "four last things" (death, judgment, heaven, hell). Moreover, his frequent observations from nature and the social world give his method affinities with Renaissance humanism and even the new science. Yet despite his differences from the continental Catholics, Hall was too widely read to be ignorant of their work, and too fair-minded to despise what was good in it. Rather than seeing Hall as adapting Ignatian practice, it is probably better to view the Protestant and Catholic methods as complementary developments stemming from the common root of late medieval spirituality. Lewalski is right to point to the *Devotio Moderna*, which emphasized deepening the interior life through meditation and extracting practical lessons from the daily study of Scripture. Although the movement began with the creation of lay communities, it led to a widespread monastic renaissance and thus influenced Ignatius, as well as Calvin, Luther, and Zwingli; see Albert Hyma, *The Christian Renaissance: A History of the "Devotio Moderna"* (Hamden, Conn.: Archon Books, 1965). Hall may well have felt its effects most closely through Thomas à Kempis' *Imitation of Christ*; Frank Huntley argues plausibly (against Martz) that à

Kempis is the "obscure nameless monk, which wrote some hundred and twelve years ago" from whom Hall claims to have received the most light (*Bishop Joseph Hall and Protestant Meditation*, 27–30).

4. *The Works of the Right Reverend Joseph Hall, D.D.*, ed. Philip Wynter, 10 vols. (1863; rpt., New York: AMS Press, 1969), 5:161. Unless otherwise noted, all quotations are from this edition, cited by volume and page.

5. Occasional Meditation No. 136 ("Upon the Sight of a Loaded Cart"); cf. Amos 2:13.

6. See Charles H. George and Katherine George, *The Protestant Mind of the English Reformation, 1570–1640* (Princeton: Princeton University Press, 1961), 149.

7. Occasional Meditation No. 121 ("Upon the Sight of a Well-Fleeced Sheep").

8. From Hall's autobiography, "Observations of Some Specialties of Divine Providence in the Life of Joseph Hall, Bishop of Norwich," *Works*, ed. Wynter, 1:xx.

9. Cf. Huntley, *Bishop Joseph Hall*, 3.

10. From the College statutes, cited by Huntley, *Bishop Joseph Hall*, 4.

11. Cf. chap. 2, n. 30, above.

12. Cited by George Lewis, *A Life of Joseph Hall, Bishop of Exeter and Norwich* (London: Hodder and Stoughton, 1886), 69.

13. Occasional Meditation No. 98 ("Upon a Child Crying").

14. Cf. the study of Alice T. Friedman, *House and Household in Elizabethan England* (Chicago: University of Chicago, 1989).

15. *Contra* Gerald Sheppard, that "Hall's own advice to wives in the light of this background appears to be a reactionary, proestablishment reaction against these growing tensions" (*Solomon's Divine Arts* [Cleveland: Pilgrim Press, 1991], 90), although Sheppard goes on somewhat to qualify his own statement.

16. Cf. George and George, *Protestant Mind of the English Reformation*, 271–74.

17. *Resolutions and Decisions of Divers Practical Cases of Conscience in Continual Use amongst Men*, in *Works*, ed. Wynter, 7:375.

18. The *Contemplations* on the Old Testament were published in eight volumes between 1612 and 1625, although Hall probably laid the groundwork in his village sermons at Hawstead. The portion on the New Testament appeared in 1633, when Hall was bishop of Exeter.

19. An Epistle "To My Lord Denny: A particular account of how our days are or should be spent, both common and holy," *Works*, ed. Wynter, 6:280.

20. Cf. White, *English Devotional Literature (Prose)*, 224.

21. Quoted by George and George, *Protestant Mind of the English Reformation*, 139n.

22. Cf. ibid., 169.

23. Quoted in ibid., 150–51.

24. Cited by Huntley, *Bishop Joseph Hall*, 107.

25. "An Apologetical Advertisement to the Reader," following *The Old Religion*, in *Works*, ed. Wynter, 8:719.

26. "Life," in *Works*, ed. Wynter, 1:xlvi.

27. From a dedicatory letter to Philip, Earl of Montgomery, *Works*, ed. Wynter, 1:400.

28. Huntley, *Bishop Joseph Hall*, 132.

29. *Hard Measure*, in *Works*, 1:lxvii–lxviii.

30. Barbara Lewalski suggests that Donne's *Devotions upon Emergent Occasions* is the first significant example of the fusion of meditation and homily; see *Donne's Anniversaries and the Poetry of Praise: The Creation of a Symbolic Mode* (Princeton: Princeton University Press, 1973), 101. However, Hall's *Contemplations* had begun to appear more than a decade before *Devotions* was written, and that Donne would have read them is entirely likely. The two writers were acquainted through their common patrons Sir Robert and Lady Drury, and Hall wrote prefatory verses for the memorial poems that Donne composed for the Drurys' daughter Elizabeth. Moreover, the poems' representation of a world in decline may well reflect Hall's youthful view, for which he became widely known through the *Satires*; cf. John Carey, *John Donne: Life, Mind, and Art* (London: Faber and Faber, 1990), 89.

31. Although the forty-two published sermons, preached mostly at court or on state occasions, contain some memorable passages, they are in general more thematic in style and have less of the narrative interest in biblical scenes and characters that make the *Contemplations* so effective.

32. Huntley, *Bishop Joseph Hall and Protestant Meditation*, 50–51.

33. "The Enemies of the Cross of Christ" (preached to James at Hampton Court, September 1624), *Works*, ed. Wynter, 5:203.

34. Cf. *Three Restoration Divines*, ed. Simon, 1:19.

35. Quoted by Huntley, *Bishop Joseph Hall*, 44. For decades, Milton held a grudge against Hall for having acted in *The Parnassus Plays* at Cambridge. The satirical plays, which Hall probably authored, include scathing attacks on all contemporary poets except Shakespeare.

36. Hall's predilection for epigrams is evident in his commentary on Proverbs, recently republished: see *Solomon's Divine Arts*, ed. Sheppard.

37. Northrop Frye, *The Great Code: The Bible and Literature* (San Diego: Harcourt Brace Jovanovich, 1982), 212.

38. From the dedicatory letter addressed to Henry, Prince of Wales (*Works*, ed. Wynter, 1:2).

39. For the contrary view, see Wayne Booth, *The Company We Keep: An Ethics of Fiction* (Berkeley: University of California Press, 1988). He revives the once-common metaphor of "books as friends" in order to explore the relationship between reading and character formation. His argument is of great pertinence to the task of teaching and preaching the biblical narratives. With respect to how religious literature in particular is designed to shape character, see Stephen E. Fowl and L. Gregory Jones, *Reading in Communion: Scripture and Ethics in Christian Life* (Grand Rapids: Eerdmans, 1991).

40. "Moses was a merciful meek man, and yet with what fury did he run thro' the camp, and cut the throats of three and thirty thousand of his dear Israelites, that were fallen into idolatry; what was the reason? 'Twas mercy to the rest to make these be examples, to prevent the destruction of the whole army" ("The Shortest Way with Dissenters" [London, 1702], 20, cited by Wayne Booth, *The Rhetoric of Fiction* [Chicago: University of Chicago Press, 1961], 318). Cf. Hall's nearly identical discussion of the mercy of Moses, *Works*, ed. Wynter, 1:131.

41. In the dedication of Book 3 to The Lord Denny, *Works*, ed. Wynter, 1:43.

42. Ian Watt, *The Rise of the Novel: Studies in Defoe, Richardson and Fielding* (Berkeley: University of California Press, 1960), 15.

43. The meditation "Nathan and David" (printed below) is especially difficult in its judgment that the death of a child is an "easy load" for David to bear. The biblical text is, of course, the real source of moral difficulty. The load can be judged "easy" (and the text rendered morally acceptable) only if this loss be weighed against the eternal loss of David's soul.

44. E. M. Forster, cited by Watt, *Rise of the Novel*, 22.

45. Joan Webber, *The Eloquent "I"* (Madison: University of Wisconsin, 1968), 7. Webber is designating a literary type (exemplified by John Donne, Thomas Browne, and Thomas Traherne); she acknowledges that individual Anglicans were aware of the passage and effect of time.

46. See the recent edition with an excellent introduction by Huntley, *Bishop Joseph Hall*.

47. Occasional Meditation No. 104.

48. *Institutes* I.v.9.

49. Cf. *The Art of Divine Meditation*, chap. 4.

50. Occasional Meditation No. 63.

51. Occasional Meditation No. 66.

52. Occasional Meditation No. 109.

53. *The Art of Divine Meditation*, chap. 3.

Chapter Four. FREDERICK W. ROBERTSON

1. "The Sympathy of Christ," *Sermons Preached at Brighton* (New York: Harper and Brothers, n.d.), 89.

2. Horton Davies, *Worship and Theology in England* (Princeton: Princeton University Press, 1962), 4:290, 293.

3. F. W. Robertson, "First Lecture on the Influence of Poetry on the Working Classes," *Lectures and Addresses on Literary and Social Topics* (Boston: Ticknor and Fields, 1859), 97.

4. *Life and Letters of Frederick W. Robertson, M.A.*, ed. Stopford Brooke, 2 vols. (Boston: Ticknor and Fields, 1865), 2:160–61.

5. "Worldliness," in *Sermons Preached at Brighton*, 337.

6. Robertson's two sermons on Balaam are especially close reflections of Newman's sermon "Obedience without Love, as instanced in the Character of Balaam" (preached April 2, 1837, a few months before Robertson became resident in Oxford); Robertson presumably had read it.

7. *Life and Letters*, ed. Brooke, 1:28.

8. Ibid., 2:208.

9. "Worldliness," 334.

10. Cf. *Life and Letters*, ed. Brooke, 2:92.

11. In a letter of November 25, 1851, he attributes the principle to Shakespeare and says that he finds the same tendency in F. D. Maurice; "therefore I love him, and so far am at one with him" (ibid., 2:9).

12. Ibid., 2:213–15.

13. Robertson, "First Lecture," 110.

14. Ibid., 142.

15. *Life and Letters*, ed. Brooke, 1:59.

16. Ibid., 1:194.

17. Ibid., 1:62.

18. Ibid., 1:106.

19. Ibid., 1:107.

20. Ibid., 1:118.

21. "An Address Delivered to the Members of the Working Men's Institute ...on the Question of the Introduction of Sceptical Publications into their Library," in *Lectures and Addresses*, 68.

22. *Sermons Preached at Brighton*, 417.

23. *Life and Letters*, ed. Brooke, 1:127.

24. "Christian Casuistry," in *Sermons Preached at Brighton*, 547.

25. Cited by James R. Blackwood, *The Soul of Frederick W. Robertson, the Brighton Preacher* (New York: Harper & Brothers, 1947), 78.

26. *Life and Letters*, ed. Brooke, 2:125.

27. *Notes on Genesis* (London: Kegan, Paul, Trench, Trübner & Co., 1892), 11.

28. Robertson's observations on the combination of the creation accounts are in fact very similar to those of Brevard Childs; see *Introduction to the Old Testament as Scripture* (Philadelphia: Fortress Press, 1979), 149–50.

29. *Life and Letters*, ed. Brooke, 1:25.

30. Ibid., 1:280–81.

31. He understood that the particular value of the Psalms is that they enable us to express feelings, such as despondency, which we are otherwise ashamed or embarrassed to express directly; see the sermon on "Religious Depression" (on Ps. 43:13), in *Sermons Preached at Brighton*, 308–12.

32. *Sermons on St. Paul's Epistles to the Corinthians* (Boston: Ticknor and Fields, 1866), 421.

33. "The Loneliness of Christ," in *Sermons Preached at Brighton*, 174.

34. "The Restoration of the Erring," in *Sermons Preached at Brighton*, 326.

35. *Life and Letters*, ed. Brooke, 1:350.

36. Ibid., 1:291.

37. The diagnosis given to Robertson was degeneration of the nerves in the cerebellum; it has been suggested to me that the symptoms as described in the letters resemble those of what is now called Huntington's Chorea.

38. *Life and Letters*, ed. Brooke, 1:64.

39. Davies, *Worship and Theology*, 4:287. His chapter on "The Victorian Pulpit" provides a good overview of the preaching of the period.

40. "Inspiration," in *Sermons Preached at Brighton*, 826.

41. The sermons as we have them are notes, taken by others or written down by Robertson (after preaching) at the request of friends. He was not eager to publish his sermons, feeling that they were composed to be heard, not read, and would open him to much misunderstanding. However, in the last year of his life he began preaching from manuscript, apparently with the thought of publishing a volume, and gave some two dozen manuscripts to a friend a few days before his death.

42. *Life and Letters*, ed. Brooke, 1:188.

43. Cited by Frederick Arnold, *Robertson of Brighton* (London: Ward and Downey, 1886), 250.

44. "The Character of Eli," in *Sermons Preached at Brighton*, 634.

45. "Prayer," in ibid., 651.

46. "Elijah," in ibid., 293.

47. "Inspiration," 831.

48. "The Character of Eli," 637.

49. Cf. "The New Commandment of Love to One Another," in *Sermons Preached at Brighton*, 184.

50. Lecture XLIII, in *Sermons on St. Paul's Epistles to the Corinthians*, 323.

51. Davies, *Worship and Theology*, 3:239.

52. From an unpublished sermon, quoted in *Life and Letters*, ed. Brooke, 2:169–70.

53. "The First Miracle: The Glory of the Virgin Mother," in *Sermons Preached at Brighton*, 391.

54. "The Character of Eli," 635.

55. "Selfishness, as Shown in Balaam's Character," in *Sermons Preached at Brighton*, 662.

56. "The Irreparable Past," in *Sermons Preached at Brighton*, 429.

57. Ibid., 433.

58. "Jacob's Wrestling," in *Sermons Preached at Brighton*, 49.

59. "Christian Progress by Oblivion of the Past," *Sermons Preached at Brighton*, 64.

60. *Life and Letters*, ed. Brooke, 1:305.

61. *Sermons Preached at Brighton*, 352.

62. *Life and Letters*, ed. Brooke, 1:297. This is in effect a statement of Robertson's first principle of teaching, from which follow all the rest (see above, p. 160).

63. "Baptism (I)," in *Sermons Preached at Brighton*, 277.

64. *Life and Letters*, ed. Brooke, 2:42.

65. *Contra* Horton Davies, who contrasts Robertson's aesthetic preaching with Newman's ethical preaching. He is more accurate in his observation that "Robertson's was a Gospel for society and the world; Newman's was for individuals and for the Church, but not for the world" (*Worship and Theology*, 4:345).

66. See "A Stray Thought," *Life and Letters*, ed. Brooke, 1:218–19.

67. The brilliant sermon by this title treats this theme in light of the non-fulfillment of God's promise of land to the patriarchs (*Sermons Preached at Brighton*, 487–95).

Elijah

68. Robertson, "First Lecture," 777.

69. Ibid., 777–78.

The Message of the Church to Men of Wealth

70. "Christ's Judgment Respecting Inheritance," in *Sermons Preached at Brighton*, 203. The sermon printed here was preached the following week to clarify Robertson's position.

71. "Typified by the Man of Sorrows, the Human Race" (preached at Christ Church, Cheltenham, April 26, 1846), in *The Preaching of F. W. Robertson*, ed. Gilbert Doan (Philadelphia: Fortress Press, 1964), 84.

Chapter Five. HENRY PARRY LIDDON

1. "Personal Responsibility for the Gift of Revelation," *Sermons Preached on Special Occasions* (London: Longmans, Green, and Co., 1897), 157.

2. *Sermons at St. Paul's and Elsewhere* (London: Longmans, Green, and Co., 1907), vvi.

3. Cited by John Octavius Johnston, *Life and Letters of Henry Parry Liddon* (London: Longmans, Green, and Co., 1904), 7.

4. From the sermon preached in memory of Edward Bouverie Pusey in St. Mary's Church, Liverpool, January 20, 1884; *Clerical Life and Work* (London: Longmans, Green, and Co., 1895), 359–60.

5. Ibid., 362.

6. Ibid., 359.

7. A letter of August 22, 1864, in Johnston, *Life and Letters*, 93–94.

8. A letter (from Pusey) of January 1853, in ibid., 28–29.

9. "Our Lord's Ascension: The Church's Gain," *Sermons Preached before the University at Oxford, First Series* (London: Rivingtons, 1884), 302.

10. "The Subject of Religion: The Soul," *Some Elements of Religion* (New York: Scribner, Welford, and Armstrong, 1872), 81.

11. "The Priest in His Inner Life," in *Clerical Life and Work*, 24.

12. A letter from Liddon to Keble, February 1858, in Johnston, *Life and Letters*, 47.

13. Letter of December 1875, in ibid., 175.

14. Ibid., 52.

15. Ibid.

16. From the sermon preached in memory of Edward Bouverie Pusey, in *Clerical Life and Work*, 361.

17. Letter of January 1872, in Johnston, *Life and Letters*, 239.

18. The Rev. E. F. Sampson, cited in ibid., 256.

19. Preface to the second edition, *The Divinity of Our Lord and Saviour Jesus Christ* (London: Longmans, Green, and Co., 1897), xv.

20. Canon Scott Holland, cited in Johnston, *Life and Letters*, 153.

21. A letter of June 1877, in ibid., 215.

22. "The Life of Faith and the Athanasian Creed," in *Sermons Preached before the University at Oxford, Second Series*, 142–43.

23. Written in 1885, cited by G. W. E. Russell, *Dr. Liddon* (London: A. R. Mowbray), 158.

24. Letter of July 1867, in Johnston, *Life and Letters*, 102.

25. Letter of Easter Monday 1868, in ibid., 126.

26. In January 1885, Lord Acton wrote in a letter the argument he had made to Gladstone: "Assuredly Liddon is the greatest power in the conflict with sin, and in turning the souls of men to God, that the nation now possesses. . . . So eminent a representative of Church principles has not occupied the See of London within living memory, and there is a balance to redress." The prime minister followed up by inquiring vaguely if Liddon would "take a Bishopric," several then being open; but Liddon would not "accept a Bishopric in the abstract" (ibid., 311).

27. Francis Paget (bishop of Oxford), in ibid., 397.

28. His traveling companion was his sister, Annie Poole King; she published *Dr. Liddon's Tour of Egypt and Palestine*, an account based on his minutely detailed journal.

29. Cited by Russell, *Dr. Liddon*, 87.

30. Preface by Charles Gore, ed., *Lux Mundi: A Series of Studies in the Religion of the Incarnation* (London: John Murray, 1890), vii.

31. Letter of November 1889, in Johnston, *Life and Letters*, 367.

32. What Liddon calls the spiritual sense of the text, Newman calls the mystical sense: "It may be almost laid down as an historical fact, that the mystical interpretation and orthodoxy will stand or fall together" (*Essay on Development of Christian Doctrine* [London: Longmans, Green, and Co., 1891], 342–43).

33. *The Worth of the Old Testament* (London: Longmans, Green, and Co., 1890), 38.

34. "The Conflict of Faith with Undue Exaltation of Intellect," *Sermons Preached before the University*, 1st ser., 172–73.

35. Ibid., 180–81.

36. From the Bristol Journal, cited in Johnston, *Life and Letters*, 56. Interestingly, Liddon's diary entry on the same sermon (preached on "Low Sunday" 1861) reads: "Preached on Phil. iii.10: 'The power of the Resurrection Life.' Felt that I was unable to really gain the attention of my audience, and had a bad headache."

37. "Growth in the Apprehension of Truth," *Sermons Preached before the University*, 2d ser., 104.

38. "Our Lord's Ascension," in *Sermons Preached before the University*, 1st ser., 286, 289.

39. *Sermons on Old Testament Subjects* (London: Longmans, Green, and Co., 1898), 138.

40. "The Law of Influence," in ibid., 196.

41. Ibid., 52.

42. Ibid., 61.

43. "Jonah," in *Sermons Preached on Special Occasions*, 168.

44. "The Attractiveness of Egypt," in *Sermons on Old Testament Subjects*, 49.

45. "Jerusalem," in ibid., 357.

46. "Impatience at the Nature of Religious Truth," in ibid., 258–59.

47. "Saul and David," in ibid., 137.

48. Johnston, *Life and Letters*, 389.

The Young Man in Dothan

49. "The Priest in His Inner Life," in *Clerical Life and Work*, 24.

50. William Paley (1743–1805), *Natural Theology: or, evidences of the existence and attributes of the Deity, collected from the appearances of nature.*

51. Confession of sin, *The Book of Common Prayer* (New York: Church Hymnal Corp., 1979).

52. Cf. *The Book of Common Prayer*, Collect 11.

Elisha at the Assumption of Elijah

53. Isaac Williams, *The Baptistery*, Part I, Image 5 (Oxford: John Henry Parker, 1842), 69.

54. Gregory VII.

55. Williams, *The Baptistery*, 73.

Chapter Six. HOLY PREACHING

1. To be precise, I mean the present cultural contexts of North America and Britain, since this book is addressed primarily to English-speaking preachers.

2. From Homily No. 1 of the *First (Edwardine) Book of Homilies* (1547).

3. Personal communication.

4. See, for example, the 1991 Baltimore Declaration produced by six Episcopal priests and the "post-liberal" response in *Reclaiming Faith: Essays on Orthodoxy in the Episcopal Church and the Baltimore Declaration*, ed. Ephraim Radner and George Sumner (Grand Rapids, Mich.: Eerdmans, 1993). An earlier version of the present essay, which includes my own critique of the Baltimore Declaration, was published in that volume.

5. Cf. Lewis Brastow's cogent observation at the beginning of the century: "Advance in any branch of scientific theology demands a corresponding advance in its practical use in the service of the Church" (*The Modern Pulpit: A Study of Homiletic Sources and Characteristics* [New York: Macmillan, 1906], 103).

6. *The Ecology of Faith*, Beecher Lectures, 1959 (Philadelphia: Muhlenberg Press, 1961), 68–69.

7. Paul Holmer, "Kierkegaard and Ethical Theory," cited by Joseph Sittler, ibid., 50.

8. Garrett Green uses this encounter to illustrate the principle: "To save sinners, God seizes them by the imagination . . . " (*Imagining God*, 149–50).

9. Personal communication.

10. Cf. Bonhoeffer's stringent comment in an address to the 1932 International Youth Conference in Gland, Switzerland: "Is it not precisely the significance of these conferences that where someone approaches us appearing so utterly strange and incomprehensible in his concerns and yet demands a hearing of us, we perceive in the voice of our brother the voice of Christ himself, and do not evade this voice, but take it quite seriously and listen and love the other precisely in his strangeness? That brother encounters brother in all openness and truthfulness and need, and claims the attention of others is the sole way in which Christ encounters us at such a conference. . . . And should some of us now have to say in all honesty: we have heard nothing, and others perhaps equally honestly have to say: we have heard no end of things, let me express to both groups a great concern which has been bearing down on me with growing heaviness throughout the whole conference; has it not become terrifyingly clear again and again, in everything that we have said here to one another, that we are no longer obedient to the Bible? We are more fond of our own thoughts than of the thoughts of the Bible. We no longer read the Bible seriously, we no longer read it against ourselves, but for ourselves" (*No Rusty Swords: Letters, Lectures and Notes 1928–1936*, ed. Edwin H. Robertson [New York: Harper and Row, 1965], 185).

11. The Baltimore Declaration, VII, see Radner and Sumner, *Reclaiming Faith*, 283.

12. *Imagining God: Theology and the Religious Imagination* (San Francisco: Harper and Row, 1989), 109–10. The term "paradigmatic imagination" is discussed more fully in n. 24 below.

13. See *Purity and Danger: An Analysis of the Concepts of Pollution and Taboo* (London: ARK, 1966), 41–57; and her refinement of this original study in *Implicit Meanings* (London: Routledge and Paul, 1975), 276–318.

14. On the function of symbolic language in Scripture, see Ricoeur's *The Symbolism of Evil* (Boston: Beacon Press, 1967), and "Biblical Hermeneutics," *Semeia* 4 (1975): 271–48.

15. *Letters and Diaries of John Henry Newman*, ed. C. S. Dessain (Oxford: Clarendon, 1975), 159–60.

16. *On Poetry and Poets* (1957; New York: Octagon Books, 1975), 137.

17. *Worldly Preaching: Lectures on Homiletics* (New York: Crossroad, 1991), 116.

18. On the danger of overpreaching, see Andrewes's Passion sermon of 1604 (*Sermons* 2:148).

19. *The Glass of Vision*, Bampton Lectures for 1948 (Westminster: Dacre Press, 1948), 42–44.

20. Ibid., 44.

21. The implications of this view of ethics for the study of literature are explored by Wayne C. Booth, *The Company We Keep: An Ethics of Fiction* (Berkeley: University of California Press, 1988). The study is highly useful for preachers, who must reckon with a text (and particularly the Old Testament) which is often ethically problematic.

22. On the value of seeing Scripture as an outsider for the maintenance of interpretive humility, see Stephen E. Fowl and L. Gregory Jones, *Reading in Communion: Scripture and Ethics in Christian Life* (Grand Rapids, Mich.: Eerdmans, 1991), 110–13.

23. *The Primacy of Faith* (New York: Macmillan, 1943), 154.

24. On the importance of the qualifier, see Garrett Green, "'The Bible as...': Fictional Narrative and Scriptural Truth," in G. Green, ed., *Scriptural Authority and Narrative Interpretation* (FS Hans Frei; Philadelphia: Fortress, 1987), 79–96; and also Garrett Green, *Imagining God*: "The paradigmatic imagination is the ability to see one thing *as* another. Kant called 'is' the copula of judgment; I take 'is' to be the 'copula of imagination.'... Imagination is the ability to say what something is like" (73).

25. *Worldly Preaching*, 129.

26. See "Ministry of the Word or Comedy and Philology," *New Blackfriars* 68 (1987): 472–83.

27. The semantic range in biblical Hebrew of the noun *mishpat* expresses the sort of flexible concept of authority I propose. The word commonly designates an exercise of divine (or divinely derived) authority. In the narrowest sense it denotes a specific ordinance (Deut. 33:10) or divine law in general (Jer. 8:7). More broadly, it denotes the operation of justice (Amos 5:24) or divine judgment (Ps. 1:5). But its meaning can be extended to include "practice" (2 Sam. 27:11, 2 Kgs. 17:33), "fitness" (Isa. 40:14), "established order" and perhaps even *modus operandi* (Job 40:8).

28. *Discovering Eve: Ancient Israelite Women in Context* (New York: Oxford University Press, 1988).

29. A. F. Kirkpatrick (citing Delitzsch), *The Book of Psalms* (Cambridge: University Press, 1902), 829.

30. *On Christian Doctrine*, 3:xv.

31. *The Priestly Kingdom: Social Ethics as Gospel* (Notre Dame: University of Notre Dame, 1984), 9.

32. See Elisabeth Schüssler Fiorenza, *Bread Not Stone: The Challenge of Feminist Biblical Interpretation* (Boston: Beacon Press, 1984): "A hermeneutics of suspicion does not presuppose the feminist authority and truth of the Bible but takes as its starting point the assumption that biblical texts and their interpretations are androcentric and serve patriarchal functions.... A feminist hermeneutics of suspicion also questions the underlying presuppositions, androcentric models, and unarticulated interests of contemporary biblical interpretation" (15–16). The term "feminist authority and truth" is unexplained.

33. Cf. Schüssler Fiorenza: "A feminist hermeneutics of proclamation must ... insist that all texts identified as sexist or patriarchal should not be retained in the lectionary" (ibid., 18).

34. "Odysseus' Scar," in *Mimesis: The Representation of Reality in Western Literature* (Princeton: Princeton University Press, 1953), 14–15.

35. Richard Eslinger dates to the 1970s the serious development of alternatives to "the old homiletic," where audiences were left stranded in "the arid scrubland of topical preaching" (*A New Hearing: Living Options in Homiletic Method* [Nashville: Abingdon, 1987], 28). This collection of sermons by several homileticians, along with Eslinger's essays on their methods, is a useful introduction to the current discussion.

36. See, for example, Paul Scott Wilson, *Imagination of the Heart: New Understandings in Preaching* (Nashville: Abingdon, 1988), and Walter J. Burghardt, S.J., *Preaching: The Art and the Craft* (New York/Mahwah, N.J.: Paulist Press, 1987).

37. "A New Look at Homiletics," *College of Preachers Newsletter* 37, no. 2 (December 1991); cf. *The Parable of Ten Preachers* (Nashville: Abingdon, 1992).

38. *The Ecology of Faith*, 66.

39. On the notion of pattern as the key to the unity and normativity of the Scriptures, see David H. Kelsey, *The Uses of Scripture in Recent Theology* (Philadelphia: Fortress, 1975), 192–97; and Garrett Green, *Imagining God*, 114–18.

40. *The Sermons of John Donne*, 2:73.

41. Cited by Czeslaw Milosz, *The Witness of Poetry* (Cambridge: Harvard University Press, 1983), 114.